Mexico

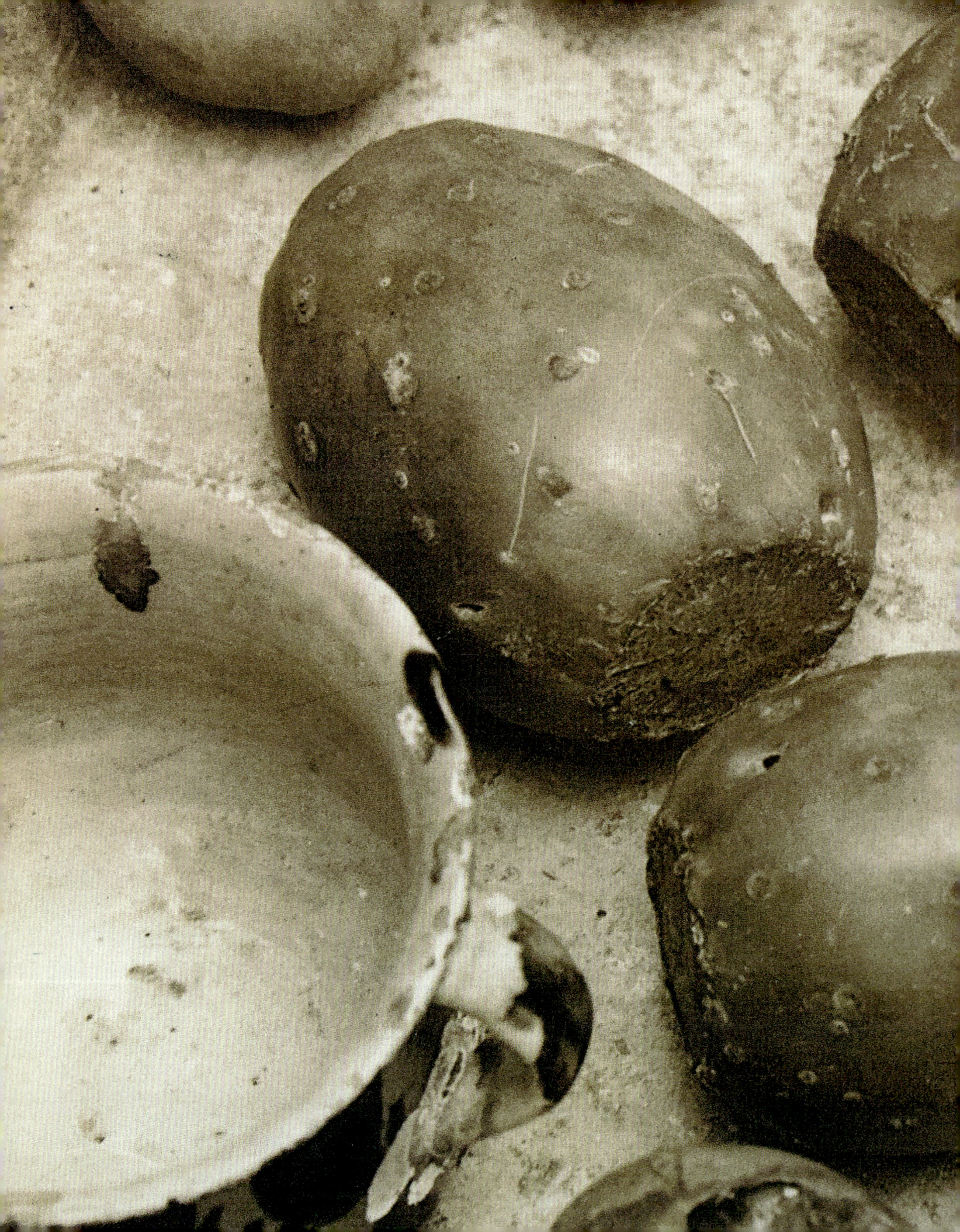

Mexico

A REVOLUTION IN ART
1910–1940

Adrian Locke

Royal Academy of Arts

'Time has told me'
Simon Owen (1963–2012)

First published on the occasion of the exhibition 'Mexico: A Revolution in Art, 1910–1940'
Royal Academy of Arts, London
6 July – 29 September 2013

The Royal Academy of Arts is grateful to Her Majesty's Government for agreeing to indemnify this exhibition under the National Heritage Act 1980, and to Resource, The Council for Museums, Archives and Libraries, for its help in arranging the indemnity.

EXHIBITION CURATOR
Adrian Locke
assisted by Sarah Lea

EXHIBITION ORGANISATION
Maeve Butler
Emma Enderby
Sunnifa Hope

PHOTOGRAPHIC AND COPYRIGHT CO-ORDINATION
Katharine Oakes

EXHIBITION CATALOGUE
Royal Academy Publications
Beatrice Gullström
Alison Hissey
Elizabeth Horne
Carola Krueger
Peter Sawbridge
Nick Tite

Copy-editing and proofreading
Nina Shandloff

Picture research
Sara Ayad

Design
Kathrin Jacobsen

Colour origination
DawkinsColour

Printed in Italy by Graphicom

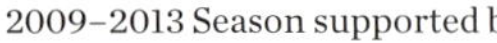

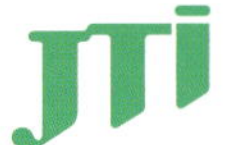

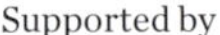

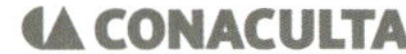

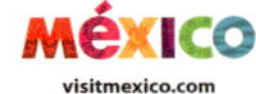

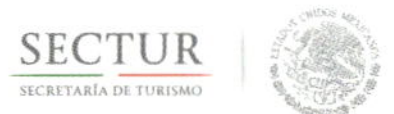

ART MENTOR FOUNDATION LUCERNE

Catherine and Franck Petitgas
James and Clare Kirkman
Mercedes Zobel

British Library Cataloguing-in-Publication Data
A catalogue record for this book is available from the British Library

ISBN 978-1-907533-31-0 (paperback)
ISBN 978-1-907533-30-3 (hardback)

Distributed outside the United States and Canada by Thames & Hudson Ltd, London

Distributed in the United States and Canada by Harry N. Abrams, Inc., New York

EDITORIAL NOTE
Measurements are given in centimetres, height before width.

ILLUSTRATIONS
Pages 2–3: Detail of cat. 69
Pages 12–13: Detail of cat. 45
Pages 18–19: Detail of cat. 6
Pages 50–51: Detail of cat. 50
Pages 102–3: Detail of cat. 83
Pages 156–7: Detail of cat. 108

CONTENTS

6 President's Foreword
8 Supporter's Statement
9 Acknowledgements
10 Map of Mexico

12 Prologue: Unleashing the Tiger
18 Mexico in Flames: 1910–1920
50 The Return of the Native: 1921–1928
102 The Clash of Sun and Shadow: 1929–1934
156 Unadulterated Artistic Creation: 1935–1940
202 Appendix

205 Endnotes
210 Bibliography
215 Lenders to the Exhibition
215 Photographic Acknowledgements
217 Index

President's Foreword

'Mexico: A Revolution in Art, 1910–1940' explores a thirty-year period of upheaval in Mexico that not only transformed the country's political, economic and social landscape but also witnessed an extraordinary flourishing of the arts. The sweeping changes that the Mexican Revolution brought about gave artists the opportunity to celebrate a previously overlooked sense of self; as a consequence Mexican artists began energetically to embrace aspects of their national identity rather than looking north to the US or east to Europe as they had hitherto. The government initially supported an ambitious and wide-ranging cultural programme through, for example, literacy campaigns and open-air art schools, and, crucially, it financed artists and provided them with public spaces in which to work. Dominated by Diego Rivera, José Clemente Orozco and David Alfaro Siqueiros, the famed mural programme that has come to define this period tells only part of the story. Unsurprisingly during such a turbulent period, numerous artists and photographers emerged, many of whom have only been recognised relatively recently. Into this rich and diverse mix of Mexican talent came an extraordinary number of international artists, photographers and intellectuals, all of them keen to participate in and experience the changes that were taking place. Mexico rapidly became even more fertile ground for artists and photographers alike. Indeed, as well as producing some of the great figures of twentieth-century art, Mexico played host to many more. The present exhibition, intelligently curated by Adrian Locke, reveals Mexico as a place of vibrant cultural exchange that made a significant, although frequently overlooked, contribution to the development of modern art.

The Royal Academy has been very fortunate to have several individuals championing this exhibition. We would particularly like to thank HE Ambassador Eduardo Medina-Mora Icaza, formerly Mexican Ambassador to the Court of St James's and now serving as Mexican Ambassador in Washington, DC, and Laura Pérez de Medina-Mora, as well as Ignacio Durán Loera and Vanessa Arelle Careveo of the Mexican Embassy, for their enthusiastic support throughout. The Royal Academy would also like to acknowledge the generous and invaluable support of a number of organisations and individuals in making this exhibition possible, including JTI, our Season supporter of exhibitions in the Sackler Wing of Galleries; Conaculta, Sectur and Visit Mexico; the Art Mentor Foundation Lucerne; Catherine and Franck Petitgas; James and Clare Kirkman; Mercedes Zobel; and the Terra Foundation for American Art. We are incredibly grateful to them all. Last, but by no means least, we owe a debt of thanks to all our lenders, who have been greatly encouraging of the exhibition and extraordinarily generous with their loans, and to those who have facilitated the loan of several significant works. We would like to acknowledge that it is only through their continuing support that the Royal Academy has been able to realise 'Mexico: A Revolution in Art, 1910–1940'.

Christopher Le Brun PRA
President, Royal Academy of Arts

Detail of cat. 32

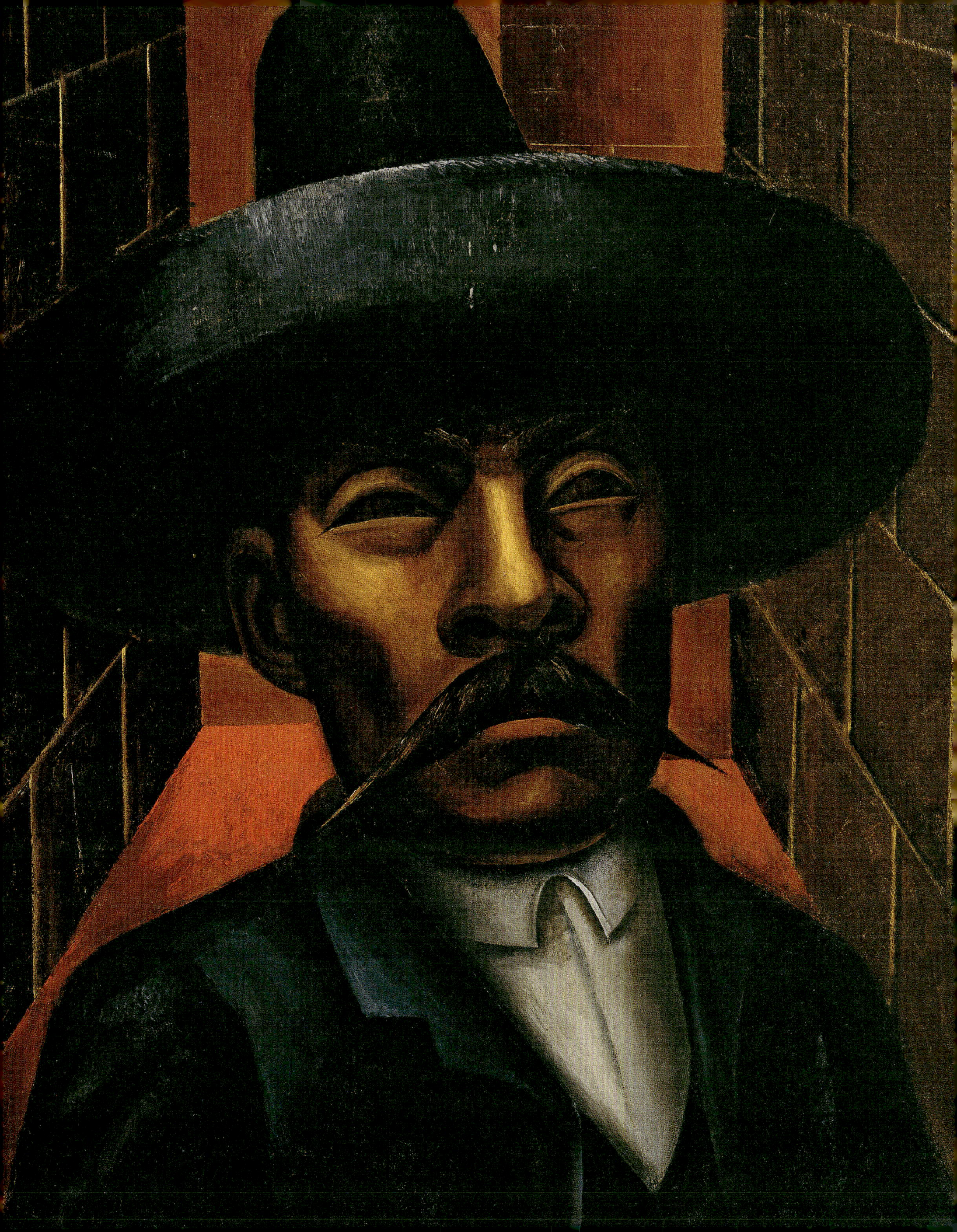

Supporter's Statement

As the long-term Season Supporter of the Sackler Wing of Galleries, JTI is delighted to support this exhibition which captures such an extraordinarily productive and diverse period in Mexico's history. The outbreak of revolution in 1910 heralded an intense thirty-year period of cultural renaissance which attracted not only Mexican artists but also international painters, photographers and intellectuals, all of whom created an inspiring record of a rich and varied country going through great political change. We're delighted to help bring such a fascinating exhibition to UK audiences.

Jorge da Motta
Managing Director UK, JTI

Acknowledgements

Put simply, exhibitions such as this would be impossible to organise without the support of friends and colleagues around the world. I would like to thank the following individuals for their help in making 'Mexico: A Revolution in Art, 1910–1940': Victor Acuña, Barbara Adams, Dawn Ades, Elizabeth Aguilar Díaz López, Leesha M. Alston, María de los Ángeles Sobrino Figueroa, Terri Anderson, Dudley Ankerson, Marisol Argüelles, Barbara and Ted Aronson, Margaret Lynne Ausfeld, Lupita Ayala, Julia T. Bailey, Austen Barron Bailly, Peter Barberie, Luisa Barrios Honey Ruiz, Rebecca Beach, Andrés Blaisten, Anthony Boadle, Vanessa Bohórquez, Clarissa and Edgar Bronfman Jr, Gerald Buck, Ashley L. Carey, Neil Casey, Deborah Chambers, Emilia Chambers, Marina Chao, Gabriela Chávez, Ana P. Christlieb Pardo, Sara Cochran, Alicia Colen, Armando Colina, Alexander Corcoran, Brenda Danilowitz, Andrée Dell, Manuel Díaz Cebrián, Richard Dorment, Michael Duncan, Lourdes Fava, Octavio Fernández Barrios, Rebecca Finlayson, Rhiannon Flemming, Polly Fleury, Nicholas Fox Weber, Samantha Gainsburg, Amy Galpin, Gabriela Gálvez Morales, Gabriela Garciadiego del Río, John Gordon Jones, Nicola Gray, Salomon Grimberg, Clementine Hampshire, Sabrina Handler, Evelyn Hankins, Joseph Holbach, Heather Hole, Vivienne Hughes, Graciela Iturbide, Jorge Jiménez, María Jiménez, Robin Kiang, Grace Kook-Anderson, Arpad Kovacs, Catherine Lampert, Rebecca E. Lawton, Dan Leers, Doïna Lemny, Heinz Liesbrock, Robert R. Littman, William Low, Anne M. Lyden, Caroline McCarthy, Mauricio Maillé Iturbe, Mary-Anne Martin, Simon Martin, Jessica May, Claire Mayoh, Betsi Meissner, Carmen Melián, Rosie Micklewright, Larry Mitchell, Diana Mogollón, Timothy Mosman, Trinity Parker, Martin Parr, María Patiño Richarte, Anne E. Peterson, Carlos Phillips Olmedo, Susie Pickering, Lilia Prado Canchola, Helga Prignitz-Poda, Aude Raimbault, Lyndsey N. Raney, Eliza Rathbone, Kate Reeve, María Elena Rico Covarrubias, Joseph J. Rishel, Norberto L. Rivera, José Antonio Rodríguez, Víctor T. Rodríguez Rangel, John Rohrbach, Cora Rosevear, Brandon K. Ruud, Consuelo Sáizar, Colin Samson, Sandra Sánchez Martínez, Peter D. Schneider, Nina Shor Fastag, Barry Sloane, S. Jackie Souryavong, Karen Lee Spaulding, Susan Fisher Sterling, Jane Stevenson, Carl Brandon Strehlke, Kerry Styles, Justine Sundaram, Michael R. Taylor, David Thomson, Spencer Throckmorton, Andreas Timmer, Hank Tusinski, Emily Underwood, Jocelyn Underwood, Joshua Underwood, Tiggy Underwood, Alexis Valticos, Jennifer Otte Vanim, Elias Vivas, Andrew Walker, Stacey Walsh, Offer Waterman, Sonia Wiffen, Michael Wilson, Rebecca Withers, Philippa Wright, Cynthia Young and Haydé Zavala.

I would also like to thank all my colleagues at the Royal Academy of Arts, past and present, for their enthusiastic support of this project and for their help in nursing the seed of an idea through to its germination as an exhibition.

I made much use of the holdings and resources of the following libraries and archives during the research and writing of this book: the Albert Sloman Library (University of Essex), the British Library, the Getty Research Institute, the Henry Moore Institute Archive, the London Library, the Museum of Modern Art Archives, the National Art Library (at the Victoria and Albert Museum), the Royal Academy of Arts Library and the Tate Archive and Library. Without these collections and their supportive staff I would have found the task infinitely more difficult, if not unfeasible.

Finally I would like to thank Joanne Harwood for both her support and her unshakeable faith in my abilities: this book is as much hers as mine. To our daughter Lily Marguerite, who has kept my feet firmly on the ground and made sure that I had my priorities right over the first five years of her life, I dedicate this book.

Adrian Locke
Curator, Royal Academy of Arts

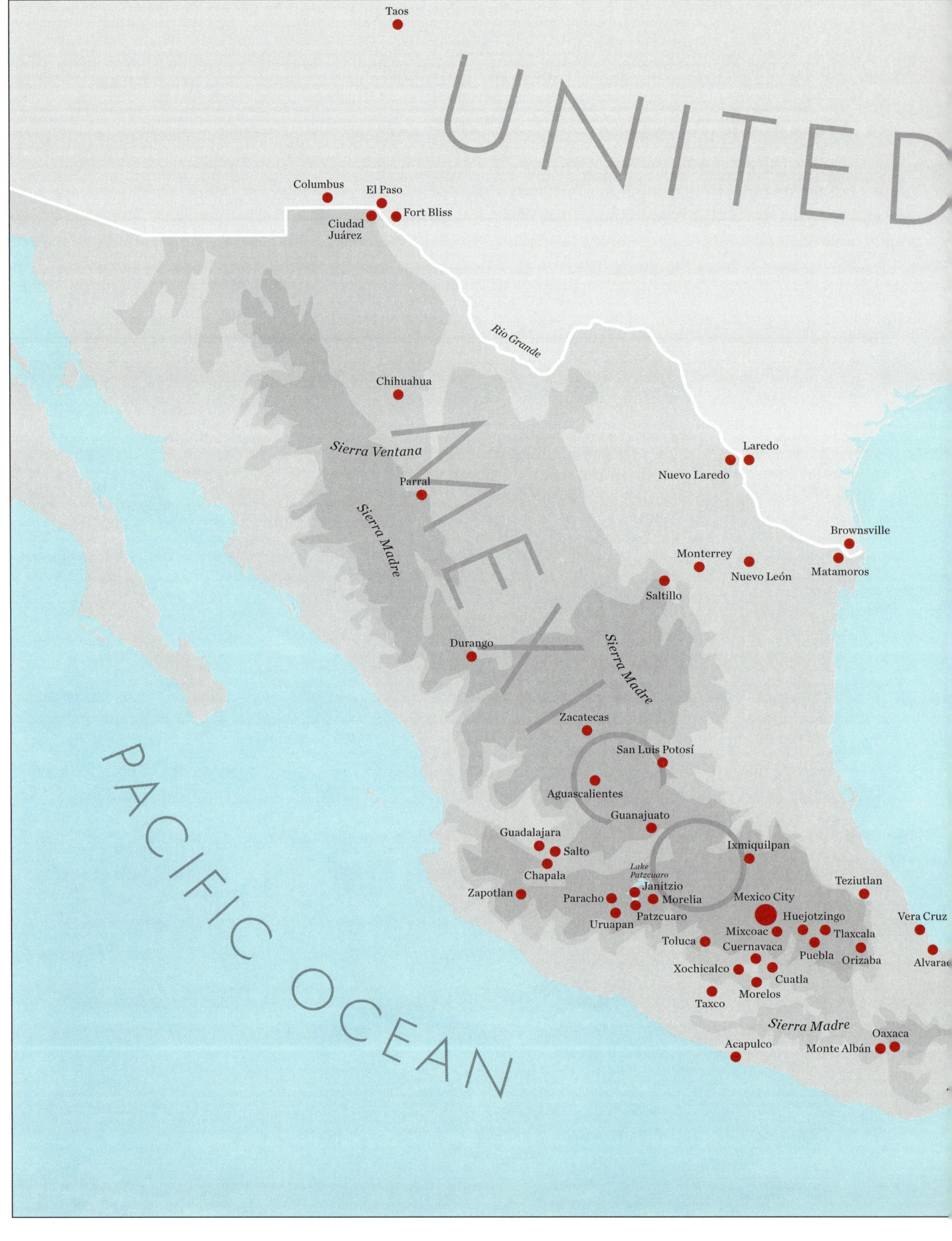

Taos
UNITED
Columbus
El Paso
Fort Bliss
Ciudad Juárez
Rio Grande
Chihuahua
MEXICO
Sierra Ventana
Parral
Sierra Madre
Laredo
Nuevo Laredo
Brownsville
Monterrey
Nuevo León
Matamoros
Saltillo
Durango
Sierra Madre
Zacatecas
San Luis Potosí
Aguascalientes
Guanajuato
Guadalajara
Salto
Chapala
Ixmiquilpan
Lake Patzcuaro
Janitzio
Zapotlan
Paracho
Morelia
Uruapan
Patzcuaro
Teziutlan
Mexico City
Huejotzingo
Vera Cruz
Mixcoac
Tlaxcala
Toluca
Cuernavaca
Puebla
Orizaba
Xochicalco
Cuatla
Morelos
Taxco
Sierra Madre
Oaxaca
Acapulco
Monte Albán
PACIFIC OCEAN

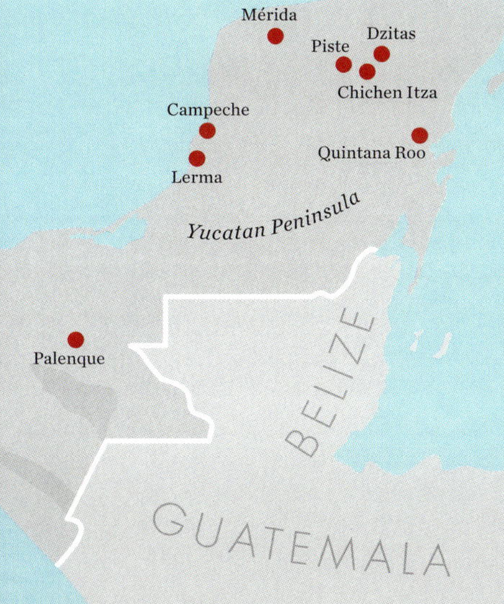
STATES
ULF OF MEXICO
CUBA
N
Mérida
Piste
Dzitas
Chichen Itza
Campeche
Lerma
Quintana Roo
Yucatan Peninsula
Palenque
BELIZE
GUATEMALA

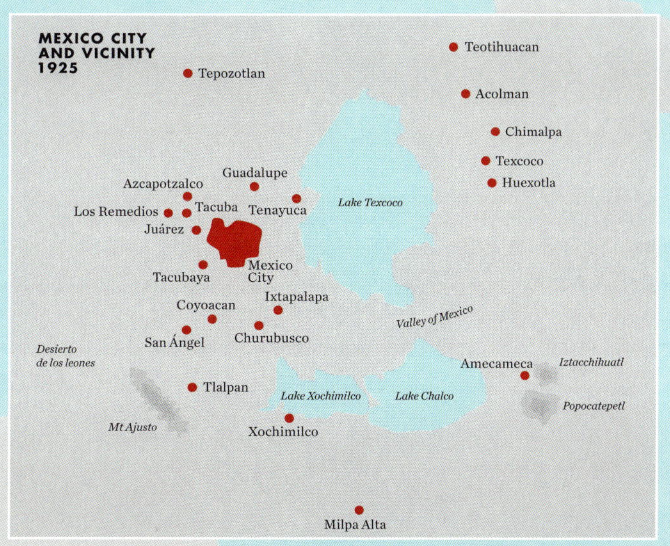
MEXICO CITY
AND VICINITY
1925
Tepozotlan
Teotihuacan
Acolman
Chimalpa
Texcoco
Huexotla
Guadalupe
Azcapotzalco
Los Remedios
Tacuba
Tenayuca
Lake Texcoco
Juárez
Tacubaya
Mexico
City
Ixtapalapa
Coyoacan
Valley of Mexico
San Ángel
Churubusco
Desierto
de los leones
Amecameca
Iztacchihuatl
Tlalpan
Lake Xochimilco
Lake Chalco
Popocatepetl
Mt Ajusto
Xochimilco
Milpa Alta

PROLOGUE

Unleashing the Tiger

Any political construction, if it is to be truly productive, must derive from the most ancient, stable and lasting part of our national being: the indigenous past.[1]

OCTAVIO PAZ

There is no thrill in the world quite equal to the thrill of knowing you are on your way to Mexico.[2]

PHILIP GUEDALLA

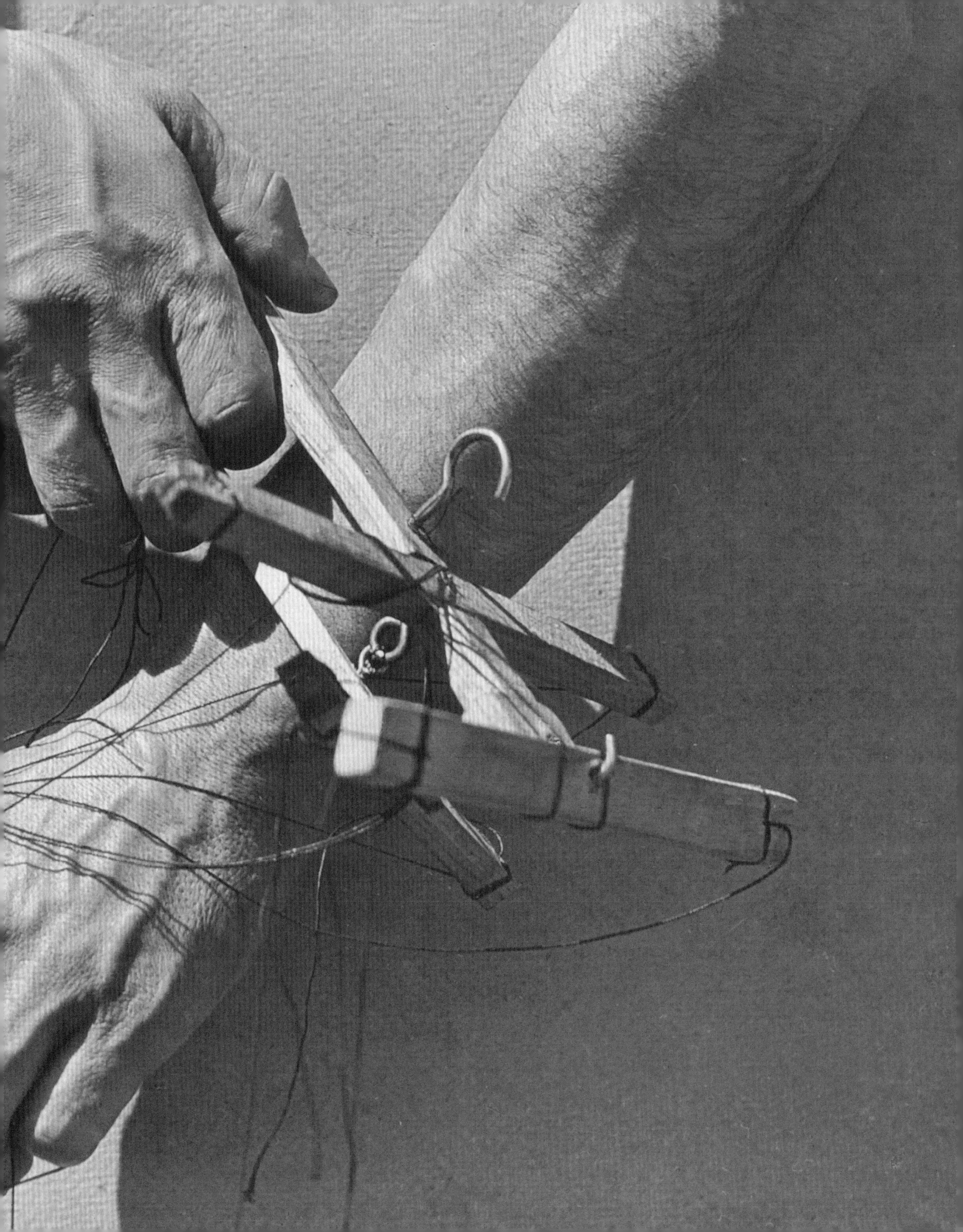

IN 1911, AS JOSÉ DE LA CRUZ PORFIRIO DÍAZ made his way to Vera Cruz – the port on the Gulf of Mexico where Hernán Cortés had landed some four hundred years earlier, claiming Mexico in the name of the King of Spain – and exile in France, he is reputed to have turned to the commander of his military escort and said, 'Madero has unleashed a tiger. Now let's see if he can control it.'[3] Porfirio Díaz was correct in the sense that his enforced departure led to a decade of bloodshed and revolution in Mexico. What he certainly did not envisage was that the same tiger would also have a voracious appetite for artistic expression. In the years from 1910 the country witnessed a flourishing of the arts that has continued to develop ever since. 'Mexico: A Revolution in Art, 1910–1940' explores a short but highly significant period that has, in many different ways and for better or worse, shaped the international perspective of twentieth-century art in Mexico.

The book has three main aims. The first is to ensure that the important role Mexico played in the history of twentieth-century art is neither overlooked nor forgotten. The second is to reveal the extraordinary wealth of art produced in Mexico during the period by both Mexican and international artists and photographers, although here limitations must be admitted, since the selection can only begin to scratch the surface of a very deep and surprisingly untapped vein of material. The third is to examine the inter-relationships that arose between artists and photographers as a result of their work during this time. Mexico boasted a dynamic and resourceful artistic community, and the connections that developed between artists and photographers are fascinating on both a personal and an artistic level. Through the works included here we can investigate these links and, in particular, attempt to show how artists, even when looking at the same subject, could see something quite differently and represent it in contrasting ways; where some created a likeness, others captured an essence.

The selection focuses on a specific period, in this case the thirty years between 1910, the outbreak of the Revolution, and 1940, the end of the presidency of Lázaro Cárdenas, arguably the last revolutionary president. The first section covers the ten-year period of the Mexican Revolution, both to provide context for the art that was produced over the following two decades and also to demonstrate that even in conflict Mexico was a country full of artistic endeavour. Indeed, perhaps unsurprisingly, the visual language of the Revolution has remained vibrant to this day. Although there may be room for debate about the extent and durability of the political, social and economic rupture that the Revolution brought about, one thing is certain: it changed permanently the art and culture of Mexico, not only in terms of the way the country looked to its pre-Columbian past but also how it represented the present and regarded the future. Hence the title of the book reflects the vibrant transformation that took place in the arts in Mexico during the first decades of the twentieth century. The gradual changes in society that came about through increased urbanisation and, thanks to augmented economic growth and prosperity, the enlargement of the middle class created an expanded appetite and demand for art. In this rarefied environment of public and private money, artists proliferated.

The proximity of Mexico to the United States was also significant. Not only did Mexican artists enjoy considerable exposure and success there, but American and other international artists, writers, photographers and film-makers flocked to Mexico from the US, drawn to the surge of creativity taking place there. In this case, at least, the old adage 'Poor Mexico! So far from God, so close to the United States' seems to have worked in the country's favour – many saw Mexico in a positive light, as a place of escape from the demands of the modern world. People came overland by car or train, or by sea. If they had money they travelled by train; travelling by sea from the US was cheaper, slower and more uncomfortable, as Graham Greene discovered. Indeed, many transatlantic passages were available from Europe via Havana.

The book examines the period through both painting and photography. The richness of the material and thigh standing of many of the artists and photographers are remarkable. Mexico was no quiet backwater, but attracted and produced some of the greatest names in twentieth-century art. In a sense, two stories cross over one another.

The first concerns the art produced by Mexican artists and photographers during this era. Carefully selected works by major Mexican artists form the spine of the selection, giving a sense of the wide range of artists working at this time and their different approaches. This reinforces the reality that artists were working as individuals rather than as a collective, despite fleeting moments of union. It was not until the foundation of the Taller de Gráfica Popular (TGP) in 1937, a subject outside the scope of this book, that a meaningful and durable artistic collective was formed in Mexico.[4] Thus the choice of works has been made with a view to revealing the power and diversity of Mexican art, providing at least a glimpse of its riches. It is hoped that this will engender a hunger to see and learn more. Furthermore, these major works help to communicate a sense of the exciting environment that awaited visitors to Mexico at the time – for art, literally in the case of the prevalent mural programme, surrounded everyone and was very much part of any tourist's itinerary, especially in Mexico City.

The second part of the narrative looks at the extraordinary number of international artists who came to Mexico and responded to what they saw and experienced there. In some instances small, focused groups of works illustrate the effect that Mexico had on people and the art they created during or after their visits. Here the cross-fertilisation that took place among artists in Mexico will be apparent, as will the various ways that artists responded to the same subject-matter. In order to provide an alternative perspective to those of artists and photographers, the experiences of a select number of novelists are also included, concentrating on British writers who travelled to and, in some cases, lived in Mexico for a time. D. H. Lawrence, Graham Greene and Malcolm Lowry all found that Mexico brought forth an intense introspection, and their novels – *The Plumed Serpent*, *The Power and the Glory* and *Under the Volcano* – are much more explorations of the self than descriptions of the country in which they are set. With all the different challenges and rewards it provided, Mexico gave artists, photographers and writers an environment that encouraged them to question their fundamental, often spiritual, values and clearly inspired creativity. Somehow it was able to give artists a freedom they had not hitherto experienced.

Even during the turbulent days of the Revolution, Mexico attracted visitors. The war correspondents and entrepreneurs who came first soon gave way to a variety of individuals attracted to a country that until relatively recently, when it gained independence from Spain in 1821, had remained largely closed to foreigners. Many were drawn by what they saw as Mexico's authenticity at a time when the US seemed to be losing its own; others went because Mexico was assumed to be a liberal country, in which attitudes towards open relationships, homosexuality, drinking and drugs were fairly relaxed. These perceptions were often misplaced, as visitors soon found on arrival; their behaviour was often inadvertently offensive to the local population and revealed a lack of understanding or respect for the country in which they were guests, where political cronyism abounded, poverty was widespread and, significantly, Catholicism remained very popular. For many, Mexico was simply cheap, and small allowances could be eked out to last longer than in the US or Europe. Some came for work, and others for holidays. A few travelled to Mexico because their visas to the US had expired, and others were drawn by left-wing politics and the apparent success of the Revolution. Many were influenced by word of mouth, encouraged by friends or colleagues who presented Mexico as a land of opportunity for artists. Although Mexico tended to be seen as a place to have fun, in which (almost) anything went, the country's extraordinarily rich cultural heritage also had great appeal – not just the wealth of its pre-Columbian cultures, but the living culture, with its wide range of regional identities complete with their own languages, traditions and creativity. Combined with the powerful and distinctive landscapes of Mexico, which often presented major challenges in terms of moving around, this ethnic diversity gave visitors a real sense of adventure and discovery. For those willing to make the effort, the feeling of achievement was palpable. Mexico preserved an aura of mystery and romance, even though the reality may have been more sobering. The country's allure did not always live up to expectations; as Vladimir Mayakovsky put it, 'And here I stand, dumbstruck, as though before my very eyes peacocks were being turned into chickens.'[5] One thing, however, is clear, despite the variety of challenges it presented and the misconceptions it suffered: Mexico made a deep and lasting impression on those who journeyed there.

Although Mexican art of this period boasts a considerable bibliography and continues to attract much valuable and recent scholarship, a surprisingly small corpus of works examines Mexico in an international context. Three of these, which have provided a source of considerable inspiration for this study and are also arguably the most important, are the pioneering *South of the Border: Mexico in the American Imagination 1914–1947* (New Haven, 1993), the catalogue for an exhibition curated by James Oles; *México: Through Foreign Eyes, 1850–1990* (Mexico City, 1993), curated by Carole Naggar and Fred Ritchin; and *Mexicana: Fotografía moderna en México, 1923–1940* (Valencia, 1998), the catalogue of the exhibition curated by Salvador Albiñana and Horacio Fernández. The present book is intended to act as a modest contribution to this body of work and to highlight the extraordinary impact that Mexico has had on modern art.

Detail of cat. 117

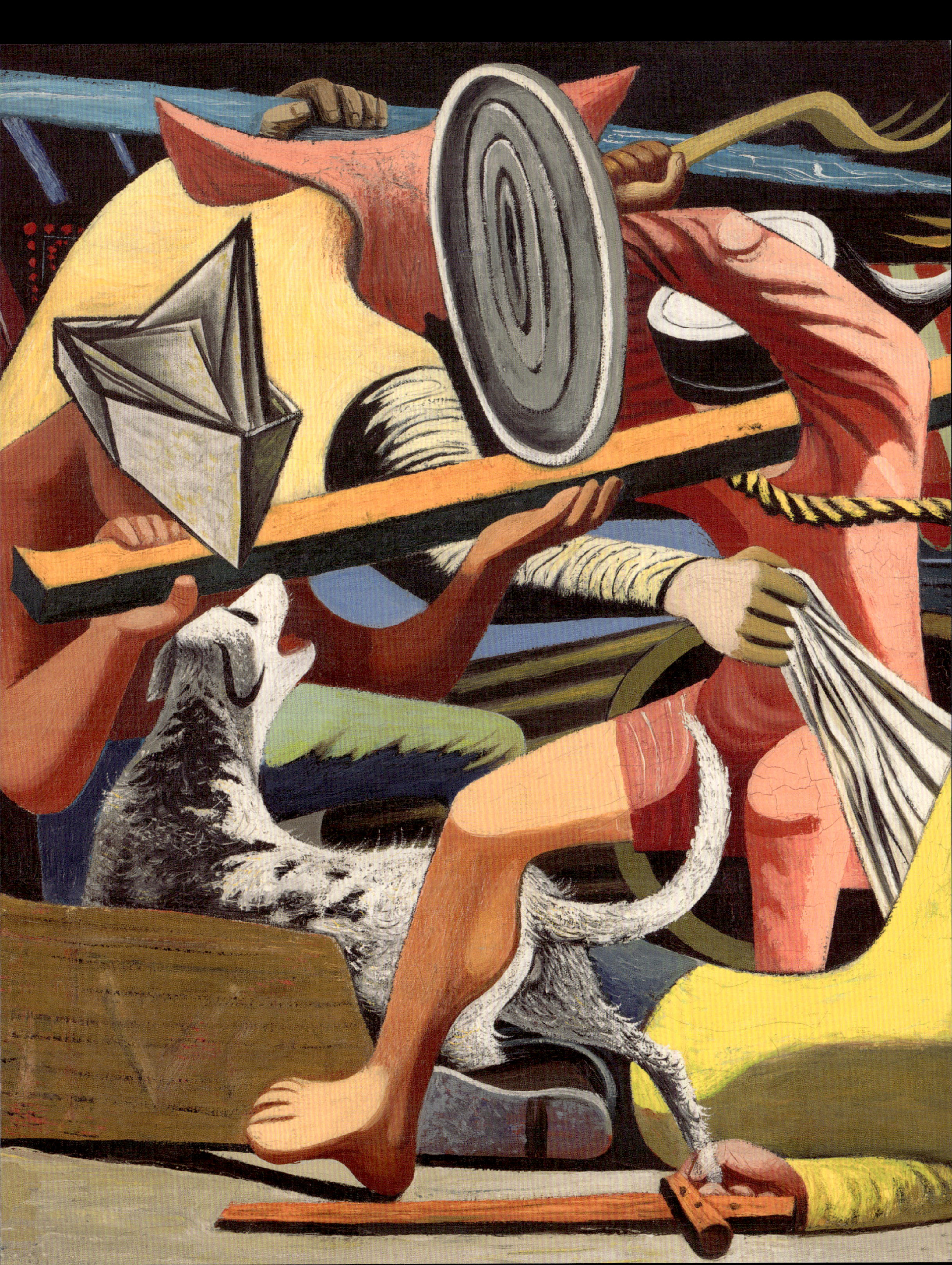

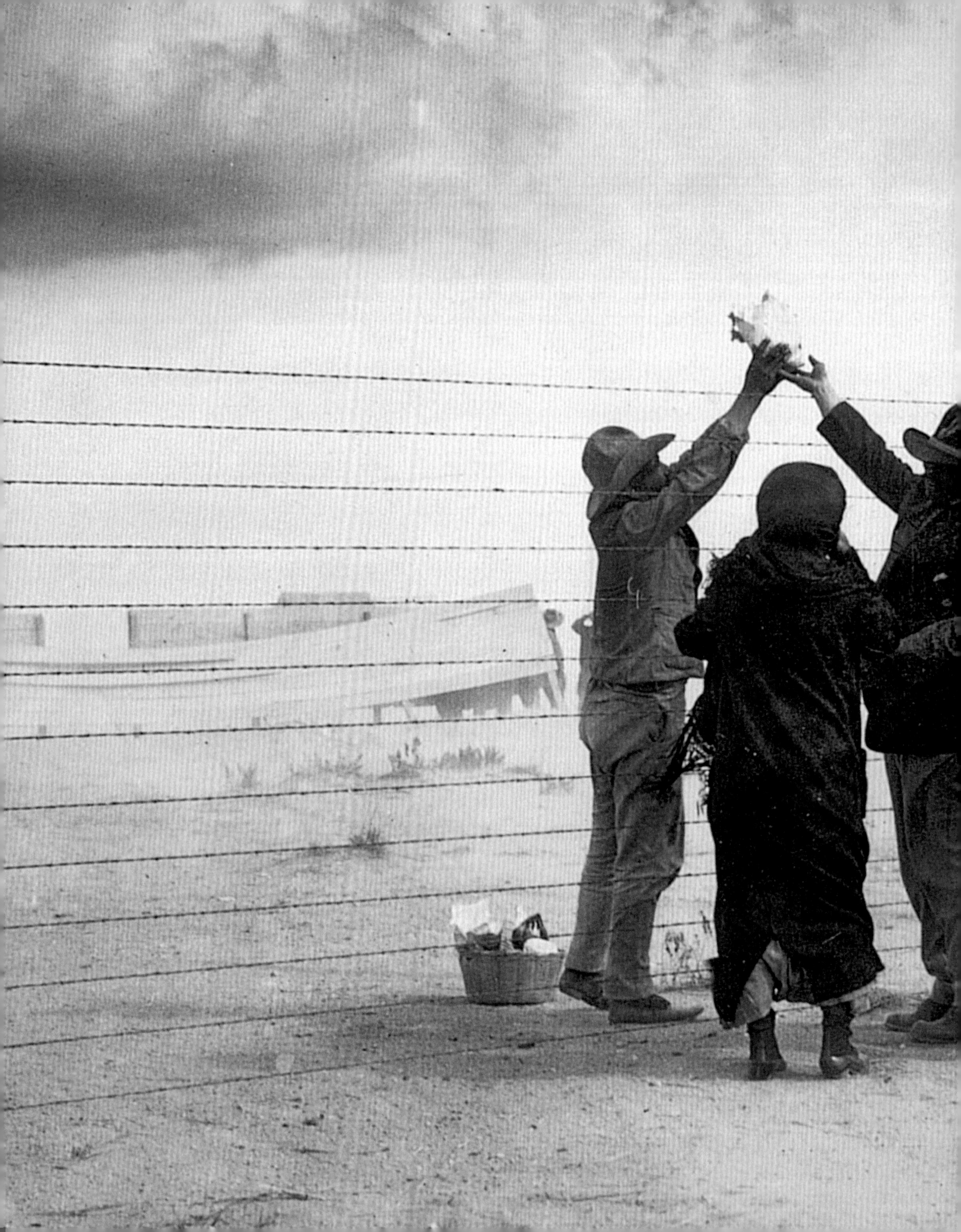

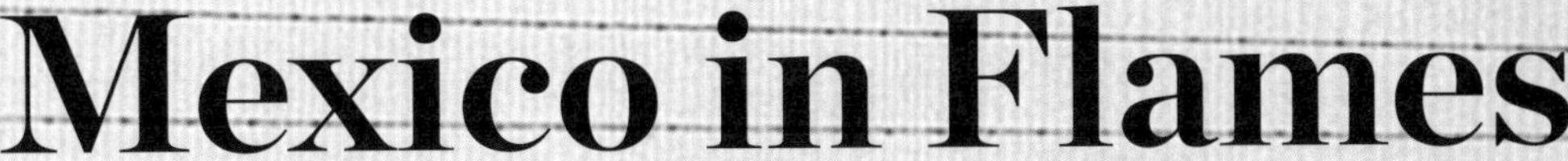

Mexico in Flames

1910–1920

For this is above all
a land of pain.[1]

FRANCISCO GOITIA

How beautiful the revolution is,
even in its savagery![2]

MARIANO AZUELA

THE YEAR 1910 WAS A MOMENTOUS ONE in the modern history of Mexico. Halley's Comet was visible in the skies above the country, causing great excitement. Initially taken as an auspicious sign, its appearance was later seen as a presage of violent change in much the same way that the Mexica (Aztec) had viewed the passage of a comet in 1517, on the eve of the arrival of the Spanish *conquistadores*, led by Hernán Cortés (fig. 1). The same year saw the centennial celebrations of the first uprising against Spanish colonial rule in the Mexican War of Independence in 1810, led by two great heroes of Mexican history, Miguel Hidalgo and José María Morelos. There were also presidential elections in 1910. The incumbent, Porfirio Díaz, was confident of winning a seventh term of office, having held the presidency for all but four years since 1876, a period known as the 'Porfiriato'. His opponent, Francisco Madero, from the north-eastern state of Coahuila, the cosmopolitan son of one of Mexico's wealthiest families, had built up a personal fortune within the Madero economic empire, which owned vast swathes of land, factories and mines.[3] Whereas Porfirio Díaz was content to maintain the *status quo*, Madero was a modernist reformer who wished to introduce political and social change as well as to improve agriculture, mining and industry through technological innovation.

Although Porfirio Díaz had presided over a period of unprecedented peace and stability in Mexico, he had also overseen the creation of a small and wealthy landowning class that dominated the country both economically and politically, with vast feudal land holdings and diverse commercial interests. Those who invested foreign capital in Mexico in the development of the railways, the telegraph system and oil, mining and smelting were allowed to make huge profits, paying little if any tax. To make matters worse, these profits were routinely taken out of the country. Porfirio Díaz's regime was not, however, a military one; the army was not autonomous, rather it responded to the wishes of the president, but not having faced a major opponent since the French in 1867, it was ill-prepared for things to come. Porfirio

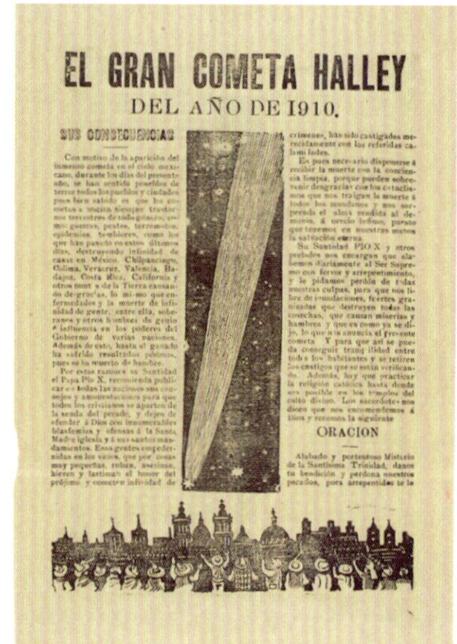

EL GRAN COMETA HALLEY
DEL AÑO DE 1910.

Fig. 1 José Guadalupe Posada, **The Great Halley's Comet of 1910 (El gran cometa Halley del año de 1910)**, 1910. Broadside, 29.9 x 19.9 cm. Art Institute of Chicago, 1943.1254

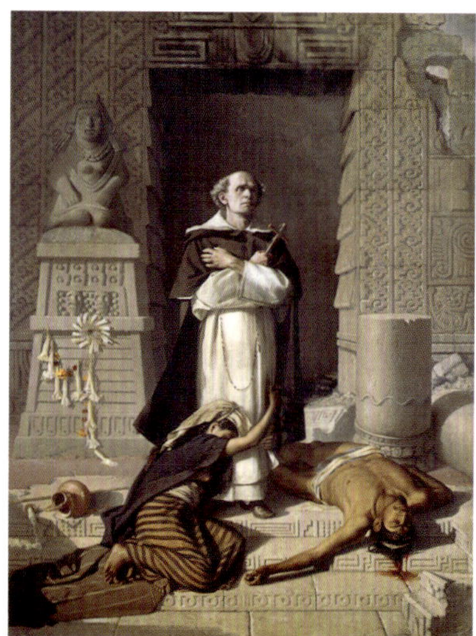

Fig. 2 Félix Parra, **Fray Bartolomé de las Casas**, 1875. Oil on canvas, 358.1 x 266.7 cm. Museo Nacional de Arte (MUNAL) – Instituto Nacional de Bellas Artes (INBA), Mexico City

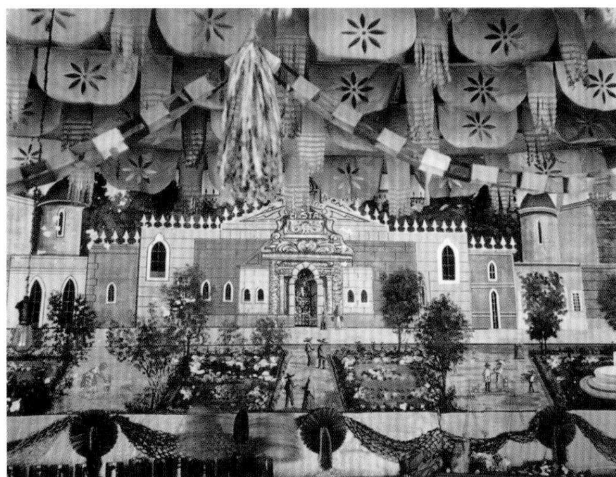

Fig. 3 Edward Weston, **Pulquería Interior**, 1926. Gelatin silver print, 19.1 x 23.8 cm. Center for Creative Photography, University of Arizona, Tucson, 82.8.61

Díaz ruled from the centre over a vast network of local political hierarchies, all of them dependent on the presidency for their position and wealth. Although these officials were often corrupt and habitually violated the rule of law, they were free to act as they pleased as long as they preserved the interests of the central government. The élite lived in luxury, imitating the Belle Epoque style of France and the East Coast cities of the United States, while the industrial and agricultural working classes laboured in poverty.

Art during the Porfiriato was the preserve of the upper classes. Paradoxically, given that they did little or nothing to further the rights of the indigenous population of Mexico, they admired, for example, great academic allegorical paintings celebrating the noble actions of the Mexica when confronted by the brutality of the *conquistadores*, or the selfless deeds of the celebrated Dominican friar Bartolomé de las Casas, who championed the human rights of the native inhabitants (fig. 2). Genre paintings were not much favoured. As the French-born painter Jean Charlot acidly commented, 'the rich thrive on alabaster statuettes, Louis XV pianos and telephones in the style of Louis XVI'.[4] In other words, art mirrored society and can be described in large part as very conservative, lagging behind the visual and technical innovations championed by the European *avant-garde*. Across Mexico, however, the popular arts were thriving in a wide variety of forms including painting, mostly anonymous. There were, for instance, decorative wall paintings produced for *pulquerías* (bars selling *pulque*, a cheap alcoholic drink made from maguey) and *ex-votos* (small paintings, usually on tin, offered to specific saints in gratitude for saving people from death or serious injury and donated to churches), as well as broadsheets that carried zinc-plate etchings of sensational events and crimes. These demonstrate that there was an appetite for artistic representation among the lower classes in Mexico and that there was a body of artists who could be approached to carry out such commissions (fig. 3). For a country with poor literacy, images remained a significant means of conveying information.

Unsurprisingly, cracks were appearing in Mexican society as the lower classes began to challenge their employers to provide better conditions. Workers' protests and stoppages were met with violent state-led repression. Over time a small liberal opposition emerged and, through Madero, challenged Porfirio Díaz for the presidency in 1910. Few were surprised when Porfirio Díaz won the election and embarked on extravagant celebrations to mark the centenary, which fortuitously coincided with his electoral victory and his eightieth birthday.

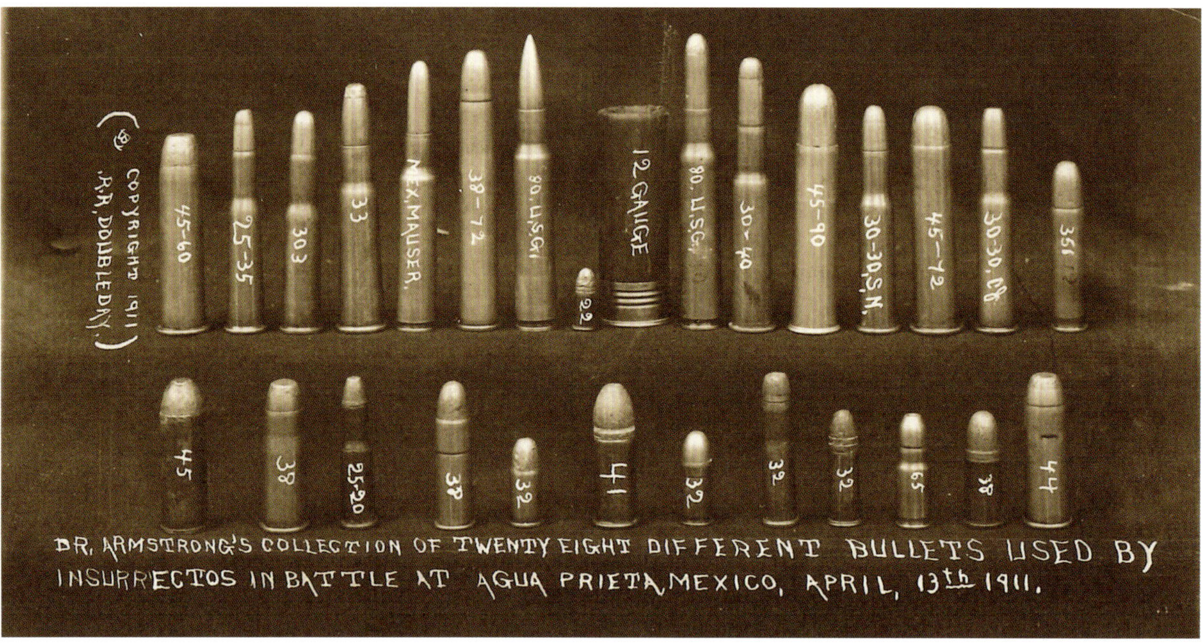

Madero, who had been arrested and jailed on the day of the election, 21 June 1910, was released on bail and subsequently escaped to the US. On his return to Mexico later in the year, Madero reluctantly conceded that the only way to get rid of Porfirio Díaz was by force. He engaged in a number of small successful military engagements before his forces laid siege to the northern frontier town of Ciudad Juárez in Chihuahua. Thus, in late 1910, the Mexican Revolution was born. Few could have predicted, however, when Ciudad Juárez fell to the rebel forces in May 1911 and Porfirio Díaz resigned from office, leaving Mexico for Paris where he died in exile in 1915, that the country would be engulfed by a bitter ten-year conflict (fig. 4, cat. 1).

Indeed Madero's victory was short-lived; having assumed the presidency in 1911 he was assassinated two years later. Rather than ushering in an era of political transition and reform, the deposition of Porfirio Díaz unleashed an armed, nationwide uprising that caused huge destruction, loss of life and population displacement (cats 2–6). The period was marked by political instability caused by frequent changes of president, often necessitated by the hand of the assassin. Although at first glance the Mexican Revolution might appear to be a multitude of disparate, local revolts, it was in fact a popular agrarian movement that 'arose in the provinces, established itself in the countryside, and finally conquered an alien and sullen capital'.[5] Ironically, the greatest

1

Walter H. Horne (1883–1921)
Dr Armstrong's Collection of Twenty-eight Different Bullets used by Rebels in Battle at Agua Prieta, Mexico, April 13, 1911, 1911.
Gelatin silver print (postcard), 8.26 x 13.34 cm. Courtesy of Arizona Historical Society/Tucson AHS 43167

single problem for the various governments from 1910 onwards remained the one that had confronted Porfirio Díaz: how to impose authority from Mexico City on the recalcitrant provinces. The principal test of each government was to overturn decades of regionalism and bring an end to the ethnic rivalry and suspicion that further fragmented the country. There were to be no quick solutions to these challenges.[6]

The Mexican Revolution was many things: complex, drawn out, fragmented, brutal and destructive. It brought about wholesale change in Mexican society, including its art world. A decisive rupture with the past ushered in a whole new era of creativity. The seeds of that creativity were sown during the Revolution and, once the conflict was over, germinated and blossomed during a period of unprecedented artistic activity from 1920 onwards. In order to reach that point, however, Mexico had to pass through a transitional decade during which a new, visceral reportage-style art emerged, thanks in the main to technical advances in photography and film. This art was documentary in style, accessible, portable and cheap. Heroic pictures of generals and presidents jostled alongside images that laid bare the extreme brutality of war. No longer bound by the conventions of taste or censorship, individuals recorded the Revolution on still and moving film. Indeed, the Revolution received more news coverage than any armed conflict prior to the Second World War.[7] The appearance of cinema, especially in the US, with its rapidly increasing audiences, coupled with the popularity of newsreel, created demand for dramatic topical events. The conflict aroused considerable interest in the US as well as justifiable concerns about

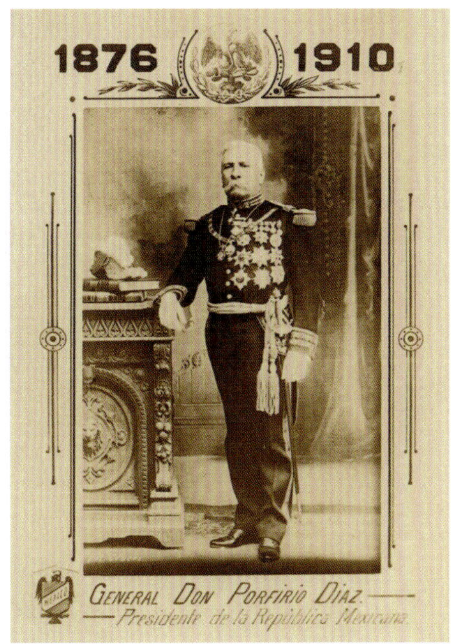

Fig. 4 Cruces, **General Don Porfirio Díaz, Presidente de la República Mexicana, 1876–1910**, *c.* 1910. Gelatin silver print (postcard), 15 x 10 cm. DeGolyer Library, Southern Methodist University, Dallas, Ag2000.1370

national security, especially as the two countries share such an extensive land border. Indeed, so close were they that residents of El Paso, Texas, were able to watch the Battle of Ciudad Juárez between Porfirio Díaz's federal army and rebels loyal to Madero in 1911 from across the Rio Grande like spectators enjoying a weekend sporting event (fig. 6). The US was anxious not only in fear of an invasion, but also because it was by far the largest foreign investor in the country. Internment camps were built across the US border to accommodate the flood of Mexican refugees (cat. 6). There was even debate in some quarters about

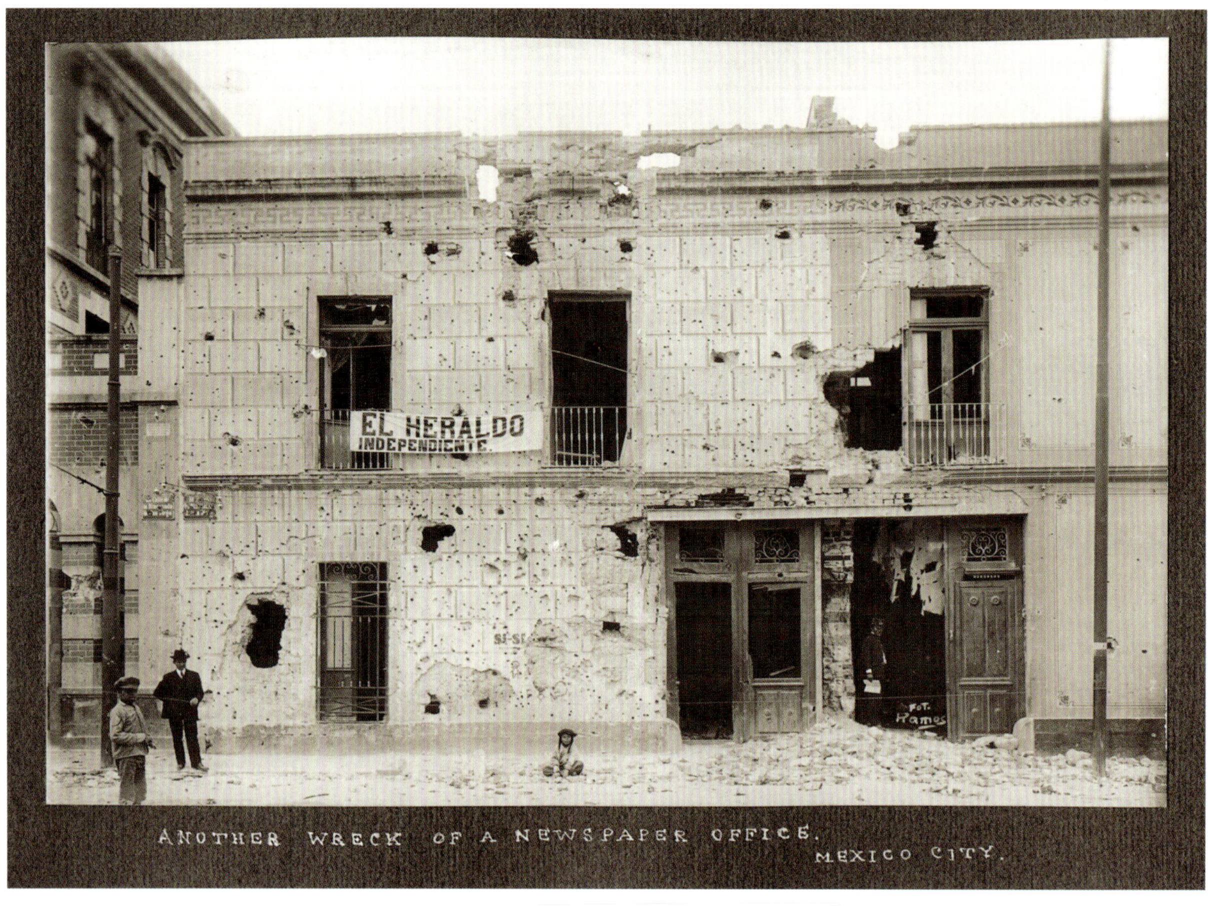

whether the US should annex Mexico to prevent the Revolution from spreading.

Perhaps nothing encapsulates better the apparently insatiable American appetite for news and images of the Mexican Revolution than the deal that Francisco 'Pancho' Villa (fig. 6) struck with the Mutual Film Corporation. The 'most famous bandit-rebel of the Revolution',[8] based in the northern frontier state of Chihuahua, Villa let it be known that he was offering motion-picture rights to cover his campaign to the highest bidder. In one of the most controversial uses of newsreel motion pictures, Villa arranged to fight battles during the hours of daylight, waiting until cameras were in place before launching attacks.[9] In return the Mutual Film Corporation secured the rights to cover Villa's campaign, paying him a staggering sum in 1914 for the privilege.[10] Villa clearly enjoyed being caught on camera and choreographed his movements to maximise the effect of his dramatic entrances on horseback at the head of his troops. Villa and Emiliano Zapata – the other great rebel figure of the Revolution, a Nahuatl-speaking

2

Manuel Ramos (1874–1945)
Another Wreck of a Newspaper Office, Mexico City, 1913.
Gelatin silver print on grey album paper, 10.2 x 15.2 cm.
DeGolyer Library, Southern Methodist University, Dallas

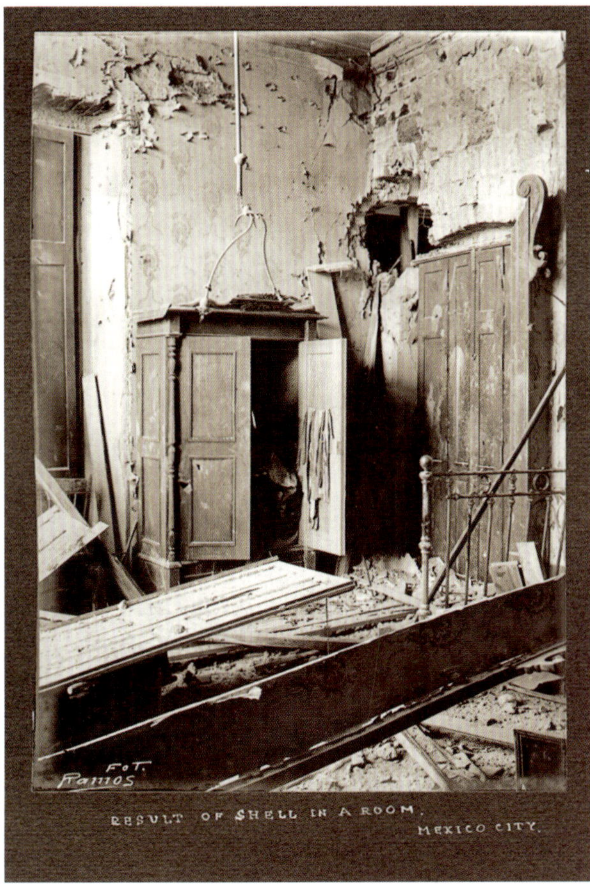

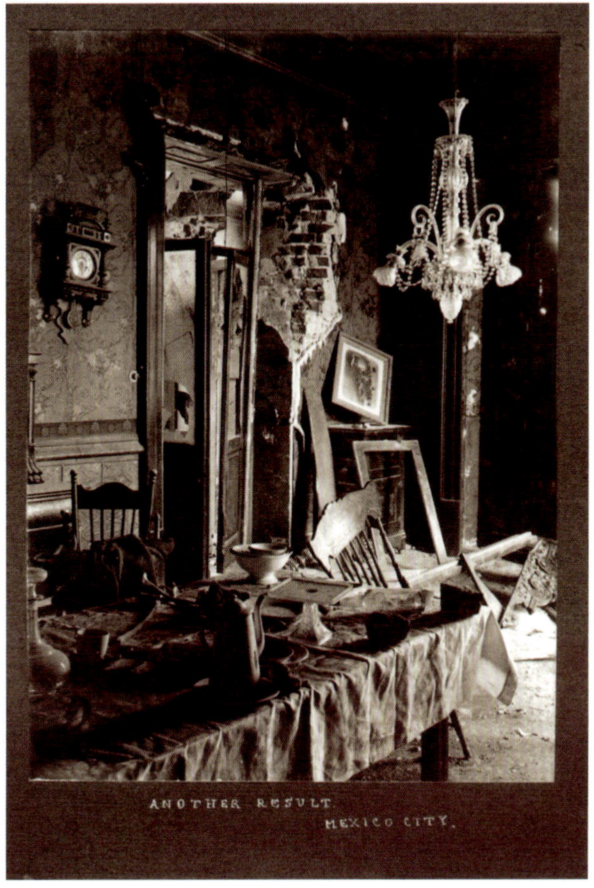

small-scale farmer and community official from Morelos who rose up against the then-President, Venustiano Carranza – came to define the archetypal visual image of the Mexican revolutionary leader as a man of the people with luxuriant moustache, wide-brimmed sombrero and bandolier (cat. 7, figs 6, 11).

Photographs capture and record events for posterity and, despite being open to manipulation and staging, are ordinarily accepted as veritable representations. In a semi-literate society such as Mexico in the 1920s, images conveyed both power and information. Photographs of the Revolution continued to resonate long afterwards, acting as a visual reminder of the individual and collective sacrifices made by the people of Mexico for an equal and just future. Furthermore, photographs could be developed and printed (in multiples) relatively quickly. Once printed, they were highly portable, easily distributed and could be sold relatively cheaply. Photographs went on to become a highly important repository of images that artists could either copy or from which they could draw inspiration.

3

Manuel Ramos (1874–1945)
Result of a Shell in a Room, Mexico City, 1913.
Gelatin silver print on grey album paper, 15.2 x 10.2 cm.
DeGolyer Library, Southern Methodist University, Dallas

4

Manuel Ramos (1874–1945)
Another Result, 1913.
Gelatin silver print on grey album paper, 15.2 x 10.2 cm.
DeGolyer Library, Southern Methodist University, Dallas

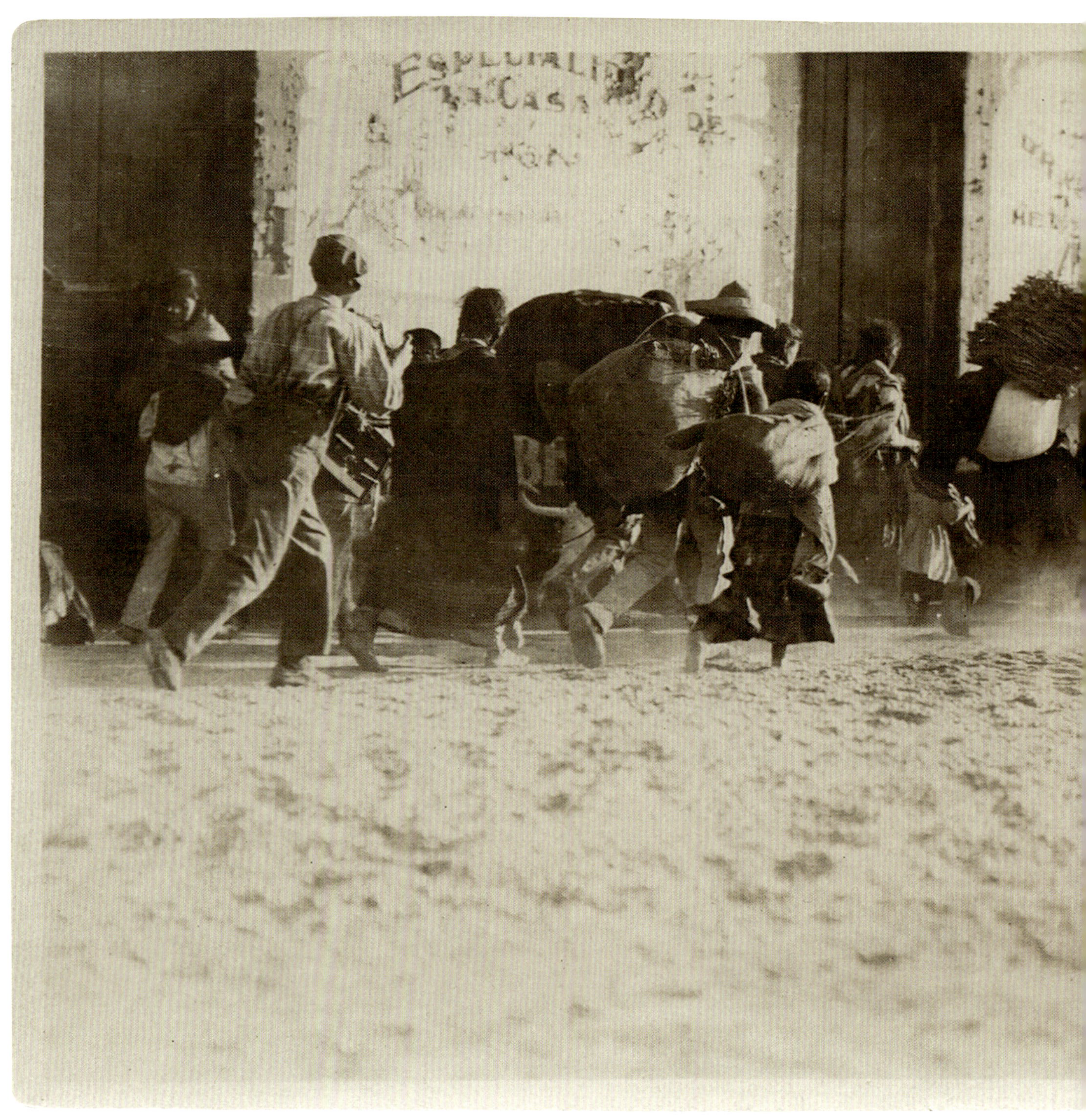

5

Mexico View Co.
Leaving the Danger Zone, February 1913.
Gelatin silver print,
11.5 x 16.5 cm.
DeGolyer Library, Southern Methodist University, Dallas

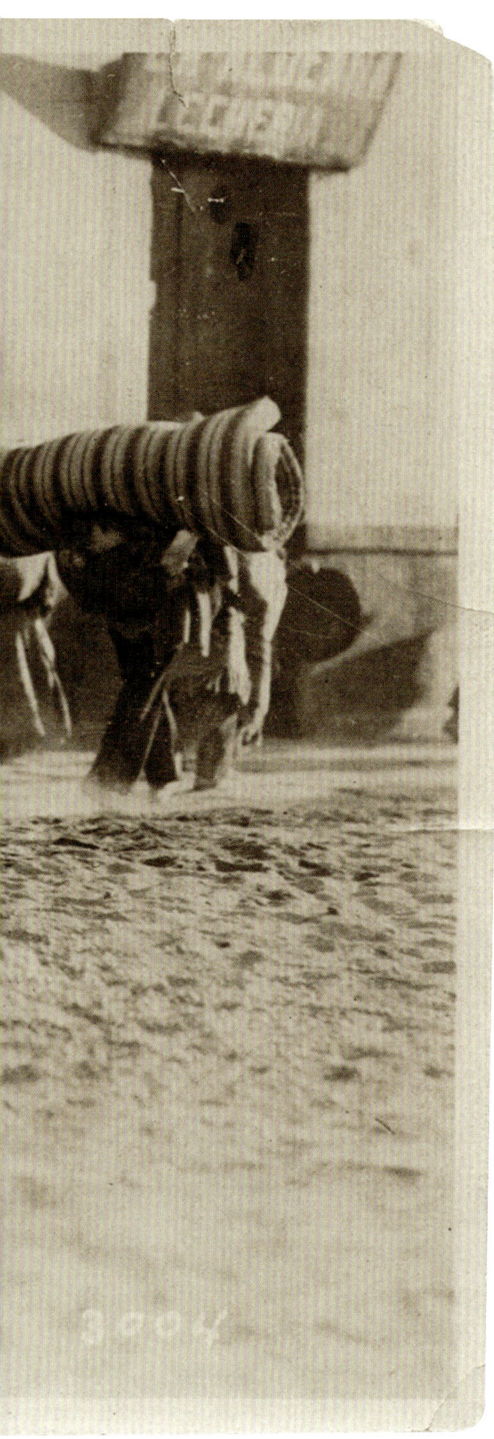

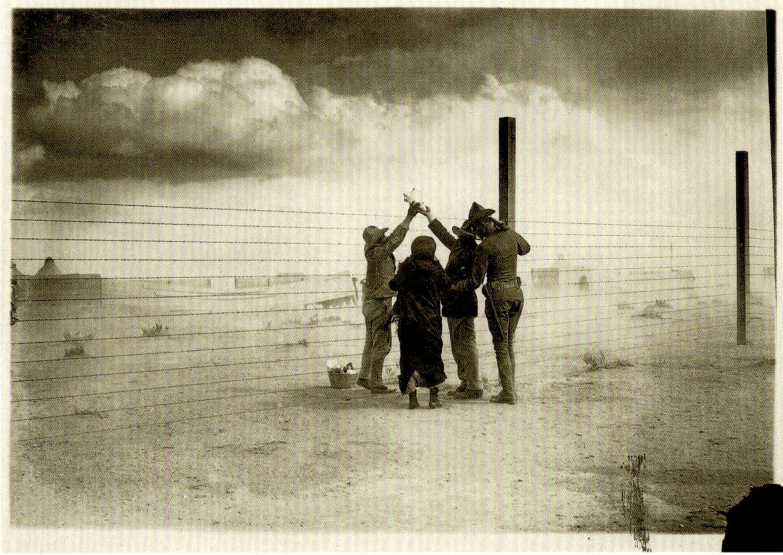

6

Unknown photographer
Fort Bliss Refugee Camp, Texas, *c.* 1914.
Black and white photograph, 12.8 x 17.4 cm.
Cushing Memorial Library and Archives, Texas A&M University, College Station

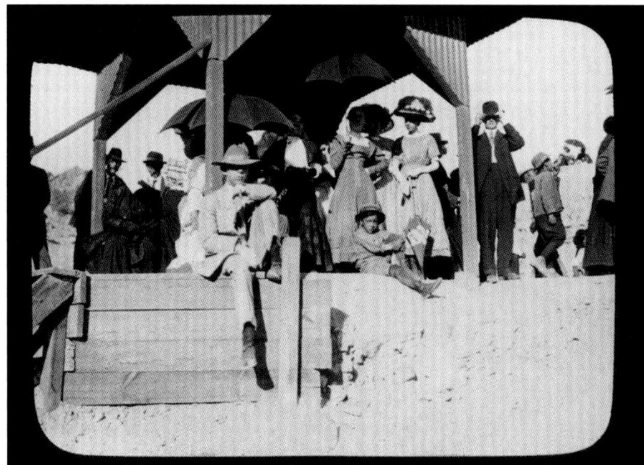

Fig. 5 James H. Hare, **Residents of El Paso Watching the Battle of Ciudad Juárez across the Rio Grande**, 1911. Lantern slide. Photography Collection, Harry Ransom Center, University of Texas, Austin, 1286

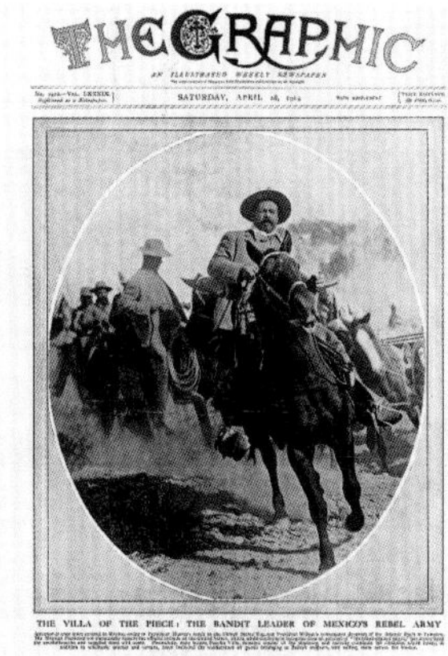

THE GRAPHIC

AN ILLUSTRATED WEEKLY NEWSPAPER

SATURDAY, APRIL 18, 1914

THE VILLA OF THE PIECE: THE BANDIT LEADER OF MEXICO'S REBEL ARMY

Fig. 6 Unknown photographer, 'The Villa of the Piece: The Bandit Leader of Mexico's Rebel Army', *The Graphic*, 18 April 1914, No. 2316, Vol. LXXXIX. Half-tone photomechanical print, 38.5 x 28.5 cm. DeGolyer Library, Southern Methodist University, Dallas, Ag2009.0009x

From the outset the Mexican Revolution was seen as an internationally important event, attracting a number of journalists, including one of the few professional war correspondents of the period, the British-born James 'Jimmy' Hare, to cover it for American newspapers and magazines. Having previously covered the Spanish-American War and the Russo-Japanese War, he reported on the Battle of Ciudad Juárez, the American occupation of Vera Cruz and the Battle of Zacatecas before leaving for Europe to report on the First World War. The American Robert Runyon (fig. 7) also made a name for himself during the Revolution. A resident of Brownsville, Texas, another significant garrison town on the opposite bank of the Rio Grande from Matamoros, Nuevo León, Runyon took up photography in 1910. In 1913 he began taking photographs of the Revolution while following the troops of General Lucio Blanco in northern Mexico. Another journalist who was directly involved was the American John Reed, who was to go on to international fame for *Ten Days that Shook the World* (New York, 1919), his account of the Russian Revolution.

Before Reed travelled to Europe in 1914 to report on the First World War, he spent several months reporting on the Mexican Revolution for the highly regarded investigative journal *Metropolitan*. On his return to the US in April 1914, Reed (fig. 8) was sufficiently moved by his experiences to write about his time there, and this was published later that year as *Insurgent Mexico* (New York, 1914).[11] His gripping first-hand account reveals the high levels of hardship and comradeship he encountered as well as his near-constant exposure to violence, destruction and the threat of death. Reed interviewed Pancho Villa – by then governor of Chihuahua and at the height of his power – portraying him as plain-speaking yet, above all, a modest, just and honest man. This image was quite different to that portrayed by others, such as the American photographer Walter Horne.

7

Unknown photographer
Gen. Villa, *c.* 1914–17.
Gelatin silver print (postcard), 15 x 10.5 cm.
DeGolyer Library, Southern Methodist University, Dallas

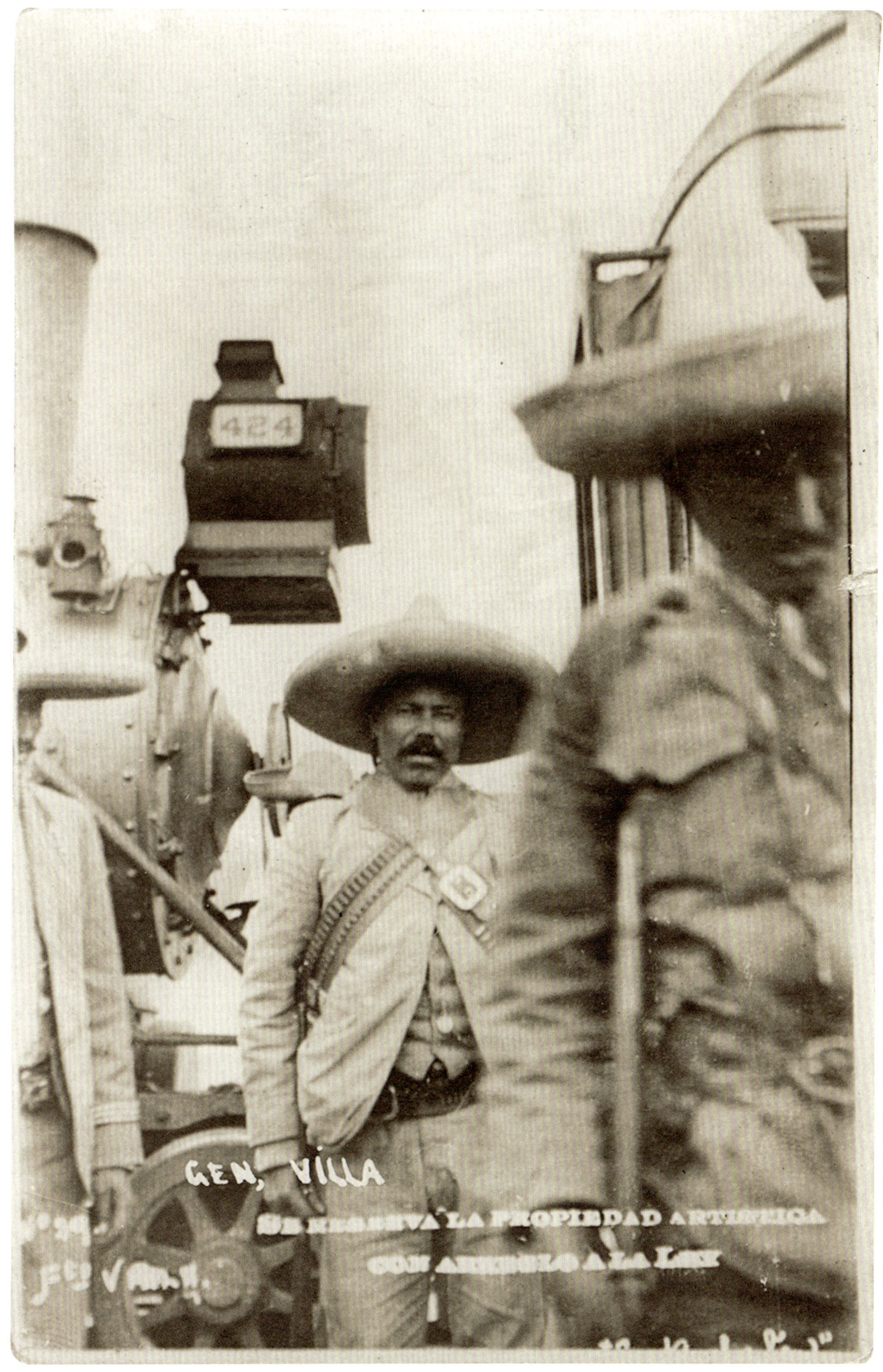
GEN, VILLA

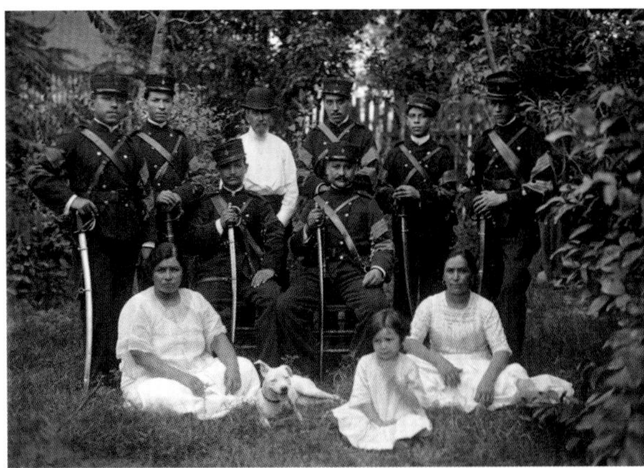

Fig. 7 Robert Runyon, **Military Band** (Matamoros, Tamaulipas), 1913–16. Glass plate negative, 12.7 x 17.8 cm. Dolph Briscoe Center for American History and General Libraries, University of Texas, Austin, 0031

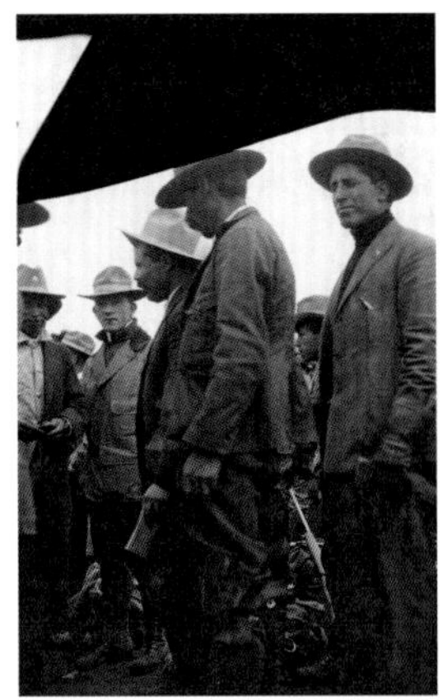

Fig. 8 Unknown photographer, **John Reed with Pancho Villa and Toribio Ortega**, 1913. Photograph, 13.6 x 18.2 cm. John Reed Papers, Houghton Library, Harvard University, Cambridge, bMS Am 1091 (1385)

Reed did not embellish or romanticise the events he had witnessed, conveying instead a sense of the impact of the conflict on the average person. Soon after he arrived in Mexico he recalled marching to the conflict zone and coming across an old man riding towards them:

> *We passed only one human being all that day – a ragged old man astride a burro, wrapped in a red-and-black checked serape, though without trousers, and hugging the broken stock of a rifle. Spitting, he volunteered that he was a soldier; that after three years of deliberation he decided he had finally to join the Revolution and fight for Libertad. But at his first battle a cannon had been fired, the first he had ever heard; he had immediately started for his home in El Oro, where he intended to descend into a gold mine and stay there until the war was over ...*
>
> *We fell silent.*[12]

Reed's narrative is very engaging, sometimes languid and at other times brisk, echoing the manner of events as they unfolded: days of waiting followed by days of intense action. His matter-of-fact style, redolent of the varied aspects of this armed conflict, can also be found in the characters and events captured in what has been called the most important novel of the Revolution, Mariano Azuela's *Los de Abajo* (El Paso, 1916).[13]

Azuela's short novel, first published in serial form between October and December 1915 in the weekly Spanish-language newspaper *El Paso del Norte*, presents the Revolution as a sequence of events in which his protagonists, a small group of revolutionary soldiers, become increasingly violent and destructive, eventually losing all sense of what they had set out to achieve. Reduced from being fierce, independent fighters full of optimism, the men and women become mere pawns in a conflict that engulfs them. They descend into a pattern

8

Walter H. Horne (1883–1921)
Gruesome Scene
(Juarez, Mexico), 1916.
Gelatin silver print (postcard), 8.5 x 13.9 cm. The Getty Research Institute, Los Angeles

of gratuitous violence, including rape, murder, theft, drinking and gambling, and become pessimistic, less liberators than oppressors. The apparent speed with which this happens is startling, and the villagers who once welcomed them as freedom fighters now hide from them in fear. The pointlessness of their sacrifice and the wilful destruction that accompanies them paint a bleak picture of the reality of life as a revolutionary: poor equipment, lack of clear instructions, hunger and despondency. Although the aspirations of the Revolution may have been noble, the day-to-day reality was very different (cat. 8):

> *At midday they came upon a hut clinging to the edge of a cliff; later on, they saw three hovels stuck on the banks of a river of charred sand; but everything was silent and abandoned. Whenever the troops drew near, the people would run off and hide in the ravines.*
>
> … *When the soldiers came to a small settlement and desperately charged through the houses and empty huts, without finding a stale tortilla, a rotten chili pepper, or even a few grains of salt to sprinkle on the despised dried beef, their brothers who had not gone to war, some as impassive as the stone faces of Aztec idols, others more human, with sordid smiles on their greasy lips and beardless faces, looked out now from their hiding places as those fierce men, who just a month earlier had made their miserable, isolated homes tremble with fright, walked dejectedly from those huts with cold ovens and dry cisterns, their heads hanging down like dogs who've been kicked out of their own houses.*[14]

Numerous surviving photographs reveal the extent of the death and destruction that beset Mexico during the Revolution. As Azuela brilliantly captured in *Los de Abajo*, the movement of troops through rural areas led to great hardship among the civilian population. Food was scarce and abuse widespread. The countryside was in constant flux during this period and many migrated to urban areas, only returning once the conflict was over. Images of the battle dead and summary executions by hanging or firing squad speak of the brutal nature of war (cats 9–13). For a country that had ceded more than half its territory to the US less than seventy years earlier in 1848, the Revolution represented another

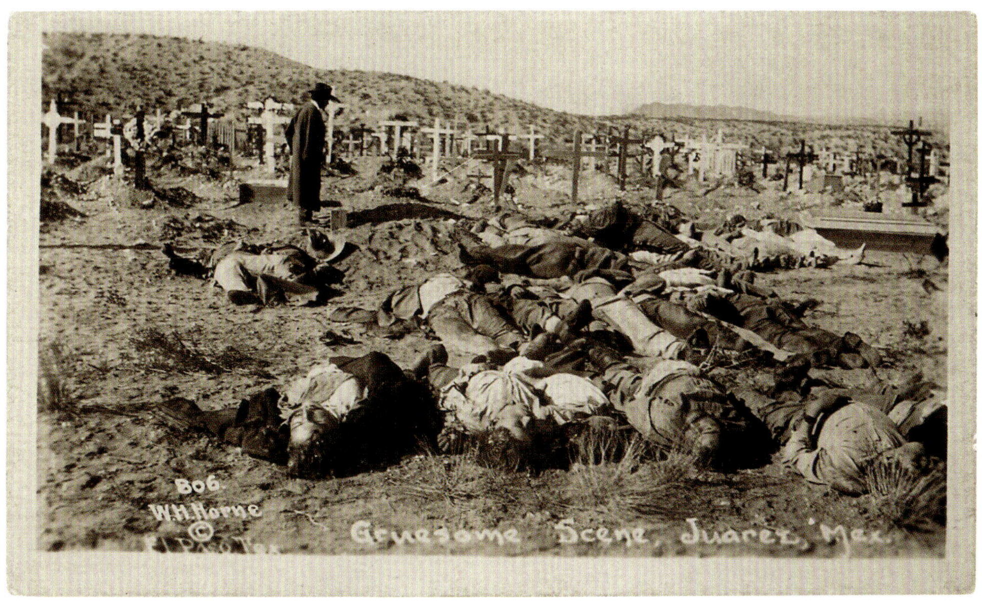

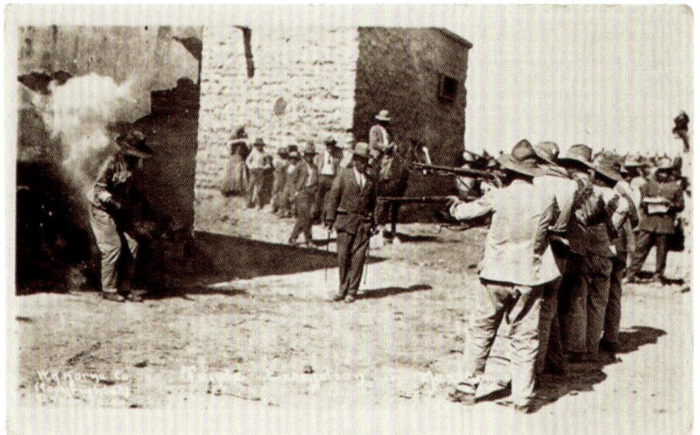

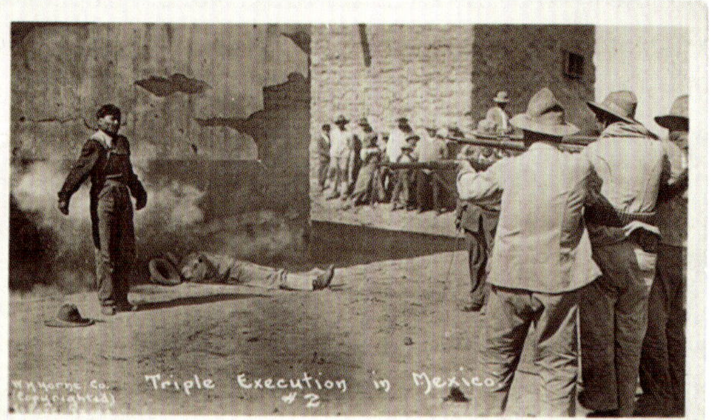

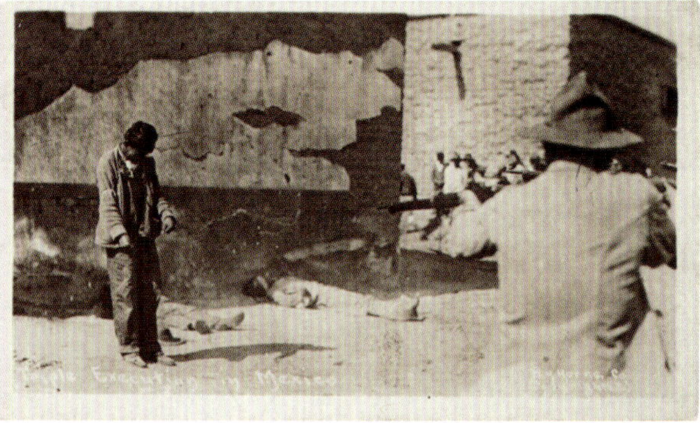

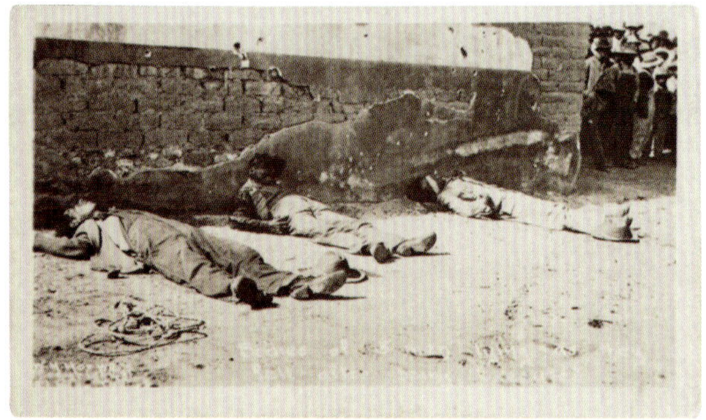

9

Walter H. Horne
(1883–1921)
Triple Execution in Mexico #1, 1916.
Gelatin silver print (postcard), 8.7 x 13.7 cm.
The Getty Research Institute, Los Angeles

10

Walter H. Horne
(1883–1921)
Triple Execution in Mexico #2, 1916.
Gelatin silver print (postcard), 8.4 x 13.7 cm.
The Getty Research Institute, Los Angeles

11

Walter H. Horne
(1883–1921)
Triple Execution in Mexico #3, 1916.
Gelatin silver print (postcard), 8.4 x 14 cm.
The Getty Research Institute, Los Angeles

12

Walter H. Horne
(1883–1921)
Bodies of the Three Men as They Fell After Being Executed, 1916.
Gelatin silver print (postcard), 8.5 x 14 cm. The Getty Research Institute, Los Angeles

period of intense turbulent change and soul-searching for what was still a young republic: Mexico had only won independence from Spain in 1821. Villa, however, was not alone in seeing the business potential in recording events. The American Walter Horne and the Mexican Agustín Víctor Casasola also both saw that profits could be made with the camera on either side of the border.

Casasola founded a commercial photo agency, the Agencia Mexicana de Información Gráfica, in 1912. He swiftly acquired a large number of images by purchasing the archive of *El Imparcial*, the official newspaper of Porfirio Díaz's regime, as well as buying up more images, contracting photographers such as Hugo Brehme to work for the agency and taking his own photographs. Casasola soon became synonymous with photographs of the Mexican Revolution and, since individual photographers were not identified by name in books or magazines and newspapers, he did little to dispel the impression that he and his brother Miguel had been personally responsible for taking all of them.[15] Anita Brenner's copiously illustrated *The Wind that Swept Mexico* (New York, 1943) is full of such photographs. A number of important Mexican photographers were, indeed, working at this time, among them Jesús H. Abitia, the Cachú brothers (Juan and Antonio Cachú Ramírez), Sara Castrejón (the first woman photographer of the Revolution), Antonio Garduño and Manuel Ramos. Although many remain anonymous, the successful monopoly created by the Casasola brothers is slowly becoming better understood, with greater recognition given to these hitherto largely overlooked photographers.

Walter Horne, suffering from tuberculosis and seeking a warm, dry climate, arrived in the Texan border town of El Paso in 1910. Not a photographer by profession, he nonetheless quickly spotted a niche business opportunity. On the opposite bank of the Rio Grande from El Paso was the Mexican town of Ciudad Juárez; the river was a strategic and very busy border crossing between the two countries. Madero's siege of the federal troops of Porfirio Díaz in Ciudad Juárez in 1911 resulted in the US Army significantly increasing the number of its troops garrisoned at El Paso: Fort Bliss saw the largest concentration of US troops since the American Civil War (cat. 6). Horne saw that these soldiers would want a cheap and effective way to communicate with their families and established the Mexican War Photo Postcard

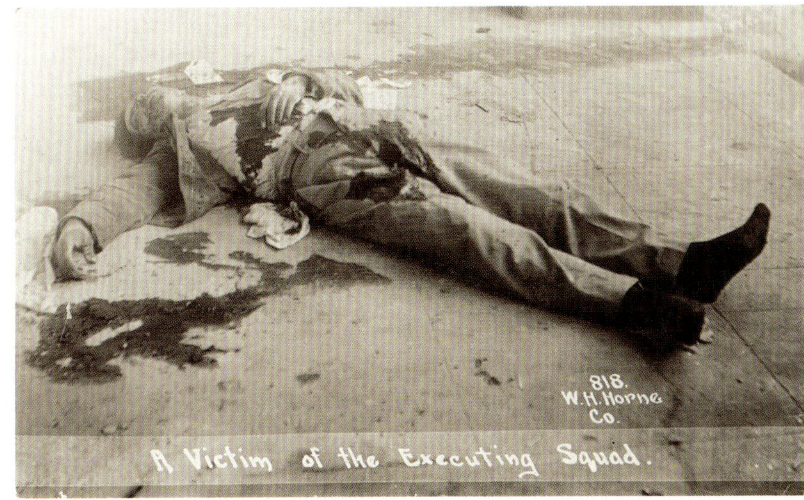

13

Walter H. Horne (1883–1921)
A Victim of the Executing Squad, 1913.
Gelatin silver print (postcard), 8.7 x 13.8 cm.
The Getty Research Institute, Los Angeles

Company. He took photographs of the garrison and significant events as they occurred, and recent developments in technology permitted these to be readily reproduced as picture postcards.[16]

When Horne proudly informed his family in December 1913 that he had taken a portrait of Villa, flushed from the success of a victorious battle, he referred to him as 'the most feared man in Mexico'.[17] By April 1915, however, defeated by the forces of Venustiano Carranza led by General Álvaro Obregón, the future president, Villa was a shadow of the once-powerful bandit leader who had dominated the northern frontier states of the country. In June 1916, desperate to shore up his rapidly waning power, Villa attacked the small American town of Columbus, New Mexico, which caused outrage in the US. President Woodrow Wilson ordered a punitive force led by General John J. Pershing into Mexico to capture Villa and his troops. Pershing may have returned empty-handed, but Horne's business thrived as a result, especially as he was the first to reach and photograph Columbus after the raid; the photographs he took in the aftermath were sold to newspapers in Chicago, New York, Boston, Atlanta and San Francisco, further cementing his reputation.[18]

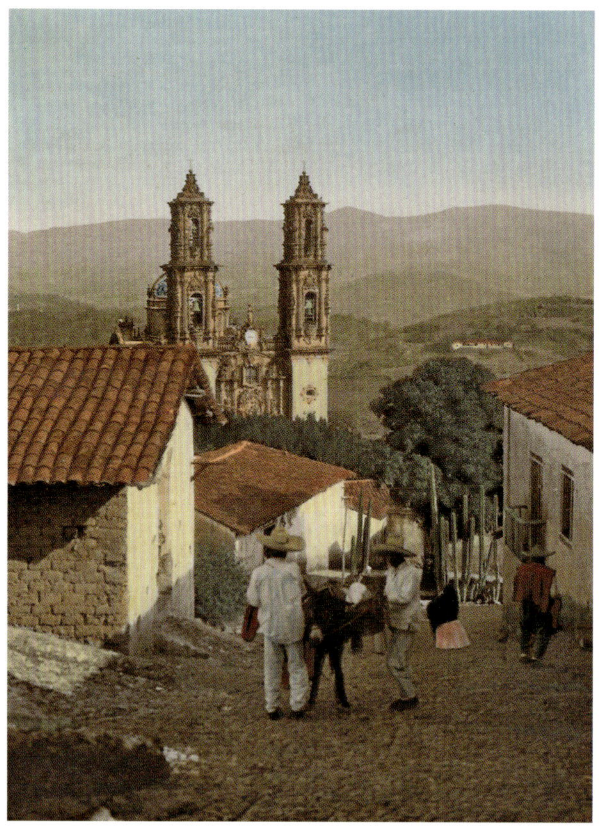

Fig. 9 Hugo Brehme, **Taxco, Gro**, *c.* 1920s. Hand-coloured gelatin silver print, 17 x 12 cm (30 x 25 cm mount). DeGolyer Library, Southern Methodist University, Dallas, Ag1988.0700

Unlike the First World War, during which a large number of official, often professional, war artists were employed by countries on both sides to record the conflict, remarkably few artists depicted scenes of the Mexican Revolution. Given the constant flux in power, the changing fortunes of the armed forces and the geographical distribution of the theatres of war, this was perhaps not surprising; after all, there was no single, united force fighting a readily identifiable enemy who was challenging the autonomy of the nation. Furthermore, there was no demand for paintings of the Revolution since its events threatened the very existence of the social, political and economic élite who had, until now, dictated the nature of the art market. There was, however, a huge appetite for photographic prints among the soldiery and general population. During the Porfiriato the depiction of poverty and misery, for example in newspapers, had not been tolerated, and the regime had insisted that photographs present only positive and optimistic images of Mexico and its people.[19] Thus photography had engaged with the picturesque and ignored the social inequality or squalid living conditions endured by the average Mexican (fig. 9). The liberalisation of art was, therefore, a direct consequence of the Revolution.

The accomplished German-born photographer Hugo Brehme moved to Mexico in 1906 and founded his studio, Fotografía Artistica Hugo Brehme, in Mexico City. Despite taking some notable photographs of Zapata and his followers for the Casasola agency, he was very successful in promoting the idyllic vision of the country preferred under the Porfiriato.[20] The manner in which two photographs by Brehme, although somewhat untypical of his style, subsequently influenced other forms of art demonstrates the contemporary significance of photography, whose impact was often immediate. His iconic photograph of Zapata in Cuernavaca in the state of Morelos in 1911, for example, was turned into an engraving by José Guadalupe Posada to illustrate a broadsheet two years before its publication as a photograph (cat. 14, fig. 11).[21] The same engraving was later reused to illustrate news of Zapata's death and burial (cats 15, 16). Diego Rivera referred to the same image when painting his mural cycle in the Palacio de Cortés in Cuernavaca in 1929, which included the portraits of two local heroes: Morelos, the War of Independence hero after whom the state and its capital were named, and Zapata (fig. 10). Numerous other examples demonstrate that this was by no means an isolated instance of cross-fertilisation.[22]

In the same year, 1911, Brehme took a photograph of four Zapatistas, clearly posing for the camera, sitting astride the cow-catcher of a stationary locomotive at the head of a troop train in Cuernavaca. This classic image of the Revolution, with its mixed group of fearless and nameless soldiers literally at the vanguard of the revolutionary struggle astride a powerful symbol of modernity that likewise seems to suggest the unstoppable momentum of Zapata and his followers, was to form the basis, three years later, of an anonymous *ex voto*. The location may have been changed from Cuernavaca to Chihuahua (ironically, the northern stronghold of Pancho Villa, yet demonstrating the geographic reach of photographs), but the image of the train is clearly the same (as is revealed by the locomotive's number, 739), although it is now running at full steam and is under attack. Brehme's photograph was also to provide the basis for another work nearly thirty years later: *Off to the Front* by Jesús Escobedo, a member of the Taller de Gráfica Popular, a graphic arts collective founded in 1937, once again takes liberties with the original image. Smoke belches from the funnel as the train, filled with soldiers off to fight for the just revolutionary cause, pulls out of the station amid a heroic send-off

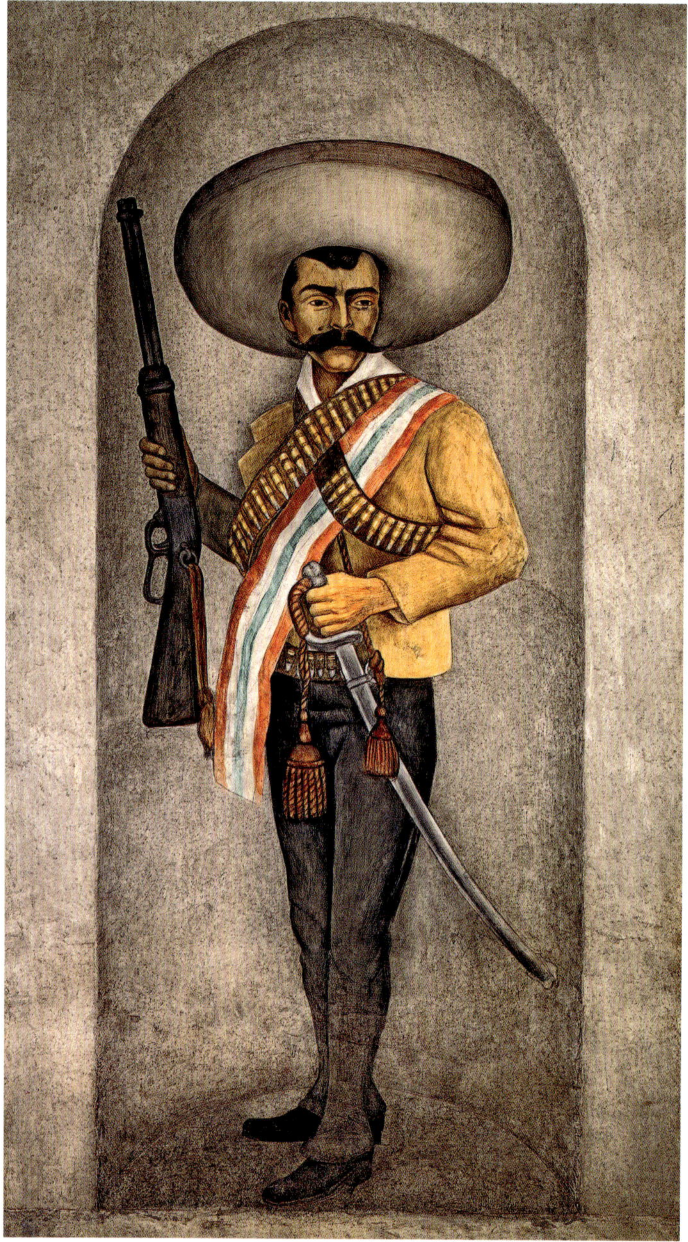

Fig. 10 Diego Rivera, **Portrait of Zapata**, 1930–31, from **History of the State of Morelos. Conquest and Revolution**. Fresco, 3 x 1.3 m. Museo de Cuauhuahuac, Instituto Nacional de Antropología e Historia (INAH), Cuernavaca, Morelos

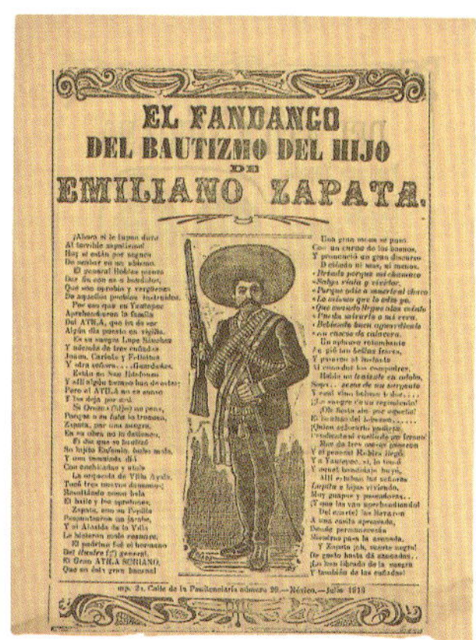

EL FANDANGO
DEL BAUTIZMO DEL HIJO
DE
EMILIANO ZAPATA.

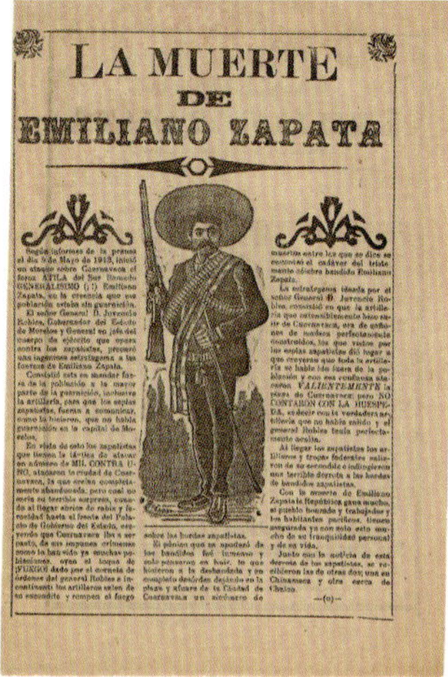

LA MUERTE
DE
EMILIANO ZAPATA

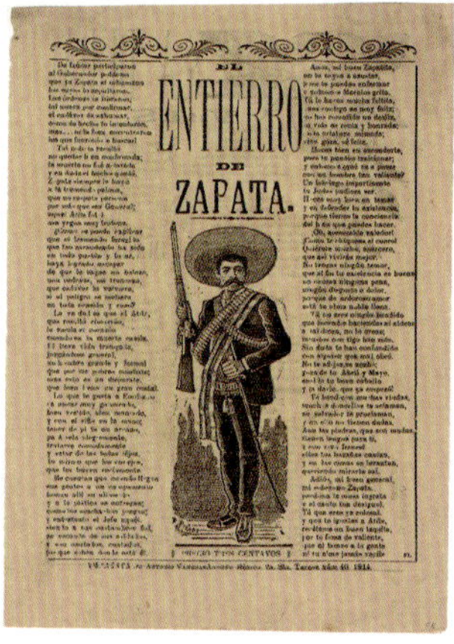

EL
ENTIERRO
DE
ZAPATA.

14

José Guadalupe Posada (1851–1913)
Baptism Party for the Son of Emiliano Zapata (El fandango del bautizmo del hijo de Emiliano Zapata), 1913.
Print on yellow grained wood paper, 27.5 x 20 cm (sheet).
DeGolyer Library, Southern Methodist University, Dallas

15

José Guadalupe Posada (1851–1913)
The Death of Emiliano Zapata (La muerte de Emiliano Zapata), 1913.
Print on yellow paper, 29.2 x 19.2 cm.
Colección Morales-Olvera

16

José Guadalupe Posada (1851–1913)
The Burial of Zapata (El entierro de Zapata), 1914.
Print on yellow paper, 29.4 x 19.2 cm.
Colección Muyaes-Ogazón

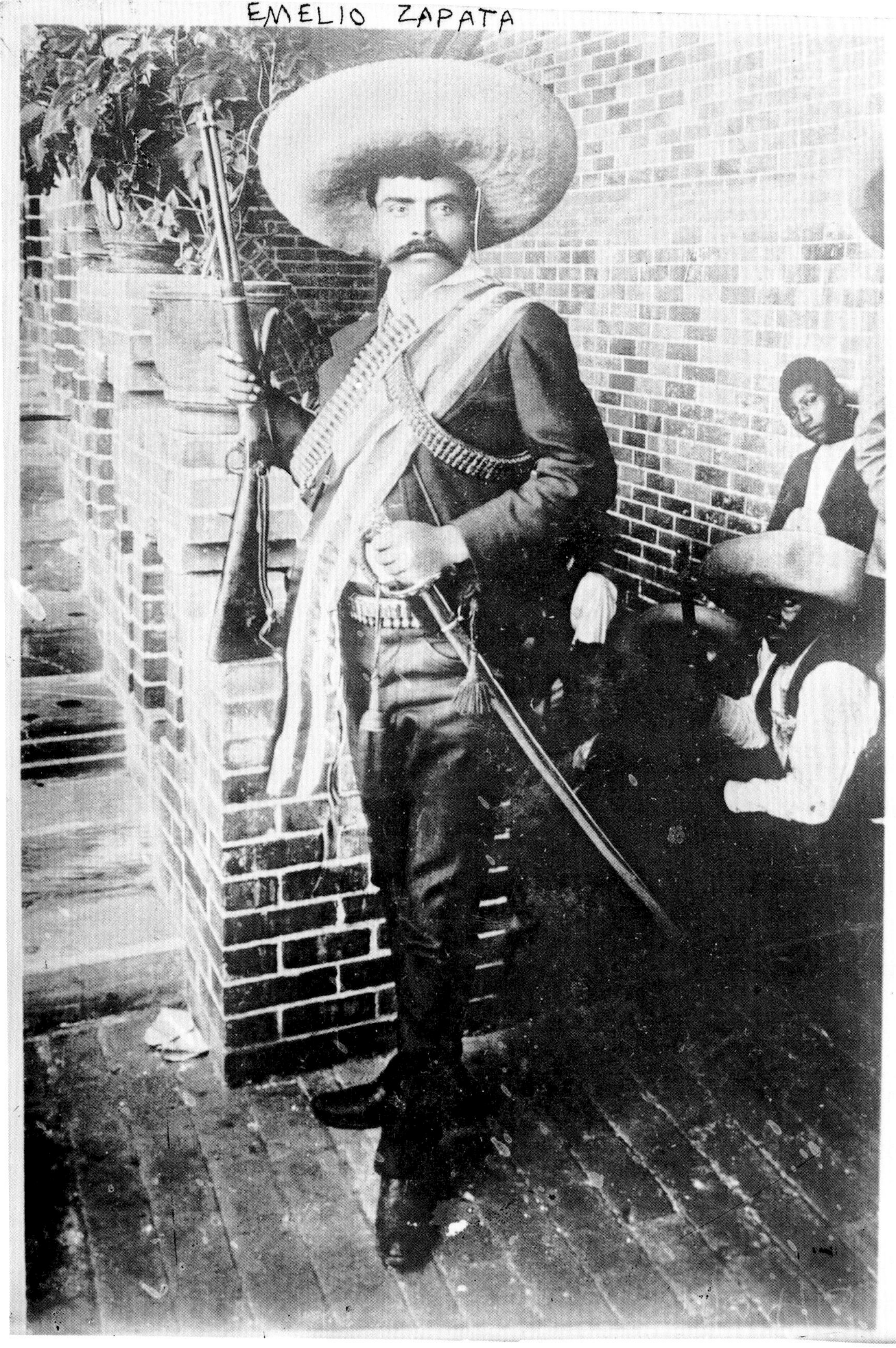

Fig. 11 Hugo Brehme, **Emelio Zapata**, 1911. Digital image from a glass negative, 17.8 x 12.7 cm. George Grantham Bain Collection, Library of Congress, Prints and Photographs Division, Washington, DC, LC-B2-2915-12

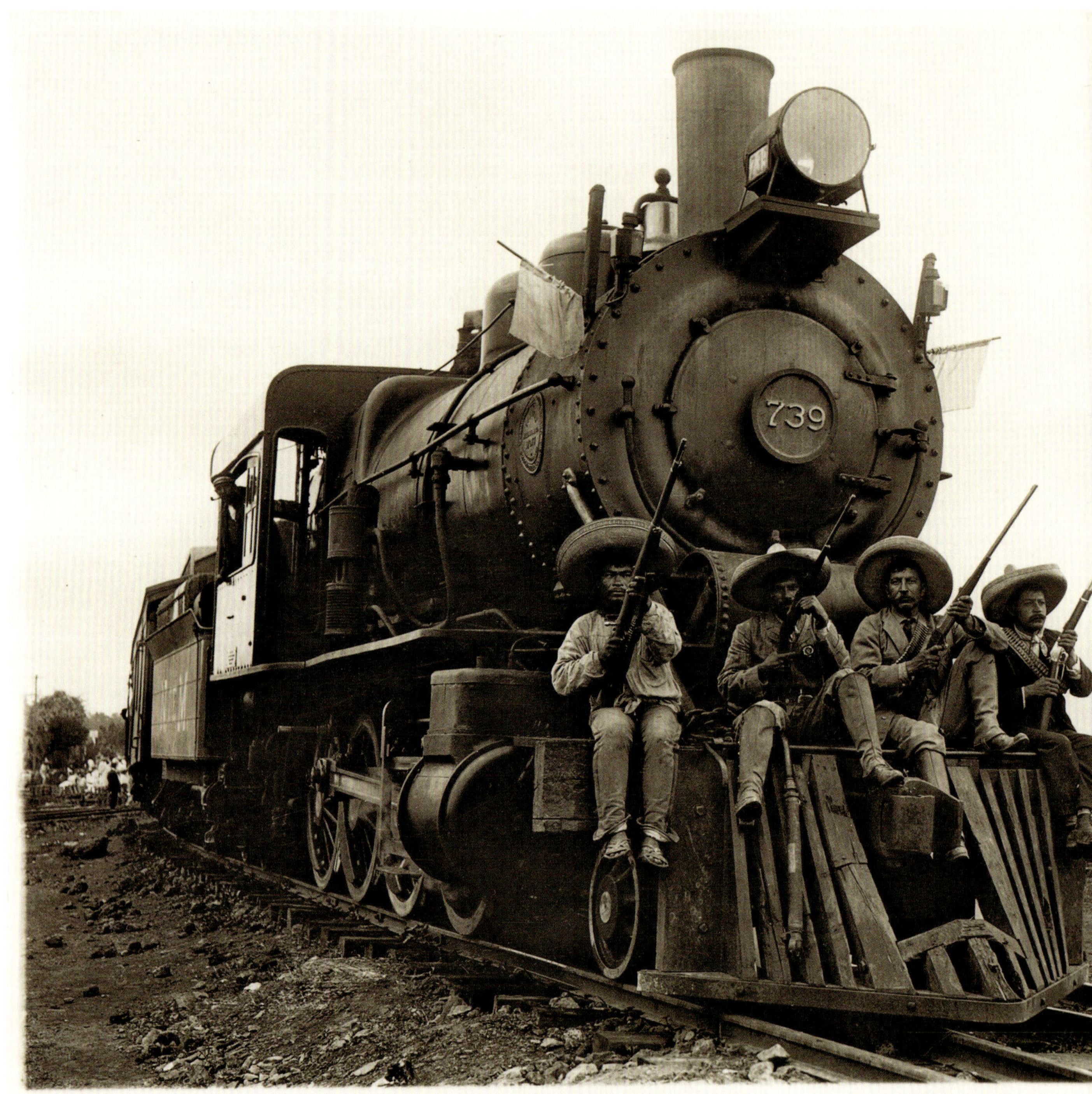

17

Hugo Brehme (1882–1954)
Untitled (Nacional de México, No. 739), *c.* 1911–17.
Gelatin silver print, 12.2 x 17 cm.
DeGolyer Library, Southern Methodist University, Dallas

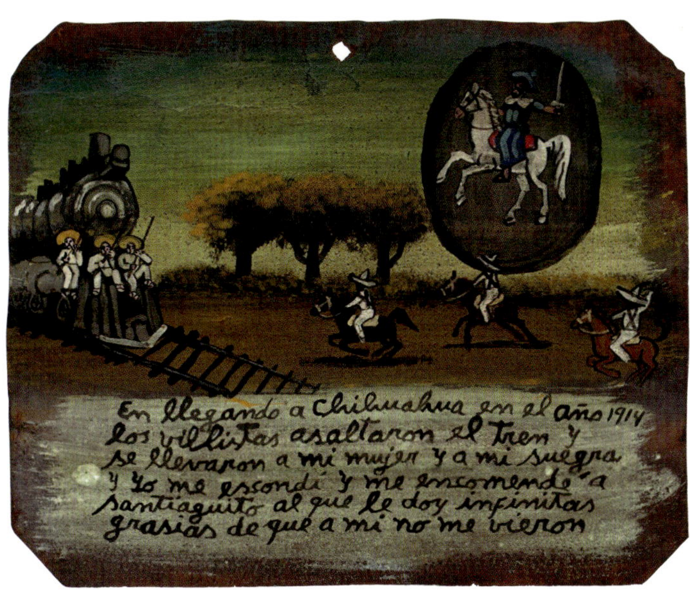

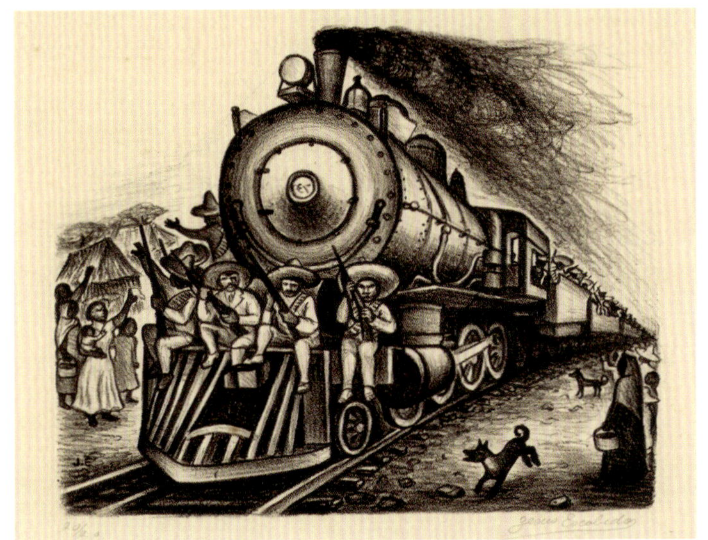

18

Unknown artist
Untitled (Ex-voto), 1914.
Oil on lamina,
20.2 x 24.1 cm.
Cano Shor Family
Collection, Mexico City

19

Jesús Escobedo (1918–1978)
Off to the Front, 1939.
Lithograph on paper,
23 x 27.5 cm.
The Trustees of the
British Museum, London

as women and children wave goodbye to their departing menfolk (cats 17–19).

In much the same way as photography, the engravings of Posada continued to inspire artists after his death. The parallels between Posada's 1899 engravings of the suicide of a young woman (figs 12, 13) and Frida Kahlo's very literal painted interpretation of 1939 of the American actress Dorothy Hale throwing herself out of her apartment in Hampshire House, New York, for instance, are evident (fig. 14). A native of Aguascalientes who moved to Mexico City in 1888, Posada died in 1913, not long after the beginning of the Revolution. By 1920 he had largely been forgotten.[23] Jean Charlot was primarily responsible for reviving interest in Posada through the publication of the first article on his work in 1925.[24] Consequently Posada became something of a hero of Mexican Modernism, a subject to be discussed in the next chapter. Posada specialised in engraving illustrations for broadsheets, popular and cheap mass-produced sheets for sale in the markets. These often carried sensational news or were printed for particular festivities, such as the Day of the Dead celebrations. Frequently satirical, they gave rise to the *calavera*, a genre of cartoon in which living people are represented by skeletons. These ephemeral broadsheets combined images with words and were passed from person to person. Although Posada was not the only artist producing engravings, his animated and distinctive style, which he successfully applied to tragic and comic material alike, combined with his considerable output, made him the leading printmaker of his generation. His skill in creating distinctive images to illustrate newsworthy stories was second to none and was to be very influential on the Taller de Gráfica Popular, most especially his use of satire. The Mexican Modernists saw Posada as an artist who could appeal to the masses without sacrificing his style or simplifying his subject-matter, while also being intrinsically and distinctly Mexican. The Surrealists later embraced his illustrations of fantastic stories, such as the woman who gave birth to an iguana. Despite being in the twilight of his career, Posada managed to create some iconic images of the Revolution, including the aforementioned portrait of Zapata and *calavera* representations of his

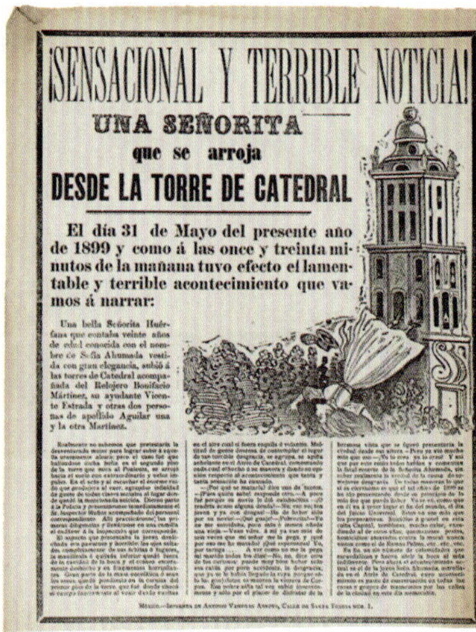

¡SENSACIONAL Y TERRIBLE NOTICIA!

UNA SEÑORITA
que se arroja
DESDE LA TORRE DE CATEDRAL

El día 31 de Mayo del presente año de 1899 y como á las once y treinta minutos de la mañana tuvo efecto el lamentable y terrible acontecimiento que vamos á narrar:

Una bella Señorita Huérfana que contaba veinte años de edad conocida con el nombre de Sofía Ahumada vestida con gran elegancia, subió á las torres de Catedral acompañada del Relojero Bonifacio Mártinez, su ayudante Vicente Estrada y otras dos personas de apellido Aguilar una y la otra Martínez.

[illegible]

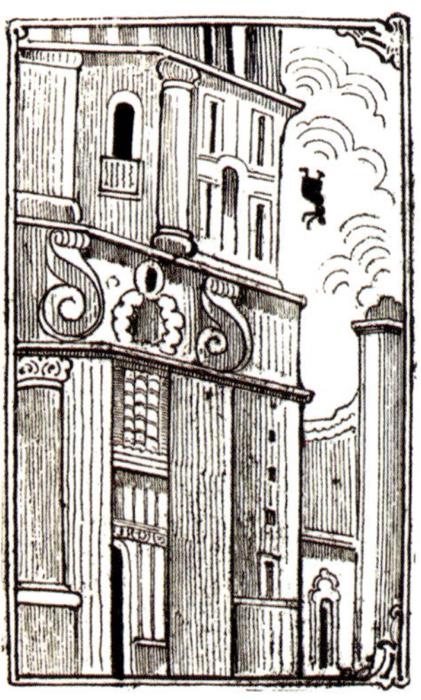

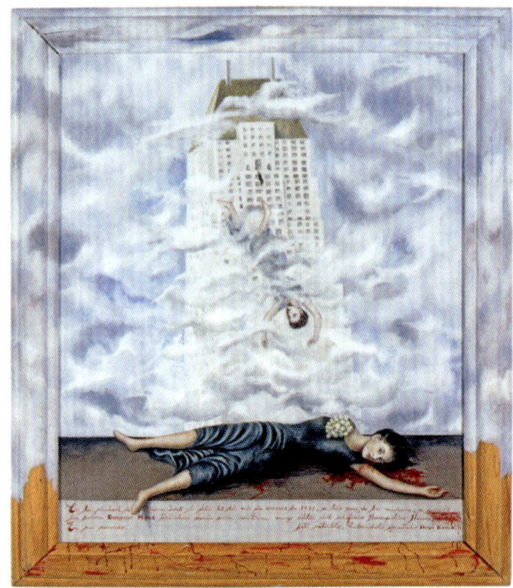

Fig. 12 An 1899 broadsheet (Stanford University Libraries, Stanford, M1238, Box 7, folder 3) reports the suicide of Maria Luisa. **Fig. 13** José Guadalupe Posada, **The Suicide of Maria Luisa (Corrido: La Suicida Maria Luisa)**, 1899. Zinc etching, 13.7 x 8.3 cm. Center for Southwest Research, University Libraries, University of New Mexico, Albuquerque, FG0195

Fig. 14 Frida Kahlo, **The Suicide of Dorothy Hale (El suicidio de Dorothy Hale)**, 1939. Oil on masonite with painted frame, 59.7 x 49.5 cm. Phoenix Art Museum, Arizona, 1960.20

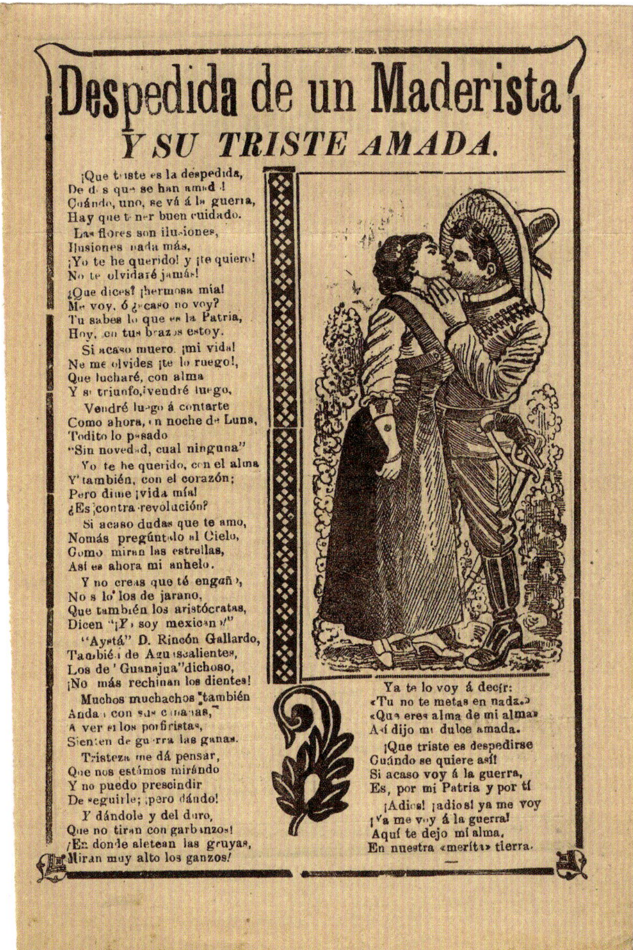

Despedida de un Maderista
Y SU TRISTE AMADA.

¡Que triste es la despedida,
De dos que se han amado!
Cuándo, uno, se vá á la guerra,
Hay que tener buen cuidado.

Las flores son ilusiones,
Ilusiones nada más,
¡Yo te he querido! y ¡te quiero!
No te olvidaré jamás!

¿Que dices? ¡hermosa mia!
Me voy, ó ¿acaso no voy?
Tu sabes lo que es la Patria,
Hoy, en tus brazos estoy.

Si acaso muero, ¡mi vida!
No me olvides ¡te lo ruego!,
Que lucharé, con alma
Y si triunfo, ¡vendré luego,

Vendré luego á contarte
Como ahora, en noche de Luna,
Todito lo pasado
"Sin novedad, cual ninguna"

Yo te he querido, con el alma
Y también, con el corazón;
Pero dime ¡vida mía!
¿Es ¡contra-revolución?

Si acaso dudas que te amo,
Nomás pregúntalo al Cielo,
Como miran las estrellas,
Así es ahora mi anhelo.

Y no creas que té engaño,
No son los de jarano,
Que también los aristócratas,
Dicen "¡Yo soy mexicano!"

"Ayetá" D. Rincón Gallardo,
También de Aguascalientes,
Los de 'Guanajua" dichoso,
¡No más rechinan los dientes!

Muchos muchachos "también
Andan con sus canañas,"
A ver si los porfiristas,
Sienten de guerra las ganas.

Tristeza me dá pensar,
Que nos estámos mirándo
Y no puedo prescindir
De seguirle; ¡pero dándo!

Y dándole y del duro,
Que no tiran con garbanzos!
¡En donde aletean las gruyas,
Miran muy alto los ganzos!

Ya te lo voy á decír:
«Tu no te metas en nada.»
«Que eres alma de mi alma»
Así dijo mi dulce amada.

¡Que triste es despedirse
Cuándo se quiere así!
Si acaso voy á la guerra,
Es, por mi Patria y por tí

¡Adios! ¡adios! ya me voy
¡Ya me voy á la guerra!
Aquí te dejo mi alma,
En nuestra «merita» tierra.

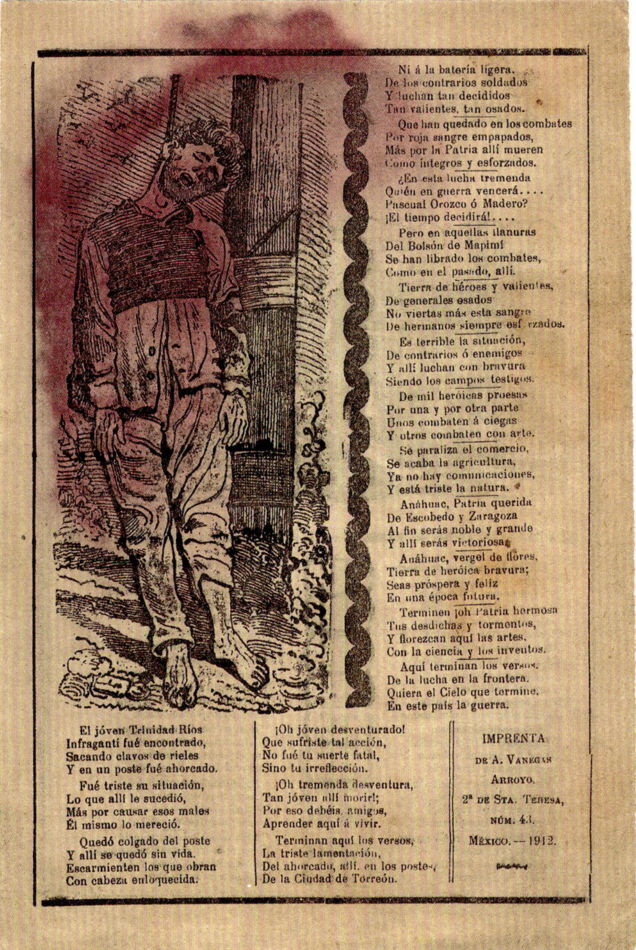

Ni á la batería ligera,
De los contrarios soldados
Y luchan tan decididos
Tan valientes, tan osados.

Que han quedado en los combates
Por roja sangre empapados,
Más por la Patria allí mueren
Como íntegros y esforzados.

¿En esta lucha tremenda
Quién en guerra vencerá....
Pascual Orozco ó Madero?
¡El tiempo decidirá!....

Pero en aquellas llanuras
Del Bolsón de Mapimí
Se han librado los combates,
Como en el pasado, allí.

Tierra de héroes y valientes,
De generales osados
No viertas más esta sangre
De hermanos siempre esforzados.

Es terrible la situación,
De contrarios ó enemigos
Y allí luchan con bravura
Siendo los campos testigos.

De mil heróicas proesas
Por una y por otra parte
Unos combaten á ciegas
Y otros combaten con arte.

Se paraliza el comercio,
Se acaba la agricultura,
Ya no hay comunicaciones,
Y está triste la natura.

Anáhuac, Patria querida
De Escobedo y Zaragoza
Al fin serás noble y grande
Y allí serás victoriosa.

Anáhuac, vergel de flores,
Tierra de heróica bravura;
Seas próspera y feliz
En una época futura.

Terminen ¡oh Patria hermosa
Tus desdichas y tormentos,
Y florezcan aquí las artes,
Con la ciencia y los inventos.

Aquí terminan los versos.
De la lucha en la frontera.
Quiera el Cielo que termine,
En este país la guerra.

El jóven Trinidad Ríos
Infraganti fué encontrado,
Sacando clavos de rieles
Y en un poste fué ahorcado.

Fué triste su situación,
Lo que allí le sucedió,
Más por causar esos males
Él mismo lo mereció.

Quedó colgado del poste
Y allí se quedó sin vida.
Escarmienten los que obran
Con cabeza enloquecida.

¡Oh jóven desventurado!
Que sufriste tal acción,
No fué tu suerte fatal,
Sino tu irreflección.

¡Oh tremenda desventura,
Tan jóven allí morir!;
Por eso debéis, amigos,
Aprender aquí á vivir.

Terminan aquí los versos,
La triste lamentación,
Del ahorcado, allí, en los postes,
De la Ciudad de Torreón.

IMPRENTA
DE A. VANEGAS
ARROYO.
2ª DE STA. TERESA,
NÚM. 43.
MÉXICO.—1912.

20

José Guadalupe Posada (1851–1913)
Farewell of a Maderista and his Sad Sweetheart (Despedida de un Maderista y su triste amada), 1911.
Print, 29.4 x 18.9 cm.
Colección Raúl Cedeño Vanegas

21

José Guadalupe Posada (1851–1913)
The Hanged Man (El ahorcado), 1912.
Print, 28 x 18.5 cm.
Colección Raúl Cedeño Vanegas

CALAVERITA GOMISTA

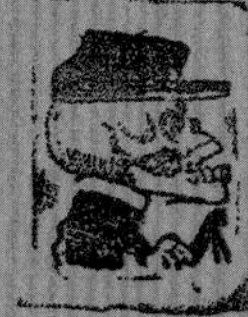

HABLA SU ASISTENTE

Ahora sí, mi General.
¡Ya nos llevó la tristeza!
y causa de tanto mal
¡ya piden nuestra cabeza!

¿Dónde nos ocultaremos
que no nos vaya a cazar
con todo lo que traémos,
ese Águila de Escobar?

La verdad, ¡estamos fritos

Con gentes tan traicioneras,
hoy todos dicen a gritos
¡que nos hagan Calaveras!

Ya mi General Almada
está decayendo mucho;
en su gran Calaverada,
quemó el último cartucho.

Dios nos guarde en hora mala
ya que a acertar no sabemos;
y nos libre de una bala,
si de ésta con bien salimos.

Con tanta Caballería
que nos sitia por doquiera;
yo opino que en este dia
¡vamos a ser Calavera!

HABLA EL DEMONIO

Mi General R. Gómez,

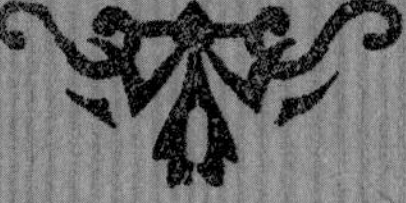

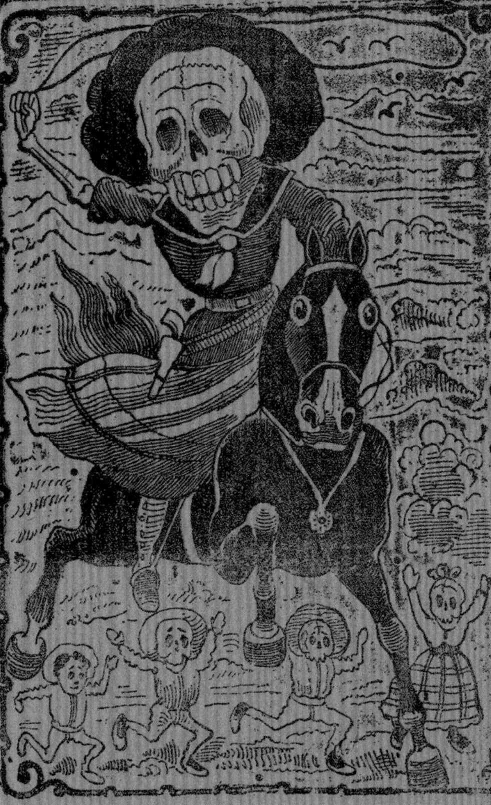

y vengo a darle refuerzo;
Cuente Ud. por pelotones
los demonios del Infierno

Soy Príncipe Lucifer
y conmigo no hay quien pueda
pues nadie me puede ver,
¡todos hablan en voz queda!

¡Vamos! no se achicopale!
¿No dicen que es muy [illegible]?
Si Ud. de mi no se vale
¡se lo harán hoy Calavera!

HABLA EL GRAL. GOMEZ

Gracias, amigo don Diablo:

Es Ud. muy honorable,
si en verdad con Ud. hablo,
¡Media vuelta y mano al sable!

¡Soy General! y me muero
en cualquier terreno que ande!
Yo necesito dinero,
y no busco quien me mande!

Yo soy capaz de bajar
a los profundos Infiernos

y empezar a fusilar
a todos los de los cuernos!!

Soy mas que Ud. don Demonio:
¿què me viene hoy con panteras?
ya lo he dicho, y no me rajo;
y lo digo deveras:
"que a un metro de tierra abajo
han de quedar Calaveras"! . . . .

HABLA EL DIABLO

Pues, Señor, me equivoqué,
Perdone Ud., me despido,
Por barbero eso saqué,
por tarugo y ofrecido

Me voy con toda mi gente
a mis profundas esferas;
ya sé que Ud. es valiente:
¡No nos haga Calaveras!

Valgo 5 centavos

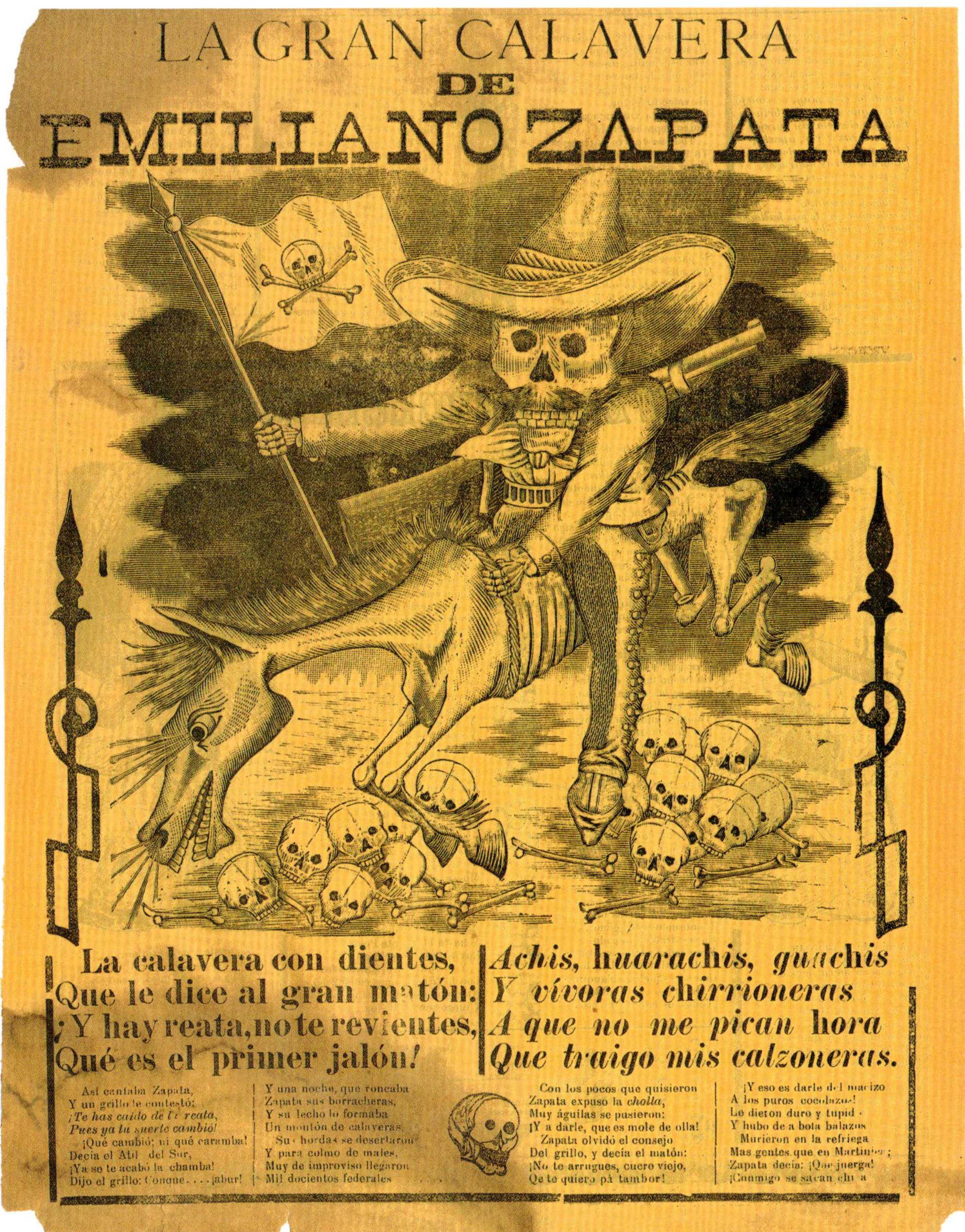

22

José Guadalupe Posada
(1851–1913)
Little Calavera of [Arnulfor] Gómez (Calaverita Gomista), n. d.
Print, 39.9 x 29.9 cm.
Colección Muyaes-Ogazón

23

José Guadalupe Posada
(1851–1913)
The Great Calavera of Emiliano Zapata (La gran calavera de Emiliano Zapata), n. d.
Print, 38.5 x 27.7 cm.
Colección Raúl Cedeño Vanegas

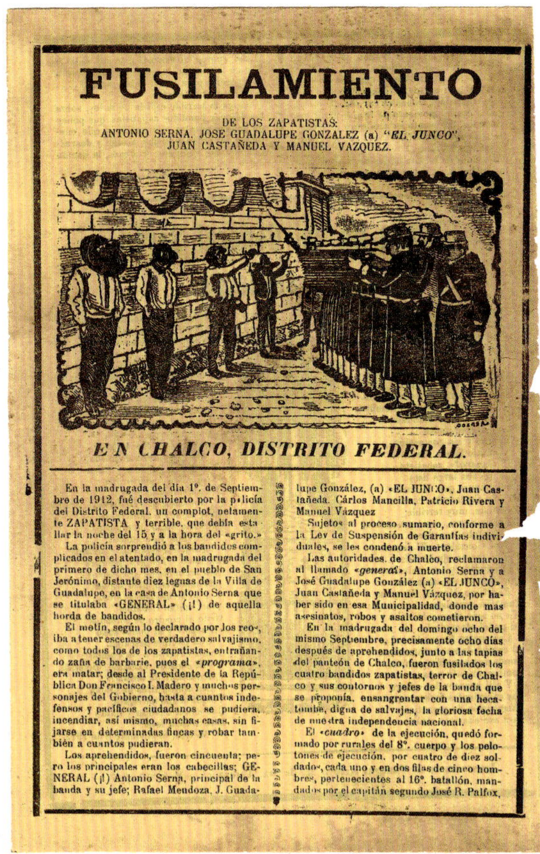

FUSILAMIENTO

DE LOS ZAPATISTAS:
ANTONIO SERNA, JOSE GUADALUPE GONZALEZ (a) "*EL JUNCO*",
JUAN CASTAÑEDA Y MANUEL VAZQUEZ.

EN CHALCO, DISTRITO FEDERAL.

En la madrugada del día 1°. de Septiembre de 1912, fué descubierto por la policía del Distrito Federal, un complot, netamente ZAPATISTA y terrible, que debía estallar la noche del 15 y a la hora del «grito.»

La policía sorprendió a los bandidos complicados en el atentado, en la madrugada del primero de dicho mes, en el pueblo de San Jerónimo, distante diez leguas de la Villa de Guadalupe, en la casa de Antonio Serna que se titulaba «GENERAL» (¡!) de aquella horda de bandidos.

El motín, según lo declarado por los reos, iba a tener escenas de verdadero salvajismo, como todos los de los zapatistas, entrañando zaña de barbarie, pues el *«programa»*, era matar; desde al Presidente de la República Don Francisco I. Madero y muchos personajes del Gobierno, hasta a cuantos indefensos y pacíficos ciudadanos se pudiera, incendiar, así mismo, muchas casas, sin fijarse en determinadas fincas y robar también a cuantos pudieran.

Los aprehendidos, fueron cincuenta; pero los principales eran los cabecillas; GENERAL (¡!) Antonio Serna, principal de la banda y su jefe; Rafael Mendoza, J. Guadalupe González, (a) «EL JUNCO», Juan Castañeda, Cárlos Mancilla, Patricio Rivera y Manuel Vázquez

Sujetos al proceso sumario, conforme a la Ley de Suspensión de Garantías individuales, se les condenó a muerte.

Las autoridades de Chalco, reclamaron al llamado *«general»*, Antonio Serna y a José Guadalupe González (a) «EL JUNCO», Juan Castañeda y Manuel Vázquez, por haber sido en esa Municipalidad, donde mas asesinatos, robos y asaltos cometieron.

En la madrugada del domingo ocho del mismo Septiembre, precisamente ocho días después de aprehendidos, junto a las tapias del panteón de Chalco, fueron fusilados los cuatro bandidos zapatistas, terror de Chalco y sus contornos y jefes de la banda que se proponía, ensangrentar con una hecatombe, digna de salvajes, la gloriosa fecha de nuestra independencia nacional.

El *«cuadro»* de la ejecución, quedó formado por rurales del 8°. cuerpo y los pelotones de ejecución, por cuatro de diez soldados, cada uno y en dos filas de cinco hombres, pertenecientes al 16°. batallón, mandados por el capitán segundo José R. Palfox,

supporters (cats 20–23, 25). Images of executions by firing squad were no revolutionary innovation: Posada had been producing them for some years (cat. 24).

Saturnino Herrán was born in Aguascalientes, like Posada, and gravitated to Mexico City, where he produced images of Mexico that celebrated the country's regional diversity as well as those who had inherited the power of the Mexica gods. Born in 1887, he was a young man during the Revolution, and was to be influential on the Mexican Modernists. Despite painting in a more conventional academic style, he was a nationalist ahead of his time, embracing a pictorial language that championed Mexico as a country with a rich past and ethnic diversity before these themes had come to dominate the artistic community (cat. 26).[25] His rich, highly evocative paintings mark the transition between the Porfiriato and post-revolutionary Mexican Modernism. Although he died tragically young, in 1918, he left behind a significant body of work, including *Our Gods* (1914–18; Museo de Aguascalientes and Collection Adriana Garduño Vda. de García Flores, Mexico City), five cartoons for an extraordinarily evocative and unrealised mural project that formed part of a competition for the Teatro Nacional (now the Palacio de Bellas Artes), which was then under construction.[26] His fifth and final panel, *Coatlicue Transformed* (fig. 15), depicts Christ crucified incorporated into the body of one of the most famous surviving Mexica sculptures of the goddess Coatlicue (She of the Serpent Skirts), then housed in the Museo Nacional. The drawing is a remarkable representation of the complexity of the Catholic faith in Mexico, with its rich mixture of European and indigenous religious traditions, and symbolises the ethnic diversity of the country.

Francisco Goitia was another artist of the revolutionary period who was to be very influential on the Mexican Modernists. Goitia, in his early

24

José Guadalupe Posada
(1851–1913)
Execution by Firing Squad (Fusilamiento), 1912.
Print, 27.4 x 17.3 cm.
Colección Raúl Cedeño Vanegas

25

José Guadalupe Posada
(1851–1913)
The Calavera of Emiliano Zapata (La calavera de Emiliano Zapata), 1912.
Paper, 38.5 x 28.3 cm.
Colección Raúl Cedeño Vanegas

LA CALAVERA
—DE—
EMILIANO ZAPATA.

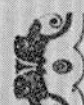

Triste y de mala manera,
Sin decir a nadie "ABUR",

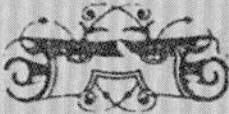

Se fué el Atila del Sur
A volverse calavera.

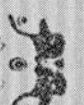

Cansado de combatir
Por aquel problema agrario,
Vió dibujarse el osario
En su obscuro porvenir.

A su mente se agolpó,
En bandada funeraria,
La legión cruel, sanguinaria,
Que tan mal nombre le dió

Y en su conciencia angustiada
Por tan fieros atentados.
Vió a sus bárbaros soldados
Levantando hacia él la espada.

Y como viera también
Mil incendios pavorosos.
Cadáveres espantosos
Y cien estragos y cien;

Que sus gentes perpetraron.
Entre oprobios y entre ofensas,
Con mujeres indefensas.
A quienes viles burlaron.

La muerte sin compasión
Cargó con el General
Que en Morelos fué fatal
Y hoy es hueso del montón.

"Ya se volvió calavera—
(Zapata reflexionó)
"Genovevo de la O.
"Titulado "*El hombre fiera.*"

"También se está corrompiendo
"Ya en la sepultura ingrata,
"Mi hermano, Eufemio Zapata
"Y yo también me estoy yendo.

"Y en la hedionda gusanera,
"Devorado de animales.
"Se encuentra el Tuerto Morales,
"Caminando a calavera."

"Todos mis fieles soldados,
"Son calaveras podridas,
"Momias en la tumba hundidas
"Y esqueletos descarnados."

Se angustió el tremendo ATILA,
Que dicen no es muy valiente,
Y se puso, prontamente.
Tembloroso como anguila.

Y fué tanta su emoción
Y vió aquel caso tan serio,
Que yendo hacia el cementerio,
Se le mojó el pantalón.

Sus cabellos se erizaron,
Y sus ojos se le hundieron,
Sus lágrimas se salieron
Y sus piernas trepidaron.

Y por la misma razón,
Por aquella angustia cruel,
Oyó resonar tras él
Una nota de trombón.

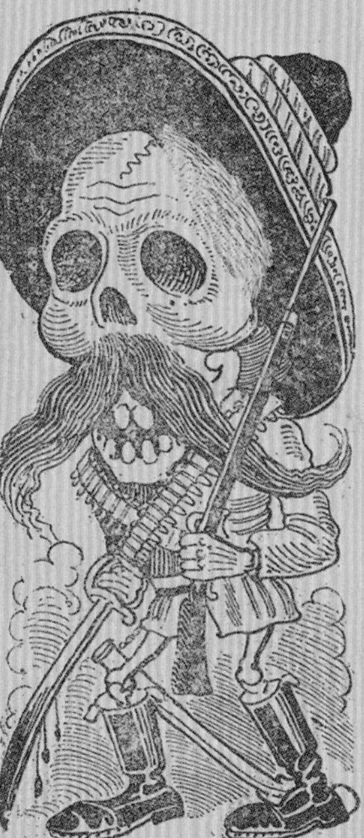

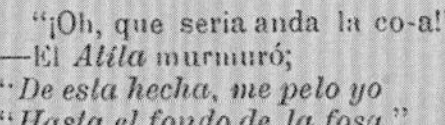

"¡Oh, que seria anda la co-a!"
—El *Atila* murmuró;
"*De esta hecha, me pelo yo*
"*Hasta el fondo de la fosa.*"

"¡Qué tremenda situación
"En la que me encuentro ahora;
"La cosa es aterradora.
"Y me declaro *coyón.*"

"La verdad que fueron *guajes*
"Los que miedo me tuvieron;
"Mis gentes, fama me dieron,
"Lo declaro sin ambajes.

"Porque hoy que me tomo el pelo.
"Delante de la pelona.
"Me juzgo yo una persona
"Que de miedo casi vuelo."

"Quién me diera ahora tener
"Aquel caballo tordillo,
"Que brincaba más que un grillo,
"Los federales al ver."

"Con qué gusto le metía
"Al malvado las espuelas,
"Diciéndole: Tú que vuelas,
"Llévame a una cueva umbría."

"Porque (la verdad desnuda)
"Yo creo que no fuí valiente.
"Si a mí me atacan sin gente.
"De lo que haría: tengo duda."

Así hablaba preocupado
Aquel señor de Morelos,
Siempre lleno de recelos
Y deseoso de soldados;

De soldados que le hicieran
En la sierra compañía,
Porque él ya se lo temía,
Que de pronto lo aprehendieran.

Mas cortó su soliloquio,
Llegando con su azadón,
Un esqueleto pelón,
Que con él trabó coloquio.

"Ahora verás, badarniz.
"Como conmigo no juegas.
"Hoy la existencia me entregas,
"Y vas a hacerte lombriz."

"Entrégame luego, luego,
"La pistola y la canana.
"El rifle y hasta la lana;
"Y prontito, que no es juego."

"Yo no soy como Madero,
"Que es un hombre bondadoso;
"Yo sí te arrojo en un pozo.
"Y me llevo hasta tu cuero."

"Conque, vamos, General,
"Que llegó la hora del rancho;
"Lo que es hoy hasta te plancho
"Y después vas al costal."

"Tú fuiste muy renombrado
"En Cuautla y Tlaltizapán;
"Pero hoy vas a donde van
"Los que ya se han restirado.

"Deja ya tu sombrerote,
"Porque este caso es muy serio,
"Y hay que entrar al cementerio
"Antes de que yo te azote."

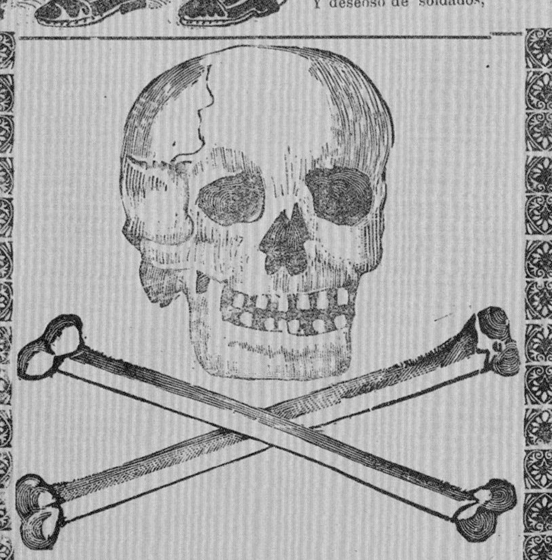

Y como el Atila aquel
Estaba temblando todo,
La muerte clavóle un codo
Y dió en la tumba con él.

Así acaban las hazañas
Con la muerte inexorable;
Ella no le teme al sable;
Al fin que no tiene entrañas.

Acabó por fin Zapata,
Que dió tanto la función,
Y hoy en un triste panteón
Deplora su suerte ingrata.

Llegó por fin su ocasión,
Y hoy medita seriamente
Que aun el hombre más valiente
Calavera es del montón.

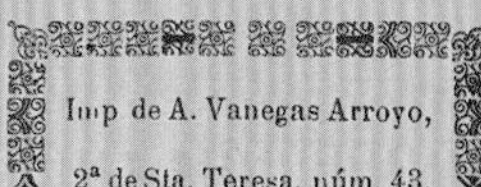

Imp de A. Vanegas Arroyo,
2ª de Sta. Teresa, núm. 43.
México.—1912.

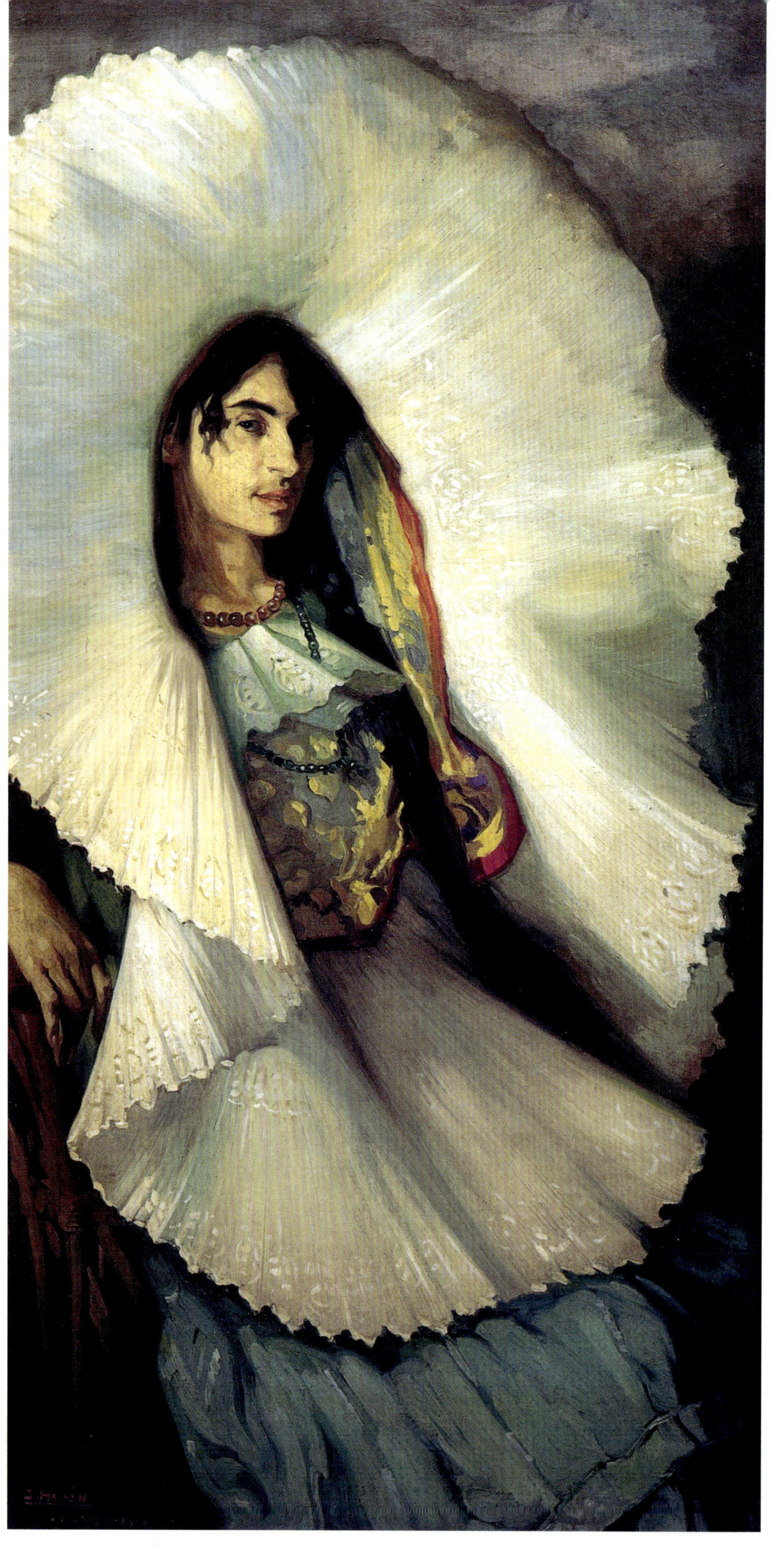

twenties, spent eight years studying art, painting and exhibiting in Barcelona and Rome, only returning to Mexico when his travel grant was rescinded in 1912. Like Herrán, Goitia is seen as a precursor of the Mexican Modernists. During his years in Europe he had studied Velázquez, Zurbarán, El Greco and Goya while also admiring the work of Delacroix, Géricault, Daumier, Millet, Courbet and the Impressionists.[27] On his return to Zacatecas, shocked by the Revolution, he approached General Felipe Ángeles, under Pancho Villa's command, wanting to contribute to the struggle, although as he later remarked, 'I did not carry weapons because I knew the mission of killing was not mine.'[28] Goitia was made an artist on Villa's staff, and witnessed among other events the Battle of Zacatecas in 1914. He left for Mexico City after Villa was crushed by Carranza's forces, led by General Obregón, the following year. His paintings of the Revolution are stark reminders of the human cost of the conflict, especially those that depict the aftermath of summary field executions. Contemporary photographs confirm that individual or mass hangings were not unusual either in the countryside or town. Whereas the corpses of the victims of firing squads were removed, the bodies of those who were hanged were often left on trees and lamp posts until they disintegrated, especially in the countryside. Such public displays were a warning to others that they would be hunted down and punished, wherever they were. Goitia's depictions of the decomposing bodies of individuals hanging from trees in the arid Zacatecan landscape, a harsh environment of dense thorny scrub, with vultures circling, are potent reminders of the low value attached to human life during war (cats 27, 28).

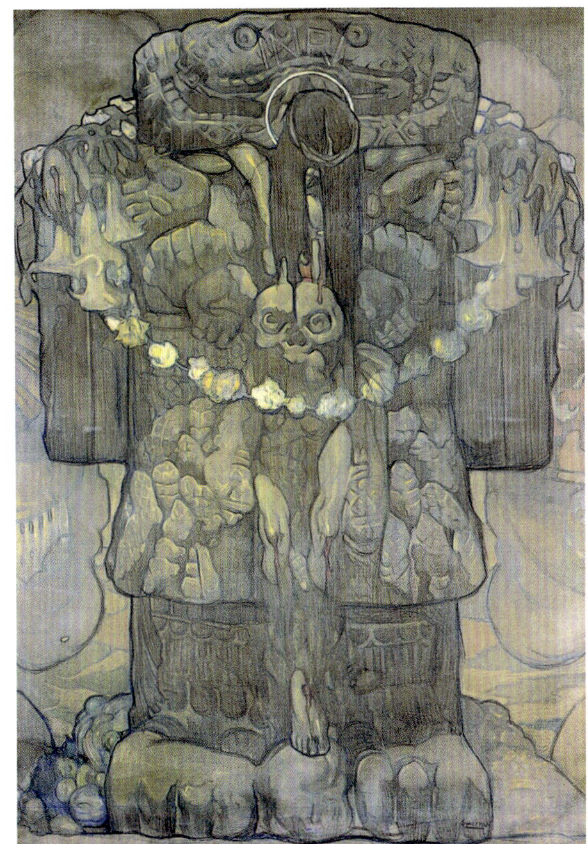

Fig. 15 Saturnino Herrán, **Coatlicue Transformed (Coatlicue transformada)**, study for the central figure of **Our Gods (Nuestros dioses)**, 1918. Crayon and watercolour on paper, 88.5 x 62.5 cm. Acervo INBA en custodia del Museo de Aguascalientes

Goitia later claimed that he personally exhumed the corpses of soldiers in Zacatecas and hung them from a tree in order to draw them, placing a hut around them and putting a caretaker there to guard them. The dry desert air, he said, helped to preserve them, making them easier

26

Saturnino Herrán (1887–1918)
Woman from Tehuantepec,
1914.
Oil on canvas, 150 x 75 cm.
Acervo INBA en custodia del Museo de Aguascalientes

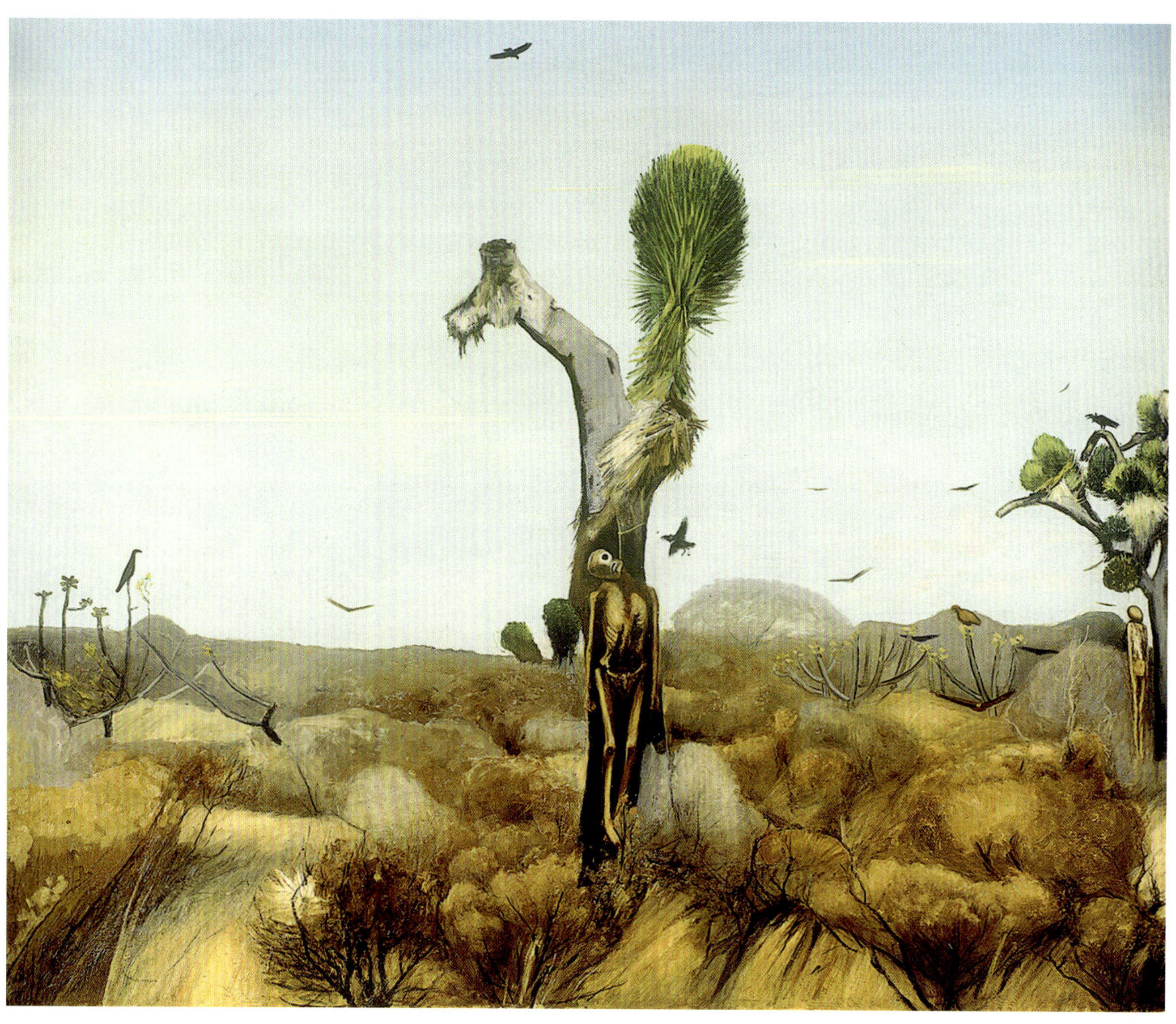

27

Francisco Goitia (1882–1960)
Zacatecan Landscape with Hanged Men II (Paisaje de Zacatecas con ahorcados II), *c.* 1914.
Oil on canvas, 194 x 109.7 cm.
Museo Nacional de Arte, Instituto Nacional de Bellas Artes y Literatura

for him to study over time.[29] Such myth-making appears quite in character with Goitia who, later in life, lived in Xochimilco, on the outskirts of Mexico City. Eschewing the modern world, this popular tourist attraction and place of relaxation was famed for its 'floating gardens', a series of highly productive raised fields known as *chinampas* that were irrigated by canals, and dated back to the time of the Mexica.

The Revolution changed many things in Mexico. As we have seen, ordinary people began to feature in representations of the country for the first time, whether in works of art, as characters in novels, in journalistic accounts of the conflict or, most significantly, in photography. No longer was art the preserve of the élite or photography constrained to representations of 'Mexican types'.[30] Technological innovations and the overthrow of the political system brought about the democratisation of art. The Revolution also created a vast and powerful visual legacy that became a fertile resource for the artists who began to emerge in its wake. General Alvaro Obregón became president in 1920 and, armed with a new constitution which had finally been ratified in 1917, he set about rebuilding Mexico. Little by little people returned to the rural areas and a new sense of optimism emerged. The engrained culture of political cronyism coupled with widespread corruption remained, however, and the threat of violence and banditry proved hard to eradicate, as many visitors to Mexico reported. Artists could now become significant participants in the government's ambitions to inspire a cultural shift through a programme of widespread reform. Seen as the perfect advocates of the new regime, artists were to find themselves, as a result of a massive public art initiative, in a position to promulgate the aspirations and achievements of the federal government. Thus art entered the mainstream of Mexican society in a way that few could have envisaged during the Porfiriato.

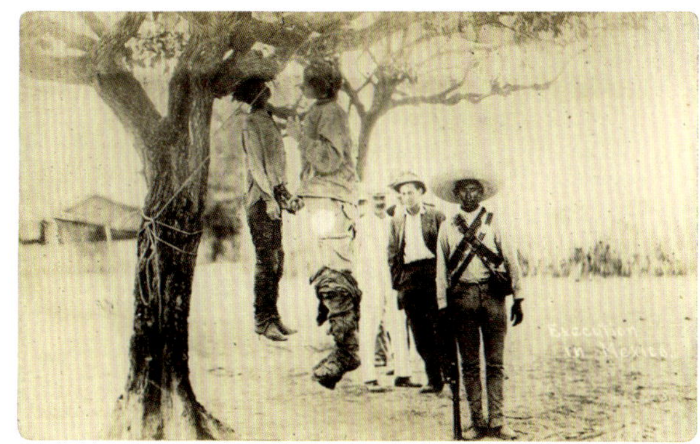

28

Unknown photographer
Execution in Mexico, c. 1910–17.
Gelatin silver print (postcard),
15 x 10.5 cm. DeGolyer Library,
Southern Methodist
University, Dallas

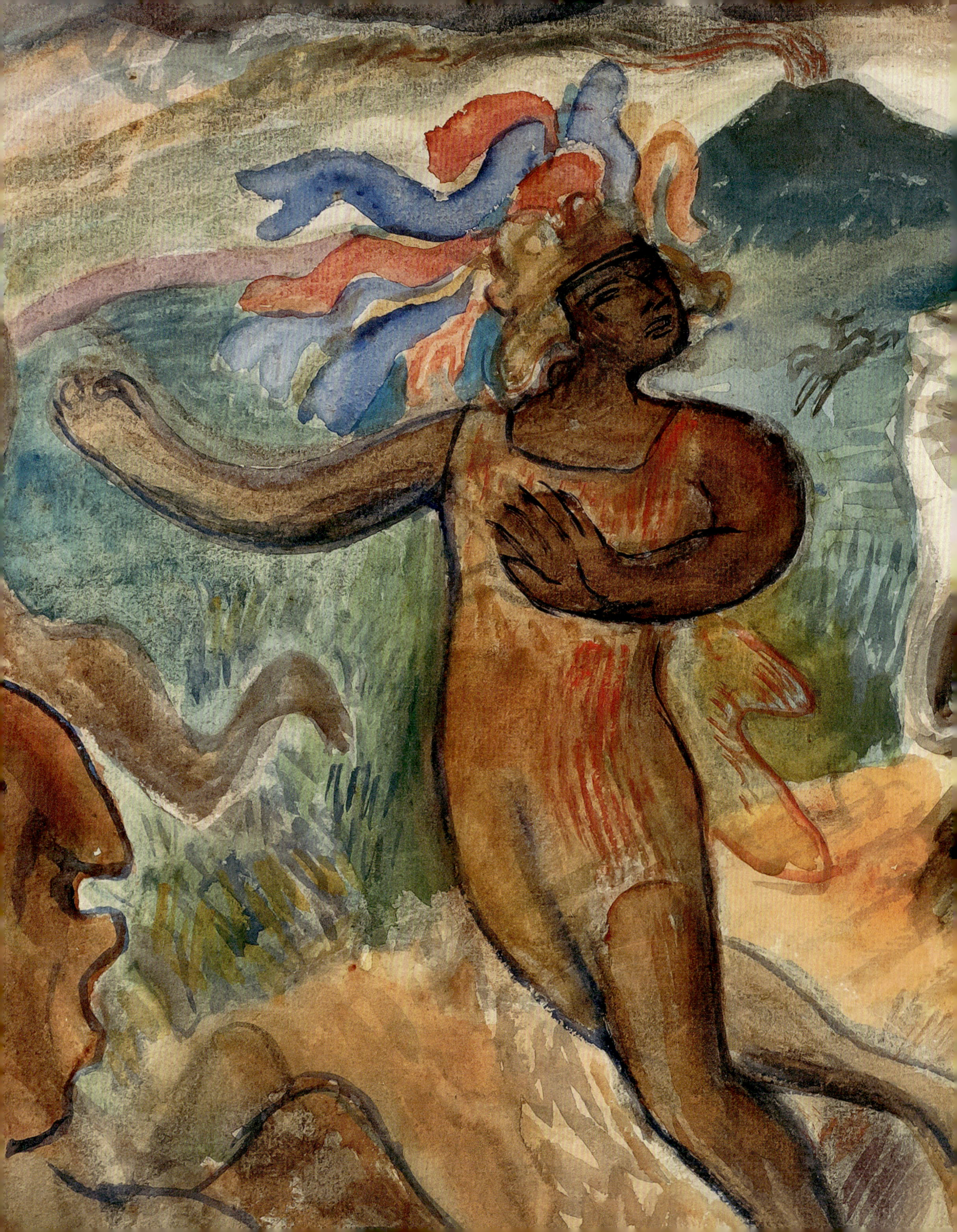

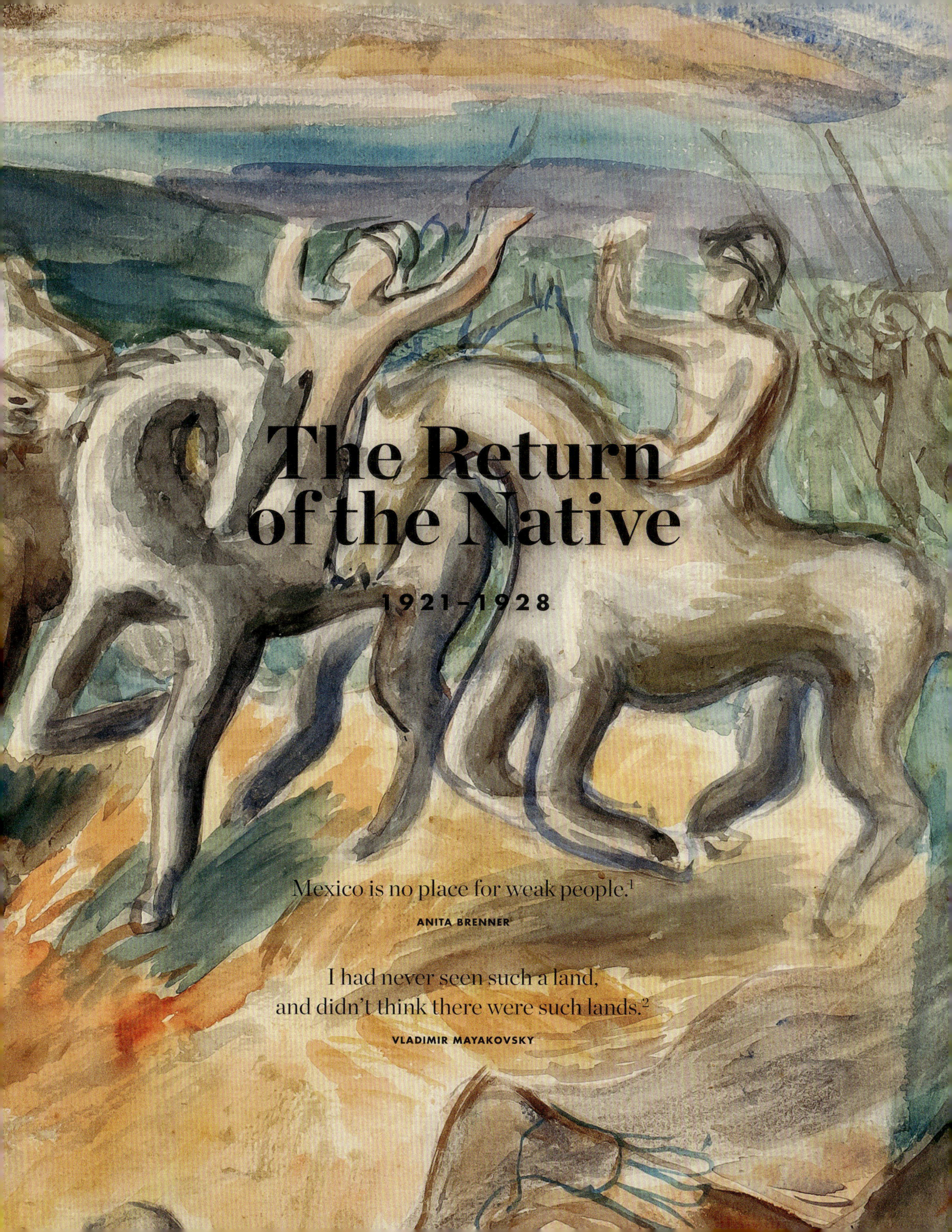

The Return of the Native

1921–1928

Mexico is no place for weak people.[1]

ANITA BRENNER

I had never seen such a land,
and didn't think there were such lands.[2]

VLADIMIR MAYAKOVSKY

AS WE HAVE SEEN, THE VISUAL ARTS DURING the Mexican Revolution were dominated by mass-produced images in response to the public demand for news. The picturesque images of Mexico that had been promoted by the Porfiriato were superseded by unsentimental visions of a war-torn country. Mexico began to see itself represented in a very different way and, as it shook off the Porfiriato's aspirations of the Belle Epoque, the country embraced a new, modern and direct visual language. As the dust of the Revolution began to settle across Mexico, the scale of the task of rebuilding the shattered nation began to be revealed; when Alvaro Obregón took office in 1920 it soon became clear that this would be a long and arduous process. Nevertheless, despite the enormity of the challenge, this was a time of celebration: the removal of Porfirio Díaz brought a new mood of optimism, characterised by an outlook full of opportunity and creativity. Given how deeply the Revolution had affected Mexico – with considerable loss of life, displacement of people and damage to the infrastructure – it is perhaps remarkable that art was able to play such a crucial role in the national rebuilding process.

Among the many problems confronting Mexico was one of its national characteristics: the power of independent regional leaders. The instability of politics during the Revolution and the significant number of changes of president from 1910 to 1920 illustrates the extent of the problem: ten men held the office of president in as many years. During his grip on the presidency Porfirio Díaz was able to control a country of strong factions and diverse interests through a wide network of supporters who were held together by self-interest. His removal in 1911 saw the collapse of this network and its replacement with a long and at times brutal fight to fill the power vacuum. The famous photograph of Villa seated on the imperial throne of Maximilian I alongside Zapata in December 1914 (fig. 16) captures the first meeting of the two most powerful regional revolutionary leaders. Although they shared a dislike of the president, Venustiano Carranza, they otherwise had little common ground: Villa returned to Chihuahua and Zapata to Morelos. The photograph suggests a unity that simply did not exist; neither man was interested in being president or in joining forces with the other. Instead they focused on resolving their own regional issues. Their independence was seen as a threat both to the imposition of central rule and to the authority of the president: the two men

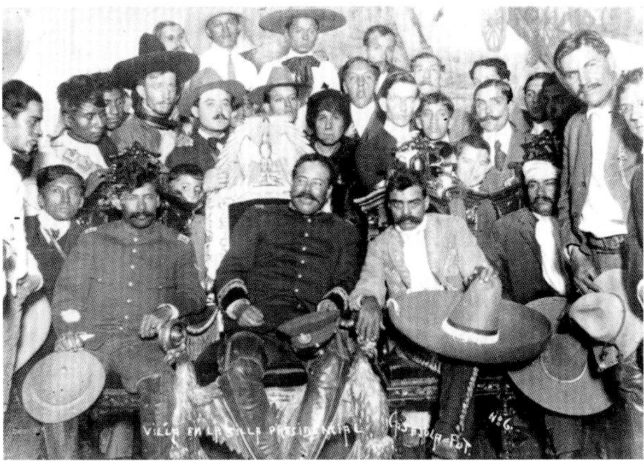

Fig. 16 Unknown photographer, **Pancho Villa on the Presidential Seat Accompanied by Emiliano Zapata**, December 1914. Photograph. SINAFO, Fototeca Nacional de Instituto Nacional de Antropología e Historia (INAH), Pachuca, 186381

29

Unknown photographer
The Assassination of Pancho Villa, July 20, 1923.
Gelatin silver print (postcard), 8.7 x 13.8 cm.
The Museum of Modern Art, New York. Gift of Edward Ranney

were potentially more popular than the president and, worse, capable of raising a fighting force to challenge his leadership or to question the imposition of new laws. Even during the Revolution these regional leaders were gradually being eliminated. On 10 April 1919 Zapata was lured into an ambush at the Hacienda de San Juan near Chinameca, Morelos, and assassinated. Four years later, on 20 July 1923, Villa was gunned down as he returned to his hacienda from Parral, Chihuahua (cat. 29). This was no short-lived campaign: powerful independent figures were still being eradicated years later. Accused of rebellion, Saturnino Cedillo was hunted down by government forces and killed on 11 January 1939 in the Sierra Ventana. Less than a year before, Graham Greene had sought him out and been granted a rare interview at his heavily guarded estate 'Las Palomas', near San Luis Potosí.

In the immediate aftermath of the Revolution, little changed in the art world. Years later, Jean Charlot (cats 30, 31) recalled that when he first arrived in Mexico from Paris in January 1921 the art scene seemed moribund. The Academia de San Carlos, founded in Mexico City in 1785, continued to play an important role. It functioned as an art school and, with an extraordinarily rich library, acted as a meeting place for artists. Significantly, however, Charlot remembered no hint that Mexico was about to undergo an artistic renaissance, least of all a mural movement. Following a six-month sojourn in France, he returned to Mexico in November 1921, to find that everything had changed during his short absence.[3] Having lived through the First World War in France, he found many similarities with war-torn Mexico; indeed the atmosphere for artists involved in the mural programme was, at times, threatening. 'The Revolution', he said, 'was still all around us then.'[4]

The change that Charlot described was inspired by Alvaro Obregón's appointment of José Vasconcelos as Minister of Public Education, a position he held from 1920 to 1924. Vasconcelos was a liberal intellectual and a key member of the

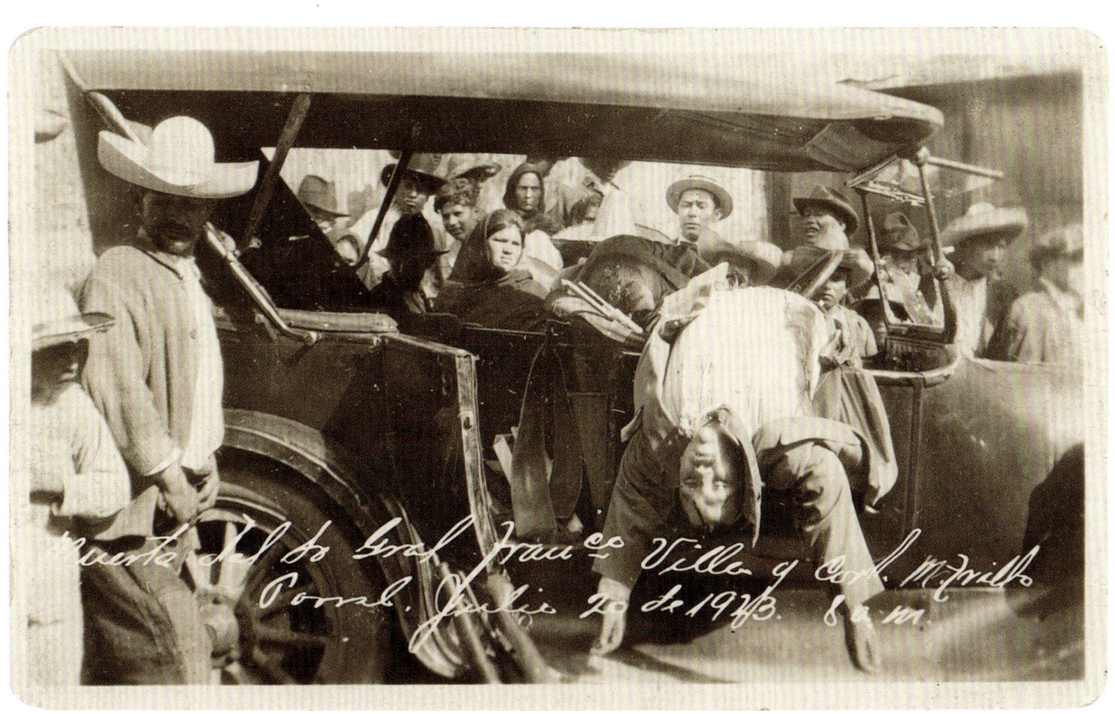

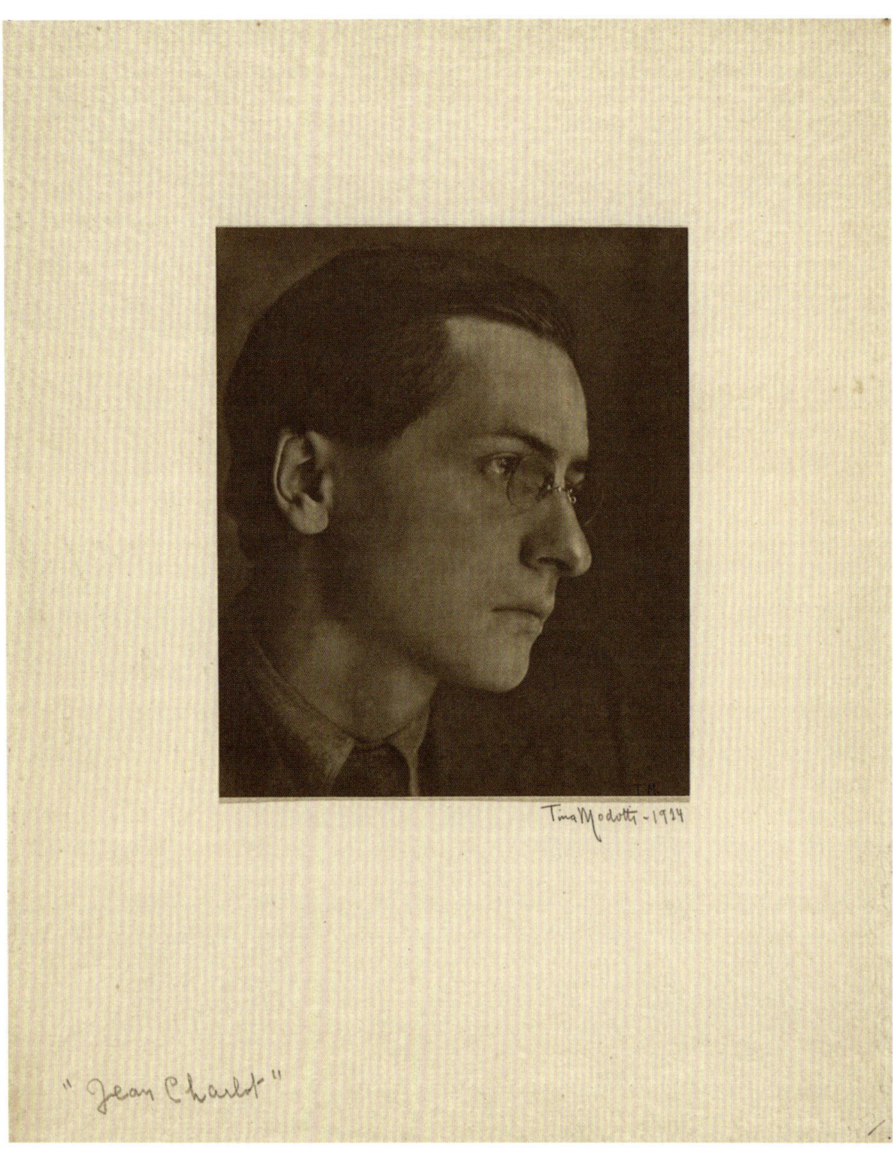

31

Henrietta Shore (1880–1963)
Jean Charlot, *c.* 1927.
Oil on canvas, 60.96 x 50.8 cm.
Los Angeles County Museum of Art. Purchased with funds provided by Mr and Mrs Robert M. Simpson, Mr and Mrs Donald W. Crocker, and Mr and Mrs Alfredo F. Fernandez

30

Tina Modotti (1896–1942)
Jean Charlot, 1924.
Platinum print, 22.9 x 18.7 cm.
The J. Paul Getty Museum, Los Angeles

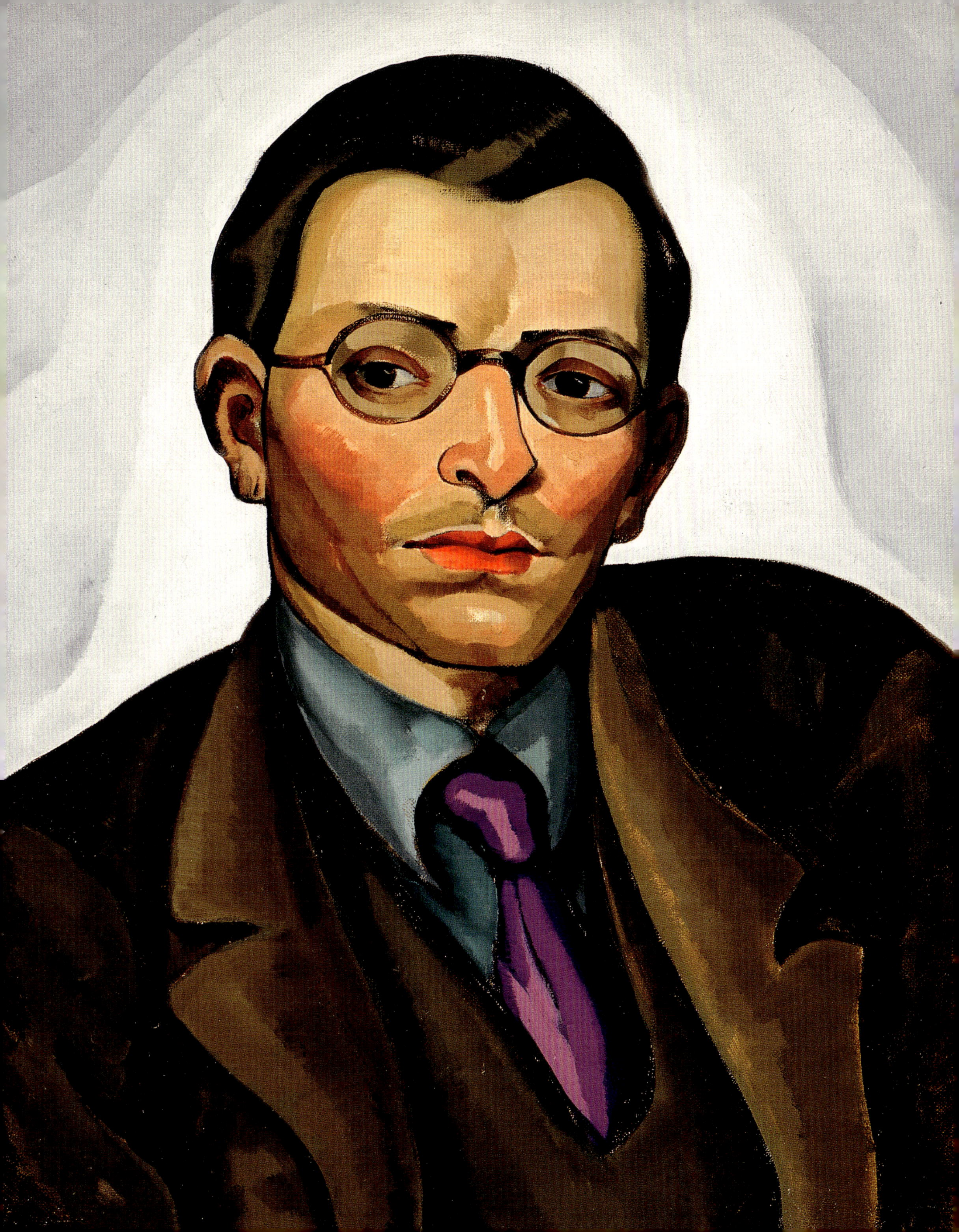

influential Ateneo de la Juventud (the writer and philosopher Alfonso Reyes was likewise a prominent member), which advocated ideological and educational reform as early as 1910. The Ateneo subscribed to José Enrique Rodó's position, espoused in his essay *Ariel* (Montevideo, 1900), which was dedicated to pan-American youth. In it he argued that intellectuals could change society through the power of ideas and that Latin America was a unity that transcended national boundaries and cultures. He saw education as fundamentally important to future success, and held the view that a higher sense of purpose existed beyond that restricted by nationalist ideals.[5]

Other significant thinkers at this time were the archaeologist Alfonso Cano; the politician Moisés Sáenz, who campaigned for indigenous rights; and the anthropologist Manuel Gamio, who studied under Franz Boas at Columbia University in New York, furthering the understanding of the history of Mexican pre-Columbian culture while also championing indigenous rights. Indeed Boas, who was a leading proponent of cultural relativism – the value of judging an object within its own context, rather than against that of another culture – founded the International School of American Archaeology and Anthropology in Mexico City in 1912.[6] The aesthetic principles adopted by Obregón's regime were, therefore, underpinned in part by cultural relativism and the anti-positivist thinking (that not all knowledge can be explained in purely scientific terms) of the Ateneo, challenging the conception that the Porfiriato was as aesthetically backward and derivative as once thought.[7]

Vasconcelos believed that creativity was the highest point of human endeavour and that humanity was destined to progress to an aesthetic stage of civilisation that would surpass the present.[8] Thus classical humanism and idealist metaphysics were harnessed to a mystical vitalism and voluntarism, in which the notion of the soul and the concept of free will play a fundamental role in the creative process.[9] As minister he introduced a far-reaching public arts programme that was sponsored by the government. This positioned the visual arts in the mainstream, making them theoretically accessible to everyone. Alongside a wide-reaching literacy campaign, which included the distribution of free books, the establishment of public libraries, the creation of open-air schools and other initiatives, artists were given wall space in public buildings on which to paint murals. The first murals commissioned by Vasconcelos – *The Tree of Life* (1920–21) by Roberto Montenegro at the ex-Convent of San Pedro y San Pablo and *Creation* (1922) by Diego Rivera at the Escuela Nacional Preparatória – reflect his humanist ideals, but this was not to last. The establishment of the Union of Technical Workers, Painters and Sculptors in 1922 advocated a socialist-inspired aesthetic that signaled a permanent rupture with Vasconcelos's ideals.[10] The Union's manifesto called for the abandonment of easel art in favour of public art, essentially asserting that muralism was the only way for artists.[11] This amounted to a type of censorship that created a real tension between the muralists and other painters who were effectively suppressed, creating a two-tier community among artists in Mexico.

Among the muralists Rivera was dominant; between 1925 and 1936 he *was* the mural movement.[12]

Mexicans had gathered much of their information from murals throughout history. In the pre-Columbian period, complex wall paintings were widespread, while in the early colonial period three mendicant orders – Franciscans, Dominicans and Augustinians – had embarked on an ambitious building programme as part of their promulgation of Christianity across the newly acquired territory of New Spain, as Mexico was then known. The interiors of their churches and convents were decorated with vibrant frescoes, designed to be both didactic and contemplative. These were often painted by indigenous Mexicans, and many cycles had sophisticated information embedded within them in pre-Columbian pictorial and phonetic language (fig. 17).

Vasconcelos believed that murals would help to unite the nation behind the government's political objectives and celebrate the achievements of the Revolution. His conviction was based less on Russian revolutionary ideas of establishing a government programme to harness the benefits of art than the aesthetic principles of the Italian Renaissance; he instructed Rivera to travel to Italy to study frescoes before returning to Mexico. In some respects the mural programme could be described as a mutually beneficial campaign in which artists were paid and given prominent public sites while the government proclaimed its achievements, or those of the Revolution, and enjoyed valuable press coverage. One inspired aspect of the initiative was that it was relatively cheap (artists and technicians were paid the equivalent of labourers' wages, thereby demonstrating the aspiration of equality across the workforce), and another was that its results were widely visible, thanks to the government's abundant

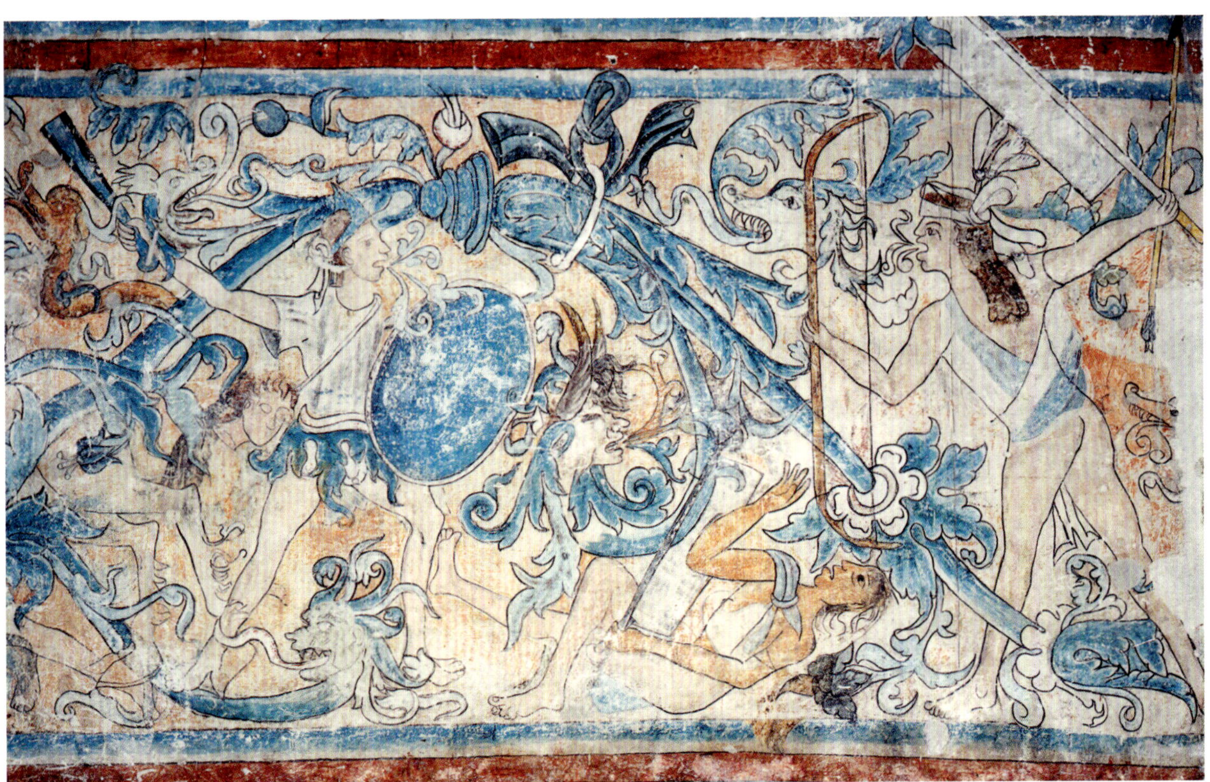

Fig. 17 Unknown Otomi artist(s), 'Battle scene', late sixteenth century. Fresco. Augustinian convent church of San Miguel Arcángel, Ixmiquilpan, Hidalgo

supply of bare-walled public buildings. Vasconcelos appreciated too that because literacy levels across Mexico needed improvement, images were the key to conveying information. The Mexican government was apparently very liberal. Its artists enjoyed considerable freedom in their choice of subject-matter and no attempt was made to curb their individuality or impose a state-approved style. Indeed, the resulting art was often more radical than the government's reforms: not only did it celebrate the heroics of the Revolution (and other episodes in Mexican history, especially those related to the suppression of the indigenous population by the Spanish), but it was to become a powerful tool in criticising the government.

In Soviet Russia, by comparison, art came to be seen as a tool of government only some time after the Russian Revolution of 1917. Although the Soviet government initially embraced its *avant-garde* artists, its support for them soon dwindled. It was not until 1932 that Socialist Realism was introduced as a state policy, one that came very much at the expense of individual creativity. Although he never visited Mexico, the English art historian Anthony Blunt expressed his surprise that 'in the recent history of the arts nothing is at first sight more puzzling than the complete failure of the Soviet Union to produce a new movement in the visual arts' equivalent to the one then underway in Mexico.[13] Aside from a visit to Mexico made by the poet Vladimir Mayakovsky, one of the founders of the Russian Futurist movement, in late 1924 *en route* to the US, and a trip Rivera made to Moscow in 1927 (fig. 18) to celebrate the tenth anniversary of the October Revolution, there seems to have been surprisingly little artistic exchange between the two nations that had brought about political regime-change through revolution in the early twentieth century.[14] Ironically, it appears that Mexico's artistic ties were stronger with the US than with Soviet Russia.

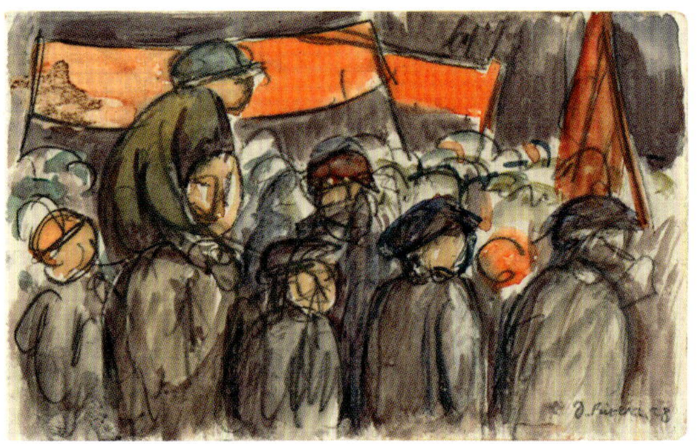

Fig. 18 Diego Rivera, **May Day, Moscow**, 1928. Watercolour and crayon on graph paper, 10.5 x 16.2 cm. The Museum of Modern Art, New York, 137.1935.32

Vasconcelos realised that his ambitious scheme would succeed only with an influential advocate. To this end he called on the services of Diego Rivera, the larger-than-life figure who was to dominate the art scene in Mexico for the next thirty years, to spearhead his programme. By this time an established artist with an international reputation, Rivera was based in Europe, where he had lived since 1907, and maintained an important position in the *avant-garde* in Paris, especially as one of the first exponents of Cubism (fig. 19). Although he was no doubt flattered to be asked to return to Mexico to assume the unofficial position of artistic 'leader' of Vasconcelos's campaign, Rivera was also completely committed to the ambitions of the minister's programme. Vasconcelos had made a shrewd choice; as a successful artist with an international profile, Rivera, who was to become a highly visible lobbyist and political activist in Mexico, attracted a great

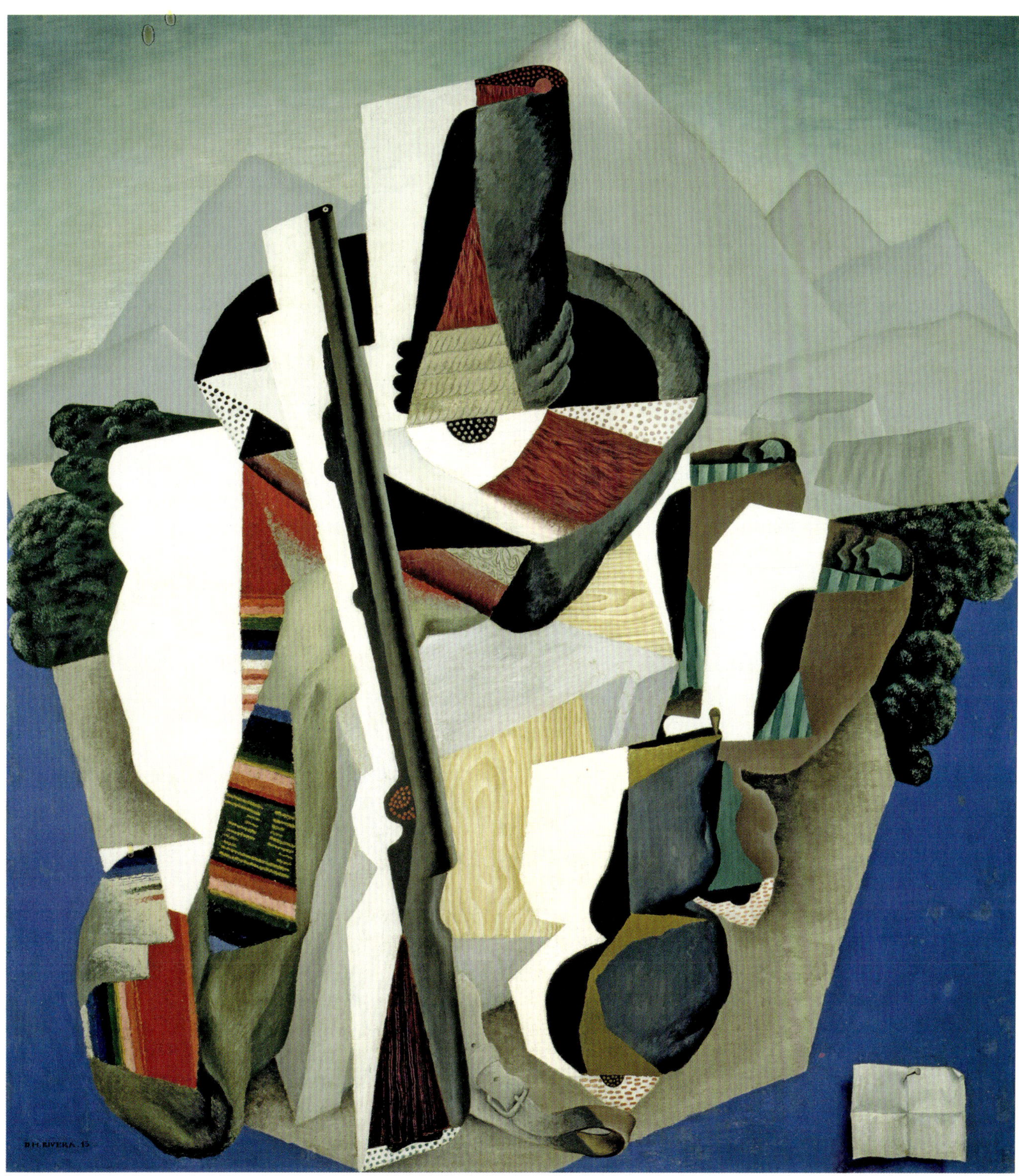

Fig. 19 Diego Rivera, **Zapatista Landscape – The Guerilla (Paisaje zapatista – El guerillero)**, 1915. Oil on canvas, 144 x 123 cm. Museo Nacional de Arte, Instituto Nacional de Bellas Artes y Literatura

deal of attention on his return to his homeland. He embraced his celebrity status and assumed the position of chief Mexican artist with relish, although he was not without his rivals and detractors. He received huge public exposure, on which he thrived. Part of his success was due to his indefatigable spirit. The photographer Edward Weston commented on Rivera's extraordinary dedication and stamina after meeting him in 1924: 'For a man to paint murals twelve hours a day – sometimes even sixteen at a stretch – and day after day working quite as a day-labourer might, not awaiting "mood" or "inspiration", it is amazing to me how much feeling he attains in his work. Only a man of great physical strength, possessed of a brilliant mind and a big heart as well, could have done what Diego has.'[15]

Rivera was ruthless in his determination to maintain his position as the greatest artist in Mexico. During the first significant public mural commission at the Escuela Nacional Preparatória, he encouraged Salvador Novo, a journalist friend, to write an article attacking the work of José Clemente Orozco, whose reputation as an artist was rapidly increasing. Orozco was easily angered, Charlot recalled, but in this case with very good reason:

> *because when* his *pictures* [Christ Destroying the Cross] *were destroyed, the students had been egged on by an article … written by Salvador Novo, I think in* El Universal Illustrado. *And Novo was a very close friend of Rivera, and obviously Rivera had asked Novo to write that article … because people were beginning to speak of Orozco in the same bracket, so to speak, with Rivera. And Rivera was quite a Machiavellian guy, and so without appearing himself, he delegated Salvador Novo to write against Orozco, and of course, the results were rather horrendous, and Orozco later on had to repair all the walls that had been not only scratched, but things had been thrown against them, and so on.*[16]

Despite the government's aspirations, the mural movement was clearly not a unified one in which everyone worked towards the same end. Art was fuelled by intense rivalries: between Rivera and Orozco over who was the greatest living Mexican artist, and between Rivera and David Alfaro Siqueiros over politics, specifically Trotskyism versus Stalinism. Charlot, disillusioned with the infighting that dominated Mexico City, accepted a job in the Yucatan in 1926 in order to get away from it all.

Rivera was not the only strong character to emerge at this time. Siqueiros, a native of Chihuahua, was to become one of *los tres grandes*, the three towering figures, of Mexican art (cat. 32), with Orozco and Rivera. As early as 1934 Siqueiros complained of 'murals painted in out of the way places and which only emerge from hiding in select monographs published for foreign amateurs', advocating that more visible advertising hoardings be given over to murals.[17] Siqueiros was not alone in criticising the murals then being painted, the most prominent target being those of Rivera.

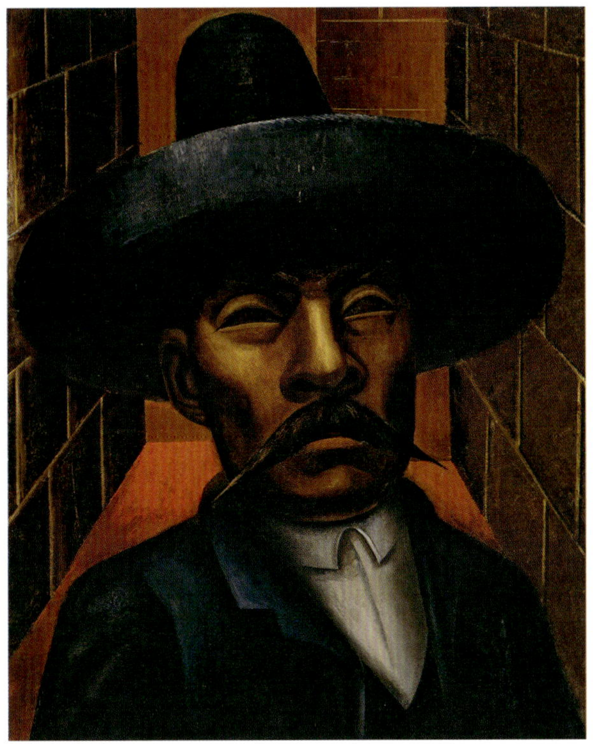

D. H. Lawrence and Edward Weston admired Rivera as an artist, but both were expressing doubts about the subject-matter of his public paintings as early as the mid-1920s. In *The Plumed Serpent,* Lawrence gave voice to his criticism through his main protagonist, Kate Leslie, who makes a point of visiting the frescoes in the *patios* of the university (undoubtedly those of the Ministry of Public Education):

> *In the many frescoes of the Indians there was sympathy with the Indian, but always from the ideal, social point of view. Never the spontaneous answer of the blood. These flat Indians were symbols in the great script of modern socialism, they were figures of the pathos of the victims of modern industry and capitalism. That was all they were used for: symbols in the weary script of socialism and anarchy.*[18]

Similarly, Weston wrote in his daybook: 'Diego, unless he gets out of his rut, has reached his limit; he is going around in circles, repeating successes, but cold and calculated in their formulisation'.[19] Cynicism about the political content of the murals and the wider role they played as a tool of government began to emerge less than five years after the programme had begun. By the late 1930s this feeling had intensified: 'We were tired of the grandiloquent plastic discourses of Orozco, Rivera, Siqueiros and their acolytes. Painted oratory we used to say.'[20]

By far the largest and most cosmopolitan city in the country as well as its capital, Mexico City drew artists in the early part of the twentieth century either to enrol in the pre-eminent national art school, the Academia de San Carlos, or to find wealthy benefactors among the urban élite. Thus numerous aspiring artists congregated there, among them Saturnino Herrán from Aguascalientes, Francisco Goitia from Zacatecas, Rufino Tamayo from Oaxaca, Rivera from Guanajuato and Orozco from Zapotlán in Jalisco. For some, Mexico City was not enough and they travelled abroad – especially to Spain, France and Italy – to continue their art education, visiting

32

David Alfaro Siqueiros (1896–1974)
Zapata, 1931.
Oil on canvas, 135.26 x 105.72 cm.
Hirshhorn Museum and Sculpture Garden, Smithsonian Institution, Washington, DC. Gift of Joseph H. Hirshhorn, 1966

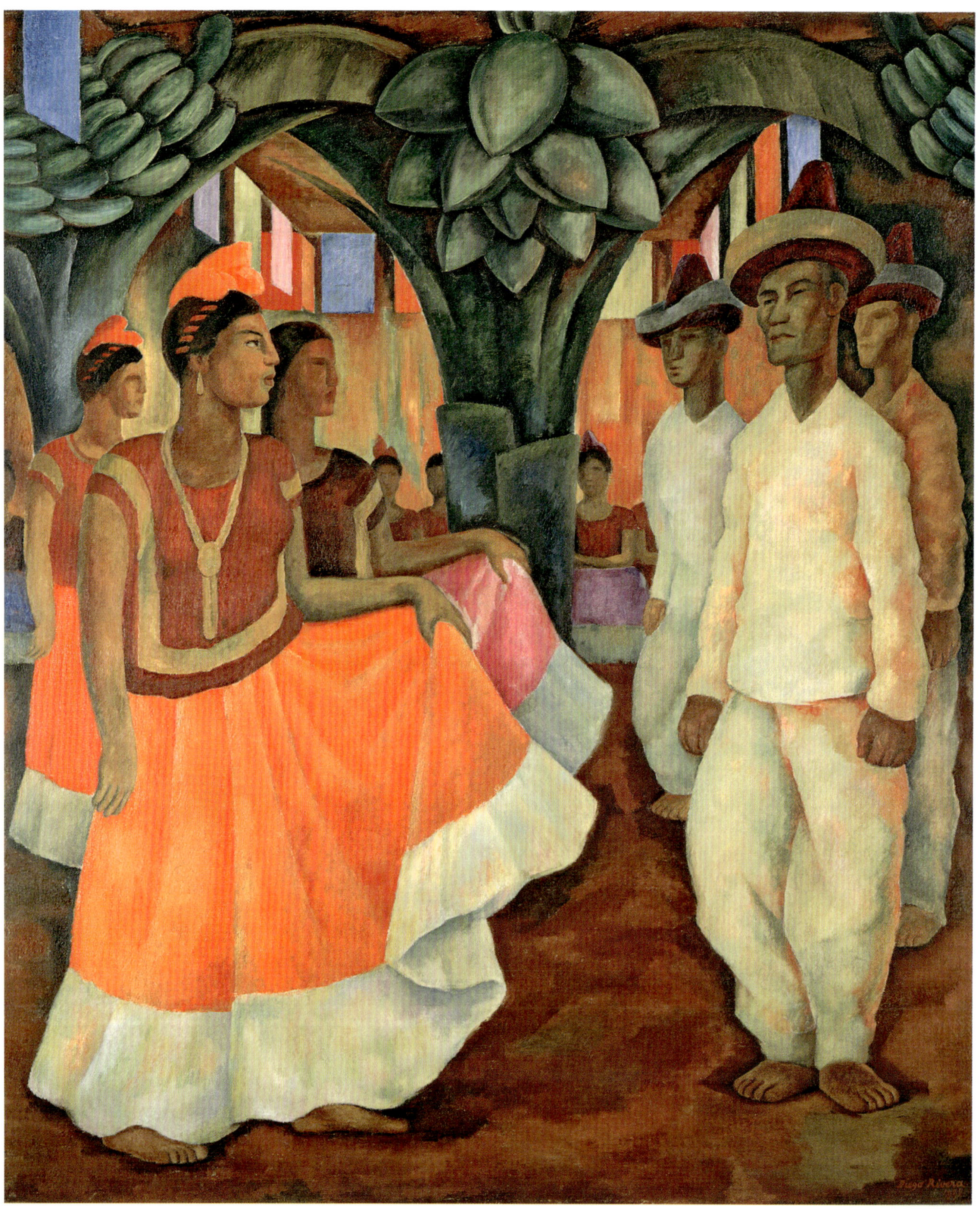

museum collections and important historical sites. Some settled in Europe, with its larger art community and market, taking studios and exhibiting their work. Roberto Montenegro from Guadalajara in Jalisco was in many ways typical. After moving to Mexico City and enrolling at the Academia de San Carlos, he was awarded a grant to travel to Europe and spent time in Madrid and Paris. The First World War prevented his return to Mexico, and, having initially sought sanctuary in Barcelona, he moved to Majorca, where he saw out the war working as a fisherman in order to survive.

Fuelled by their experiences in Europe and charged with a newfound sense of national pride, Mexican artists looked inward rather than outward for inspiration on their return. Most found that their initiation into contemporary art involved a rupture with the past as well as a break with traditional academic training.[21] Henceforth Mexican artists began to eschew Europe and America, instead embracing the beauty, diversity and history of their own country. Their celebration of Mexico's past through the often highly visible remnants of pre-Columbian civilisations, combined with the rich ethnic diversity of the present population, produced a powerful new artistic movement, which for the purposes of this text I have referred to as 'Mexican Modernism'. The art of this period has been described elsewhere as the 'Mexican Renaissance', a 'Mexican school of painting' and even an extreme 'phase two' of modernism.[22] Mexican artists set out to create an original and independently Mexican version of modernism, whose origins lay in their rejection of both the Beaux-Arts academicism of the Porfiriato and Socialist Realism. Indeed, they tried to find a third path that would be modernist and figurative without being *avant-garde* or academic, in which folk or popular art was an integral part of their political and aesthetic strategies.[23] Towns with strong regional identities, such as Tehuantepec in Oaxaca, Patzcuaro in Michoacan and Taxco in Guerrero, became very popular among the artistic community and were often the subject of artists' work (cats 33, 34, 54). The British diplomat, folklorist and ethnomusicologist Rodney Gallop celebrated the diversity of Mexico in *Mexican Mosaic: Folklore and Tradition* (London, 1939), which although it was published later is representative of the appetite that people had for experiencing and recording the rich traditions of Mexico. Illustrated with photographs

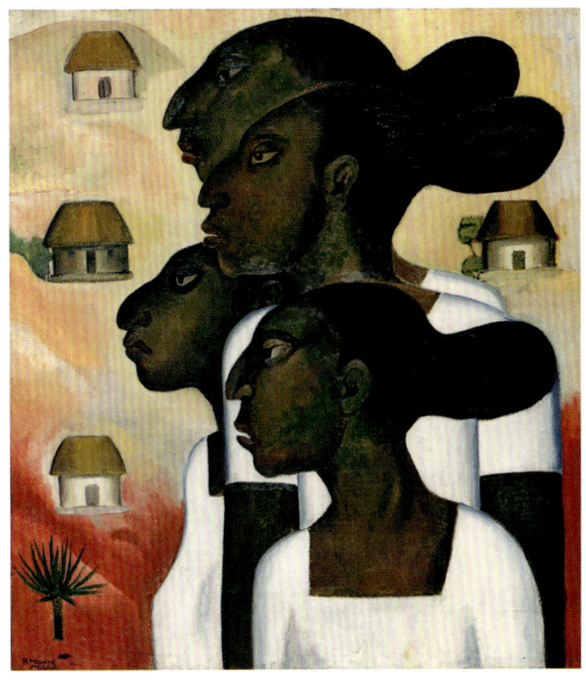

33

Diego Rivera (1886–1957)
Dance in Tehuantepec (Baile in Tehuantepec), 1928.
Oil on canvas, 200.7 x 163.8 cm.
Collection of Clarissa and Edgar Bronfman Jr

34

Roberto Montenegro (1887–1968)
Maya Women (Mujeres mayas), 1926.
Oil on canvas, 80 x 69.8 cm.
The Museum of Modern Art, New York. Gift of Nelson A. Rockefeller, 1941

by the author and drawings by his wife, this was no ordinary travel book: like many artists at the time, the Gallops were deeply drawn to the cultural heritage of Mexico and spent most of their free time visiting remote parts of the country and recording the people and traditions they encountered. Travelling within Mexico at this time was often arduous and required real determination, since the transport network was very limited and roads often impassable. The challenge of travelling and utilising various forms of transport added to the sense of adventure, enriching the experience and ultimately making the journey more satisfying (fig. 20). Mexican Modernism was not a conscious movement, rather an opportunity for artists to celebrate national and regional pride and identity without being bound by any restrictions or conventions. The work of Rivera and Montenegro, for instance, celebrated regional identity in markedly different ways; Rivera captured the colour and movement of La Zandunga, the regional dance of the semi-tropical Tehuantepec, a famous matriarchal society, while Montenegro reflected on the nobility and beauty of the people and the distinctive landscape of the Yucatan, providing an unspoken link with the Maya forebears of the region (cats 33, 34).

Another central tenet of Vasconcelos's radical mural programme was a determination to raise the profile of the hugely rich fields of archaeology and anthropology in Mexico. Vasconcelos felt that a clearer understanding of Mexican history would advance the incorporation of the indigenous population into post-revolutionary society and help to create a sense of Mexico as one nation, rather than an assemblage of distinct regions, with a shared source of national pride and a common identity. A number of high-profile archaeological excavations and restorations were funded through Monumentos Prehispánicos, part of the Ministry of Public Education, often in partnership with external institutions such as the Carnegie Institute, which brought both funding and expertise (cat. 35). Many

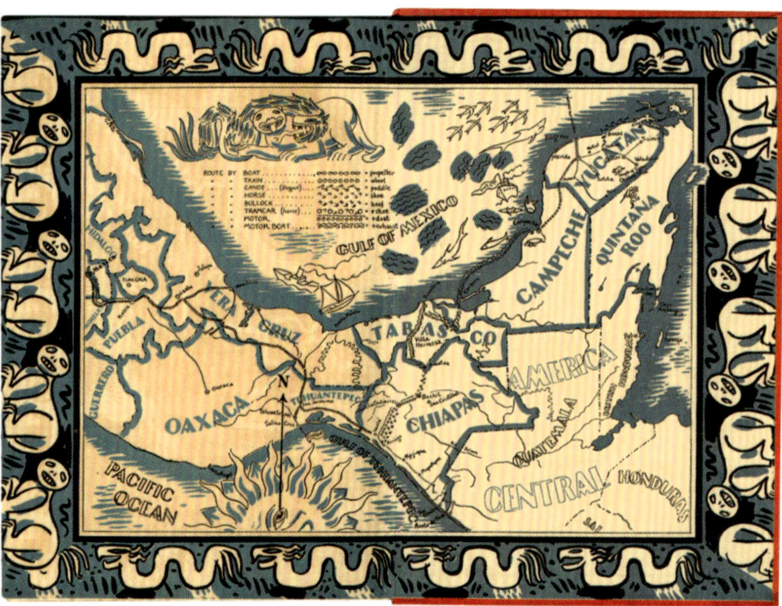

Fig. 20 Leon Underwood, endpapers of Phillips Russell, **Red Tiger: Adventures in Yucatan and Mexico**, published by Hodder and Stoughton (London, 1929). Printed book, 24.2 x 15.9 cm. Royal Academy of Arts, London

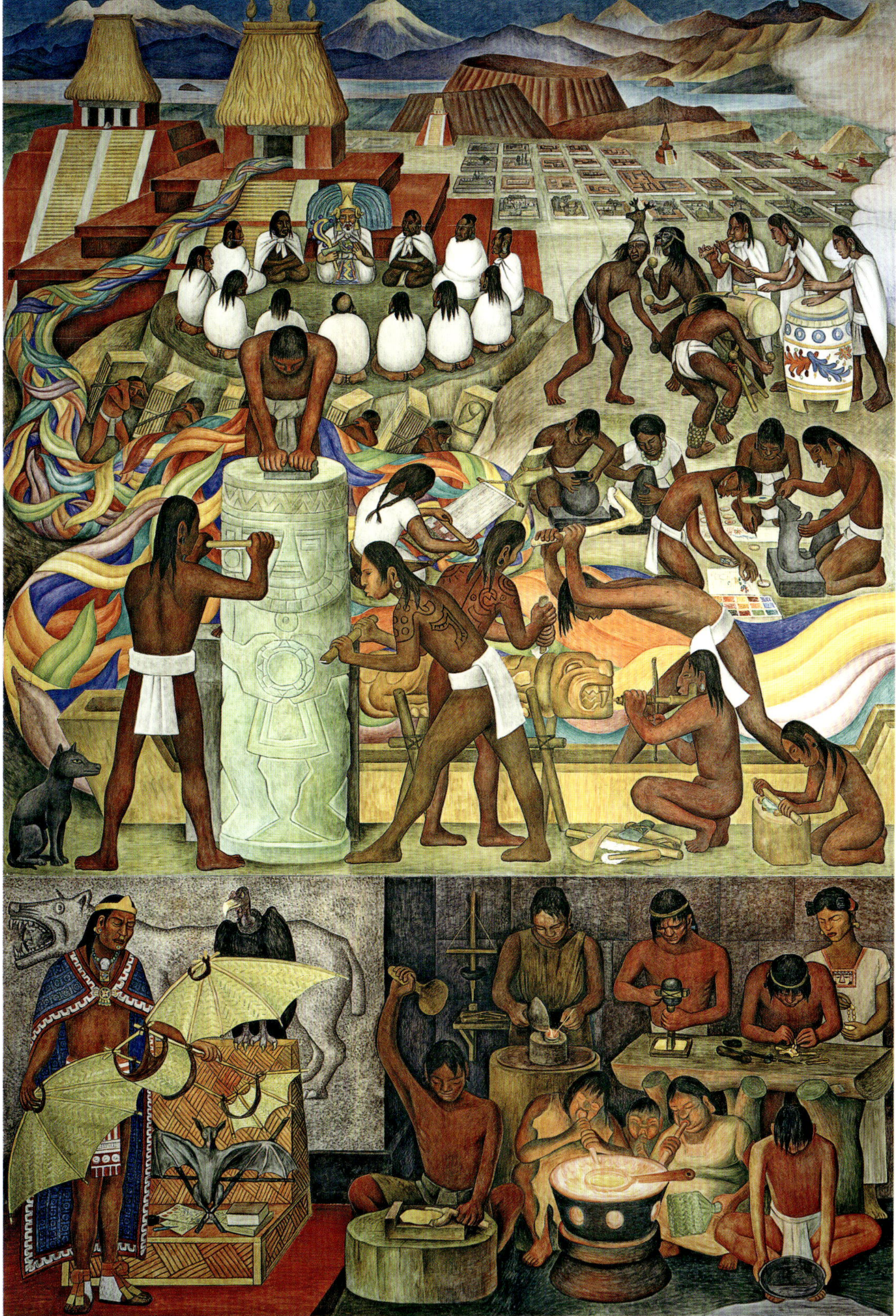

Fig. 21 **The Creative Genius of the South Growing from Religious Fervour and a Native Talent for Plastic Expression**, 1940. Two removable panels of **Pan American Unity. The Marriage of the Artistic Expression of the North and of the South on the Continent**. Fresco, 8.26 x 4.84 m. City College of San Francisco

artists collected pre-Columbian artefacts and gave them prominence in their homes and studios. Rivera even went so far as to build a special museum to house his vast collection, the Anhuacalli, designed by Juan O'Gorman, which was completed only after his death in 1957.

The popular arts – practical, decorative and ritual objects – were likewise celebrated as indications of the inherent creativity and industry of the Mexican people; indeed, they came to be seen as an integrated whole with the fine arts, without distinction between disciplines. The painter and vulcanologist Gerardo Murillo, who was known as Dr Atl, after the Nahuatl word for water, headed a national commission to promote the popular arts through an exhibition that opened in Mexico City and travelled to the US. He wrote a lavishly illustrated two-volume publication, *Las Artes Populares en México* (Mexico City, 1922), assisted by René D'Harnoncourt (fig. 22), later Director of the Museum of Modern Art, New York, and Anita Brenner, who was to publish *Idols behind Altars* (New York, 1929), which, among other things, championed the work of Mexican popular artists and was richly illustrated with photographs by Edward Weston and Tina Modotti. Weston, Modotti and, later, Manuel Álvarez Bravo photographed many works of popular art for the English-language journal *Mexican Folkways*, which was edited by the American Frances Toor.

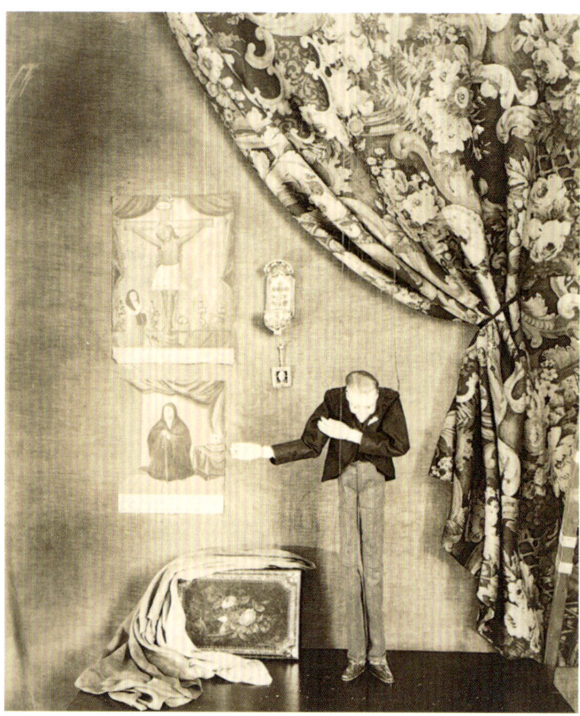

Fig. 22 Tina Modotti, **René D'Harnoncourt Puppet**, 1929. Gelatin silver print, 23.6 x 19.05 cm. Center for Creative Photography, University of Arizona, Tucson, 93.27.8

The art world, despite its many artistic and ideological rivalries, remained small, however, and was largely centred on professional relationships and personal friendships. These were subject to constant frictions. Nevertheless the camaraderie in the years immediately after the Revolution was tangible, as Weston and Brenner captured in their respective diaries. During June 1926, for instance, Weston, Modotti, Rivera and Toor travelled widely throughout Mexico together to photograph the popular paintings that decorated the exterior and interior of *pulquerías* for an article by Rivera to be published in *Mexican Folkways* (fig. 23).[24] In the 1940 exhibition 'Twenty Centuries of Mexican Art' at the Museum of Modern Art, New York, which is discussed further in Chapter Four, popular art formed a central component of the exhibition, and in the accompanying catalogue Antonio Castro Leal credited it with reinvigorating Mexican artists:

> *Mexican popular art reveals a people unusually gifted for self-expression in forms of aesthetic significance, and the vitality explains why the plastic arts that were becoming debilitated in cultured environments acquired a new vigour and feeling when they drew near to the taste and inspiration of the people.*[25]

Not everyone embraced the popular arts with such enthusiasm. Ever the political animal (he was later to participate in the Spanish Civil War), Siqueiros was unequivocal in his opposition, and, in 'Towards a Transformation of Plastic Arts', written in New York, he thundered: 'We must put an end to superficial *folk art*, of the type called '*Mexican Curious*' which predominates in Mexico today, and substitute it for an art which is internationally valid though based on local antecedents and functional elements.'[26]

D. H. Lawrence was one of the first novelists to visit Mexico after the Revolution, and between March 1923 and March 1925 he spent some twelve months there, spread over three trips.[27] He and his wife Frieda Weekley were living in the US in the Taos art colony, which had been established in New Mexico in 1919 by Mabel Dodge Luhan. They needed to leave

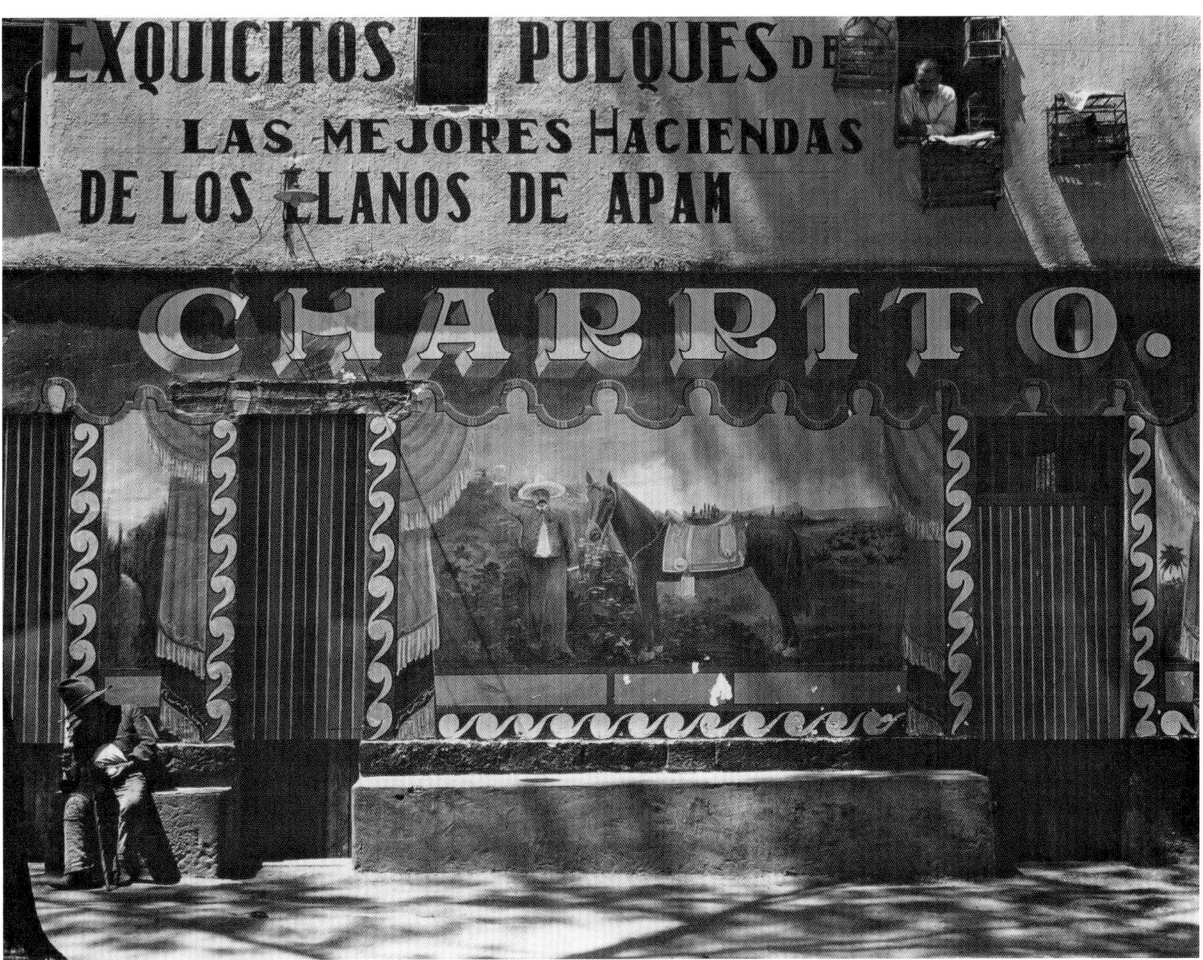

Fig. 23 Edward Weston, **Charrito (Pulquería), Mexico**, 4 October 1926. Gelatin silver print, 19.2 x 24.2 cm. Center for Creative Photography, University of Arizona, Tucson, 76.10.29

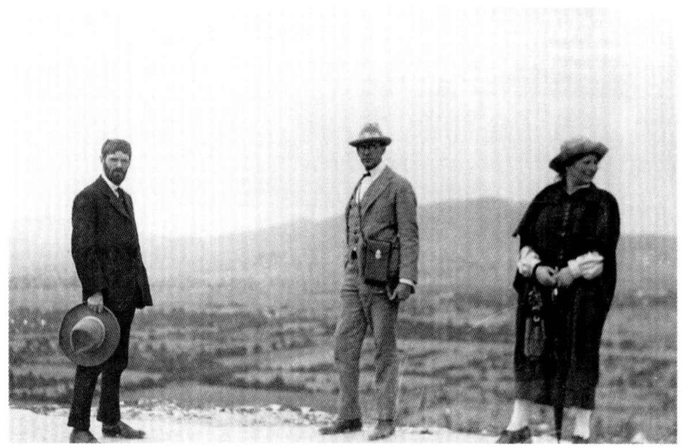

Fig. 24 Willard Johnson(?), **D. H. Lawrence, Witter Bynner and Frieda Weekley on the Pyramid of the Sun, Teotihuacan**, 1923. Photograph, half-plate black and white negative, 8.3 x 14 cm. Manuscripts and Special Collections, University of Nottingham, La WB 1/25

the US as their six-month visas were due to expire, and Mexico seemed the obvious destination, especially as events there were generating considerable interest in Taos. Famed for the alternative lifestyle it promoted, the Taos community also attracted visitors from Mexico: the composer Carlos Chávez met the photographer Paul Strand there.

Lawrence first visited Mexico in March 1923 with Frieda, the American poet Witter Bynner and his companion Willard Johnson.[28] On an excursion to Teotihuacan (fig. 24), he was inspired by Manuel Gamio's recent excavations and immediately decided to write a novel set in Mexico, naming it after the god Quetzalcoatl, to whom the temple that had made such a deep impression on him was dedicated. Bynner recalled: 'In the great quadrangle of Quetzalcóatl, we saw Lawrence stand looking and brooding. The coloured stone heads of the feathered snakes in one of the temples were a match for him'.[29]

Soon after his arrival in October 1924 with Frieda and the British artist Dorothy Brett on his final visit, Lawrence lunched with W. Somerset Maugham, who had only just arrived in Mexico; Lawrence disliked him.[30] Maugham had planned to set a novel in Mexico but having become disenchanted with Mexico City he left for Guatemala shortly afterwards. Lawrence was later introduced to Edward Weston, recently arrived. 'My first impression was a most agreeable one. He will sit for me Tuesday', noted Weston in his daybook.[31] Two days later, as agreed, Lawrence came to Weston's studio in Calle Lucerna in the Juárez district of Mexico City:

> *The sitting of D. H. Lawrence this morning. A tall, slender, rather reserved individual with a brick-red beard. He was amiable enough and we parted in a friendly way, but the contact was too brief for either of us to penetrate more than superficially the other: no way to make a sitting. Perhaps I should not have attempted it; now I actually lack sufficient interest to develop my plates.*[32]

Weston's three portraits (cat. 36, fig. 25) show Lawrence as preoccupied and aloof. He sent prints to Lawrence, now settled in Oaxaca, who responded: 'Thank you very much for the photographs. I like them very much: think I like the one with the chin up better than the other looking down: but like both of them.'[33]

Lawrence spent the next six weeks working on his manuscript, taking a short break in mid-December to write four pieces about life in Oaxaca that together form the core of *Mornings in Mexico* (London, 1927).[34] By then 'Quetzalcoatl' was almost

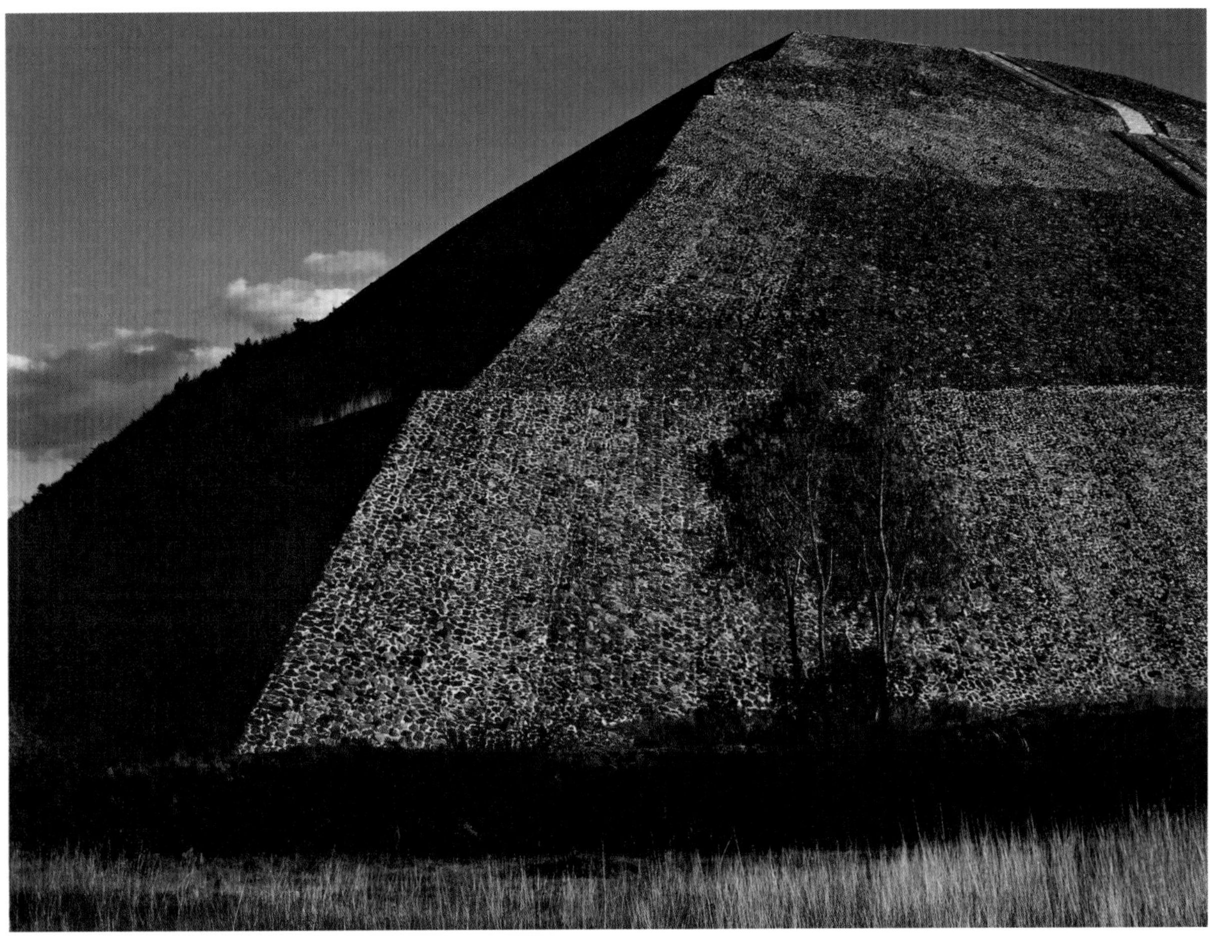

twice the length of the first draft and its author was becoming increasingly ill. When he finished the final draft on 29 January 1925 Lawrence suffered a physical collapse. Too ill to travel to Europe as he had planned, he stayed in Mexico City for a month's recuperation before his return to the US. Lawrence's feelings towards his book fluctuated. Early on he thought 'Quetzalcoatl' one of his greatest works but later reflected, 'I'd rather not have it published at all.'[35]

In the end *The Plumed Serpent*, an extraordinary novel centred on a religious revolution that aimed to resurrect pre-Columbian gods and practices through the cult of Quetzalcoatl, was published in 1926. The book captures many of Lawrence's experiences in Mexico, as well as the many places he visited, but the writing throughout has an undercurrent of primitive power, a dark menace that reflects the unease Lawrence felt and articulated while he was there.

35

Edward Weston (1886–1958)
Pyramid of the Sun, Mexico (Pirámide del Sol, Mexico),
1923.
Gelatin silver print, 19 x 23.7 cm.
Center for Creative Photography, University of Arizona, Tucson.
Gift of Ansel and Virginia Adams

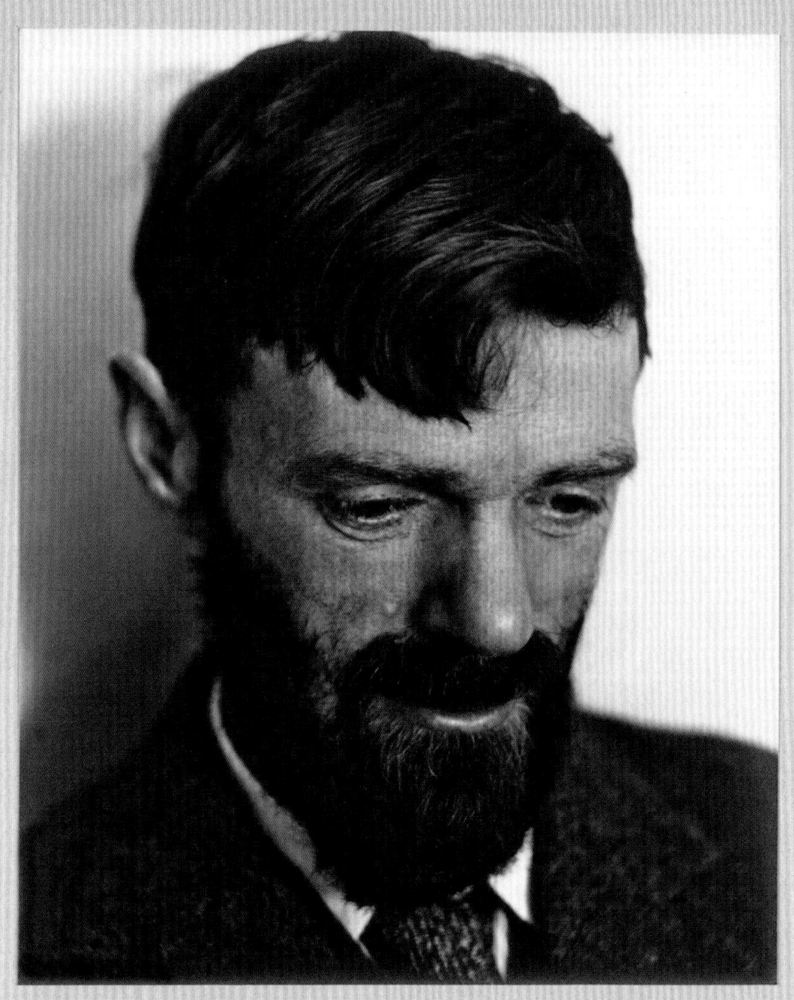
D. H. Lawrence
Edward Weston
Mexico 1924

The novel is less a description of the country and its people than a psychological exploration of belief and death. On the novel's publication Lawrence's vision was criticised by those who knew Mexico well. The American journalist Carleton Beals described the book as 'an absurd farce', adding 'there is no possibility of the return of the old gods because the old gods have never entirely departed'.[36] Anita Brenner was even more outspoken: 'Been reading the most gosh-awful book ever, *Plumed Serpent*. Hysterics and nasty humour, less pettiness of an old and sick woman is the tone. Keen observer, silly interpreter, and the whole thing unpleasant.' She concluded: 'Mexico is no place for weak people.'[37] Weston was very excited to be given a copy by D'Harnoncourt while he was staying in Patzcuaro, but was likewise disappointed with it:

> *Throughout the book apparently trivial inaccuracies persist, and form a wrong or one-sided impression of Mexico. Lawrence was bewildered by Mexico, he was frightened, but he over-dramatised his fear. There are fine descriptive passages, intelligent analyses, accurate prophecy, but such a padding of tiresome allegory about Quetzalcóatl that excellent material has been used to create a volume of unconvincing mysticism.*[38]

Knowing that any work by Lawrence would receive a great deal of interest, Beals, Brenner, Weston and others who felt the same way thought that he had failed to do justice to the country about which they

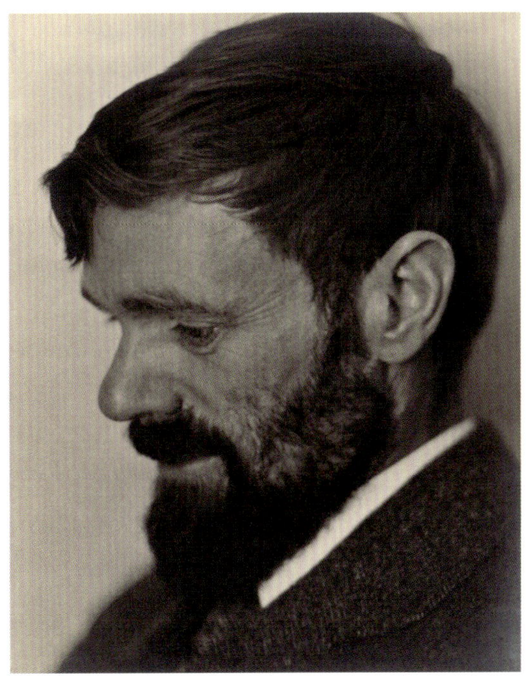

Fig. 25 Edward Weston, **D. H. Lawrence**, 4 November 1924. Gelatin silver print, 24.2 x 18.8 cm. Center for Creative Photography, University of Arizona, Tucson, 76.5.8

were passionate. The fact is that Lawrence was ill at ease in Mexico and mistrustful of the locals, and this sentiment permeates the work he created there. A sentence about the novel's protagonist, Kate Leslie, might just as well have been about himself: 'And in this Mexico, with its great under-drift of squalor and heavy reptile-like evil, it was hard for her to bear up.'[39] Lawrence's eventual departure, after initially being turned back at the US border, was that of a beaten man. He was reduced to wearing rouge

36

Edward Weston (1886–1958)
D. H. Lawrence, 1924.
Vintage chlorobromide print, 24.3 x 19.3 cm. National Portrait Gallery, London

to disguise the tell-tale signs of his tuberculosis, and was never to return.[40]

Weston arrived in Mexico with great enthusiasm, hoping to rediscover his creative inspiration (cat. 37). He was burnt out and bored by his work as a successful studio photographer in California. An exhibition of his photographs at the Academia de Bellas Artes in Mexico City the previous year was seen as a good omen and encouraged him to explore the possibilities that Mexico offered.[41] He arrived with his lover Tina Modotti and his eldest son Chandler, then aged thirteen, in August 1923 (cat. 38).

Modotti had already been to Mexico, albeit under very different and trying circumstances. Her then partner, the American poet and actor Roubaix de l'Abrie Richéy, known as Robo, had heard about the cultural renaissance taking place after the Revolution from the Mexican archaeologist Ricardo Gómez Robelo in Los Angeles, and travelled down in late 1921 seeking new opportunities. Robelo, a close friend of Vasconcelos, had been appointed a government minister and offered his friend a teaching position, a studio and an exhibition. On board a train on her way to Mexico in February 1922 for a long-awaited reunion with Robo, Modotti heard of his sudden death from smallpox.

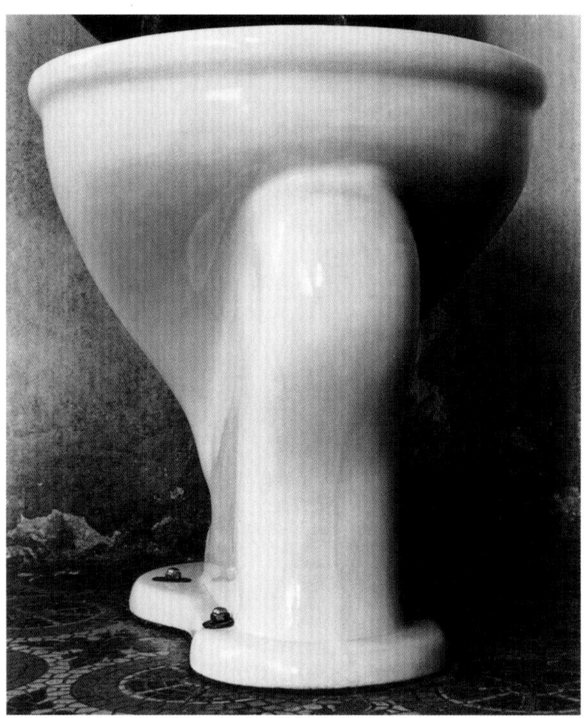

In Mexico City she met many of Robo's friends and was introduced to several others by Robelo. Weston photographed Robelo, who later became Director of the Ministry of Public Education's Department of Fine Arts (fig. 26). Intoxicated by the atmosphere and the intensity of the cultural activity

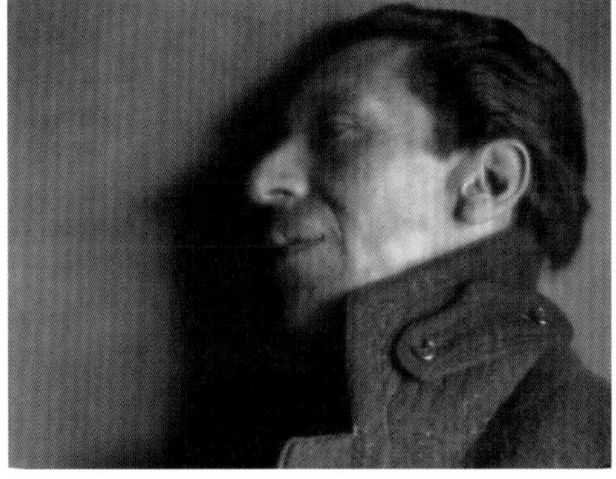

Fig. 26 Edward Weston, **Ricardo Gómez Robelo**, 1921. Gelatin silver print, 19.2 x 24.3 cm. Center for Creative Photography, University of Arizona, Tucson, 81.276.2

37

Edward Weston (1886–1958)
Excusado, 1925.
Vintage gelatin silver print, 50.8 x 40.5 cm.
Wilson Centre for Photography, London

38

Unknown photographer
Edward Weston and Tina Modotti, 1924.
Gelatin silver print, 57.5 x 42.3 x 3 cm (framed).
Victoria and Albert Museum, London

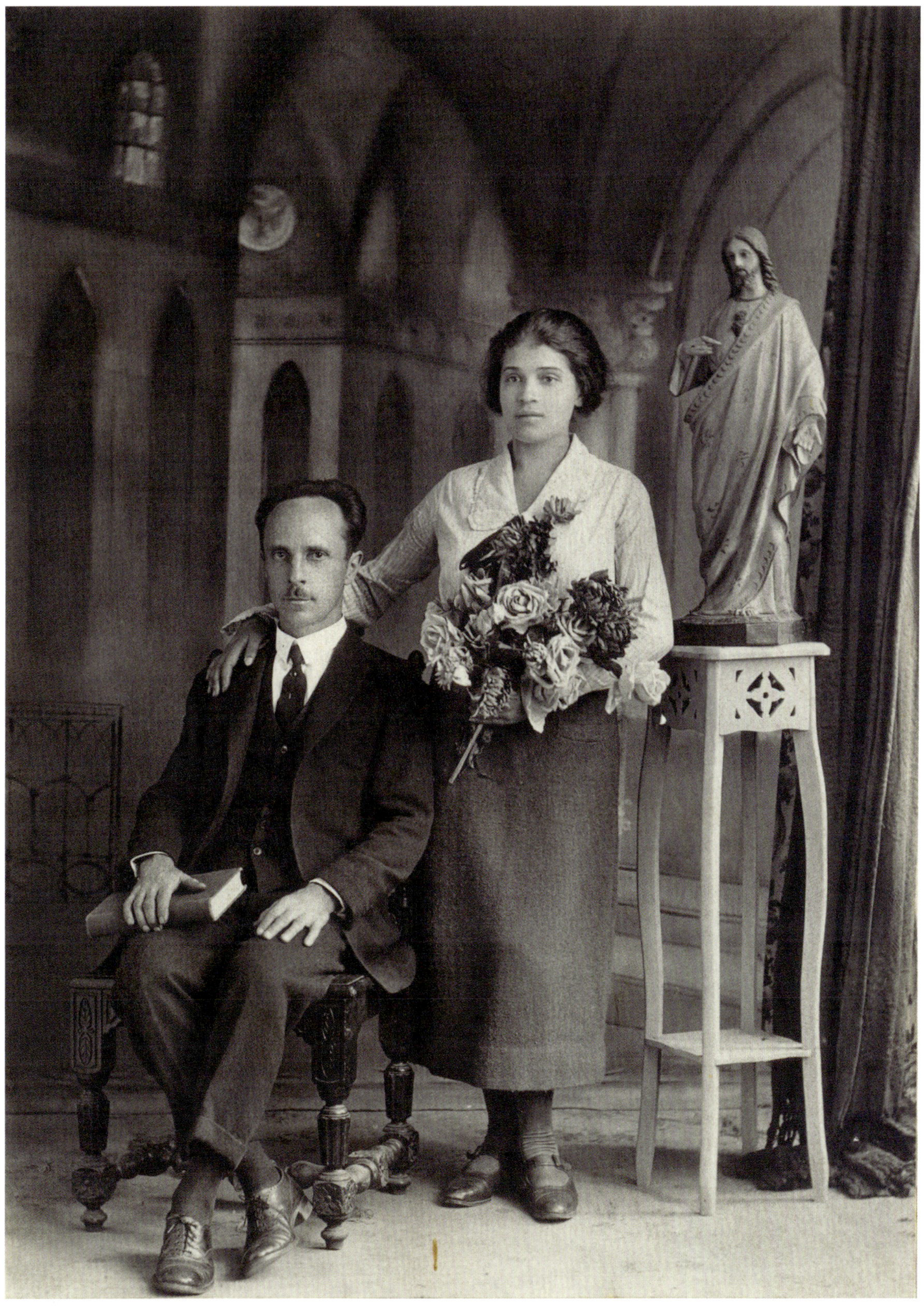

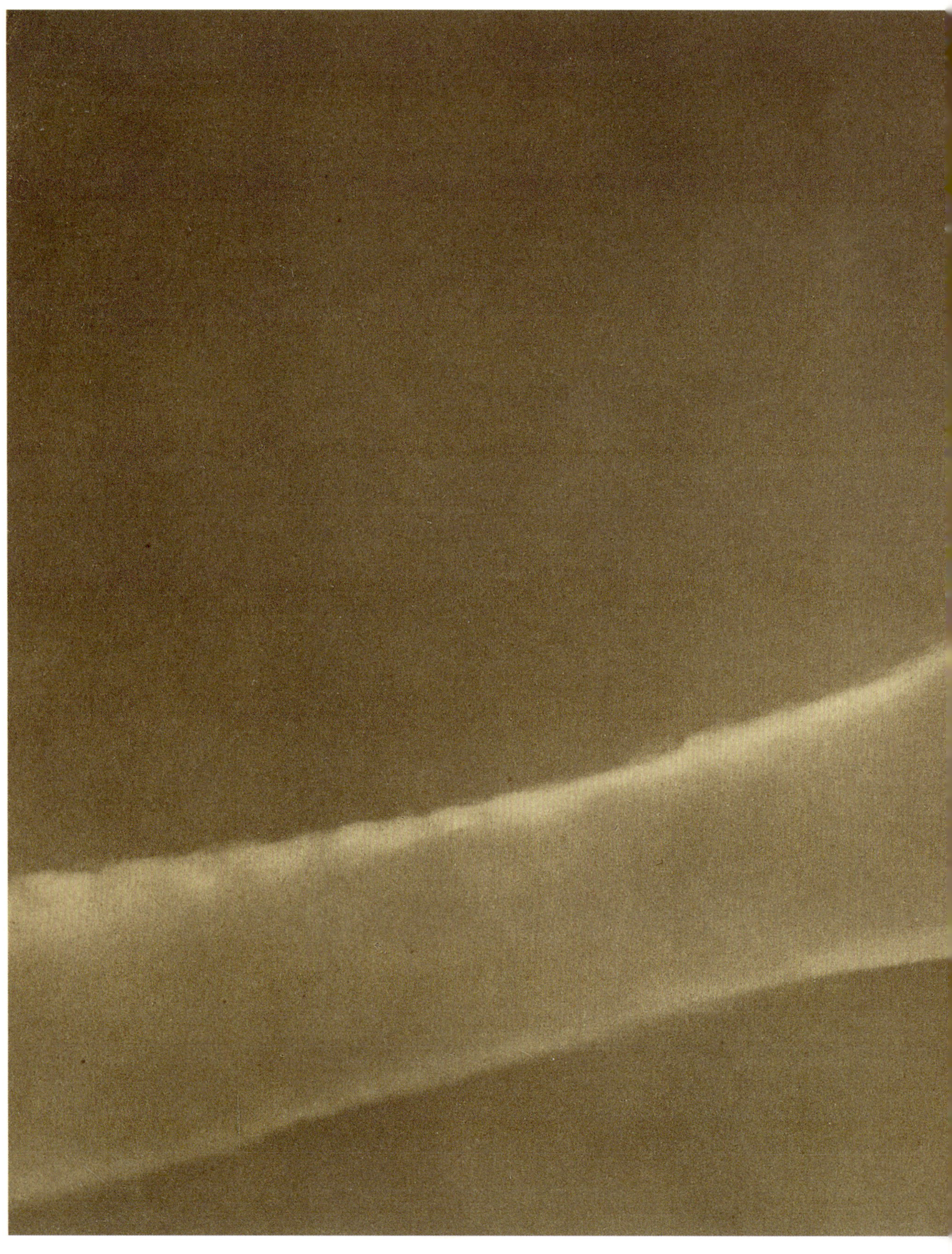

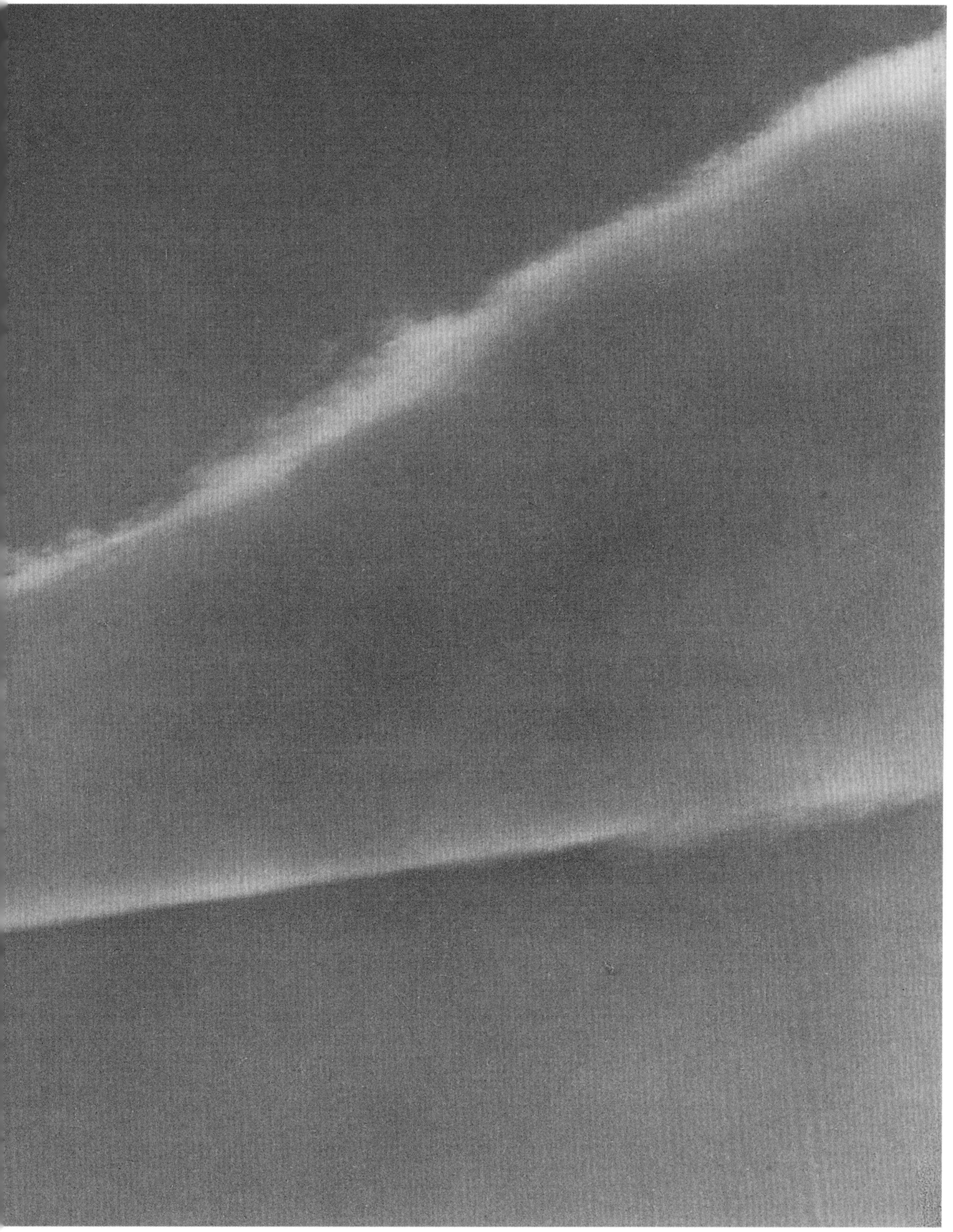

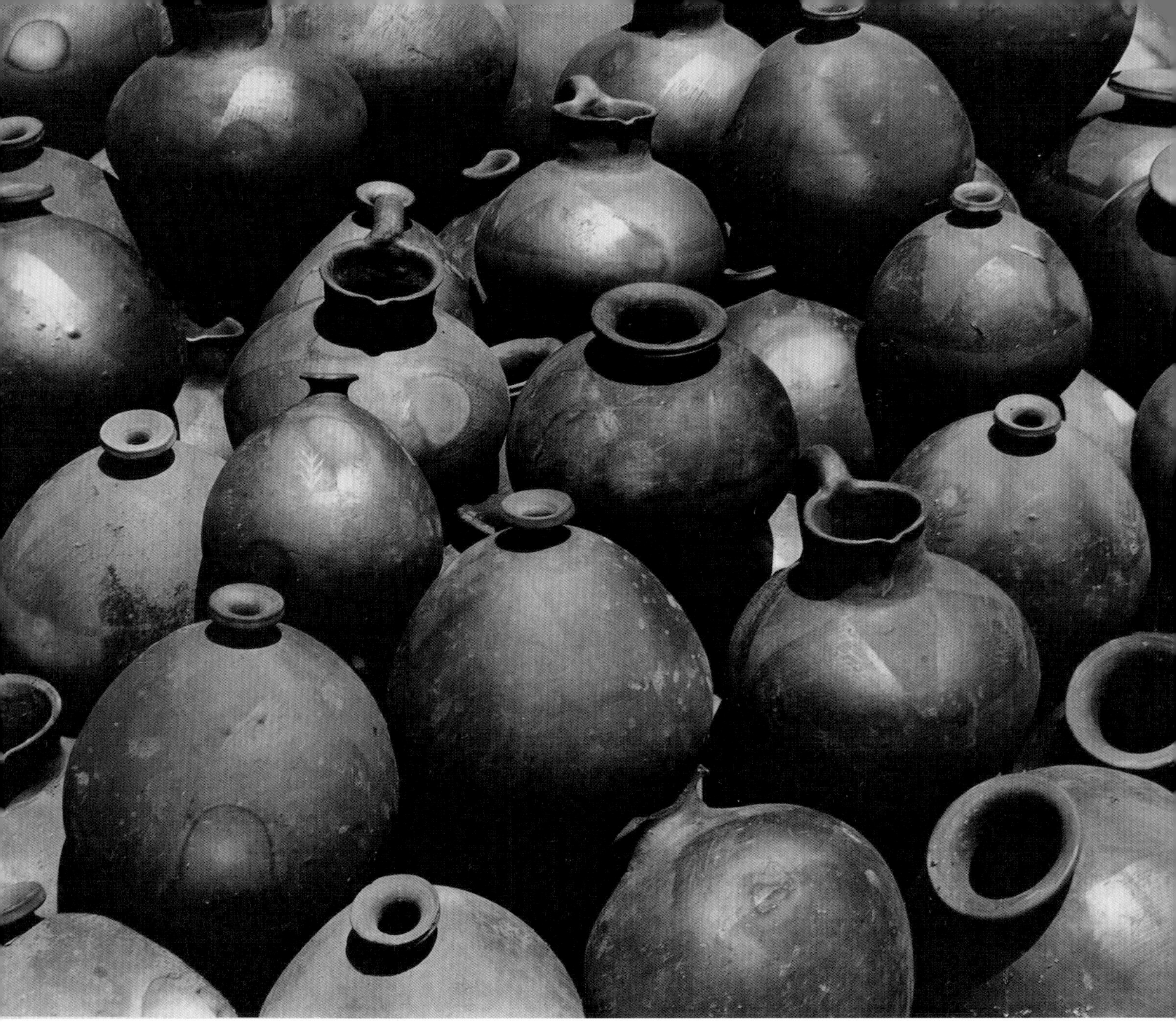

39

previous pages:
Edward Weston
(1886–1958)
Cloud, Mexico, 1926.
Palladium print,
14.9 x 24 cm.
The J. Paul Getty Museum,
Los Angeles

40

above:
Edward Weston (1886–1958)
Heaped Black Pots
(Ollas de Oaxaca), 1926.
Vintage gelatin silver print,
40.5 x 50.8 cm (mounted).
Wilson Centre for Photography,
London

Fig. 27 Tina Modotti, **St Francis Helping the Poor**, detail of a mural in the Escuela Nacional Preparatória by José Clemente Orozco, 1923(?). Gelatin silver print, 19 x 24 cm. Jean Charlot Collection, University of Hawaii at Manoa Library, JCCMT21

in Mexico, Modotti was determined to return permanently. Weston had initially planned to go to Mexico and share a studio with Robo but had kept postponing his decision.[42]

No doubt Weston was motivated to move by the success of his exhibition, but as his relationship with Modotti deepened she must have finally persuaded him to do so.[43] By this time Modotti had decided to become a photographer and, since Weston offered to teach her, she assumed the position of his assistant (cats 56, 57).[44]

On their arrival in August 1923 Modotti introduced Weston to a number of artists and they were soon a popular and celebrated couple in Mexico City's vibrant art scene (cats 40, 41).[45] Indeed, they were the only photographers who consorted with the muralists, and considered themselves to be their colleagues.[46] Testament to this is the large body of photographs that Modotti took of their work (fig. 27). In November they met the French artist Jean Charlot, with whom Weston struck up an immediate rapport.[47]

Charlot's maternal great-uncle, Eugène Goupil, was born in Mexico. He lived in Paris and boasted an important collection of pre-Columbian objects and manuscripts. Charlot moved to Mexico from Paris with his mother in 1921. He stayed in Coyoacan, where he shared a studio with the painter Fernando Leal, and began working as an assistant to Rivera on *Creation* at the Escuela Nacional Preparatória. Charlot was very popular among the artistic community in Mexico and enjoyed some

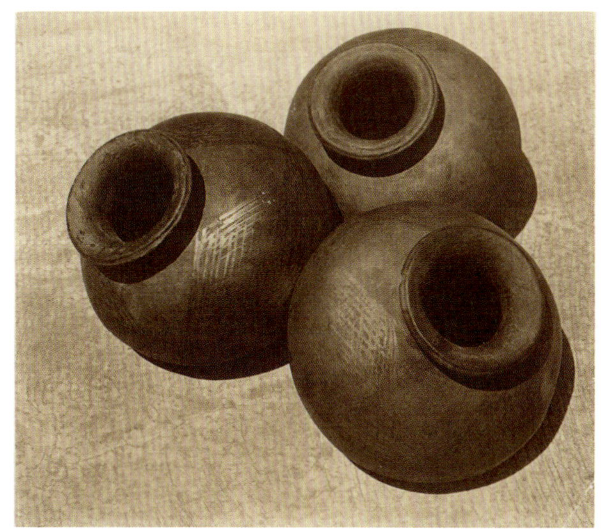

success while he was there (cats 30, 31).[48] Indeed, such was his standing in Mexico that, alongside Pablo O'Higgins (who was born Paul Higgins in San Francisco) and the Guatemalan-born painter Carlos Mérida, he was one of only three foreign-born artists to be included in the book *Modern Mexican Artists* (Mexico City, 1937), which, incidentally, surprisingly omitted Frida Kahlo. Charlot was art editor of *Mexican Folkways* and had a close relationship with Brenner, who visited him at Chichen Itza when he began work there in 1926 recording Mayan frescoes as they were being uncovered. Charlot left Mexico for Washington, DC in 1929 to work on his study of the Temple of the Warriors at Chichen Itza with Ann Axtell Morris. He settled permanently in the US that

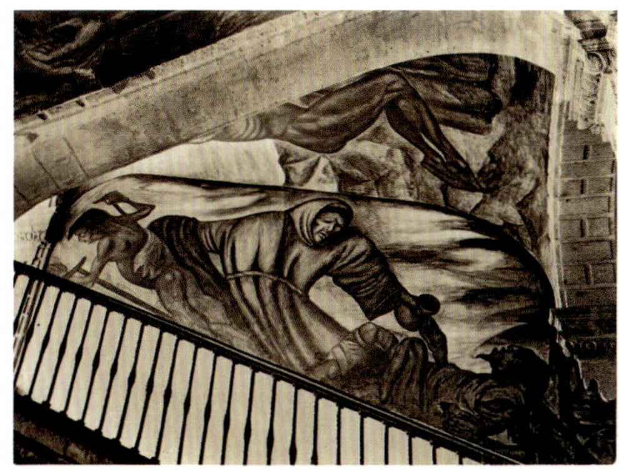

41

Edward Weston (1886–1958)
Three Oaxacan Pots (Tres ollas de Oaxaca), 1926.
Platinum print, 18.5 x 20.6 cm.
Philadelphia Museum of Art.
Gift of Anne d'Harnoncourt and Joseph Rishel in memory of Theodor Siegl, 1976

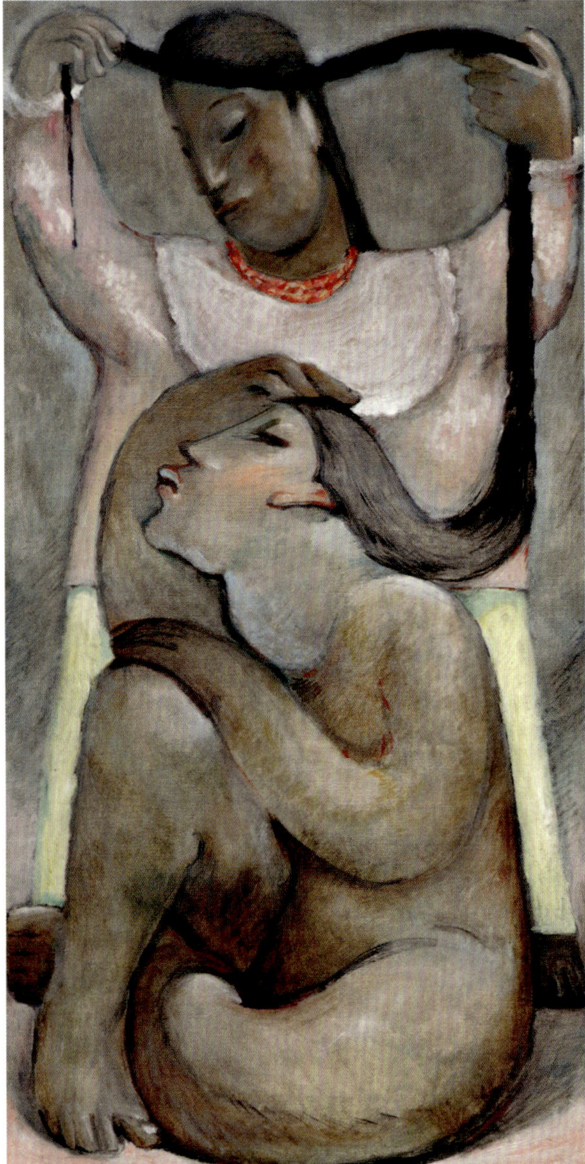

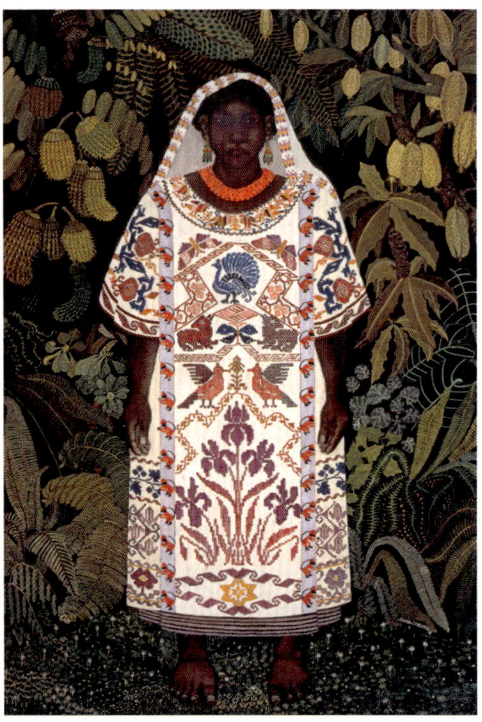

Fig. 28 Ramón Cano Manilla, **India Oxaqueña**, 1928. Oil on canvas, 152.4 x 101.5 cm. Museo Nacional de Arte, Instituto Nacional de Bellas Artes y Literatura

42

Jean Charlot (1898–1979)
Coiffure (Trenzando el pelo), 1930.
Oil on canvas, 122.5 x 61.5 cm.
Colección Andrés Blaisten

43

Tina Modotti (1896–1942)
Untitled (Workers, Mexico), *c.* 1926–30.
Gelatin silver print, 16.8 x 21.1 cm.
Amon Carter Museum of American Art, Fort Worth

same year and continued to explore Mexican themes in his art (cat. 42).[49] Charlot was drawn to the indigenous population of Mexico and worked extensively with 'Luz' (Luciana Jiménez), a model from Milpa Alta, a suburb in the extreme south-east of Mexico City, whom he painted on numerous occasions and to whose family he became close. The manner in which artists worked with indigenous Mexicans, presenting them as equals and celebrating their regional identity and traditions, was a central tenet of Mexican Modernism (fig. 28).

Weston returned to the US permanently in late 1926, anxious to spend more time with his family in California. He and Modotti had grown apart, a process accelerated by their dalliances with other people during their relationship. Weston never went back to Mexico. Following his departure, Modotti became fully committed to a political agenda. Although her early experiments with photography reflect the influence of Weston's aesthetic preoccupations, her mature work changed to focus on images of workers, on the one hand as suppressed and exploited, and on the other as noble and heroic, responsible for rebuilding the country (cats 43–45). Modotti also engaged with overt political still-lifes in which the hammer and sickle, emblems of Soviet communism – a theme embraced by numerous Mexican artists, many of whom were members of the Mexican Communist Party – were juxtaposed with other iconic objects, such as

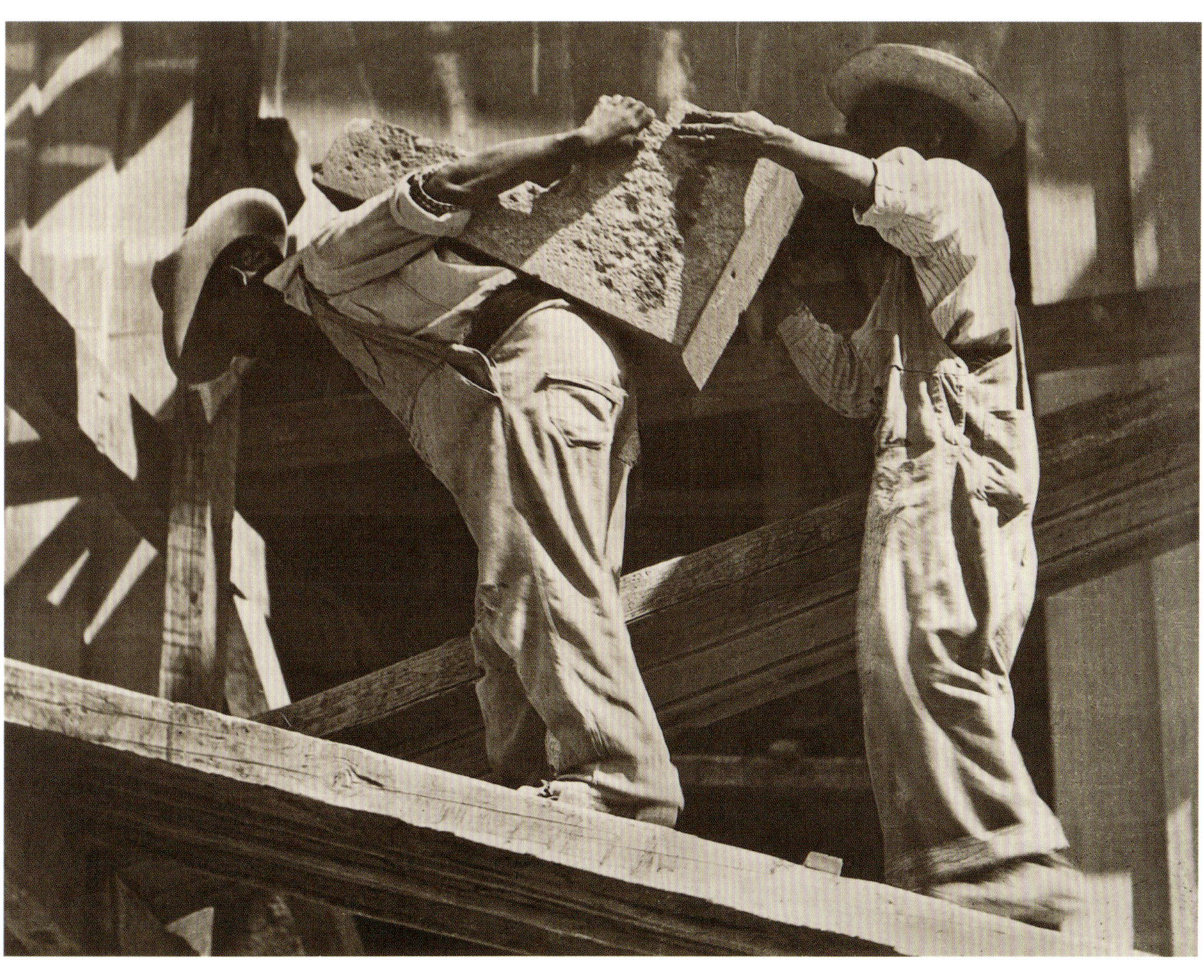

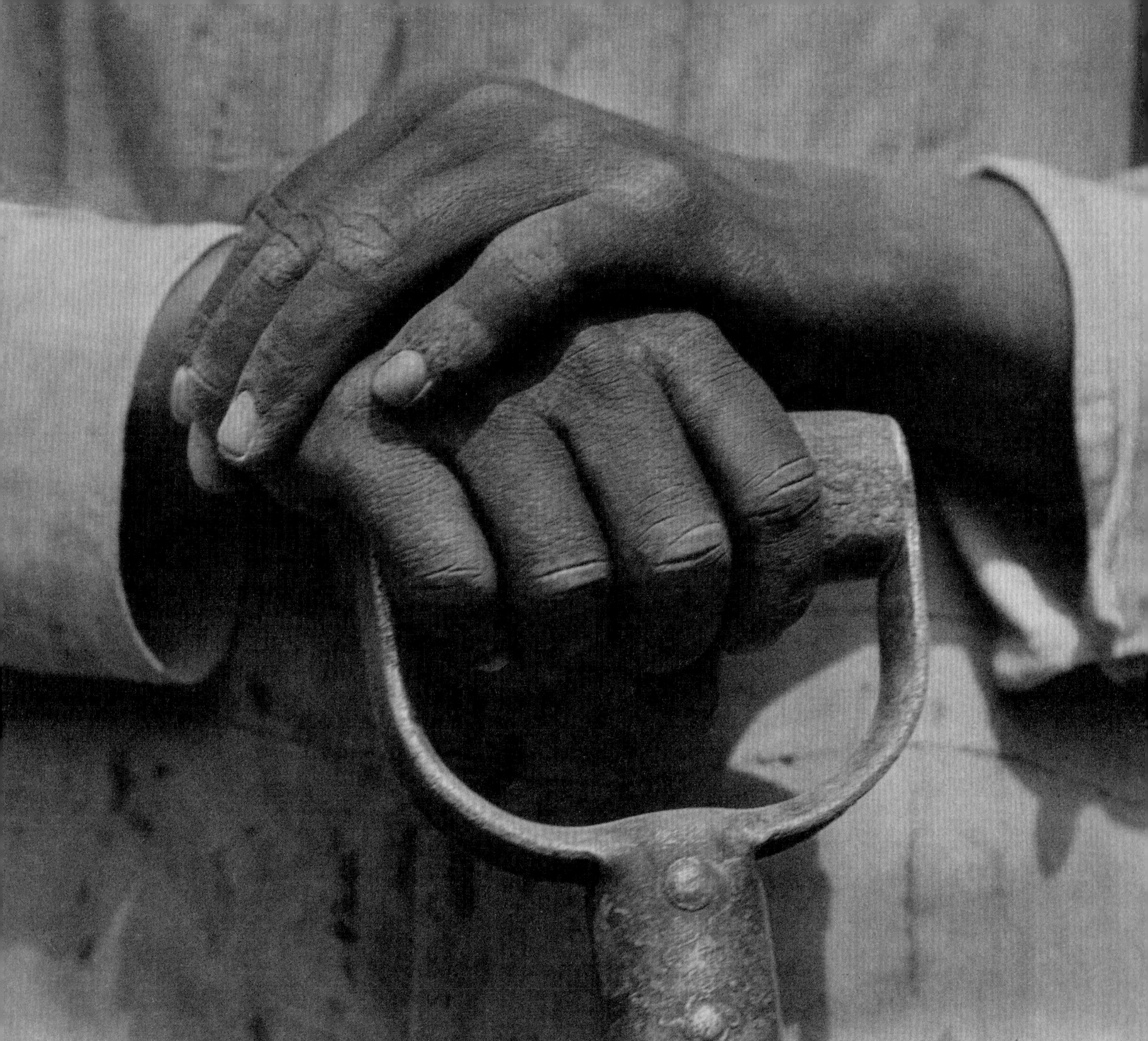

44

Tina Modotti (1896–1942)
Hands Resting on Tool, 1927.
Palladium print, 19.7 x 21.6 cm.
The J. Paul Getty Museum,
Los Angeles

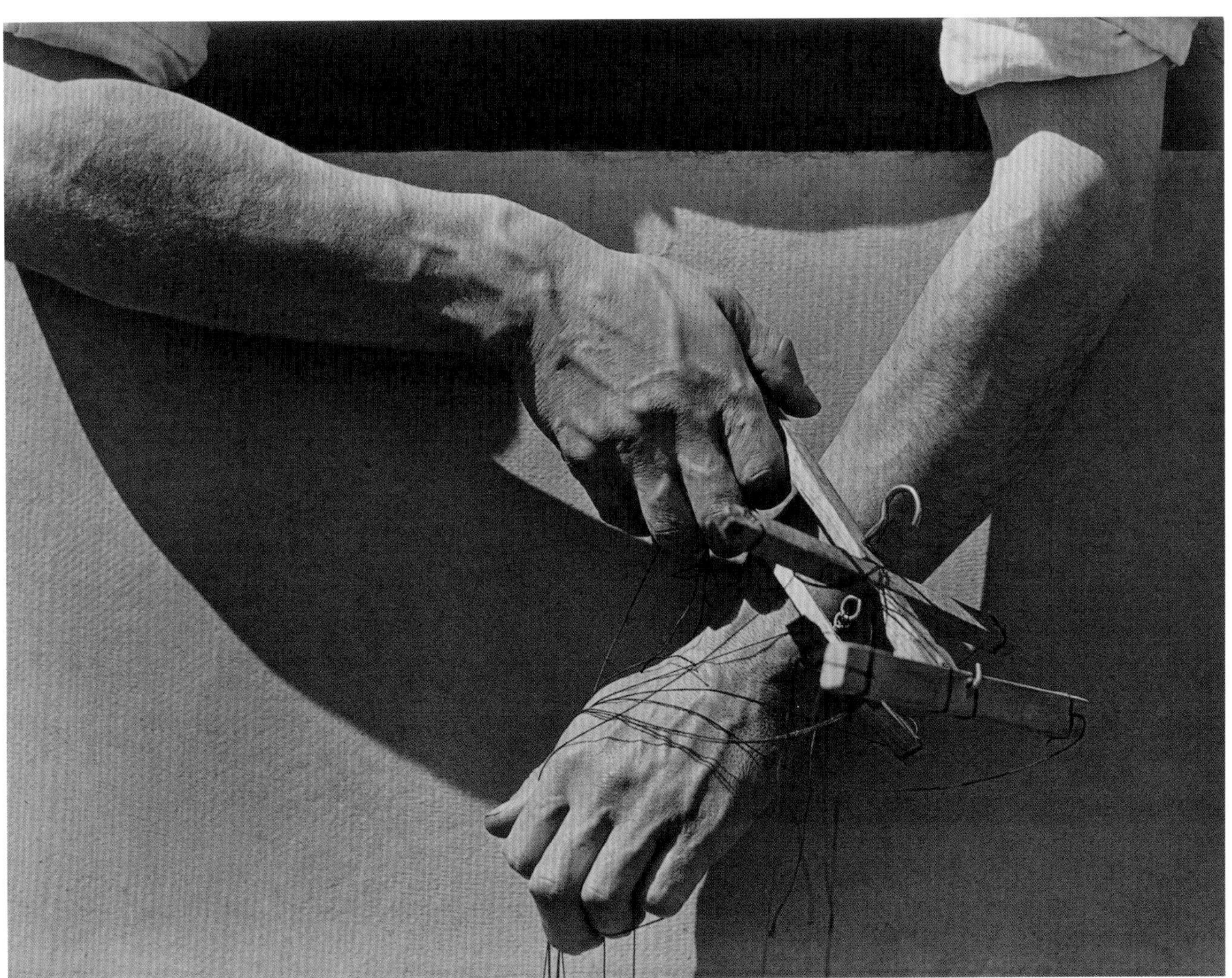

45

Tina Modotti (1896–1942)
Hands of a Puppeteer, 1929.
Vintage gelatin silver print,
50.8 x 40.7 cm. Wilson Centre for
Photography, London

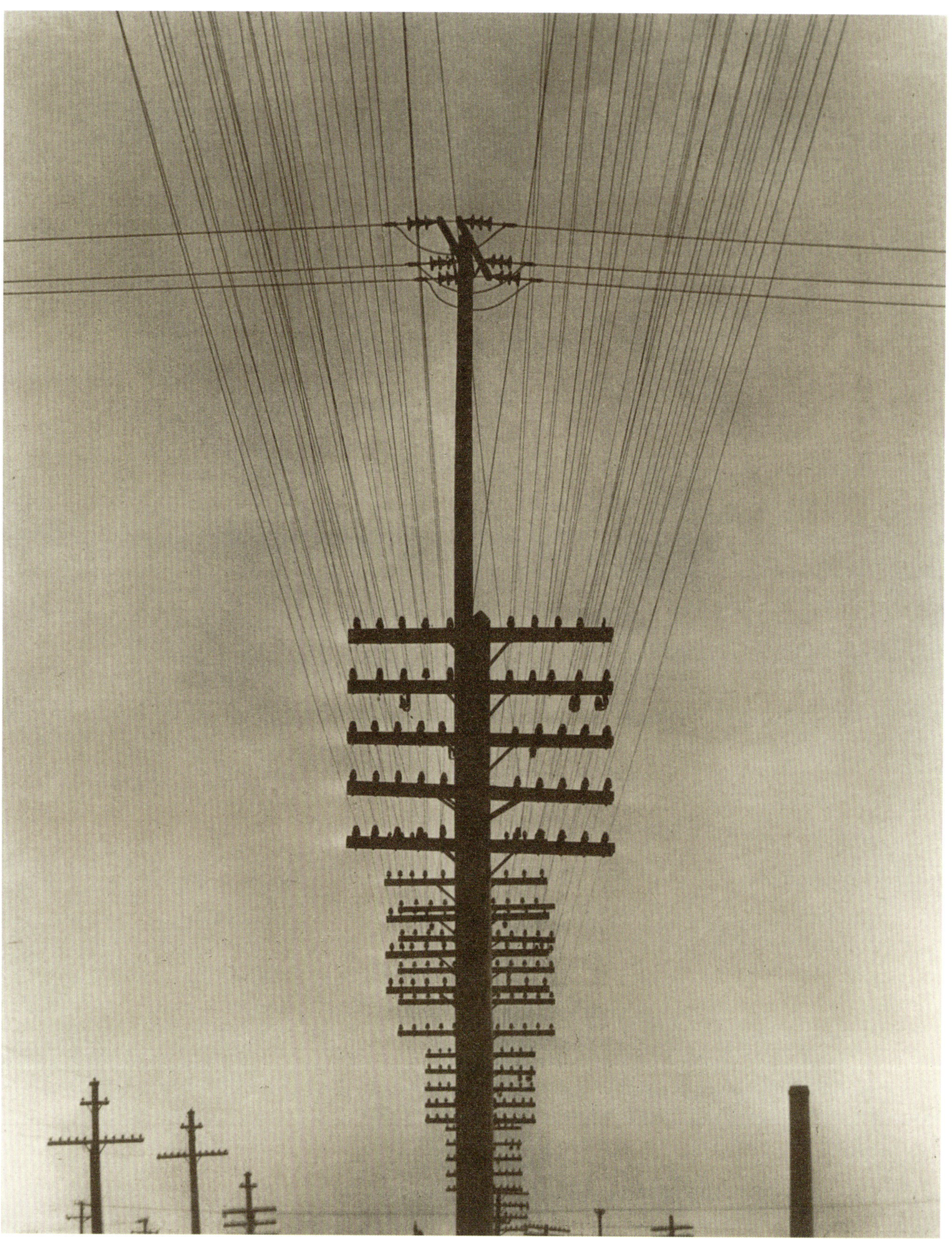

bandoliers, sombreros, guitars and ears of corn (fig. 29) and symbols of modernism (cat. 46). Corn was more than just a staple of the Mexican diet; in the Mayan origin myth transcribed in the *Popol Vuh*, it was the material from which mankind was created.

Much admired by other artists, Francisco Goitia was seen as something of a mystic. One of his paintings (cat. 47) shows an old man seated on a rubbish tip. Apparently a self-portrait, it presents a very different view of modern Mexico to Modotti's, marked by discarded items rather than achievements: the conspicuous detritus of wealth. This was a time of increased waste and consumerism, the ultimate price of development. Here the artist sits astride the rubbish as if seated on a throne, his staff of office grasped firmly in his left hand. Behind him lies a shack, similar perhaps to the one where Goitia lived in Xochimilco, as a vulture glides in. Goitia said of the work: 'The old man sitting on a garbage heap ... was the happiest man I ever saw. He owned not a thing in the world, not even a hat, and he sat there every day and enjoyed the blue sky. You see a kind of irony goes through my work. I think that old man would be well, hanging in the office of an American millionaire.'[50]

Modotti was not destined to spend long in Mexico. Her public profile and outspoken views as a communist at a time when the Communist Party was banned led to her being considered an undesirable (cat. 48). Her new companion, the Cuban communist leader Julio Antonio Mella, was fatally shot as they returned home on the night of 10 January 1929 (fig. 30). Modotti was also spuriously linked to the assassination attempt against Pascual

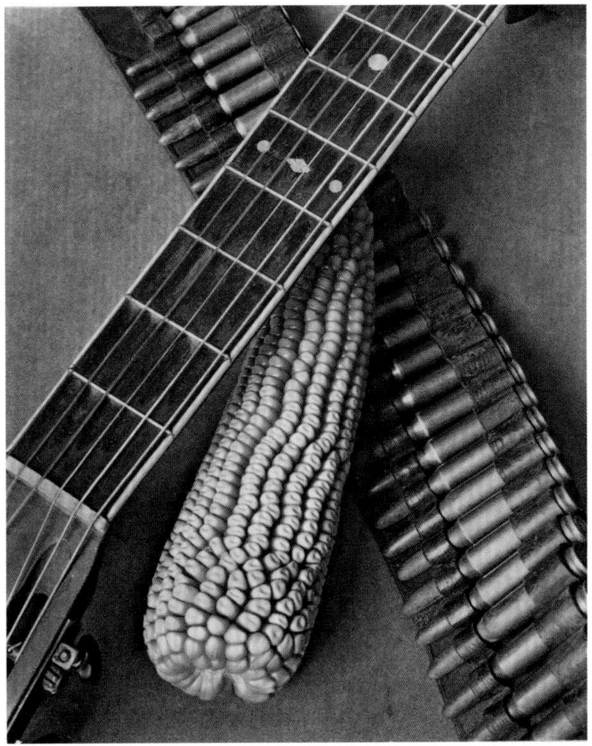

Fig. 29 Tina Modotti, **Illustration for a Mexican Song**, 1927. Gelatin silver print, 23.4 x 18.6 cm. The Museum of Modern Art, New York, 341.1965

Ortíz Rubio in early 1930, soon after he had assumed the presidency. Although supported by Rivera, she was deported in February 1930. In April 1939, after a number of years in Germany and the Soviet Union, she returned to Mexico under the assumed name of Dr Carmen Ruiz Sánchez, one of many seeking asylum there from Spain, where she had been fighting for the Republican cause during the Spanish Civil War. Three years later, in January 1942, she died

46

Tina Modotti (1896–1942)
Telegraph Wires, *c.* 1925–28.
Gelatin silver print on paper,
25.4 x 20.32 cm.
Throckmorton Fine Art, Inc.
New York

of a heart attack in the back of a taxi at the age of 45, having successfully restored her reputation and been pardoned but without having taken another photograph of the country that so fascinated her.[51]

In late 1927 the British artist and art teacher Leon Underwood arrived in Mérida in the Yucatan from the US, where he had been working, at the beginning of what turned out to be a five-month adventure. Underwood was fascinated by the clash of cultures, in this case those of the Europeans and the indigenous Mexicans in the sixteenth century, and the impact such events could have on material culture (cats 49, 51, 52). He was also intrigued by notions of the primitive. Earlier that year he had persuaded the American publisher Lowell Brentano to commission a book, which Underwood would illustrate and his friend Phillips Russell would write, retracing the steps of the artist Frederick Catherwood and the travel writer John Lloyd Stephens, who had gone in search of the Maya civilisation nearly a century earlier.[52] At the start of their journey Russell and Underwood visited Chichen Itza, which was undergoing excavation and restoration.[53]

Underwood was in his element, although Field Director Earl H. Morris 'asked me with great delicacy and regret not to make use of sketches of any of the interior paintings or carvings in the temples ... at the moment we met I was a little annoyed but could not show it'.[54] Morris had

47

Francisco Goitia (1882–1960)
Man Seated on a Trash Heap (Viejo en el muladar), 1926–27.
Oil on canvas, 52.5 x 57 cm.
Museo Nacional de Arte/Instituto Nacional de Bellas Artes y Literatura

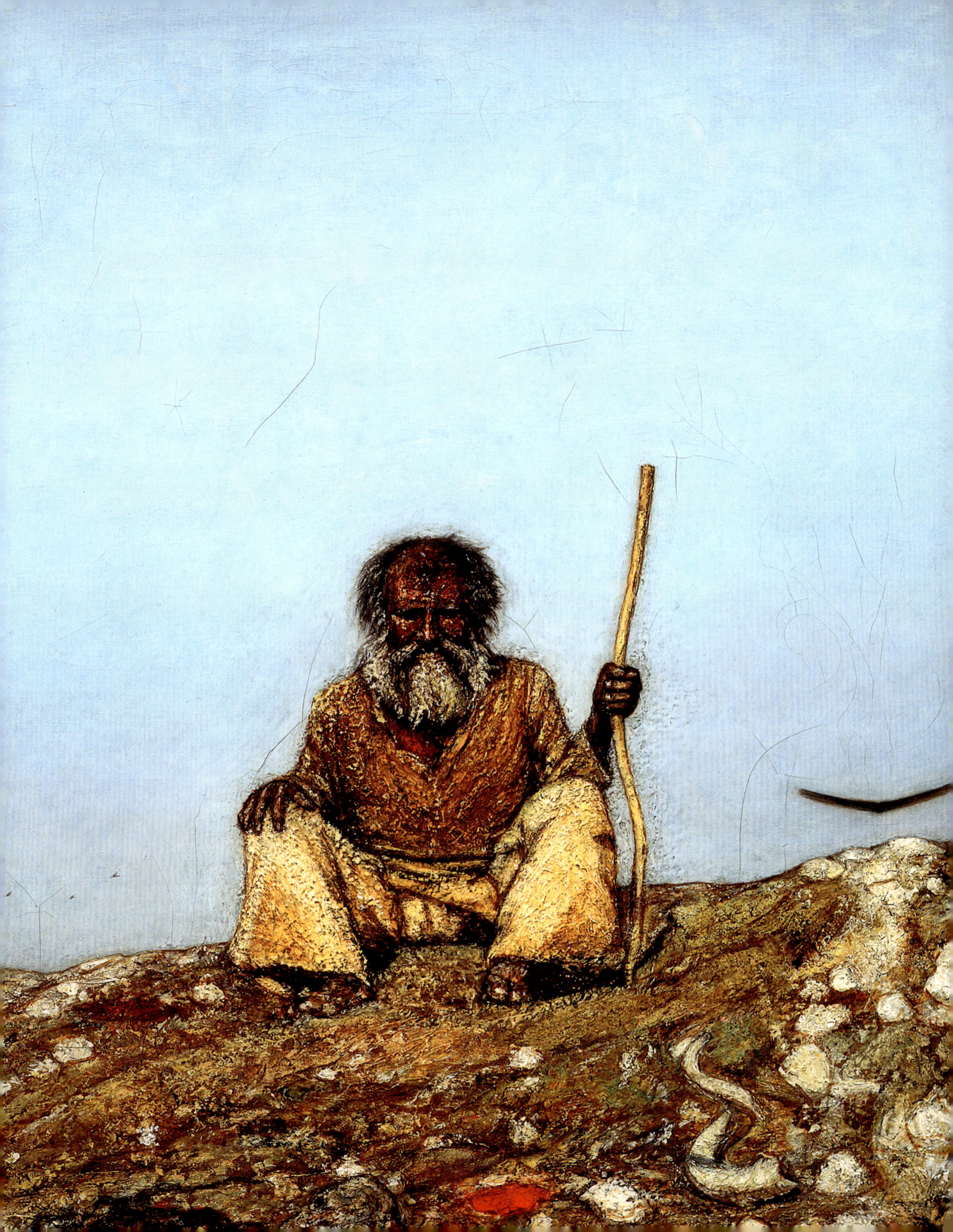

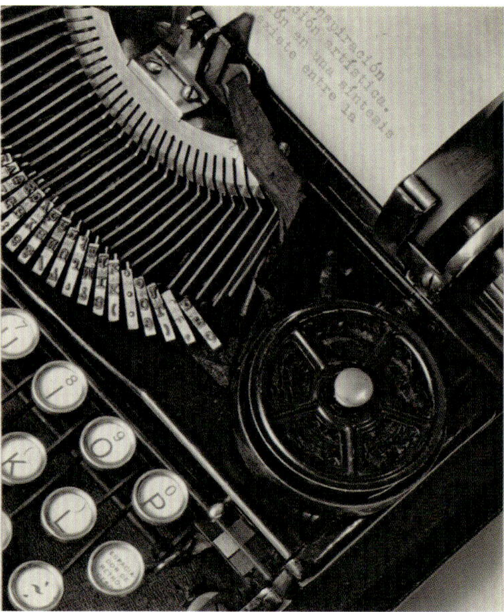

Fig. 30 Tina Modotti, **Mella's Typewriter**, 1928. Gelatin silver print, 24 x 19.2 cm. The Museum of Modern Art, New York, 353.1965

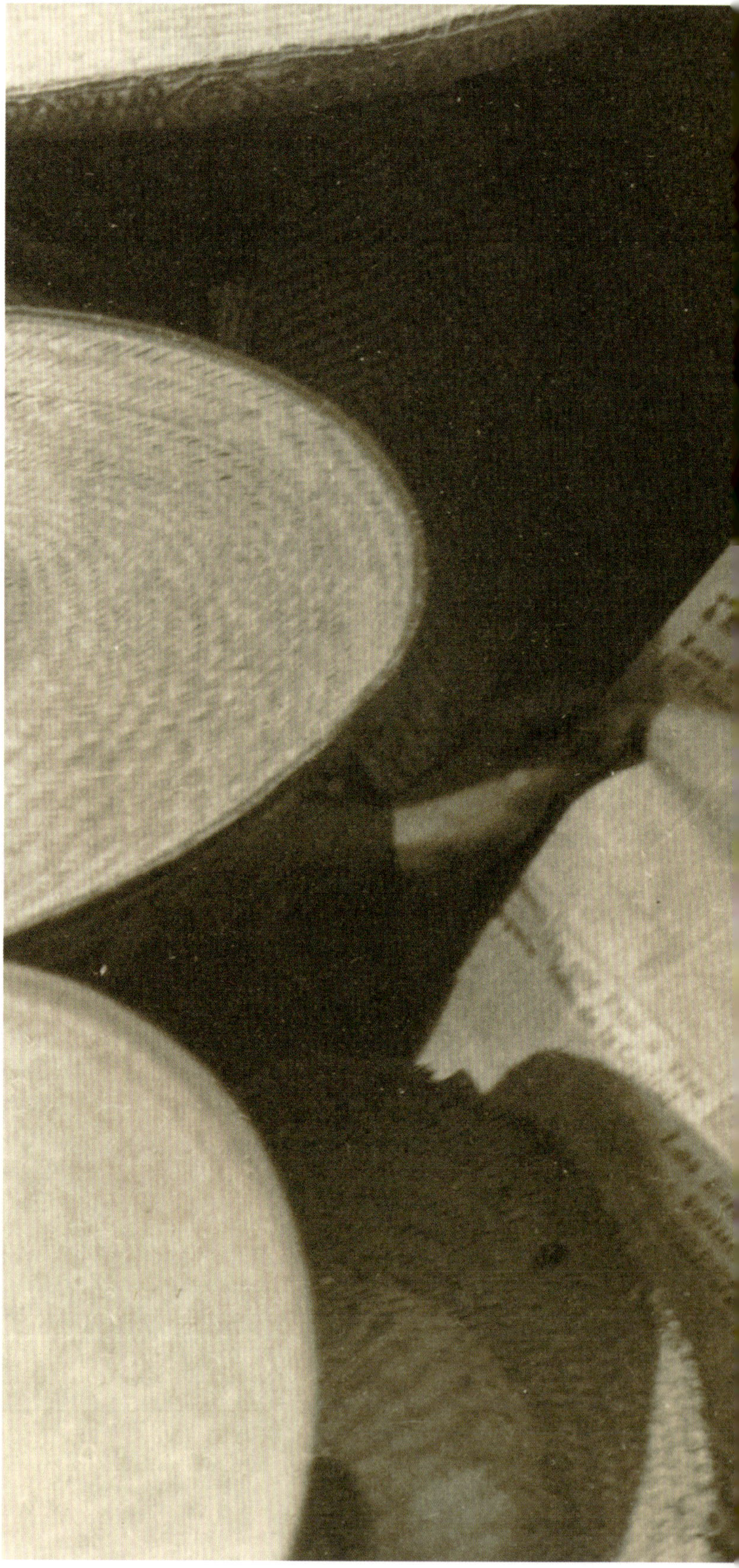

48

Tina Modotti (1896–1942)
Workers Reading
El Machete, c. 1929.
Platinum print, 7.92 x 10.46 cm.
Throckmorton Fine Art, Inc.,
New York

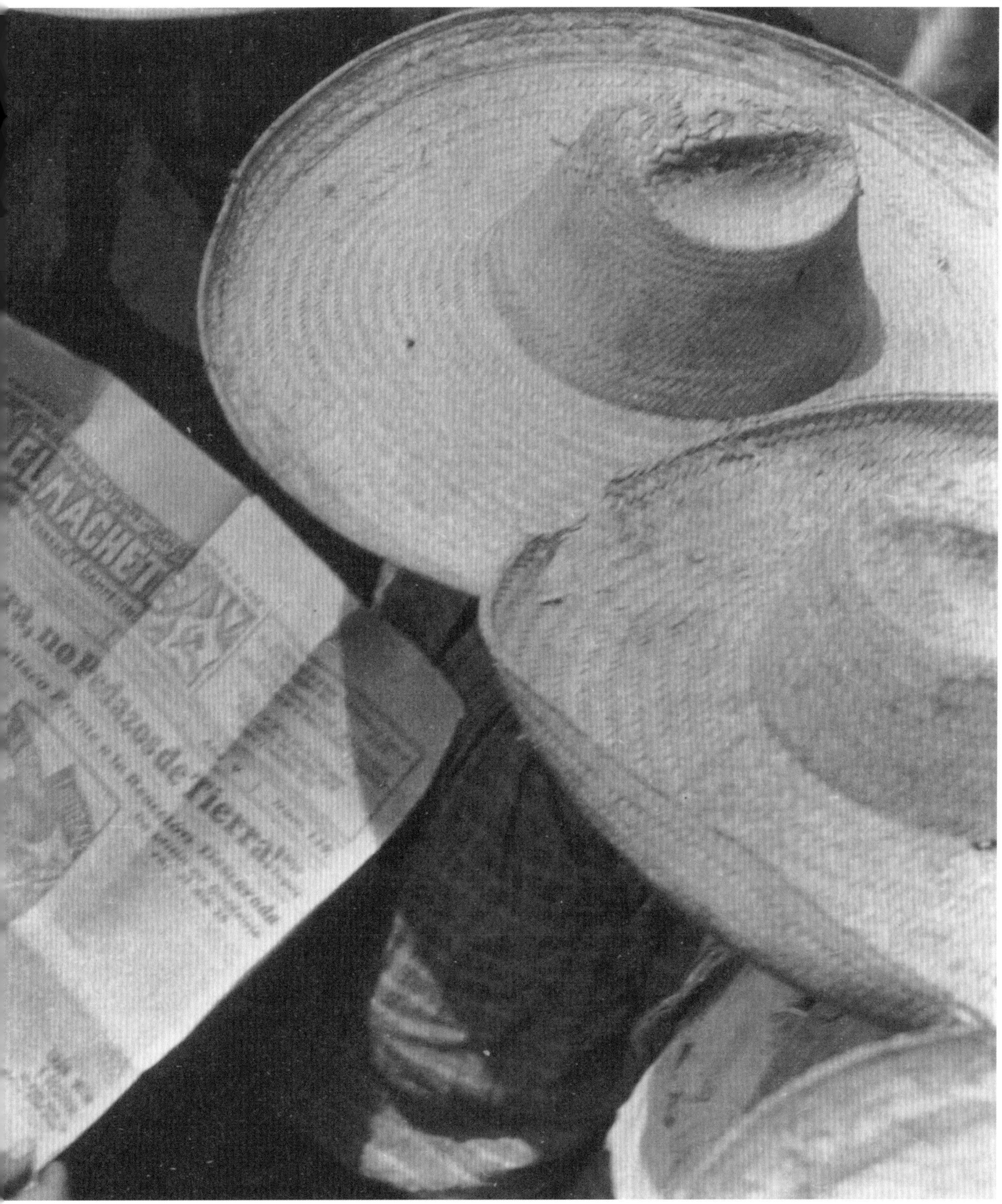
de Tierra

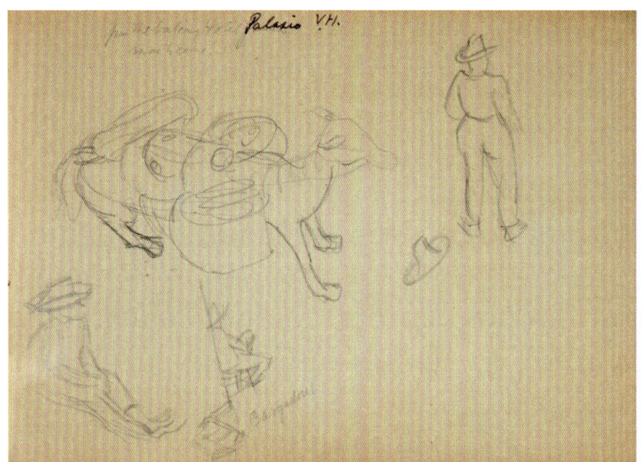

Fig. 31 Leon Underwood, **From the Balcony Hotel Palasio, V. H.**, *c.* 1928. Pencil on paper, 24 x 16.6 cm. Henry Moore Institute Archive, Leeds, 2000.46

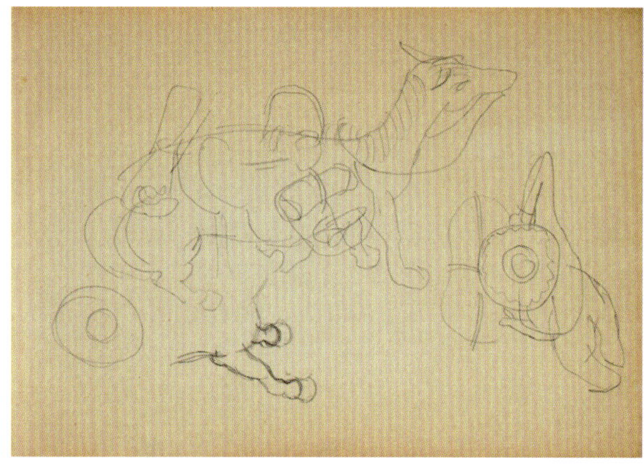

Fig. 32 Leon Underwood, **Untitled** (sketch from the balcony of Hotel Palasio, Villa Hermosa, Tabasco), *c.* 1928. Pencil on paper, 24 x 16.6 cm. Henry Moore Institute Archive, Leeds, 2000.46

already employed Charlot to record the expedition's discoveries, with his wife Ann Axtell Morris. These were exciting times for Mexican archaeology. A smaller temple was discovered in April 1925 inside the Temple of Kukulkan (also known as El Castillo; fig. 35), which was found to contain a fine Chacmool and, in August 1926, the red *balam* (jaguar) throne that gave Russell and Underwood the title of their book: *Red Tiger: Adventures in Yucatan and Mexico* (New York, 1929).[55] A photograph records Underwood making a cast of 'the exquisite figure, called the Red Tiger' in the Mérida Museum (fig. 33).[56] He recalled: 'I went to Charlot's quarters and saw some photographs of the work of modern painters I look forward to in Mexico City',[57] undoubtedly a reference to Charlot's collection of photographs by Modotti of murals in Mexico City.[58]

Underwood, who like Jacob Epstein became a serious collector of African tribal art, was interested in the skills and techniques of local popular artists. His poetic record of a visit to a local potter in Lerma (fig. 34), in the state of Campeche, reflects his fascination with process:

> *The potter sat there holding with his feet a small round chok* [sic] *of wood (4' diam), which he turned upon the chimney end of two boards with his big toe of the right foot and the heel of the left. In weaving a pot he would make a complete revolution of his chok* [sic] *in about 30 to 40 seconds. I say weaving a pot because the process is so different to what I have seen, the pot seems to grow with such life like changing of forms as the opening of a flower, seen on a slow-motion cinema film.*[59]

It was not until Underwood returned to England at the end of 1928 that he began to draw on his experiences in Mexico, producing paintings, watercolours, woodcuts, linocuts and at least two sculptures that were largely based on sketches made there (cat. 49, figs 31, 32). His work was to retain a Mexican theme for the next ten years, during which he illustrated episodes from his time there, taken

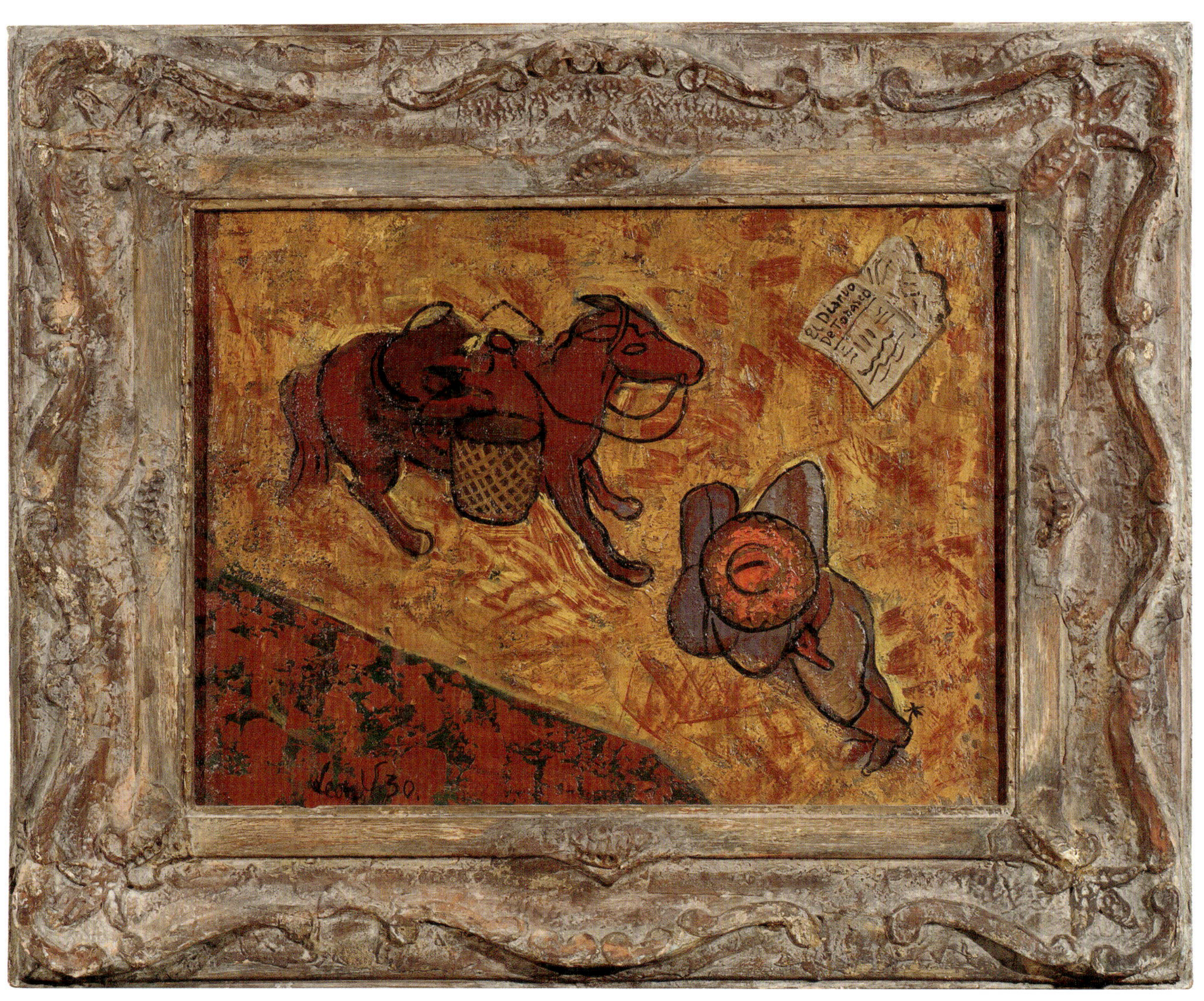

49

Leon Underwood
(1890–1975)
From the Balcony, *c.* 1930.
Oil on canvas, 30.5 x 40.5 cm.
Private collection

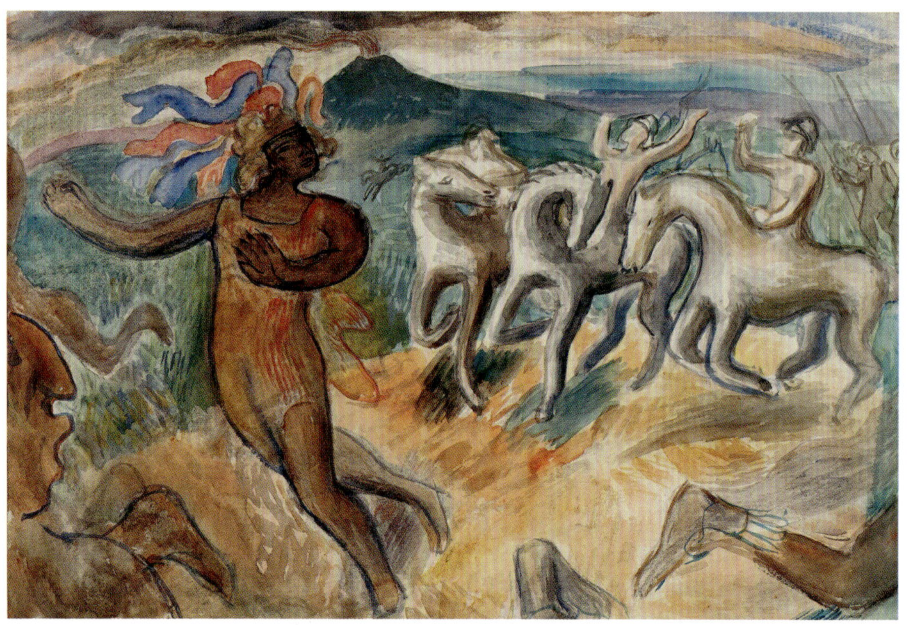

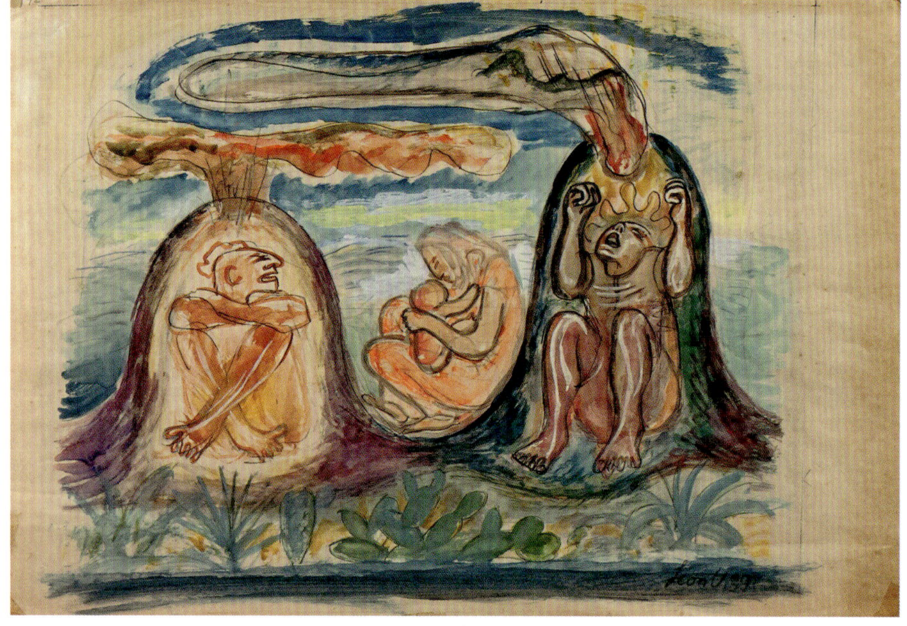

50

Leon Underwood
(1890–1975)
Untitled, *c.* 1930.
Watercolour on paper,
43.3 x 60 cm.
Private collection

51

Leon Underwood
(1890–1975)
Untitled, 1939.
Watercolour on paper,
49.5 x 59.4 cm.
Private collection

52

Leon Underwood
(1890–1975)
Moctezuma's Voices, 1930.
Watercolour on paper,
62.9 x 47.7 cm.
Private collection

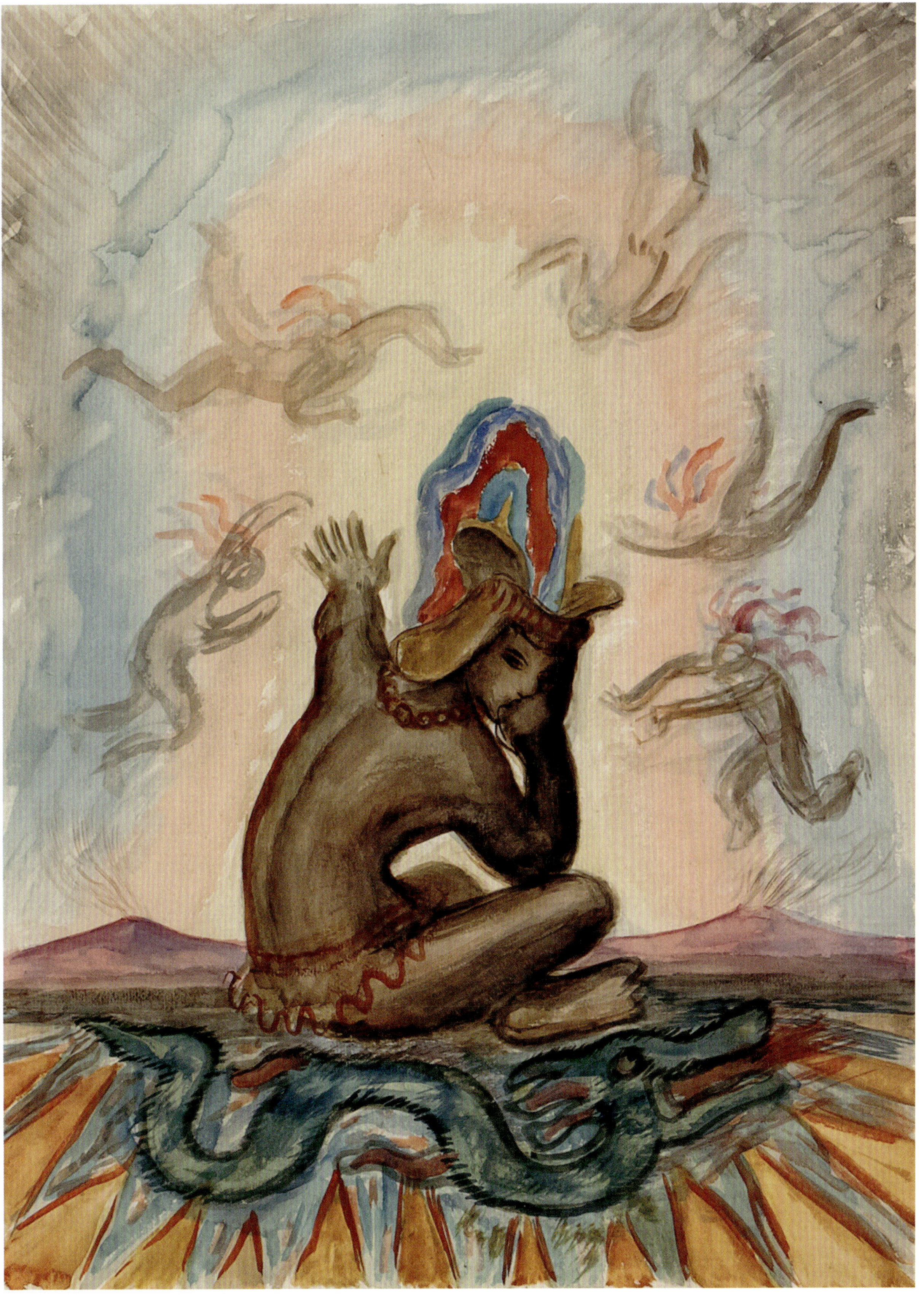

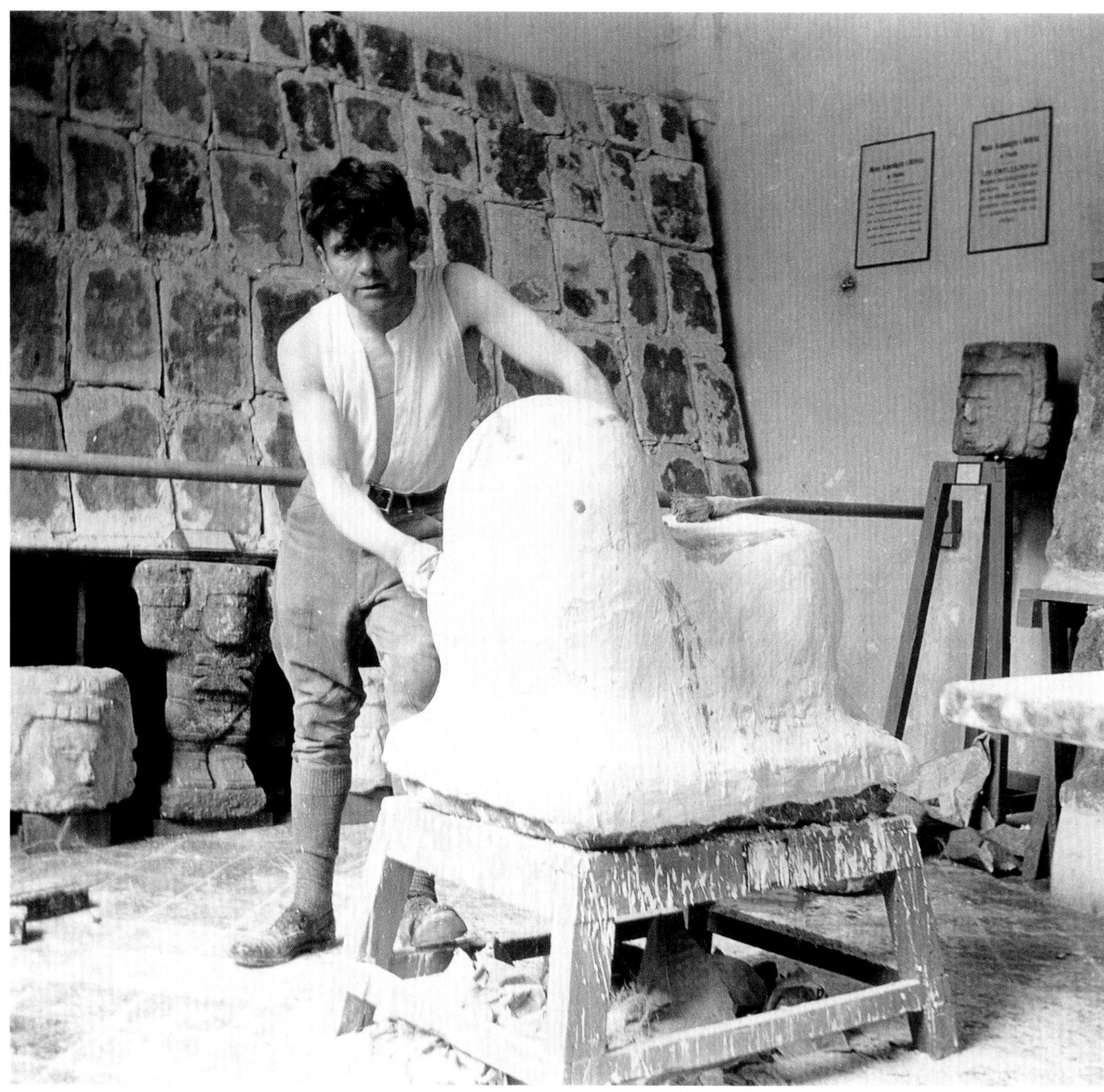

Fig. 33 Unknown photographer, **Leon Underwood casting the Red Tiger, at the Mérida Museum, Mexico**, 1928. Conway Collection, Courtauld Institute of Art, London

from his sketchbooks, almost as an explorer. He captured the exotic, depicting Mexico as a tropical idyll populated with beautiful, lithe women, and also engaged with the impact of the Europeans' arrival on the spiritual equilibrium of the country. He was clearly influenced by colour, which he freely translated into his work, and by the murals of Orozco. Many examples are narrative images of the everyday, but he also explored more complex cultural issues. In a series of bold watercolours he gave free rein to his interest in the religion of the pre-Columbian civilisations and the violent cultural clash that took place between the Mexica and Spanish in the sixteenth century. Volcanoes spew furious plumes of smoke into the atmosphere as Underwood depicts the irreparable damage done by the Spanish invasion to the harmonious balance that had hitherto existed between the physical and spiritual worlds inhabited by the Mexica (cats 49, 51, 52).

Chaac-Mool's Destiny (cat. 53), one of Underwood's most ambitious paintings of this period, dates from the year in which Henry Moore, a former student of Underwood's at the Royal College of Art, created one of his best-known early sculptures (fig. 36).[60] Both artists were drawn to the form of the Chacmool, the ceremonial sacrificial altar of the Toltec, which is also associated with the Maya and the Mexica. Having seen the recently excavated Chacmool at Chichen Itza, Underwood had a considerable advantage over Moore, who had only seen reproductions in books and possibly the small receptacle at the British Museum.[61] In *Chaac-Mool's Destiny*, Underwood reveals

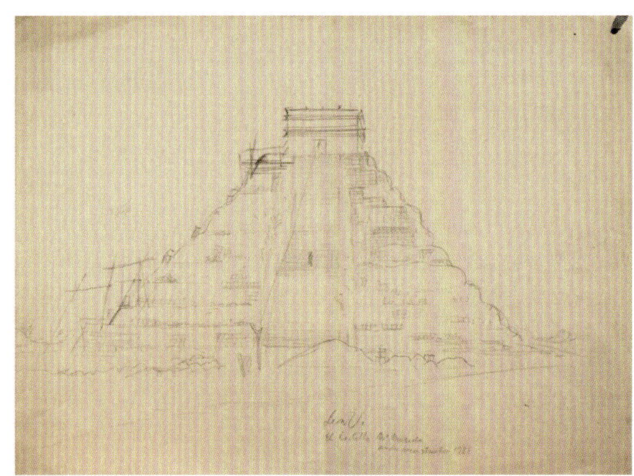

Fig. 35 Leon Underwood, **El Castillo nr Merida under Reconstruction**, 1928. Pencil on paper, 37.7 x 50.5 cm. Private collection

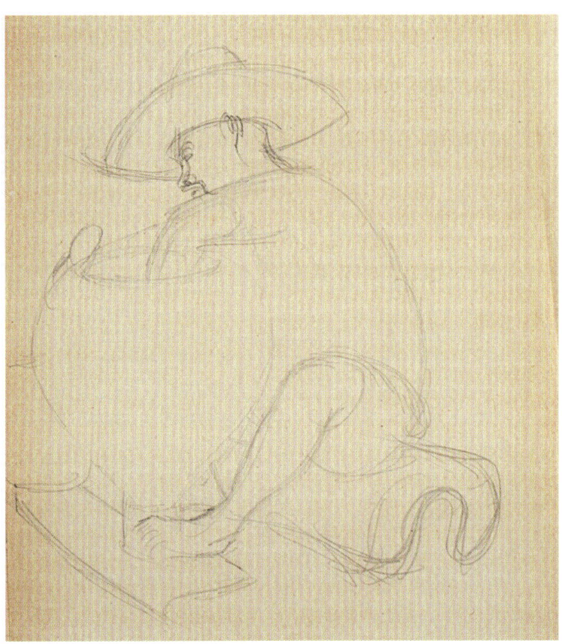

Fig. 34 Leon Underwood, **Untitled** (drawing of a potter, Lerma, Campeche), *c.* 1928. Pencil on paper, 22 x 16.5 cm. Henry Moore Institute Archive, Leeds, 2000.46

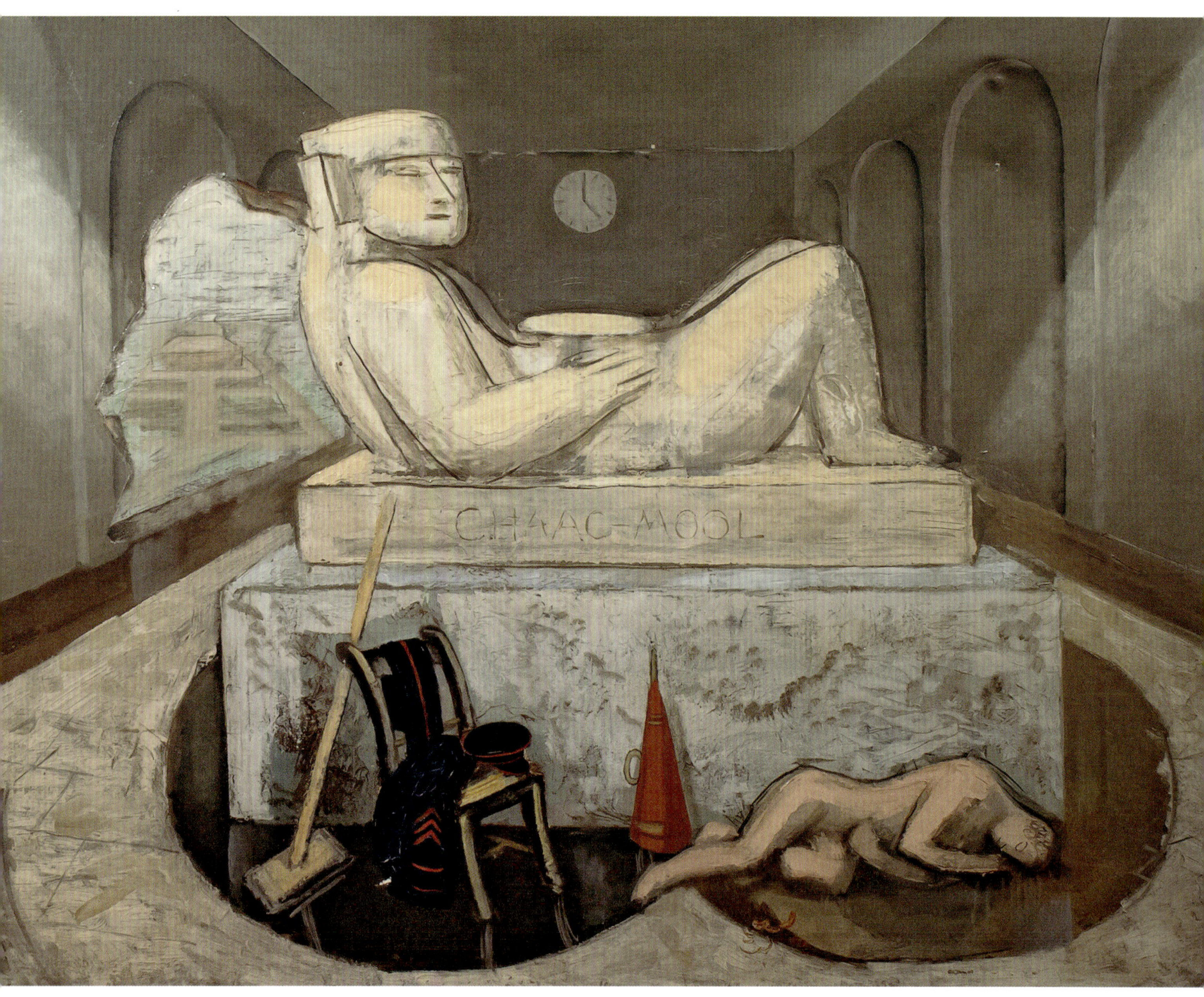

53

Leon Underwood (1890–1975)
Chaac-Mool's Destiny, 1929.
Oil on canvas, 77.44 x 102.87 cm.
Private collection

his preoccupation with the idea 'that subject-matter and expression were linked to belief and technology'.[62] The painting, which has been described as influenced by de Chirico, shows Underwood flirting with Surrealism. He pays homage to the original purpose of the Chacmool, whose spiritual power remains potent despite the sculpture's relocation and cannot be contained by the museum's walls.

The Canadian-born Henrietta Shore, a founder member of the New York Society of Women Artists, is a good example of the way in which word of mouth encouraged artists to visit Mexico. Shore returned to Los Angeles from New York in 1923 with a considerable reputation as a contemporary artist. She met Edward Weston in early 1927 and the two soon became close friends; Weston admired the deep emotional attachment to be found in her paintings. Inspired by her friend's evocative descriptions, Shore travelled to Mexico later that year with the painter Helena Dunlop, returning to the US in early 1928. She was well received by the art community in Mexico, no doubt armed with introductions to many of Weston's friends, Modotti among others. Although she described Modotti's work as 'structureless' in comparison to Weston's, Shore's opinion was perhaps subjective, given her fondness for him.[63] Shore also met, and painted, Charlot, whom she described as 'an artist in his judgement and in his feeling'.[64] The whereabouts of her portrait of Orozco, another artist she greatly admired, are presently unknown. In a letter to Weston, Shore wrote of Rivera: 'I prefer his earlier work – the earliest. It is most unfortunate that I am unable to fully appreciate his work. I grant its excellence – but I am bored by it. Orozco and Charlot both interest me more.'[65] In an earlier letter she had written to Weston: 'I like Mexico and I know why you love it.'[66] Although she did not paint much while there, her *Women of Oaxaca* (cat. 54) and *Mexican Bathers* (fig. 37) of 1927–28 reveal her affinity with and deep appreciation for Mexican Modernism. The surroundings are reduced to the minimum, focusing the viewer's eye on her subject: women going about their daily tasks. Shore presents them as noble and timeless, a reflection of the society in which they live. The modest size of both works belies their impact.

The extent of cultural exchange between Mexico and the US continued to grow throughout the 1920s. Dwight Morrow, American ambassador from 1927 to 1930 and a passionate lover of things Mexican, maintained a house in Cuernavaca. In 1928 he commissioned Rivera to paint a series of frescoes, depicting the history of Cuernavaca, in the Palacio de Cortés, now the Museo

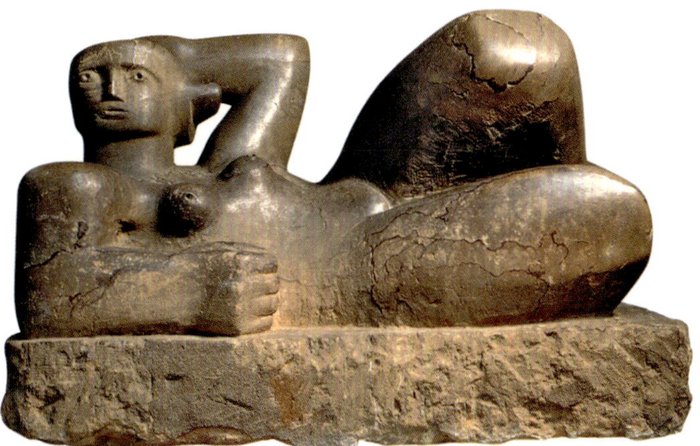

Fig. 36 Henry Moore, **Reclining Figure**, 1929. Hornton stone, length 83.8 cm. Leeds Art Gallery, LH59

de Cuauhuahuac (fig. 38). The year before he had persuaded Charles Lindbergh, fresh from his transatlantic crossing from New York to Paris, to fly the *Spirit of St Louis* from America to Mexico as a gesture of goodwill between the two nations. The flight caused huge excitement in Mexico and a reciprocal flight from Mexico City to New York was arranged the following year. Tragically, the pilot, the Mexican flying ace Emilio Carranza Rodríguez, died after his plane was struck by lightning and crashed in New Jersey while he was returning to Mexico on 12 July 1928. An unexpected consequence of Lindbergh's flight to Mexico was his marriage to Morrow's daughter Anne, which took place in May 1929. When the couple returned to Mexico, they were continually mobbed by reporters, finding solace only when they took to the skies.[67] They flew over the Yucatan and Quintana Roo, looking for and photographing Mayan ruins with Alfred V. Kidder. Anne wrote: 'The thick jungle trails over mounds and masonry like a blanket of snow' (fig. 39).[68]

The American archaeologist and anthropologist Zelia Nuttall, who made Mexico

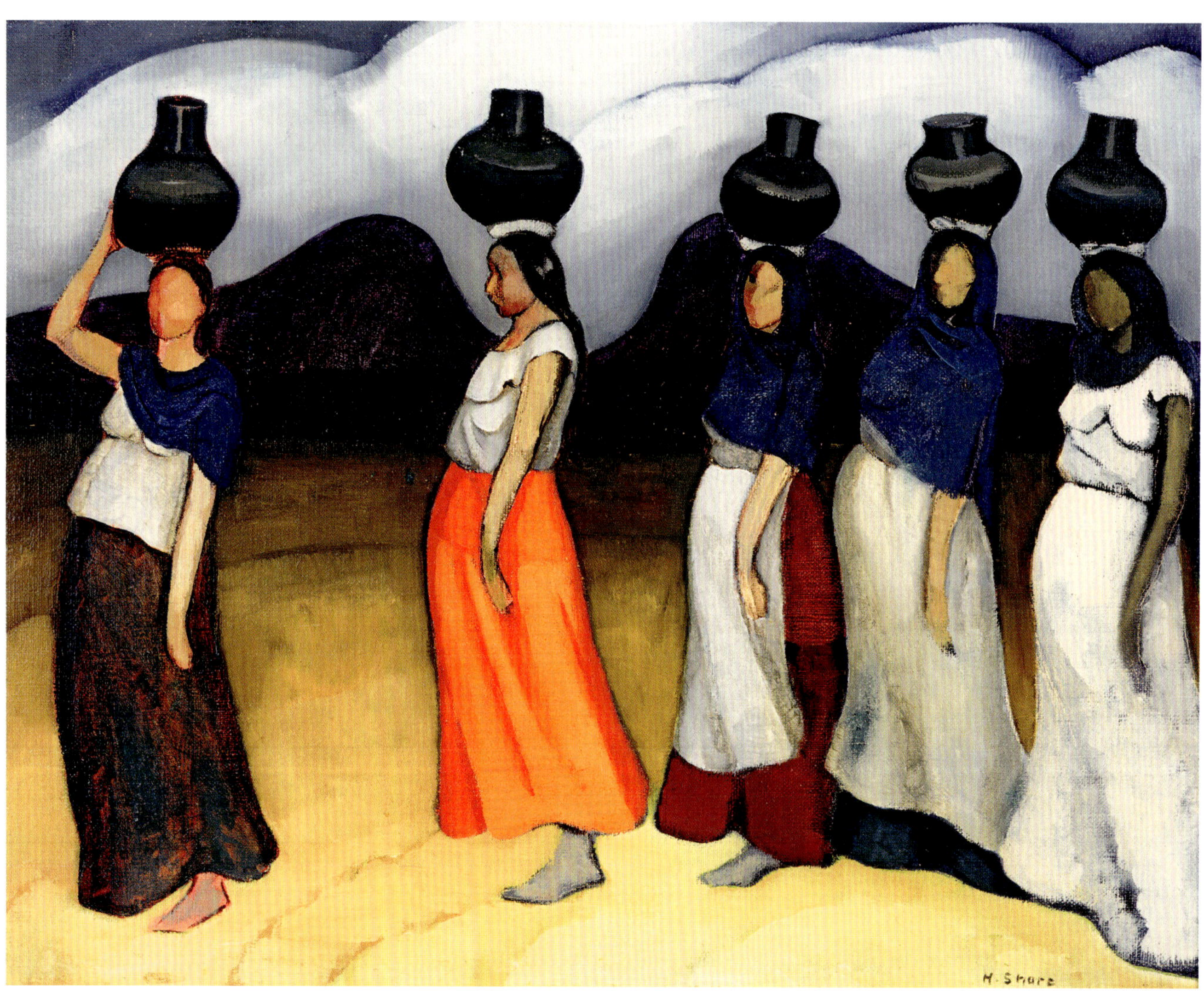

her home in 1902, epitomises the attraction that Mexico had for foreign visitors.[69] An associate of the Peabody Museum at Harvard University, Nuttall lived in Coyoacan on the outskirts of Mexico City in a sixteenth-century house that had once belonged to Pedro de Alvorado, lieutenant of Hernán Cortés. Intensely gregarious, she delighted in bringing together people from different walks of life. Lawrence lunched with her and adapted the episode for *The Plumed Serpent*. The British watercolourist Adèle Breton (fig. 40), a frequent visitor to Mexico, stayed with her. Anne Morrow Lindbergh described to her husband an invitation she had received from Nuttall to spend the day at Xochimilco for the celebration of Santa Anita, also known as the Festival of Flowers (fig. 41).[70]

When the Russian Futurist poet Vladimir Mayakovsky disembarked at Vera Cruz in late 1924 on his way to the US, he was disappointed to find that none of the glamour he had expected, and which he had built up in his mind from reading the novels of James Fenimore Cooper and Mayne Reid, was evident. The exotic was reduced to the ordinary: 'And here I stand, dumbstruck, as though before my very eyes peacocks were being turned into chickens.'[71] In Mexico City he was met by Rivera. Coming from Soviet Russia, Mayakovsky was very taken with the Mexican landscape but unimpressed by what he could see of Mexican politics: 'A Mexican revolutionary is anyone who, weapon in hand, may overthrow the reigning authority – indifferent to whatever it may be. And since, in Mexico, everyone has either overthrown or is overthrowing, or wants to overthrow the current regime – they are all revolutionaries' (fig. 42).[72]

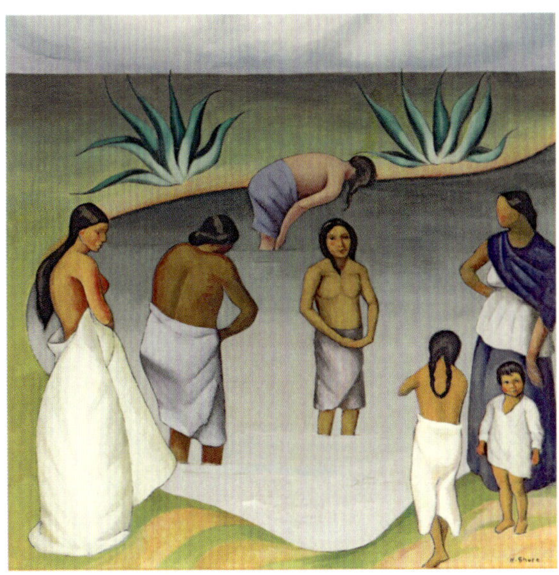

Fig. 37 Henrietta Shore, **Mexican Bathers**, 1927–28. Oil on canvas, 66 x 66 cm. Andrée Dell Collection, Toronto

In 1924 Obregón left office, having been replaced by Plutarco Elías Calles, whose tough, uncompromising approach made him a ruthless president. Although he only held the presidency until 1928, Calles ruled from behind the scenes and effectively held power until 1934. As well as professionalising the army, he implemented a number of hitherto unenforced anticlerical articles from the constitution, which led to a strike. For three

54

Henrietta Shore (1880–1963)
Women of Oaxaca, *c.* 1927.
Oil on canvas, 40.6 x 50.8 cm.
The Buck Collection,
Laguna Beach, CA

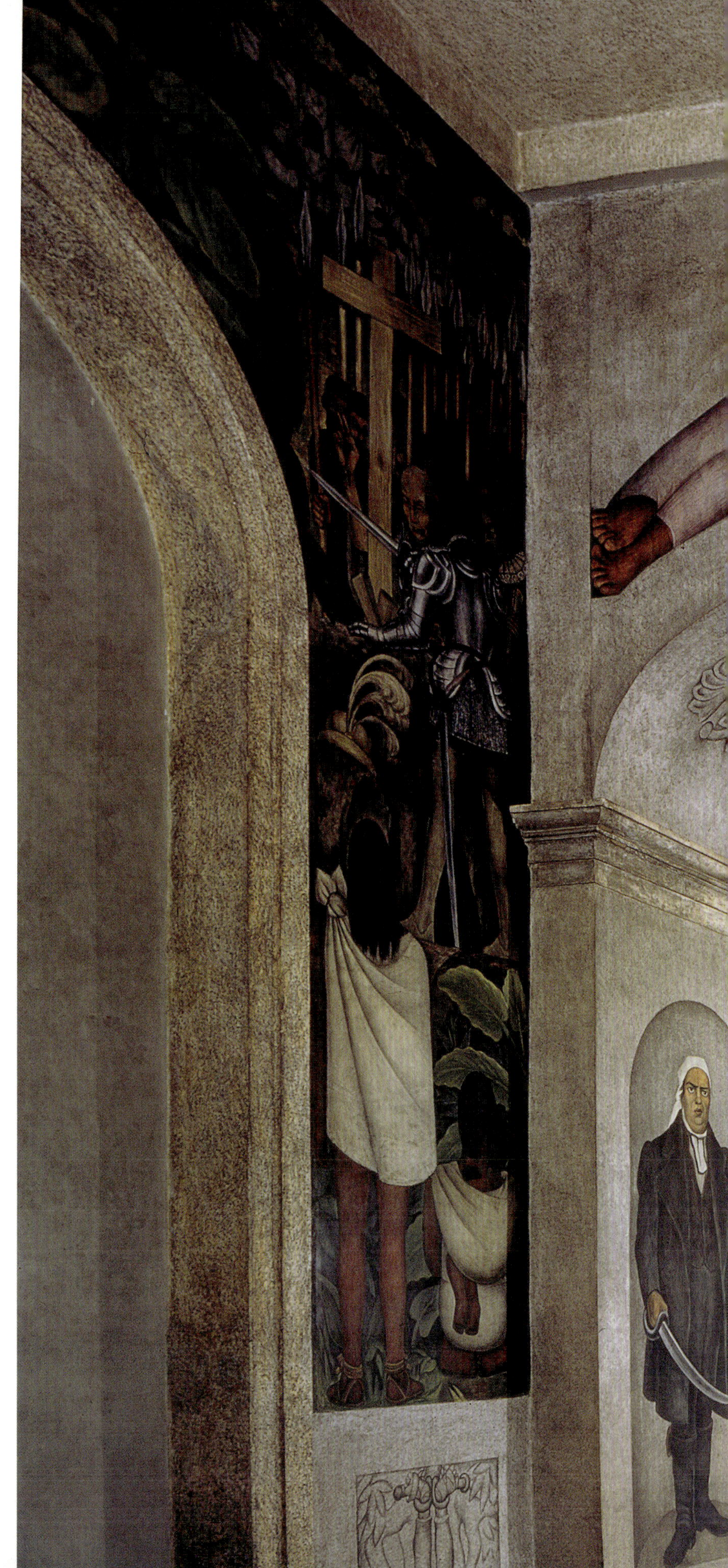

Fig. 38 Diego Rivera, **History of the State of Morelos. Conquest and Revolution**, 1930–31. Mural, 148.6 sq. m. Museo de Cuauhuahuac, Instituto Nacional de Antropología e Historia (INAH), Cuernavaca, Morelos

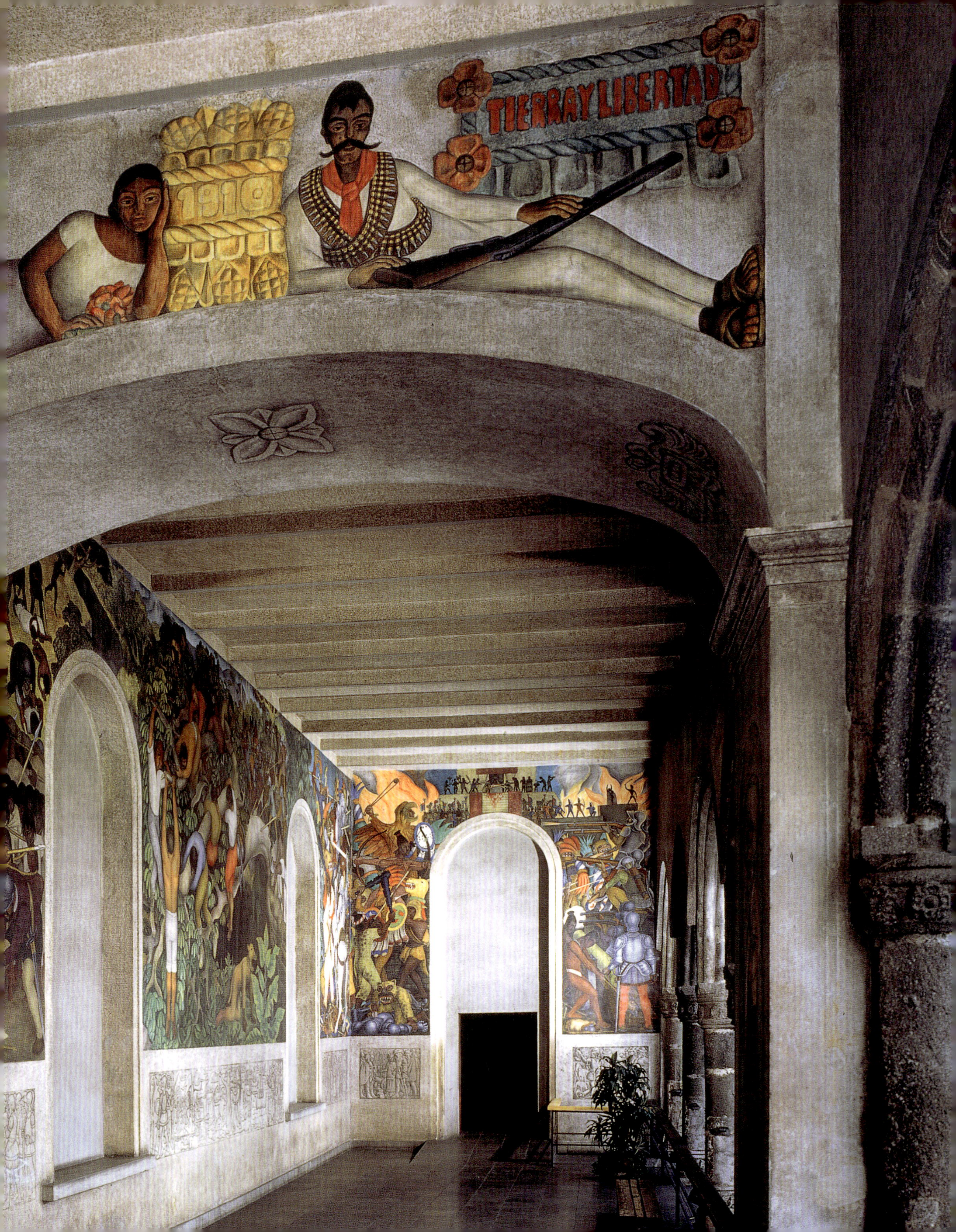
TIERRA Y LIBERTAD
1910

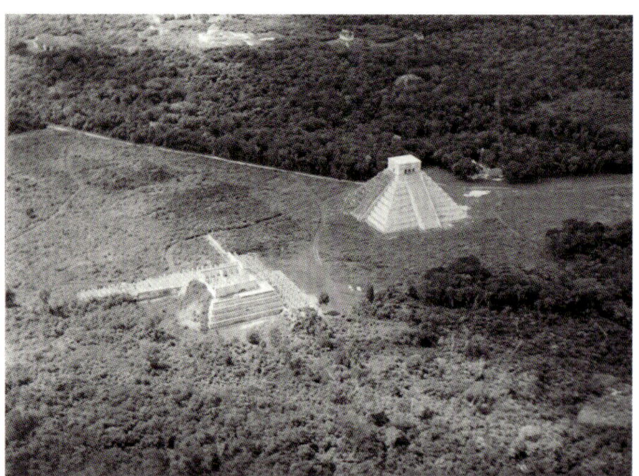

Fig. 39 Alfred V. Kidder, **Aerial View of the Temple of the Warriors and El Castillo, Chichen Itza**, 1942. Photograph, 10.2 x 12.7 cm. Peabody Museum of Archaeology and Ethnology, Harvard University, Cambridge, 58-34-20/72823

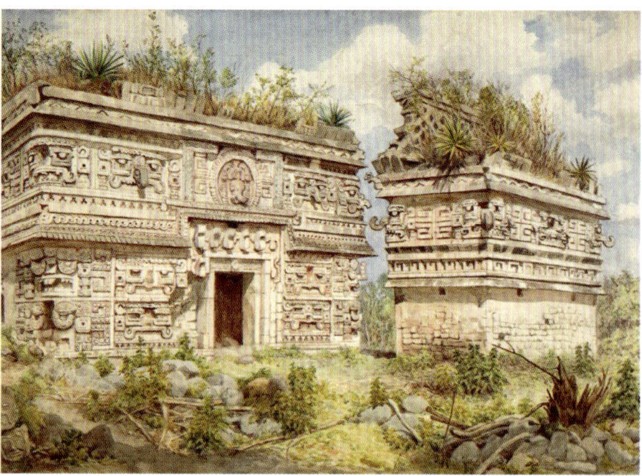

Fig. 40 Adèle Breton, **The Annexe of the Nunnery (Chichen Itza)**, March 1900. Watercolour, 59 x 42 cm. Bristol Museum and Art Gallery, Ea8492

years Catholic priests refused to hold masses and baptisms, or to administer the last rites and other religious ceremonies. To the battle cry of 'Viva Cristo Rey', an armed uprising known as the Cristero Rebellion broke out, as religious extremists took up arms in protest against these government-imposed measures. The government was showing signs of becoming increasingly reactionary. In 1929, for instance, the Nicaraguan revolutionary leader Augusto Sandino and his entourage sought political sanctuary in Mexico. Fearful of the US, which was hostile to Sandino, the government ordered his confinement under strict conditions in Mérida in the Yucatan. Unable to travel to Mexico City, Sandino had had enough by April 1930 and returned to Nicaragua.

Vasconcelos had accomplished much as Minister of Public Education. His stewardship had brought about significant expansion in the number of rural schools and allowed art to take centre stage in Mexico. His vision had achieved sufficient momentum to ensure that it would survive his leaving office. The resources and exposure given to art in the wake of the Revolution laid firm foundations for the future. Vasconcelos's mural scheme, which became known as the 'Mexican Renaissance', continued and remains a potent reminder of his visionary ideas. Indeed, so successful was the programme that Mexico began to export murals, especially to the US, where the work of such artists as Orozco and Rivera was in great demand and public art, an arm of the New Deal programme, was embraced enthusiastically.

However, painting in Mexico was not restricted to great public art projects. Not everyone had heeded Siqueiros's call in 'A Declaration of Social, Political and Aesthetic Principles', written for the Union of Technical Workers, Painters and Sculptors, to 'repudiate so-called easel painting' in favour of 'monumental art in all its forms, because it is public property'.[73] New, young artists began to emerge, among them Rufino Tamayo, Frida Kahlo and Maria Izquierdo, who embraced the modern

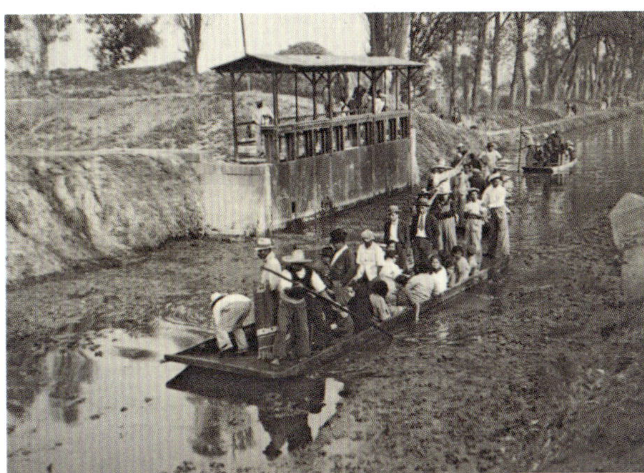

Fig. 41 Esther Born, **Fiesta, Día de las Flores, Mexico City (Canal to Xochimilco)**, c. 1936. Gelatin silver print, 15.2 x 20.3 cm. Center for Creative Photography, University of Arizona, Tucson, 2008.68.4

pictorial language but adapted it to reflect their own specific identity as Mexican artists. To them, art was a form of personal expression rather than a vehicle for political motivations; the art scene in Mexico was beginning to mature and diversify. The introduction of modern photography by Weston and Modotti likewise had a profound impact, giving rise to a new generation of progressive photographers, such as Manuel Álvarez Bravo, Emilio Amero and Agustín Jiménez, who grasped new technology and approaches to photography and celebrated the elements of Mexico that made it different from other lands. They took their places at the forefront of the debate started by Modotti about whether photography should be considered an art form. In a short article she wrote for *Mexican Folkways*, Modotti argued that photography was the most eloquent, most direct means for recording modern times. She concluded by stating, 'To know whether photography is or is not an art matters little. What is important is to distinguish between good and bad photography.'[74]

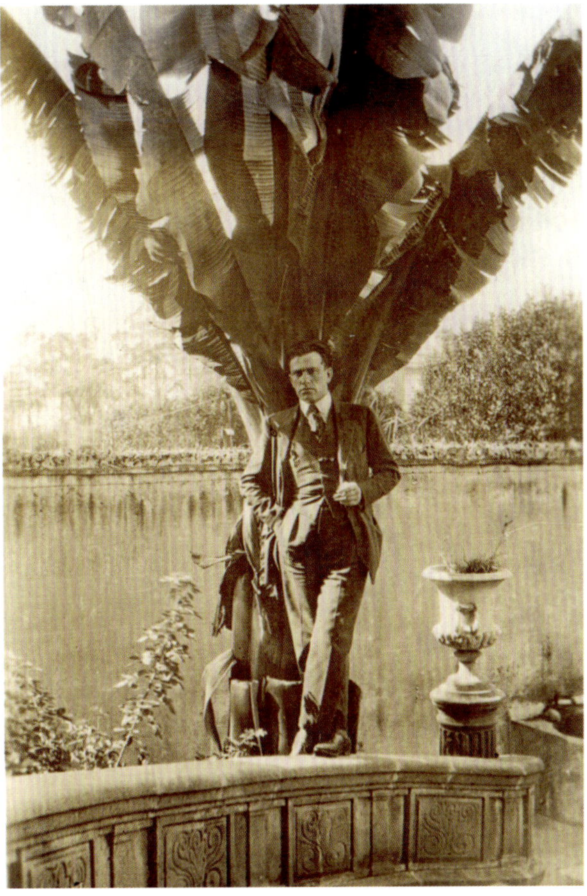

Fig. 42 Unknown photographer, **Vladimir Mayakovsky in Mexico, 1925**. Photograph. Society for Co-operation in Russian and Soviet Studies Photo Library, London, SCRSS002123

Mexico continued to attract foreign artists eager to experience at first hand the country and the changes it was undergoing. The armed struggle of the Mexican Revolution may have been over, but ranks of new revolutionaries had taken its place: a vanguard of artists and writers equipped with new technology with which to do battle and to promulgate the ambitions of a nation.[75]

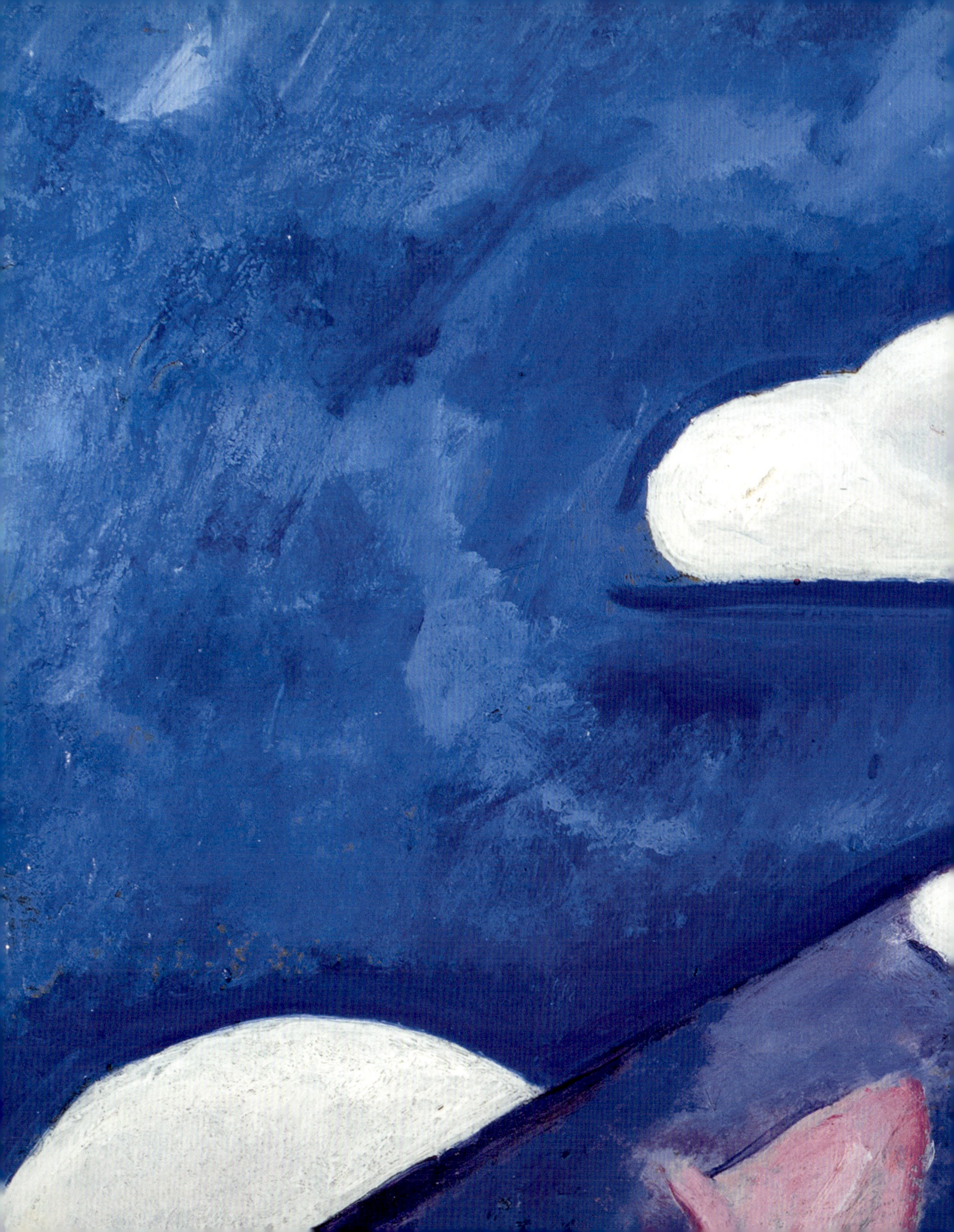

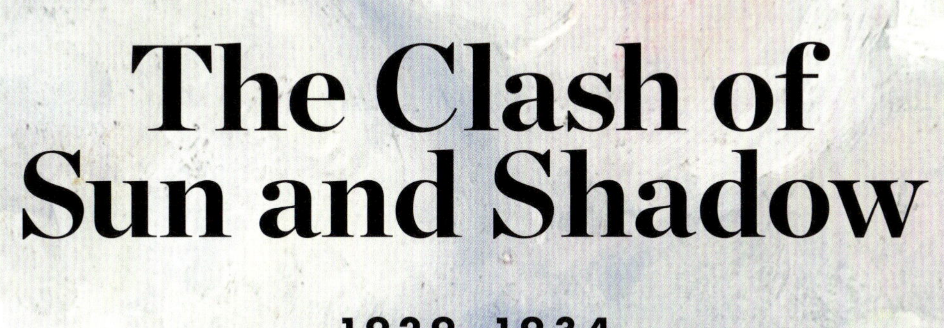

The Clash of Sun and Shadow

1929–1934

The most amazing light
eye has ever encountered.[1]

MARSDEN HARTLEY

[Mexico] is not a curiosity to be visited
but a life to be lived.[2]

HENRI CARTIER-BRESSON

BY 1929 THE MEXICAN MURAL MOVEMENT was dominated by Rivera. Vasconcelos's absence was keenly felt, especially as the new minister, Bernardo Gastelum, removed much of the government support from the mural programme and thereby alienated many artists. Siqueiros, for instance, dedicated himself to the Communist Party and therefore to political opposition to the government.[3] Consequently Mexican artists accepted commissions in the US, while conversely numerous American artists undertook mural projects in Mexico. Although a deep-rooted belief in the enduring power of public art and the social responsibility of the artist remained, opportunities were noticeably reduced. One of the most important places where artists and writers met was the Café Paris, run by Madame Hélène between 1930 and 1945. 'It was', the Mexican poet Octavio Paz recalled, 'a society within a society', in which different groups sat at separate tables and rarely mixed. It was at the Café Paris that a group – led by Juan Soriano and including Maria Izquierdo, Lola Álvarez Bravo and Lupe Marín (Rivera's second wife) – met.[4] The artistic community in Mexico City was a divided one, whether on political or personal lines. Indeed there were a number of practising artists, such as Izquierdo, Manuel Rodríguez Lozano, Abraham Angel, Agustín Lazo and Julio Castellanos, who remained overshadowed by 'los tres grandes' ('the three greats', Rivera, Orozco and Siqueiros) and whose work was only to emerge much later.

Diego Rivera painted murals in San Francisco, Detroit and New York; José Clemente Orozco in New Hampshire, where he lectured at the Ivy League university Dartmouth College, and Pomona in California (cat. 55); while David Alfaro Siqueiros painted three murals in Los Angeles, including *The Street Meeting* (1932) at the Chouinard Art Institute, where the Mexican José Chávez Morado was studying painting, and *Portrait of Present Day Mexico* (1932) for the Pacific Palisades residence of the film director Dudley Murphy.

The murals of Rivera, Orozco and Siqueiros were not, however, universally embraced in the US, and indeed they attracted numerous detractors.[5] The occasionally radical viewpoints they expressed, whether championing communism or criticising American imperialism, were not always welcomed. Because each artist was essentially working as an individual rather than playing a part in an ideologically and artistically united collective, the style and content of the murals varied widely. The three artists did not represent a radical political group, actively fomenting social change through art, but were expressing their personal beliefs, and as a result their work was often viewed with suspicion. The message of Siqueiros's *América Tropical* (fig. 43), a 1932 mural at the Italian Hall in Los Angeles, dominated by an eagle descending on a crucified indigenous Mexican, was an unambiguous critique of American regional imperialism; it was

55

José Clemente Orozco
(1883–1949)
Barricade (La trinchera), 1931.
Oil on canvas, 139.7 x 114.3 cm.
The Museum of Modern Art, New York. Given anonymously, 1937

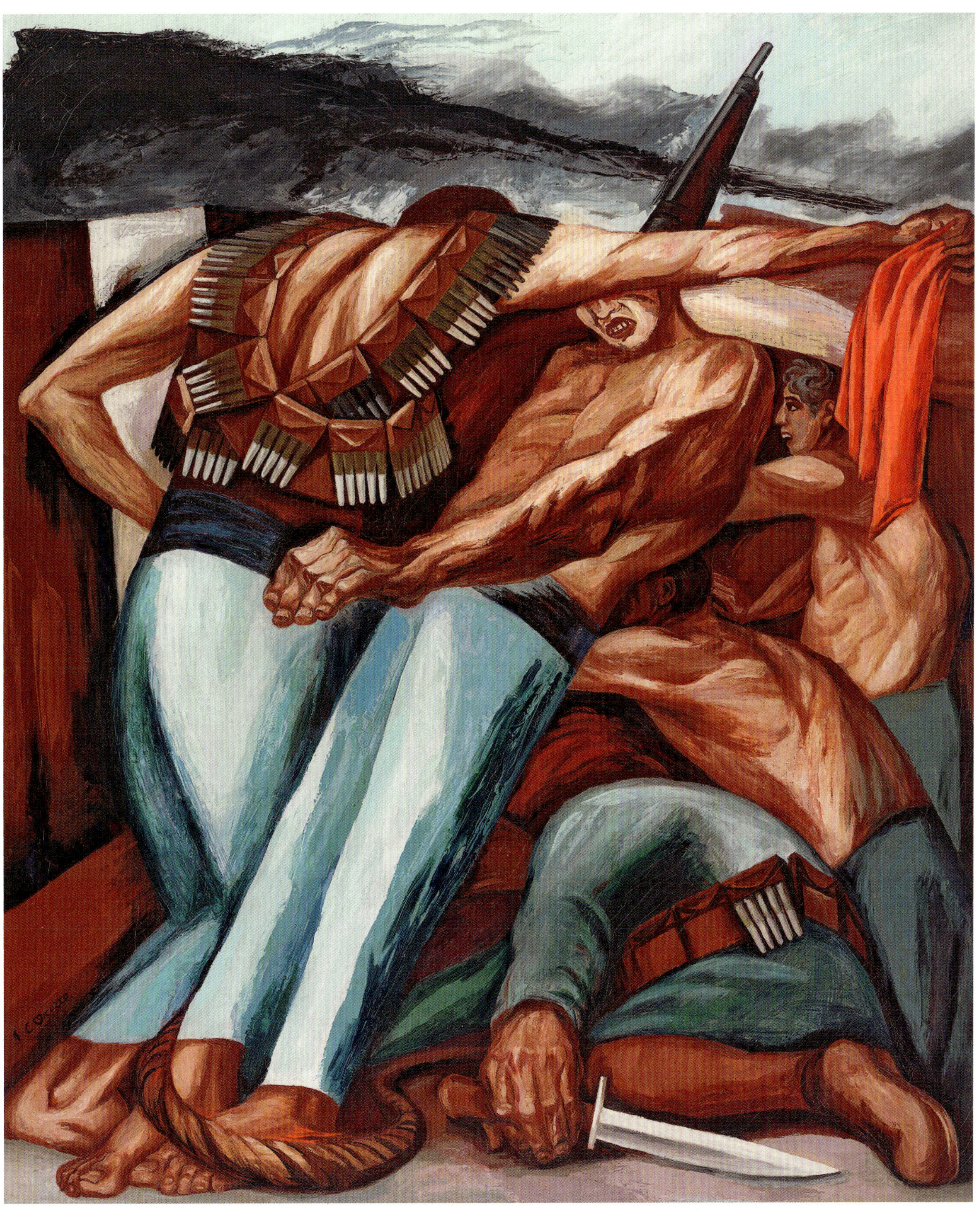

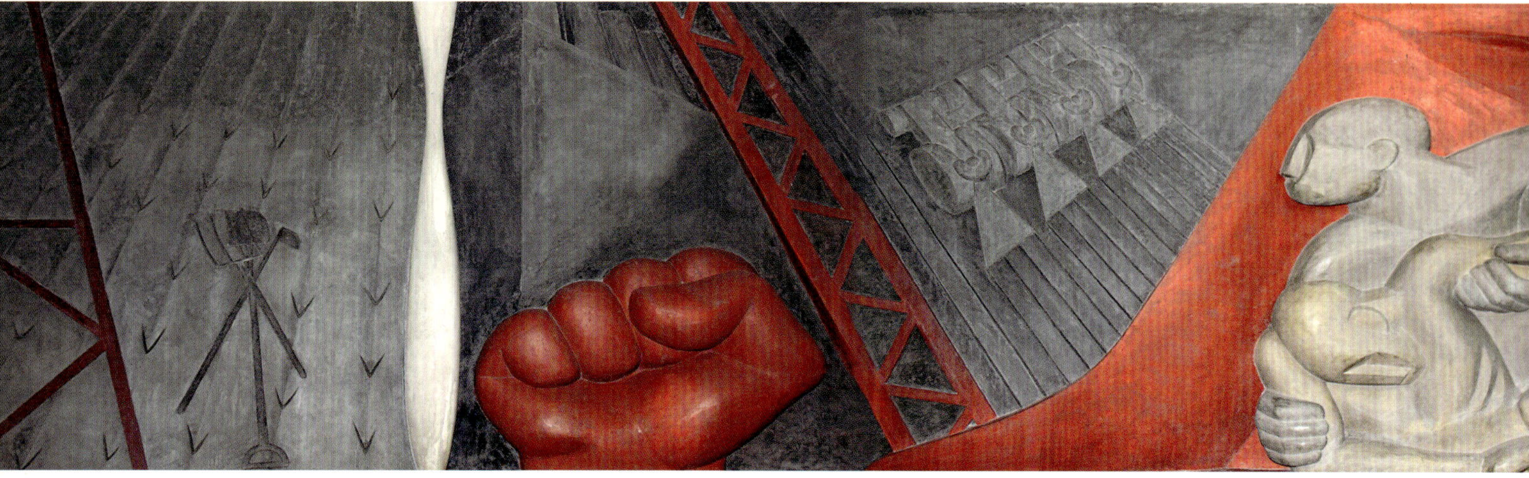

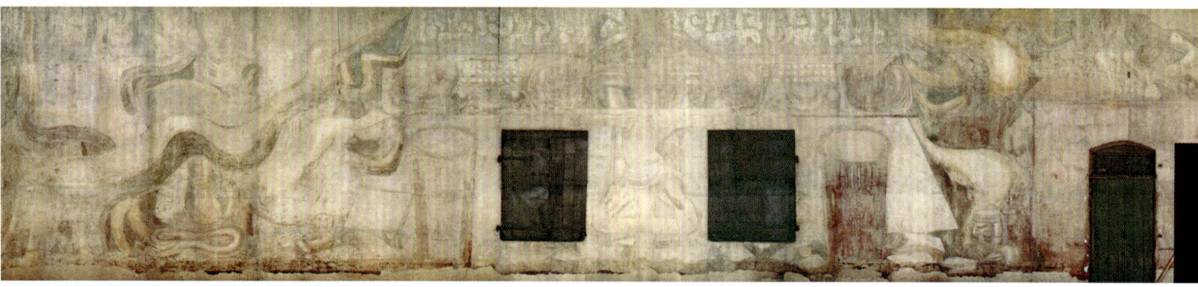

Fig. 43 David Alfaro Siqueiros, **América Tropical**, 1932. Mural applied with airbrush on cement, 5.48 x 24 m. Italian Hall, Olvera Street, Los Angeles.

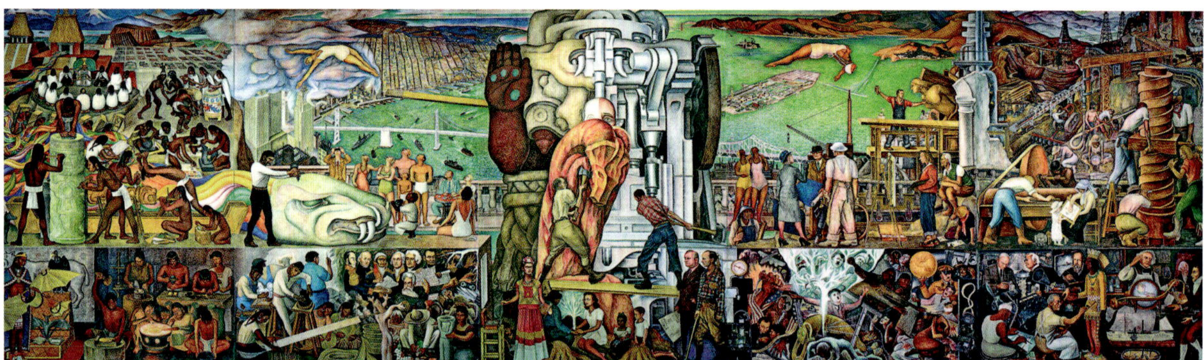

Fig. 44 Diego Rivera, **Pan American Unity. The Marriage of the Artistic Expression of the North and of the South on the Continent**, 1940. Fresco on ten removable panels, 175.4 sq. m. City College of San Francisco

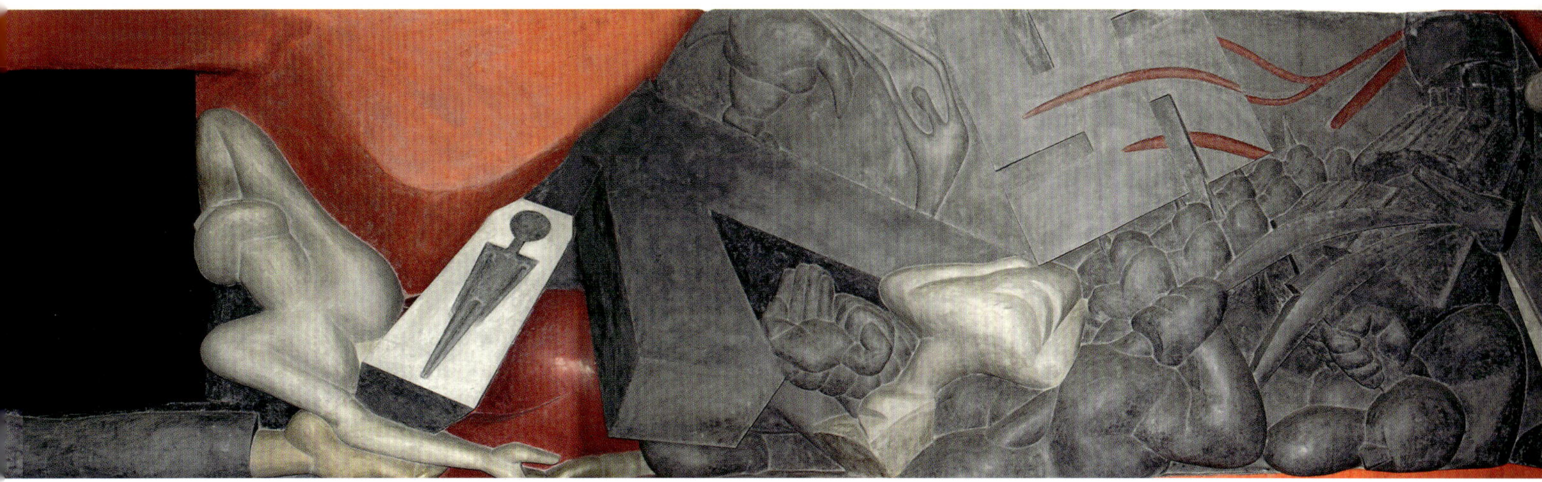

Fig. 45 Isamu Noguchi, **History as Seen from Mexico in 1936**, 1936. Tinted cement, concrete and brick, 2.2 x 22 m. Abelardo L. Rodríguez Market, Mexico City

quickly whitewashed. It is significant, however, that Mexican artists were content to travel north to the US to accept private commissions, often from very wealthy individuals and corporations; evidently they did not see these as compromising their revolutionary credentials. Rivera's 1940 *Pan American Unity* at City College of San Francisco (fig. 44), for instance, cannot be called a revolutionary image. As Rivera discovered in Moscow when he was there in 1927 for the tenth anniversary of the October Revolution, Soviet Russia allowed artists little room to challenge the authorities; despite having received a commission to paint a mural for the Red Army Club, he was encouraged to leave because of his public support of artists. It is clear that the Mexicans' commitment to the revolutionary cause was, at times, compromised by their desire to further their artistic careers.

By 1933 the Mexican government had provided wall space for such American artists as Marion and Grace Greenwood, Ryah Ludins, Isamu Noguchi and Pablo O'Higgins. Both Marion Greenwood (fig. 46) and Noguchi (fig. 45), recipient of a Guggenheim Fellowship in 1935,[6] worked at the newly constructed covered food market in Mexico City named after the former president, Abelardo L. Rodríguez, in 1936. In the US the Federal Art Project, part of the Works Progress Administration, a component of President Franklin D. Roosevelt's New Deal (a federal initiative to help America recover from the Great Depression), funded many public art projects between 1935 and 1943, including mural paintings by such artists as Howard Cook (a Guggenheim Fellow in 1932), Phillip Goldstein (as Philip Guston was then known) and Henrietta Shore,

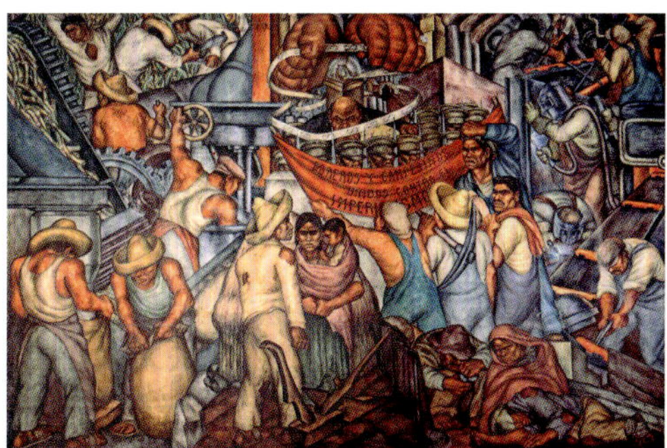

Fig. 46 Marion Greenwood, **The Industrialisation of the Countryside**, 1935. Mural. Abelardo L. Rodríguez Market, Mexico City

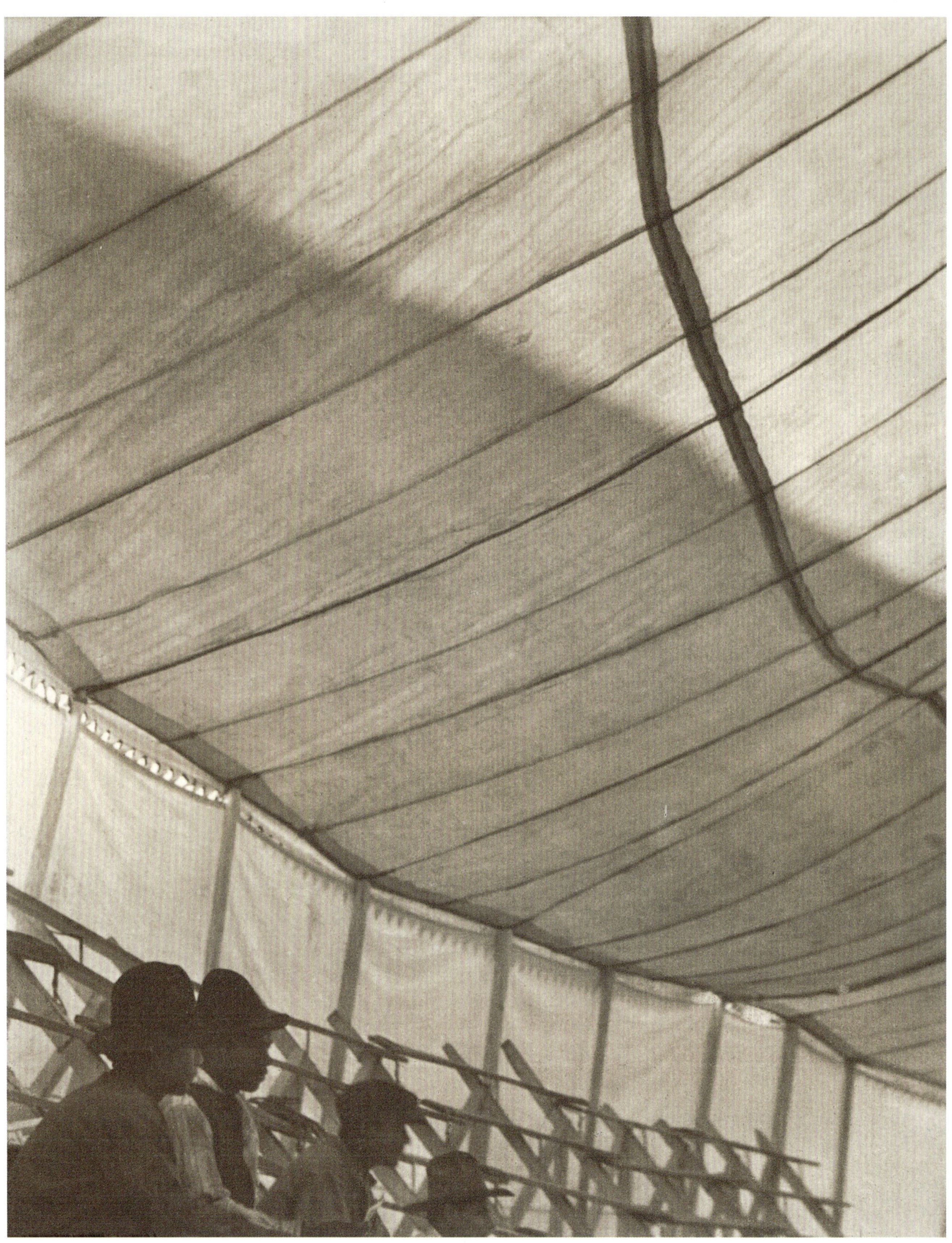

all of whom knew Mexico, demonstrating the regional interest in public art.

Although the mural movement remained dominant in Mexico, plenty of artists ignored the rallying cry of Siqueiros and the Union of Technical Workers, Painters and Sculptors, whose 1922 manifesto called on them to abandon easel art in favour of public art projects. Rufino Tamayo and Maria Izquierdo, for example, believed that art was intensely personal and that individuals should be free to express themselves artistically as they saw fit. Their approach was not so much a rejection of the nationalist language that had come to define Mexican Modernism as a dismissal of a prescriptive way of selecting and representing subject-matter, especially if that meant embracing a Socialist-Realist style. As Octavio Paz astutely observed, Frida Kahlo and Maria Izquierdo came from opposite ends of Mexican society: Kahlo was from a well-off, urban family with European blood while Izquierdo came from a poor, rural background with indigenous blood. Although Kahlo passionately wanted to be Mexican, Izquierdo did not: a tension that was manifest in their art.[7]

Originally from Oaxaca, Tamayo was orphaned at an early age and sent to live with his aunt in Mexico City. An aspiring young artist and, like many, a graduate of the San Carlos Academy, he became head of ethnographic drawings at the National Museum of Archaeology in 1921. His appointment led to a lifelong passion for Mexican pre-Columbian art, and he became a serious collector, as did a number of other notable artists at this time, among them Miguel Covarrubias and Diego Rivera. Tamayo set up a studio that he shared for four years with Izquierdo, who came from Jalisco, until they separated in 1934. The similarity of their early work reflects their intimate bond as lovers working in the same space. By 1933 Tamayo was spending a great deal of time in New York and finally moved there in 1936.

Like many artists of the time, Izquierdo was drawn to the popular arts and forms of entertainment. Her delicate still-lifes incorporate examples of regional popular art that could be bought in the markets of Mexico City and which artists eagerly collected on their journeys across the country. Another subject that she favoured, and

56

Tina Modotti (1896–1942)
Circus Tent, Mexico, *c.* 1924.
Platinum print, 23.4 x 17.7 cm.
Center for Creative Photography, University of Arizona, Tucson. Purchase

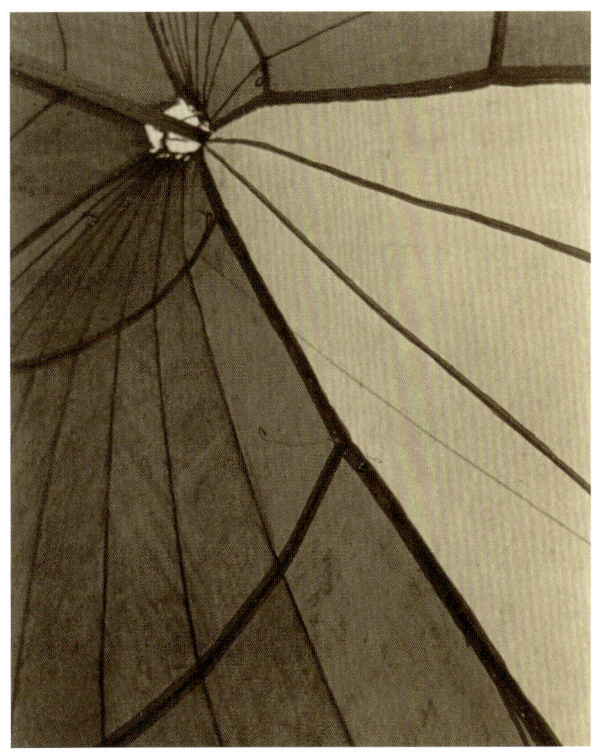

57

Edward Weston
(1886–1958)
Circus Tent, Mexico, 1924.
Gelatin silver print,
9.8 x 7.5 cm. The J. Paul Getty Museum, Los Angeles

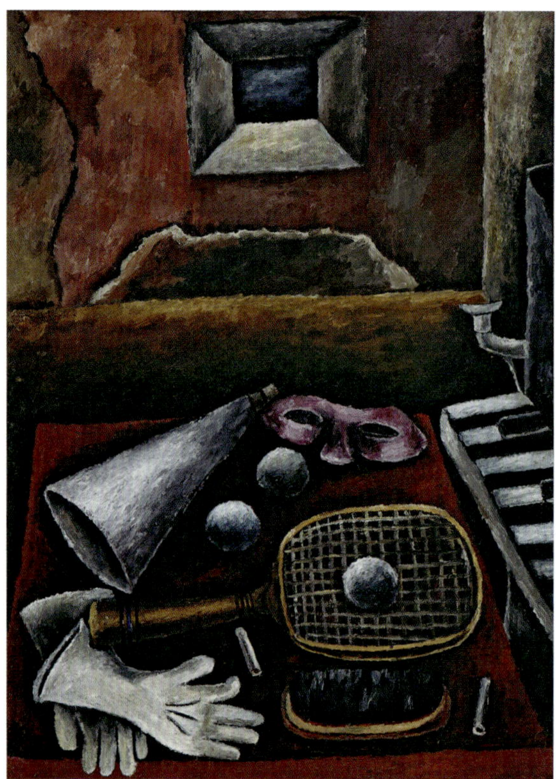

which was also of interest to photographers as well as painters abroad, was the travelling circus, then a huge attraction in Mexico, especially in rural areas. Once ensconced under the big top, viewers could escape from the humdrum and marvel at the acrobats, for instance, whose routines were not only highly skilled and daring but extraordinarily creative (cats 56, 57).

Izquierdo was the first Mexican artist to have a solo exhibition in the US. The show took place in 1930 at the Art Center in New York, and was organised by Frances Flynn Paine, an American art-dealer and a passionate promoter of Mexican art. After Izquierdo's separation from Tamayo, she took a house in Calle Venezuela in the historic centre of Mexico City, sharing it with Lola Álvarez Bravo after her separation from her husband Manuel (cat. 58). Izquierdo was very close to Antonin Artaud during his stay in Mexico. Indeed, he took four of her paintings back with him to France. Many years later, in conversation with Octavio Paz, Artaud said, 'In her paintings the real Mexico, the ancient one, not Rivera's ideological one, appears with the heat of blood and lava.'[8] Paz himself described Izquierdo as someone who painted with a unique light, more lunar than solar.[9]

Later in life, Tamayo recalled that time in Mexico and the challenges with which artists were confronted:

> *When they [Mexican artists] returned [from abroad], because of the revolution, they and those of us at home were all trying to liberate ourselves politically and economically. In that atmosphere the artists turned strongly nationalist. At that moment it was necessary for us to be very nationalist. That meant we could go back to our roots and absorb from them whatever we could. We had to become sure of ourselves. Before the revolution the Mexican government didn't really believe in Mexico's artists. They thought that because we had no experience we knew nothing, and therefore anything of quality could only come from foreigners.*
>
> *The trouble was that the painters portrayed only a surface nationalism. They painted the facts of Mexico's history and culture, all leading to the facts of the revolution. But revolution*

58

Maria Izquierdo (1902–1955)
The Racket (La raqueta), 1938.
Oil on canvas, 70 x 50 cm.
Museo Colección Andrés Blaisten

59

Rufino Tamayo (1899–1991)
Mandolins and Pineapples, 1930. Oil on canvas, 50.16 x 69.85 cm.
The Phillips Collection, Washington, DC

is not a Mexican phenomenon. It happens all over the world. I'm not opposed in theory to what they did. It was natural for them. But I myself felt something beyond that. I was a rebel, not against the revolution, but against the Mexican mural movement which was conceived to celebrate it. It is impossible, I feel, in this time when communications are so open, to set out deliberately to make an art which is Mexican, or American, or Chinese, or Russian. I think in terms of universality. Art is a way of expression that has to be understood by everybody, everywhere. It grows out of the earth, the texture of our lives and our experiences.[10]

Mandolins and Pineapples (cat. 59) reflects Tamayo's concerns. The painting expresses a deep longing for the land of his birth. Despite being an experimental still-life – the viewer's gaze is drawn through the open window – the subdued palate is typical of Tamayo's work from this period. The subject-matter, however, is quintessentially Mexican and refers specifically to his hometown of Oaxaca, a city with a rich and diverse history. The region boasts numerous musical customs and festivals, including some that mix the indigenous with the Catholic. The painting features the mandolin – most likely the *tricordia*, a triple-stringed version of the mandolin, known in Europe as the *mandriola* – an instrument closely associated with Mexican folk

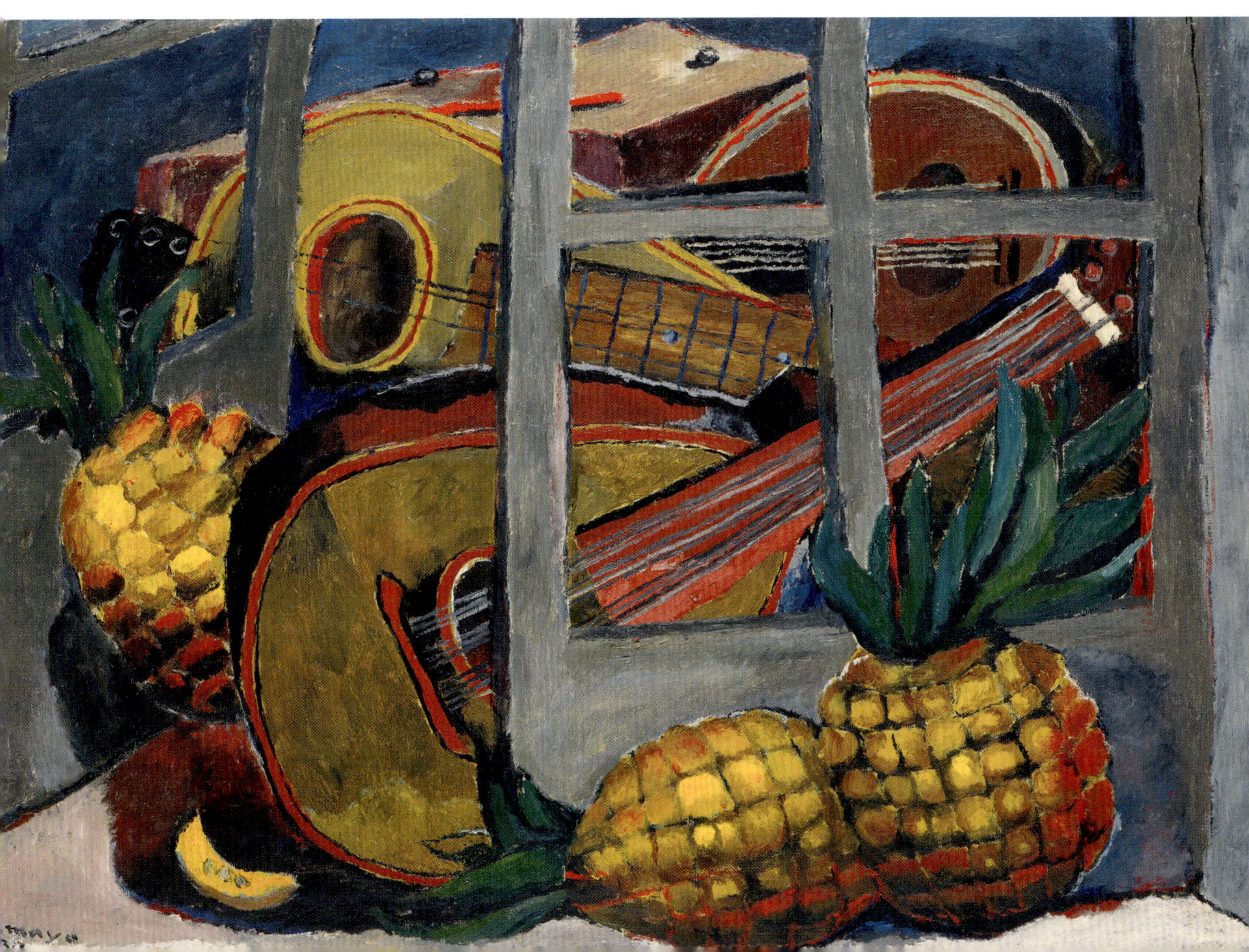

music. In the background, mallets rest on the closed case of a *marimba*, another traditional instrument especially connected with Oaxaca. The inclusion of pineapples, ubiquitous in Mexico where they are savoured fresh with powdered chilli, completes this nostalgic vision of Oaxaca, centre of pineapple-growing in the country. The painting was most probably painted in New York for an exhibition at the Julien Levy Gallery in 1930. Although not overtly political, it remains full of yearning, and its Mexican subject-matter positions it comfortably alongside the work of his contemporaries. The Chilean poet and Nobel laureate Pablo Neruda described Tamayo as 'complex and passionate, as Mexican as the fruit or woven goods in the markets'.[11]

Having introduced new techniques and approaches to photography in Mexico, both Weston and Modotti had left the country by 1930, albeit in very different circumstances. The foundations had been laid for Mexican photographers to take centre stage. Abandoning the conventional approach of posing people to photograph them, which was little more than outdoor studio photography, or shooting views of the idyllic landscape, photographers began now to work in more challenging ways. They explored new angles and viewpoints, allowing details to fill the frame, creating symbolic and often politically charged images, capturing people unawares and recording unusual random juxtapositions. Photography was becoming more a creative art form than a means to record a place, a person or an event. Photographers were experimenting also with the printing process, cropping images to suit their needs, and with the titling of their works.

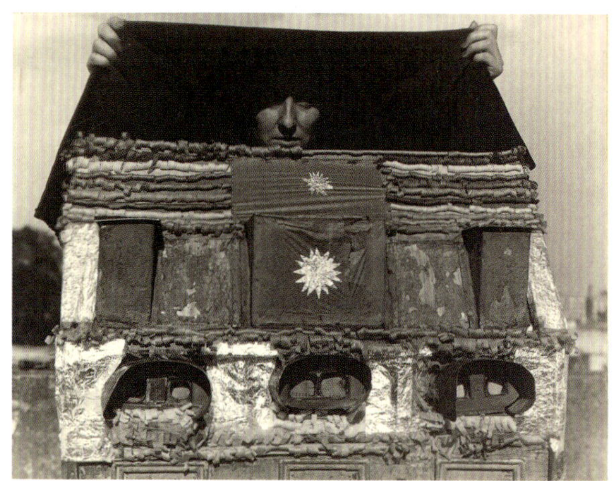

The young, aspiring Manuel Álvarez Bravo, who worked as a tax inspector, epitomises this new generation of energetic and ambitious photographers. He secured his reputation as an emerging talent by appearing in the vast 'Primer salón Mexicano de fotografía' in 1928, organised by the photographer Antonio Garduño and the artists Carlos Mérida and Carlos Orozco Romero in the Palacio de Bellas Artes. A native of Mexico City, Álvarez Bravo had witnessed many changes there. He could recall, for instance, seeing dead bodies, victims of the Revolution, lying in the streets on his way to school. The city had subsequently exploded in size, doubling its population to reach one million inhabitants by 1925 (cats 60, 61).

As a photographer Álvarez Bravo was first inspired by Hugo Brehme, the German-born photographer known for his pictorial images of Mexico, whose style he mimicked early on but soon abandoned.[12] In 1927 he met Tina Modotti,

60

Manuel Álvarez Bravo
(1902–2002)
Box of Visions
(Caja de visiones), *c.* 1930.
Gelatin silver print,
18.8 x 23.5 cm.
Philadelphia Museum of Art.
125th Anniversary Acquisition. The
Lynne and Harold Honickman Gift
of the Julien Levy Collection, 2001

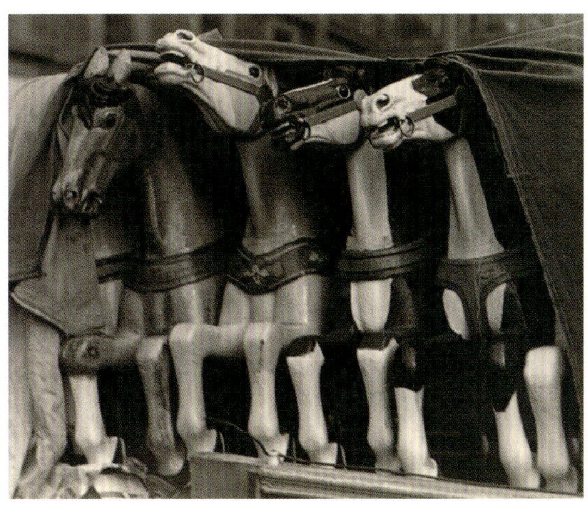

61

Manuel Álvarez Bravo
(1902–2002)
The Obstacles
(Los obstáculos), 1929.
Gelatin silver print,
18.9 x 22.6 cm.
Philadelphia Museum of Art
125th Anniversary Acquisition. The
Lynne and Harold Honickman Gift
of the Julien Levy Collection, 2001

an encounter that was to have a profound impact on his life. They forged a strong friendship that lasted until her deportation three years later. On the eve of her departure, Modotti gave Álvarez Bravo her camera. Undoubtedly he learned much from her photography, although she was relatively new to the discipline. Modotti had made enormous progress over a short period, during which she created a very distinct style, full of the confidence that came from her political convictions. Although both artists based their work on the culture and people of Mexico, Modotti's subjects were full of political and social connotations, whereas Álvarez Bravo worked with subjects that emerged from his imagination and sharp eye but were rooted in the essence of everyday life. Álvarez Bravo delighted in walking the streets and markets, capturing images of the humdrum that appealed to his aesthetic and sense of humour. His work can be divided into two principal themes: the first looks at Mexican history, culture and identity, and the second embraces photography as a fluid medium of observation in which episodes of daily life are distilled into emblems or fables of existence (cats 62, 63).[13]

After Modotti's deportation, Álvarez Bravo took over her duties as photographer for *Mexican Folkways* and began to take photographs of the murals in Mexico City. These proved very popular and he sold prints of them for 50 cents each to make a living, but his life was changed in 1931 when he won the Tolteca competition, which allowed him to dedicate himself, temporarily at least, to full-time photography.[14]

In August 1931 the British-owned cement manufacturer Cementos Tolteca announced an open art competition for painters and photographers to produce the best representation of their modern new plant in Mixcoac, a suburb of Mexico City. Diego Rivera was one of the jurors. This brilliant marketing campaign placed modernity and progress centre stage, with both their state-of-the-art plant and its product, cement, which symbolised modern, progressive Mexico. The ensuing campaign used the new discipline of photography to promote the corporate sector in Mexico.[15] Numerous photographers, including Manuel Álvarez Bravo, Agustín Jiménez and Lola Álvarez Bravo, entered the photographic category; in total there were 282 entries. Manuel Álvarez Bravo took first prize in the photography category with his *Tríptico Cemento 2* (fig. 47), also known as *La Tolteca*. Other prizewinners included Jiménez, Lola Álvarez Bravo and Aurora Eugenia Latapí. Modotti, now in Berlin, was sent copies of the winning entries, demonstrating the regard with which she was still held in the world

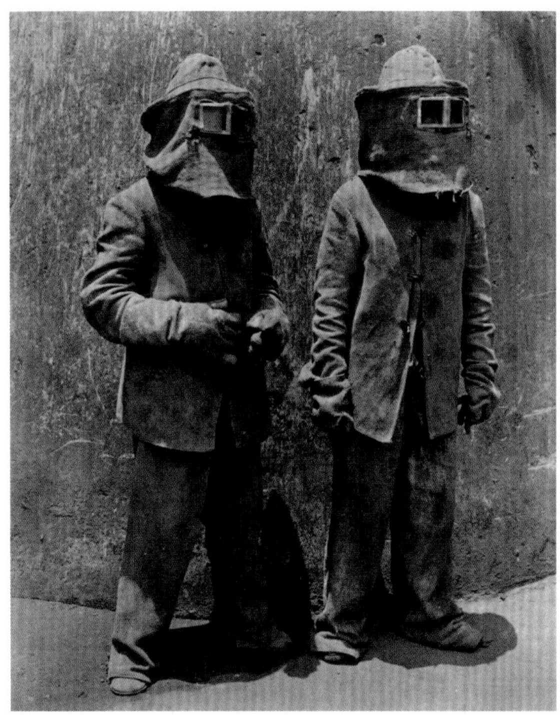

of Mexican photography; Modotti felt that Lola Álvarez Bravo should have won first prize.[16] The competition was marked both by the photographers' dramatic approach to their subject and their use of shadow and light and oblique angles to great effect: a modern response to a modern subject (cat. 64).

As an emerging photographer, Álvarez Bravo benefited from meeting two great masters of the art while they were visiting Mexico: the American Paul Strand and the Frenchman Henri Cartier-Bresson. He forged strong friendships with both. He also met Sergei Eisenstein in 1932, travelling with him to various locations, and André Breton in 1938 when the writer was in Mexico. Although Álvarez Bravo never really considered himself a Surrealist, he enjoyed the exposure the movement gave him; Breton was greatly taken with his work and purchased thirteen of his photographs. These were included in Breton's 1939 exhibition 'Mexique' at the Galerie Renou & Colle in Paris, in which Álvarez Bravo's work appeared alongside eighteen paintings by Frida Kahlo and examples of Mexican popular art.[17] Such was his standing with Breton that Álvarez Bravo's *Girl Looking at Birds* (fig. 48) featured on the cover of the exhibition's catalogue, as did his *About Winter* (*Sobre el invierno*, 1939) for the 'Exposición internacional del surrealismo' the following year. As we shall see, Breton considered Mexico to be 'the Surrealist place par excellence'. He wrote in *Minotaure*: ' ... in Mexico ... artistic creation is not adulterated as it is here [in Europe]'. Art, he believed, was still authentic in Mexico, thanks to its deep connections with myth and ritual, the country's diverse ethnography, and the vibrant and expressive traditions of popular art.[18] This meant that Mexico retained the kind of diversity that was becoming increasingly scarce in Europe and the US as the pace of development swept aside ancient customs and traditions, replacing them with a more uniform and conventional society. Mexico must have seemed like another world to those coming from Europe, with the increasing power of the Fascist regimes presiding over Germany, Italy and Spain (cat. 68).

Following a run of five exhibitions in 1931, including a solo show at the Sala de Arte of the Ministry of Public Education, Agustín Jiménez came to be seen as 'the best promise that Mexico

62

Manuel Álvarez Bravo
(1902–2002)
Furnace Men (Trabajadores del fuego), 1935.
Platinum print, 57.5 x 42.3 x 3 cm (framed). Victoria and Albert Museum, London

63

Manuel Álvarez Bravo
(1902–2002)
Lords of the Dance (Reyes de danza), 1931.
Platinum print, 57.5 x 42.3 x 3 cm (framed). Victoria and Albert Museum, London. Given by Dorothy Bohm

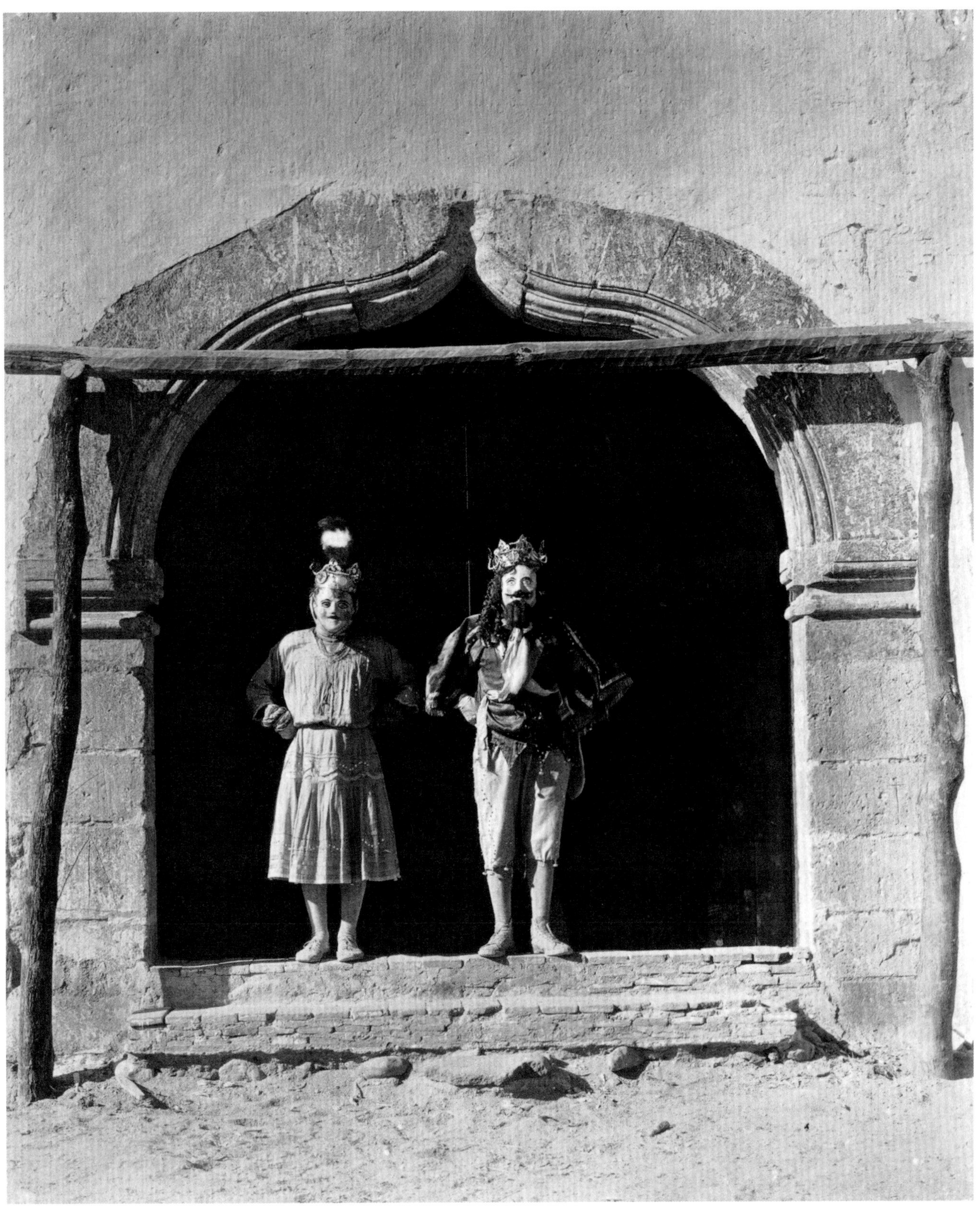

has of a Mexican school of photography'; *Mexican Life* likened him to the American photographer Edward Steichen (cat. 65).[19] Jiménez's work had also been shown in New York, at the Delphic Studios. He was a student of architecture, and his interest in buildings is evident from his early work, although he later worked as a teacher at the Escuela Nacional de Bellas Artes, Mexico City, where he tutored a promising group of students, foremost among them Aurora Eugenia Latapí (cats 66, 67). Despite his apparent success, he detached himself from the cultured setting of the art gallery in 1931 and moved into the more commercial world of newspapers, magazines, posters and photographic commissions, effectively becoming a professional photographer as opposed to a photographic artist.[20]

Jiménez developed a keen interest in the fledgling film industry in Mexico, no doubt inspired by his friendship with Sergei Eisenstein, whom he visited on set in Mexico City, photographing some props (fig. 49). Although he continued to take photographs, Jiménez began to concentrate on film, working with the celebrated artist and director Adolfo Best Maugard, firstly on *Humanidad* (1933) and then on the controversial *La mancha de sangre* (1937). Erotic scenes and a plot that centres on a prostitute taking care of a young man who has just arrived in Mexico City from the provinces resulted in a government ban on the release of *La mancha de sangre* until 1943. Jiménez also worked with Juan Bustillo Oro on *Dos monjes* (1934), a film highly praised by André Breton. This was stylishly shot by Jiménez, showing the influence of Eisenstein and German Expressionist cinema with its use of strongly contrasting light and dark shadows and unconventional camera angles (cats 69–71). Its plot follows the tragic tale of two men who love the same woman. Following her death, both enter the Church, where they meet again. During confession they recount different versions of the same story, giving Bustillo Oro the opportunity to use flashbacks. Much later Jiménez worked with the Spanish-born film director Luis Buñuel, who moved to Mexico in 1946, on *Ensayo de un crimen* (*The Criminal Life of Archibaldo de la Cruz*, 1955).[21]

After Eisenstein's death in Moscow in February 1948, a telegram from the prominent American author and socialist Upton Sinclair was found pinned to his desk. Dated April 1932, it had reached Eisenstein as he left New York for Moscow. In it Sinclair undertook to send the finished reels of film that Eisenstein had been making in Mexico on the following boat. But he never kept his promise, and Eisenstein saw none of the film. The telegram served to remind Eisenstein of his huge disappointment about this, not just as a director, but as someone who was passionate about Mexico.

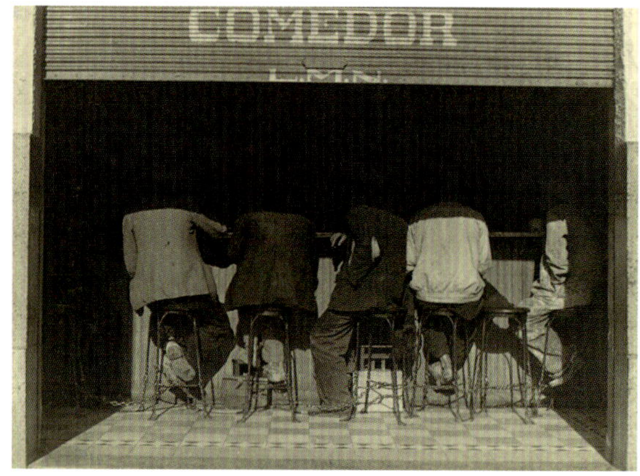

64

Manuel Álvarez Bravo (1902–2002)
The Crouched Ones (Los agachados), 1934.
Gelatin silver print, 17.8 x 23.8 cm. The J. Paul Getty Museum, Los Angeles

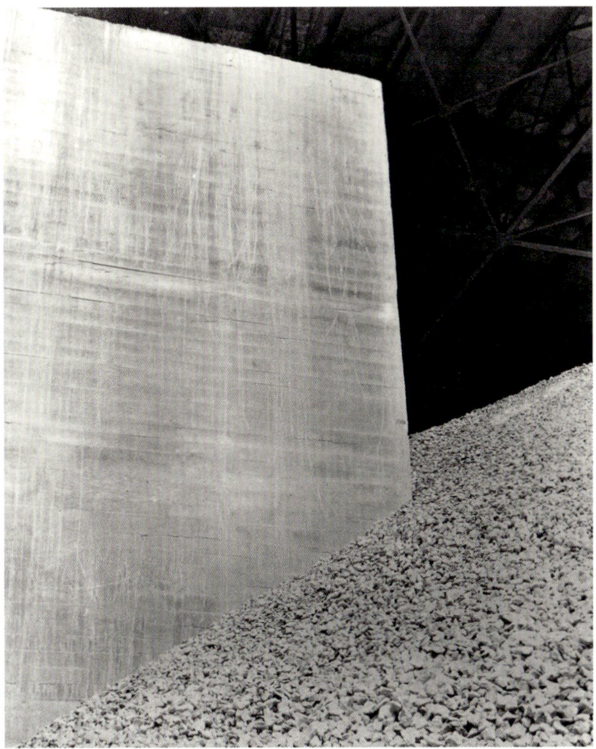

Fig. 47 Manuel Álvarez Bravo, **Tríptico Cemento 2** (also known as **La Tolteca**), 1931. Gelatin silver print, 20.3 x 25.4 cm. Asociación Manuel Álvarez Bravo, Mexico City

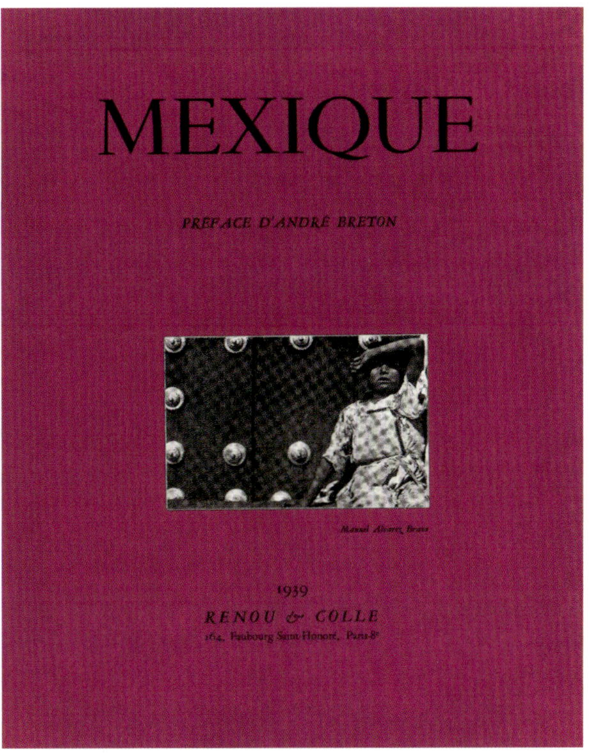

Fig. 48 Catalogue of **Mexique**, featuring Manuel Álvarez Bravo's **Girl Looking at Birds (Muchacha mirando pájaros)**, 1931. Galerie Renou & Colle, Paris, March 1939

He wrote to the Argentinian writer Victoria Ocampo, expressing his frustration: 'I so loved Mexico and it is painful not to be able to express it in this film that's now destroyed.'[22]

Although he had signed a contract with Paramount Pictures in April 1930 to produce a film in Hollywood, Eisenstein realised that the agreement would never lead to any realisable project.[23] Instead, he headed south. He owned a number of books on Mexico, including Anita Brenner's *Idols behind Altars* (New York, 1929), and was further encouraged to visit by his friendship with Rivera, but his love of the country had been kindled many years before, in 1921, when he was directing a production of Jack London's *The Mexican*, a short story about the Revolution first published in 1911, at the Proletcult Theatre in Moscow. When Rivera was in Moscow in 1927 he likened Eisenstein's films to murals, and Eisenstein thought murals possessed a cinematic

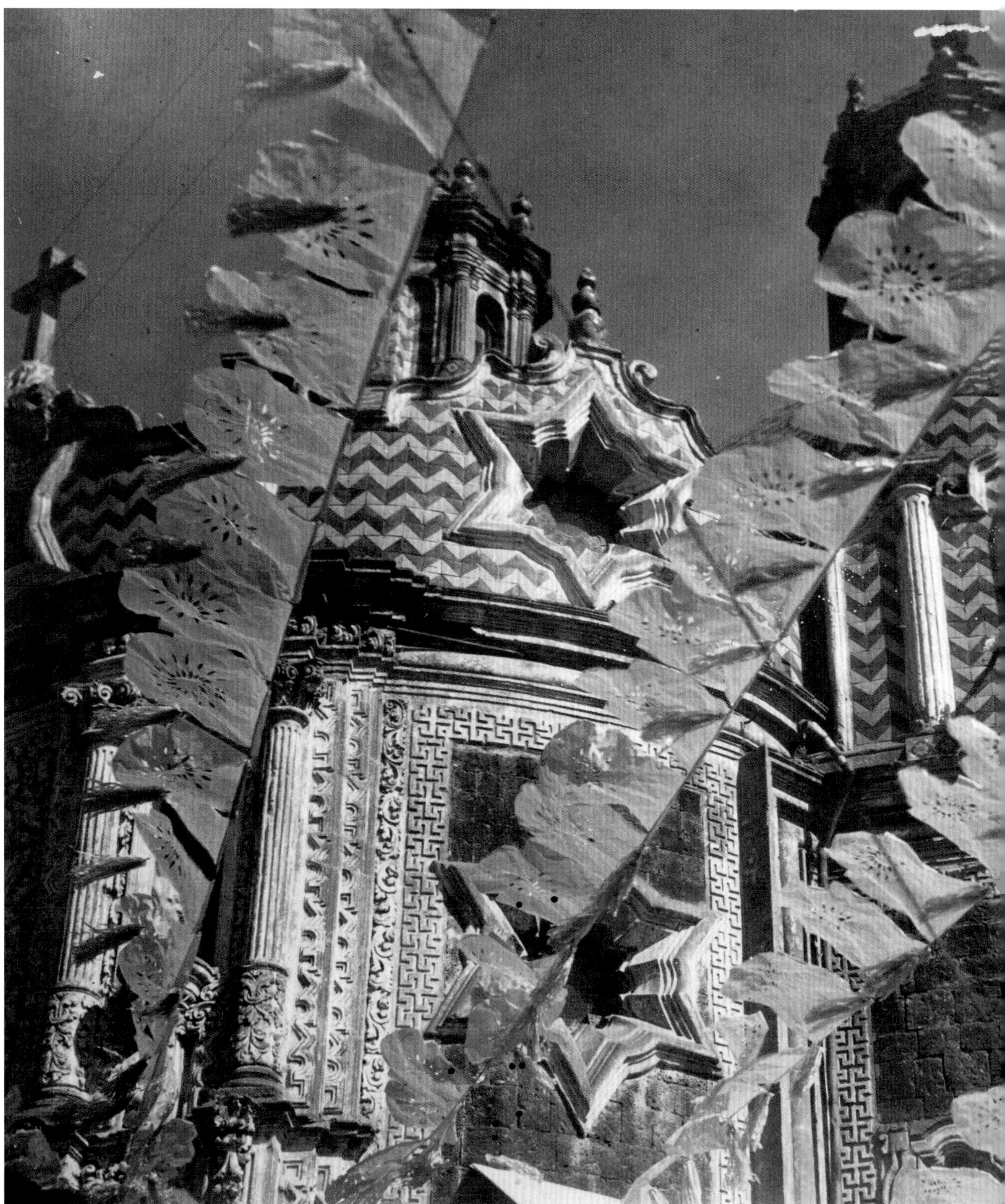

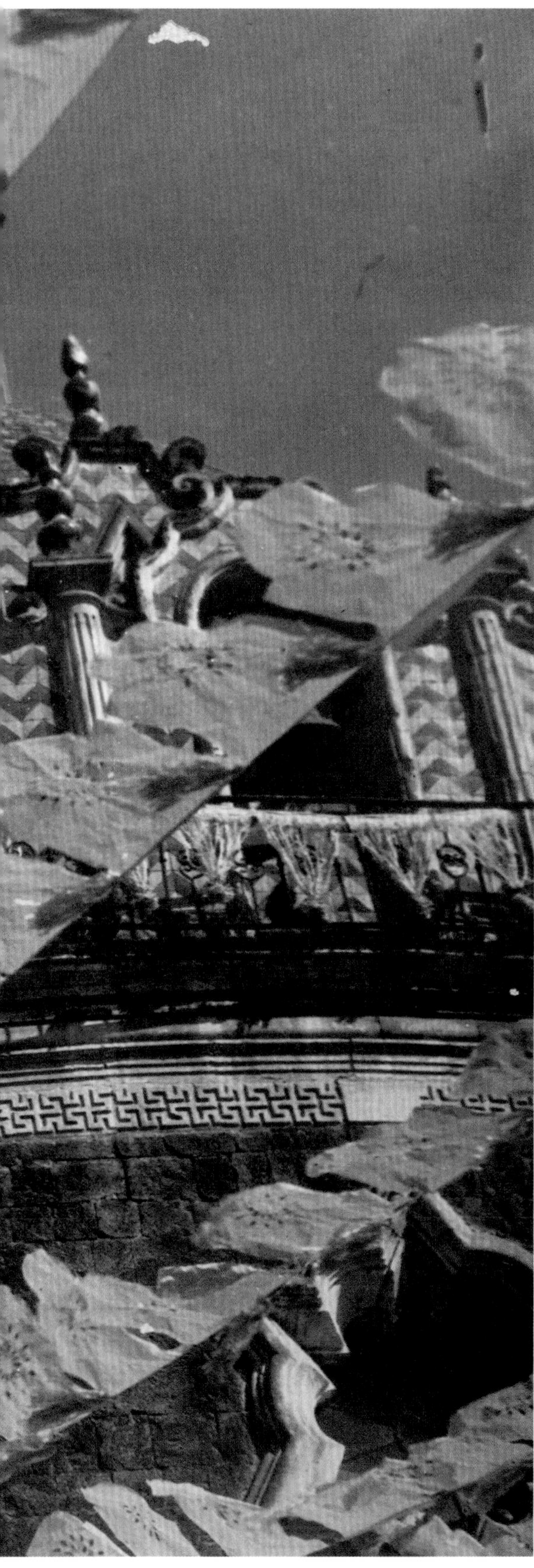

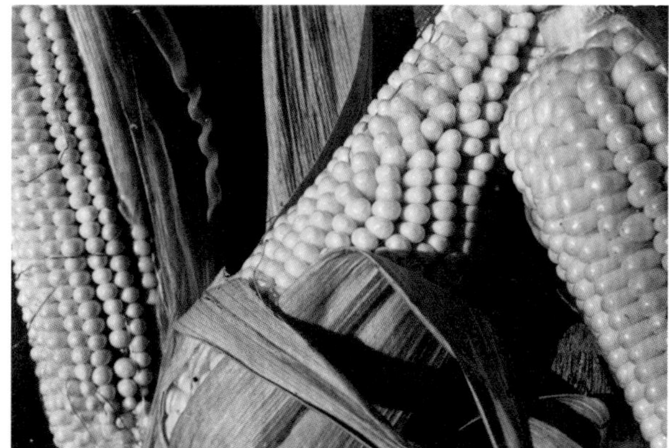

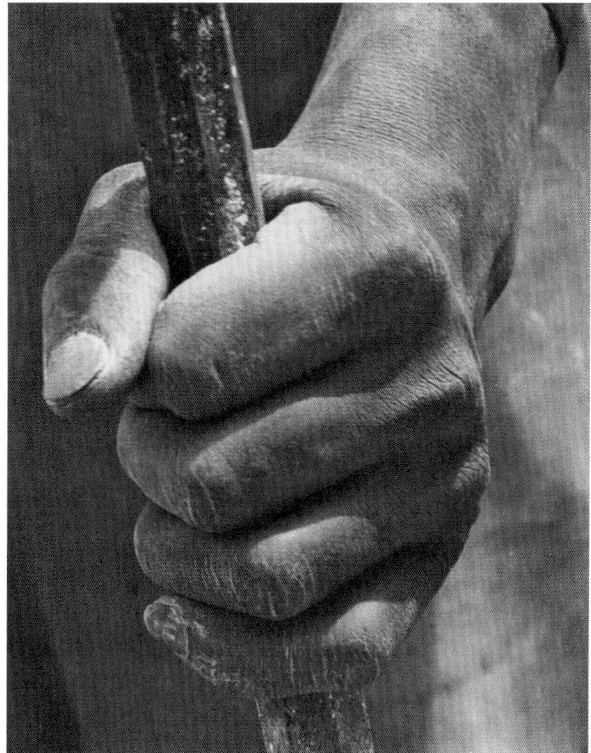

66

Aurora Eugenia Latapí
(1915–2000)
Corncobs (Elotes), 1924.
Gelatin silver print, 16.8 x 11.8 cm.
Archivo fotográfico Agustín Jiménez

65

Agustín Jiménez
(1901–1974)
The Basilica (La Basílica), 1931.
Gelatin silver print, 24.3 x 18.4 cm.
Archivo fotográfico Agustín Jiménez

67

Aurora Eugenia Latapí
(1915–2000)
Worker (Obrero), 1931.
Gelatin silver print, 19.5 x 15 cm.
Collection José Antonio Rodríguez, Mexico City

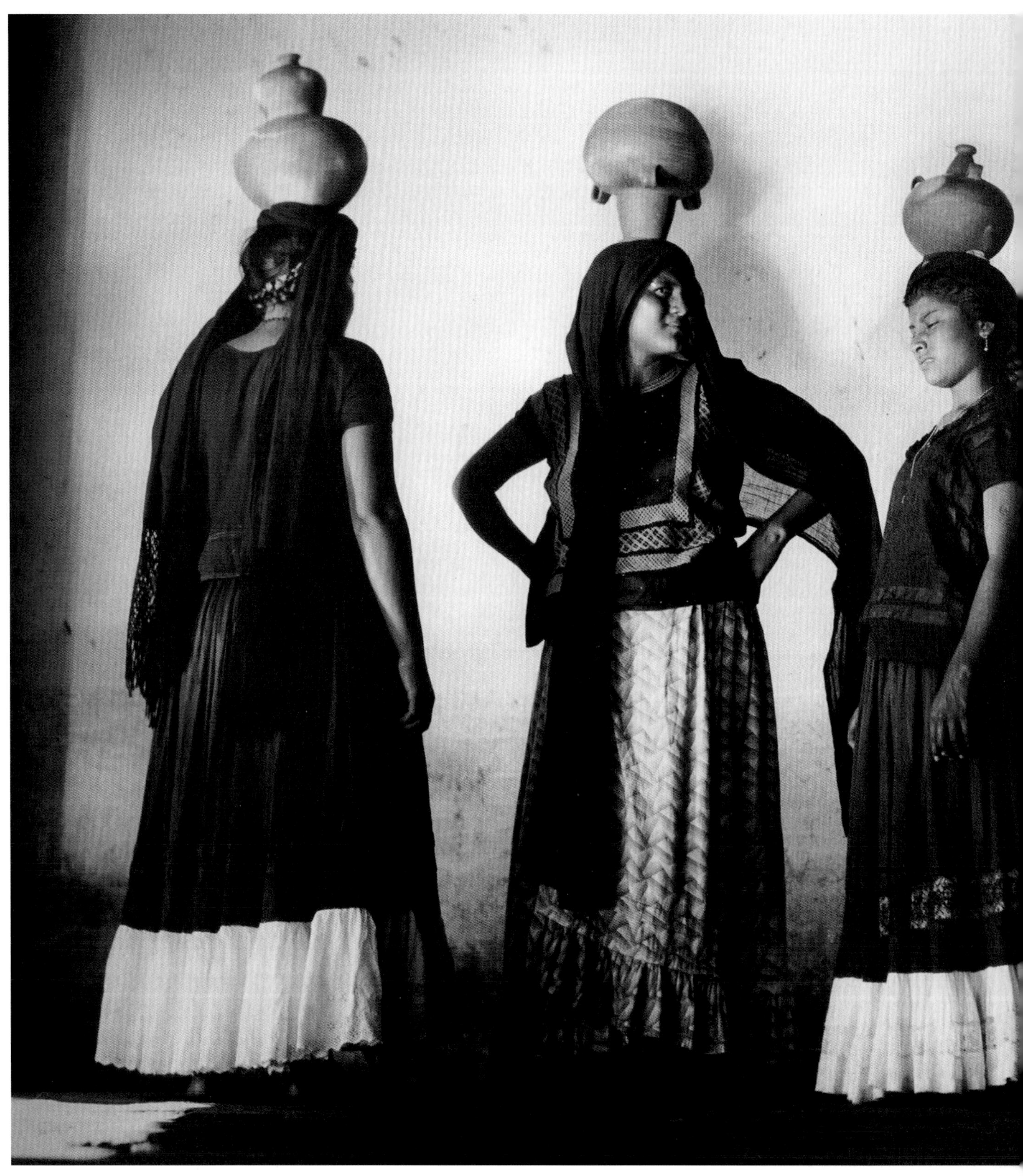

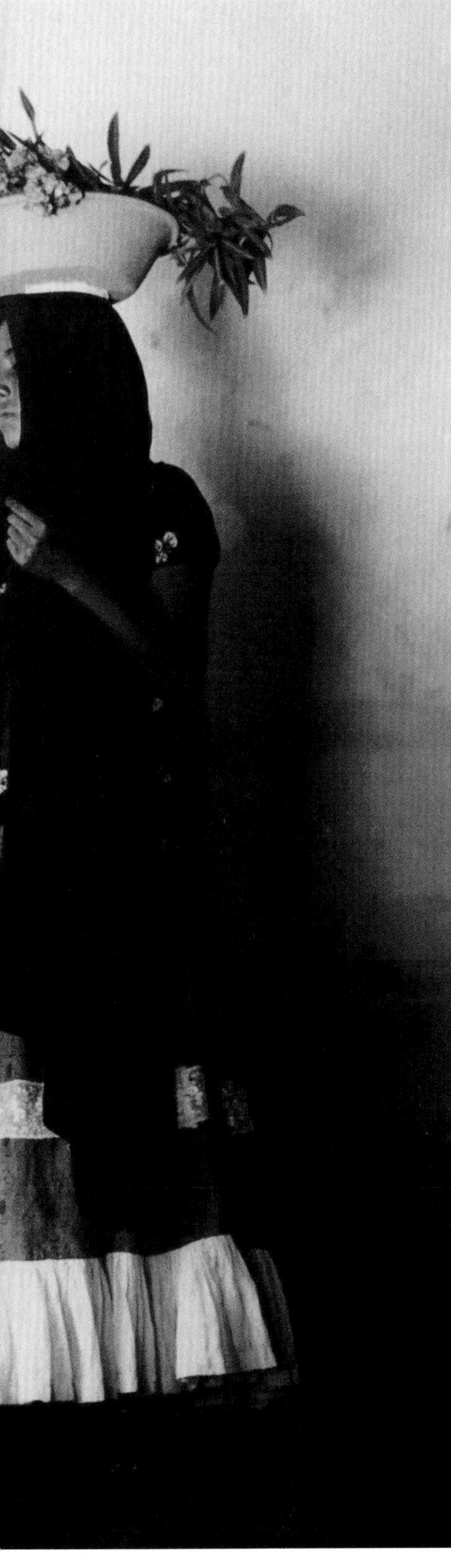

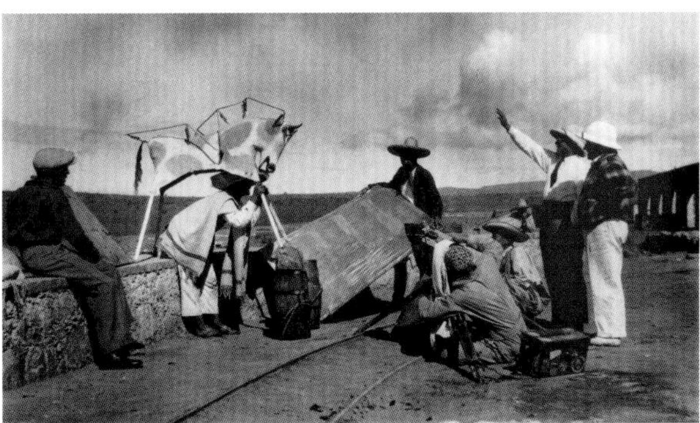

Fig. 49 Agustín Jiménez, **Untitled** (from **¡Qué viva México!** shoot), 1931. Gelatin silver print, 25 x 30 cm. Archivo fotográfico Agustín Jiménez

quality; the two artists understood and valued each other's work. Eisenstein, however, felt that Orozco's murals came closest to film.[24] Eisenstein described his films as 'my moving frescoes (for we also work on walls!)'.[25]

Abandoning California, Eisenstein arrived in Mexico on 9 December 1930 with his assistant director Grigory Alexandrov and cameraman Edouard Tissé. Over the following fourteen months he worked on an ambitious film tentatively called *¡Qué viva México!* At Charlie Chaplin's suggestion, Eisenstein had secured finance for the film from Sinclair, and had signed a binding contract with him before leaving the US. The film was broadly supported by the Mexican government, which also had an agreement with Eisenstein guaranteeing access to the plot; the government appointed Best Maugard to ensure that the film presented Mexico in a positive light. Eisenstein never finished the film and it became the most famous of his many unrealised projects. Sinclair refused to carry

68

Agustín Jiménez (1901–1974)
Tehuanas (from the film project Tehuantepec), 1934.
Gelatin silver print, 17 x 24 cm.
Archivo fotográfico
Agustín Jiménez

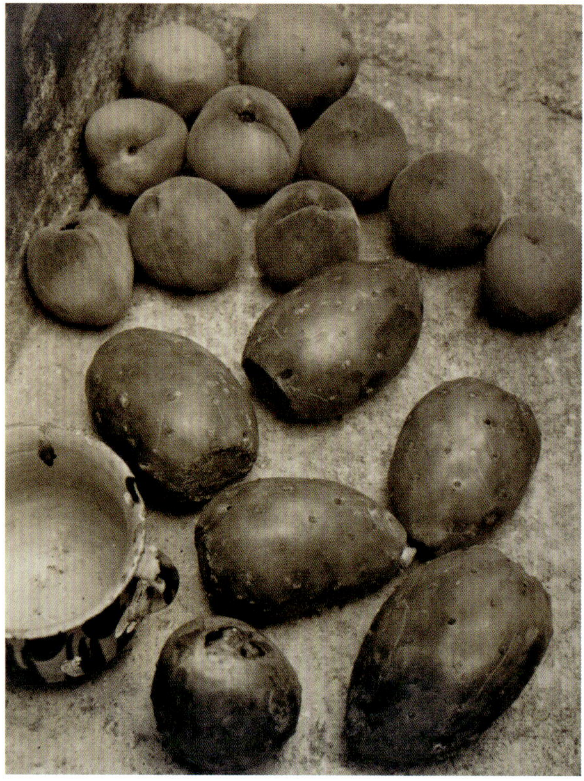

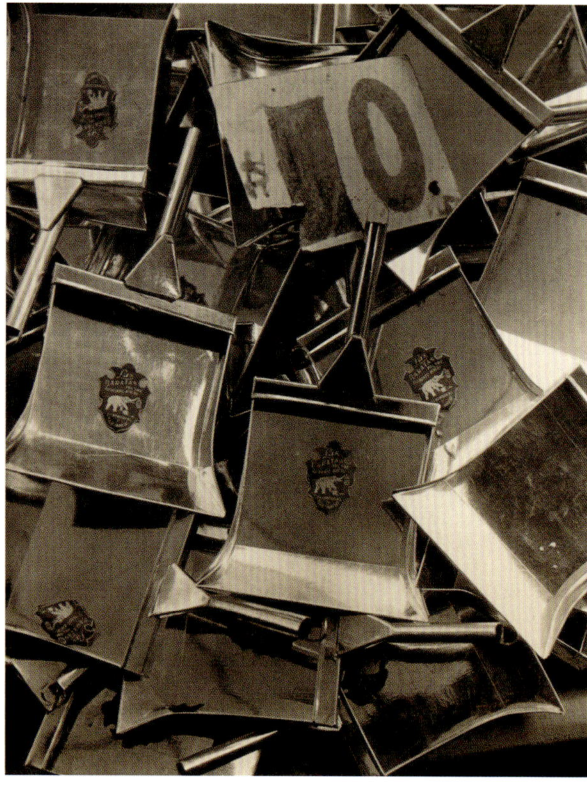

on financing the production, and Stalin, fearing Eisenstein would stay in the West, ordered his return. As far as the authorities in Soviet Russia were concerned, a film about Mexico served little or no political purpose and would be meaningless to ordinary Russian citizens.

Eisenstein was enchanted by Mexico's intense colours, powerful light and deep shadows. He loved the heady mixture of cultures, from the pre-Columbian pyramids through the exuberant baroque churches of the colonial era to the modern spectacle of the bullfight and the festive carnivals.[26] The Day of the Dead celebrations likewise fascinated him. After a break of nine years he returned to sketching; Mexico made him more contemplative, more aware of the world around him and more attuned to nature. He also found himself, for the first time, free from social, political or religious constraints. It is little wonder that he viewed Mexico as his spiritual homeland.[27] His film was to comprise four sections – 'Sandunga', 'Fiesta', 'Maguey' and 'Soldadera' (the only episode of the film that was never shot) – plus a prologue, which juxtaposed indigenous Mexicans with Maya and Mexica buildings and sculpture, and an epilogue, which

69

Agustín Jiménez (1901–1974)
Peaches and Prickly Pears (Duraznos y tunas), 1930.
Gelatin silver print, 24 x 18 cm.
Archivo fotográfico Agustín Jiménez

70

Agustín Jiménez (1901–1974)
Dustpans (Recogedores), *c.* 1932.
Gelatin silver print, 20 x 24.5 cm.
Archivo fotográfico Agustín Jiménez

71

Agustín Jiménez (1901–1974)
Explosion (Explosión), 1932.
Gelatin silver print, 18.9 x 24.3 cm. Archivo fotográfico Agustín Jiménez

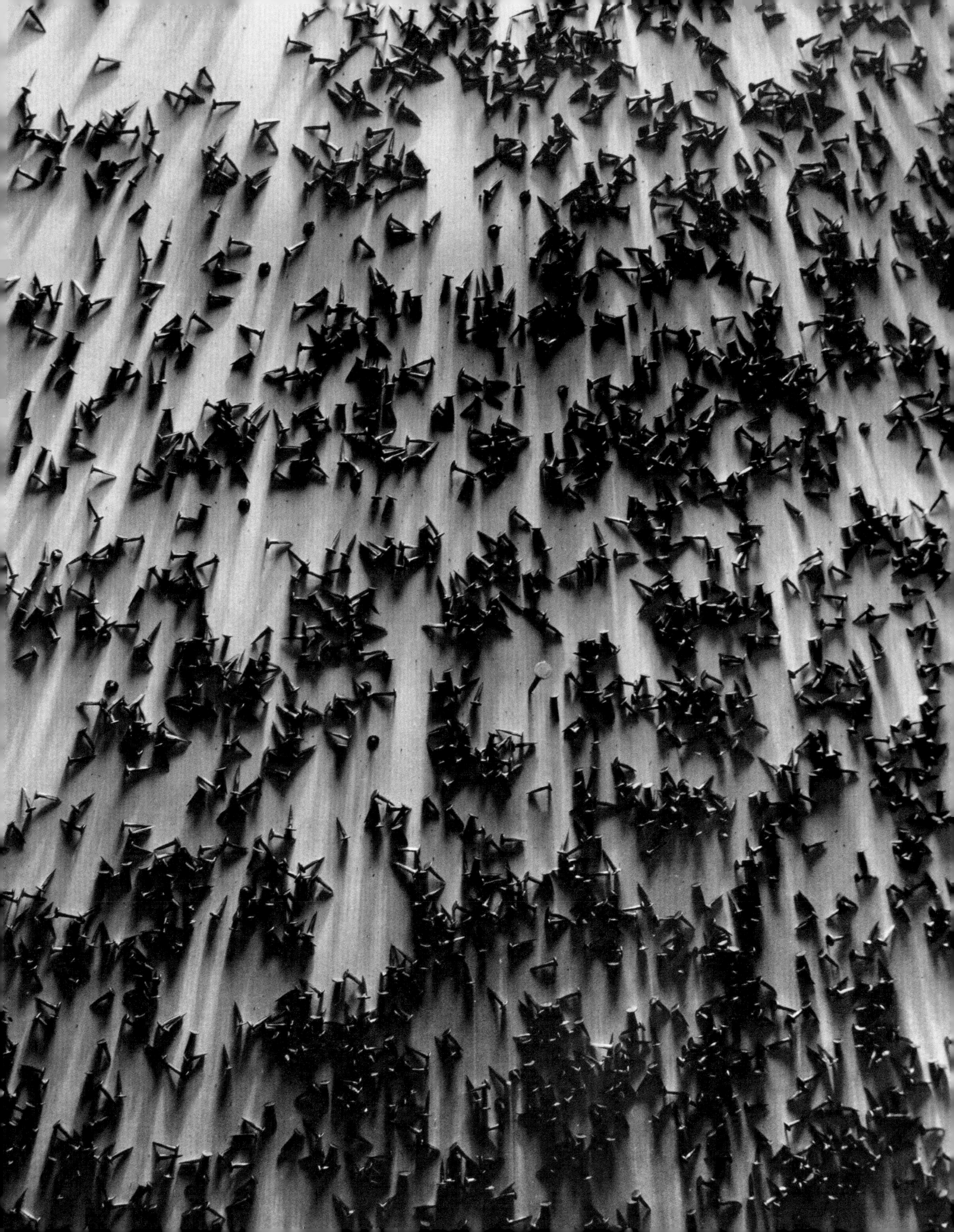

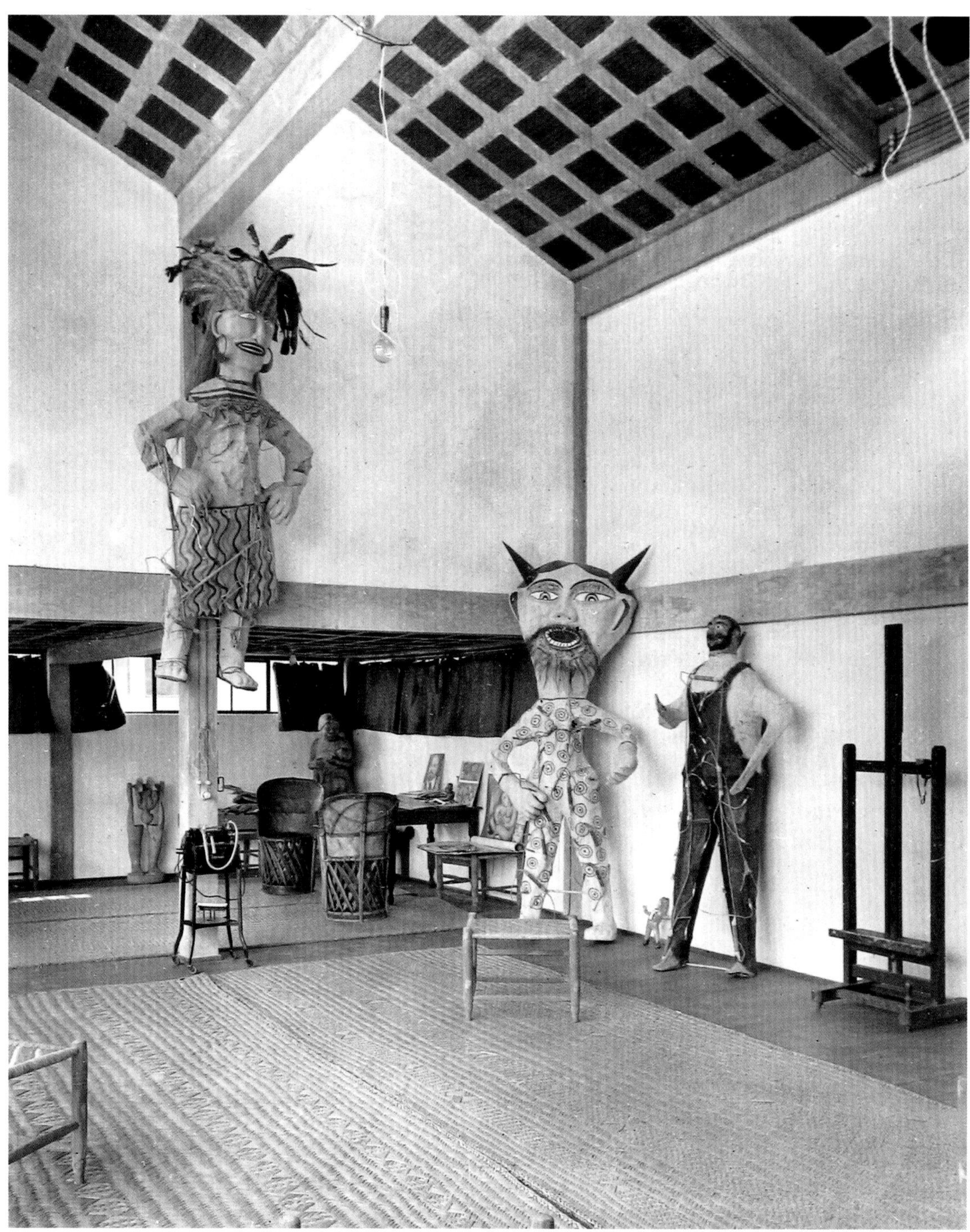

72

Martin Munkácsi (1896–1963)
Rivera's Studio, c. 1934.
Gelatin silver print, 30.48 x 24.13 cm.
Howard Greenberg Gallery,
New York

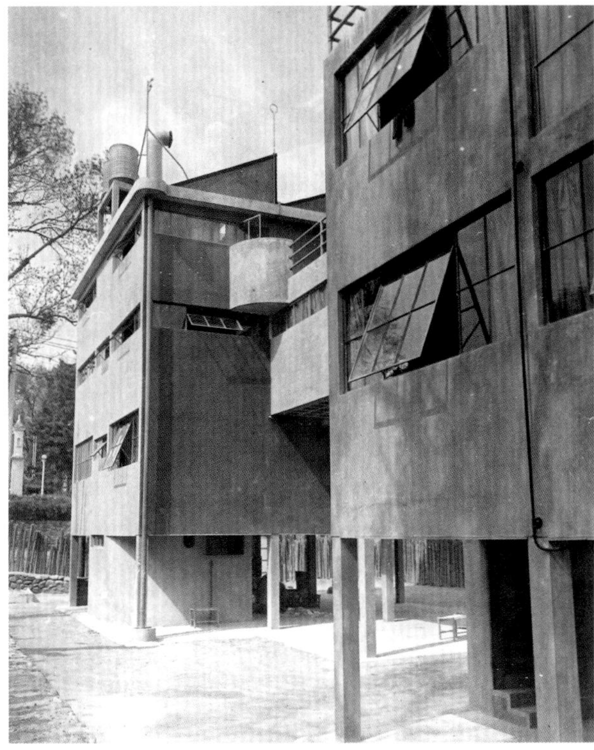

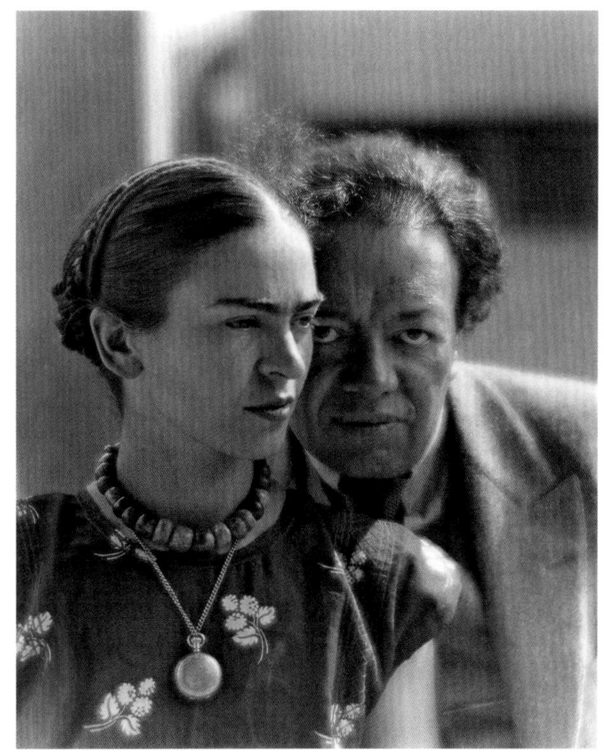

focused on the Day of the Dead. Eisenstein was so taken with Mexican contemporary art that he dedicated each section of his film to a prominent artist.[28]

On his return to Soviet Russia Eisenstein was deeply depressed at being thwarted on this project, and he vowed never to make another film. Although he did go back to film-making six years later, it was Mexico that had given him a new angle from which to view the world: to look to the future, to relive the past and to see that there was more than the dialectical process of class struggle.[29] Mexico's influence on his subsequent output is most apparent in *Ivan the Terrible* (1945), which reflects the fascination for religious ritual that he developed during his time there.

Fig. 50 Martin Munkácsi, **Frida Kahlo and Diego Rivera, Mexico**, 1933. Gelatin silver print, 30.5 x 22.5 cm. International Center of Photography, New York, 2009.6.47

In November 1933 the Hungarian photographer Martin Munkácsi visited the East and West coasts of the US before travelling on to Mexico early the following year. It is not entirely clear why he went to Mexico, but his employers, the German publishers Ullstein Verlag, actively encouraged him to join the exodus of Hungarians to Western Europe and the US, where he was to settle the following year. The final report of his trip to Mexico for Ullstein Verlag contained photographs of military uniforms, but these were never published.[30] In Mexico, Munkácsi visited the newly completed house

73

Martin Munkácsi (1896–1963)
Rivera's Studio, Mexico, *c.* 1934.
Gelatin silver print, 30.48 x 24.13 cm.
Howard Greenberg Gallery,
New York

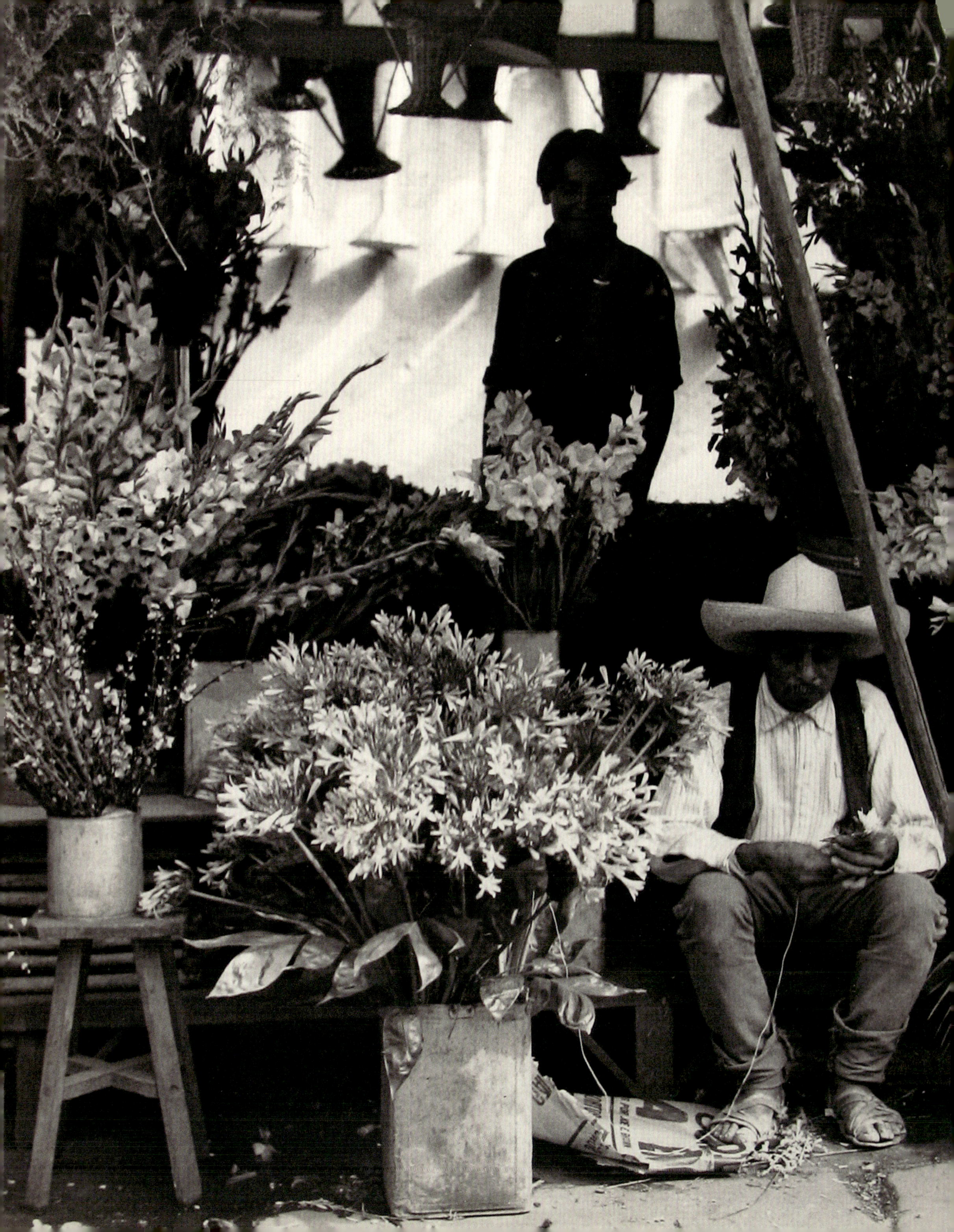

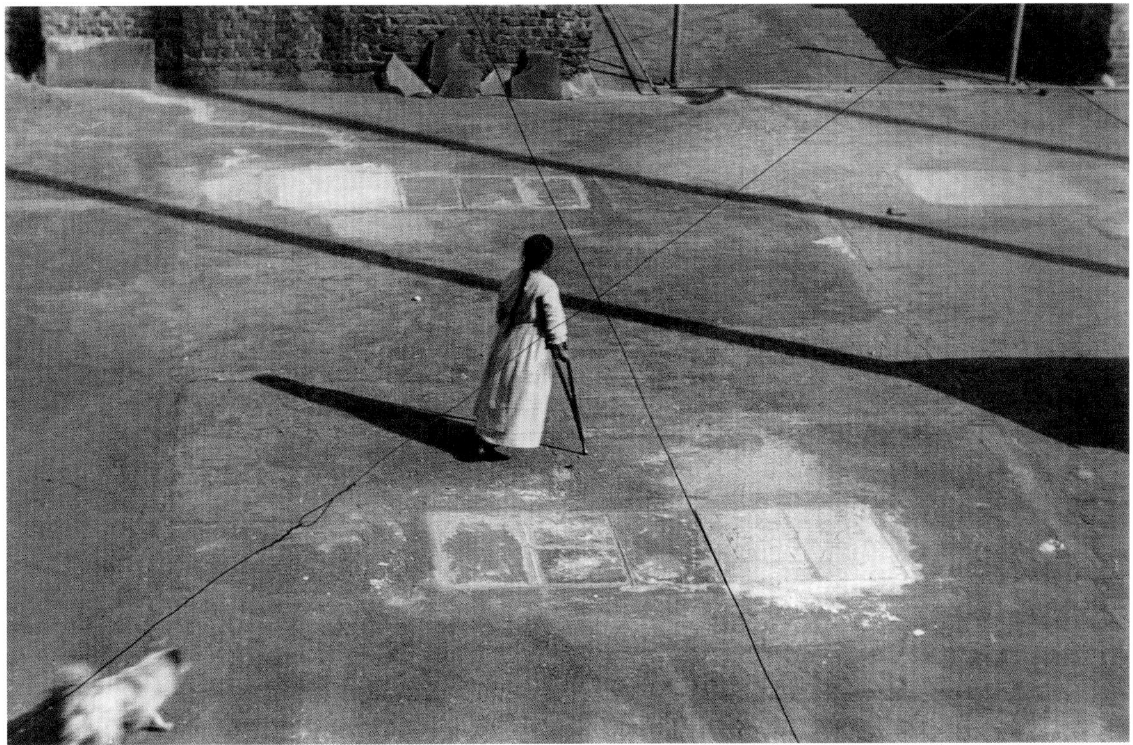

designed by Juan O'Gorman for Diego Rivera and Frida Kahlo in San Angel on the outskirts of Mexico City, into which they had just moved. He took a series of photographs of the building (cats 72–74), which boasted two separate, colour-coded dwellings with studios for each artist and an elevated walkway that communicated between the buildings. Whether he was on a special assignment or took these photographs for a speculative future article remains unclear. Munkácsi also took the most alluring double portrait of Mexico's best-known artistic couple (fig. 50).

The Spanish-speaking Afro-American poet Langston Hughes returned to Mexico in December 1934 following the death of his father, who had lived there and with whom Hughes had had a troubled relationship. During his time in Mexico, Hughes mingled with the artistic crowd and shared an apartment with Henri Cartier-Bresson. In an article published in Mexico about Cartier-Bresson's 1935 exhibition in Mexico City, discussed below, Hughes wrote: 'There is the clash of sun and shadow, like modern music, in a Cartier-Bresson picture' (cat. 75).[31]

74

Martin Munkácsi (1896–1963)
Mexico, *c.* 1927–34.
Gelatin silver print, 29.21 x 23.18 cm.
Howard Greenberg Gallery,
New York

75

Henri Cartier-Bresson (1908–2004)
Mexico, 1934.
Gelatin silver print, 23.2 x 34.6 cm.
Collection Fondation Henri
Cartier-Bresson, Paris

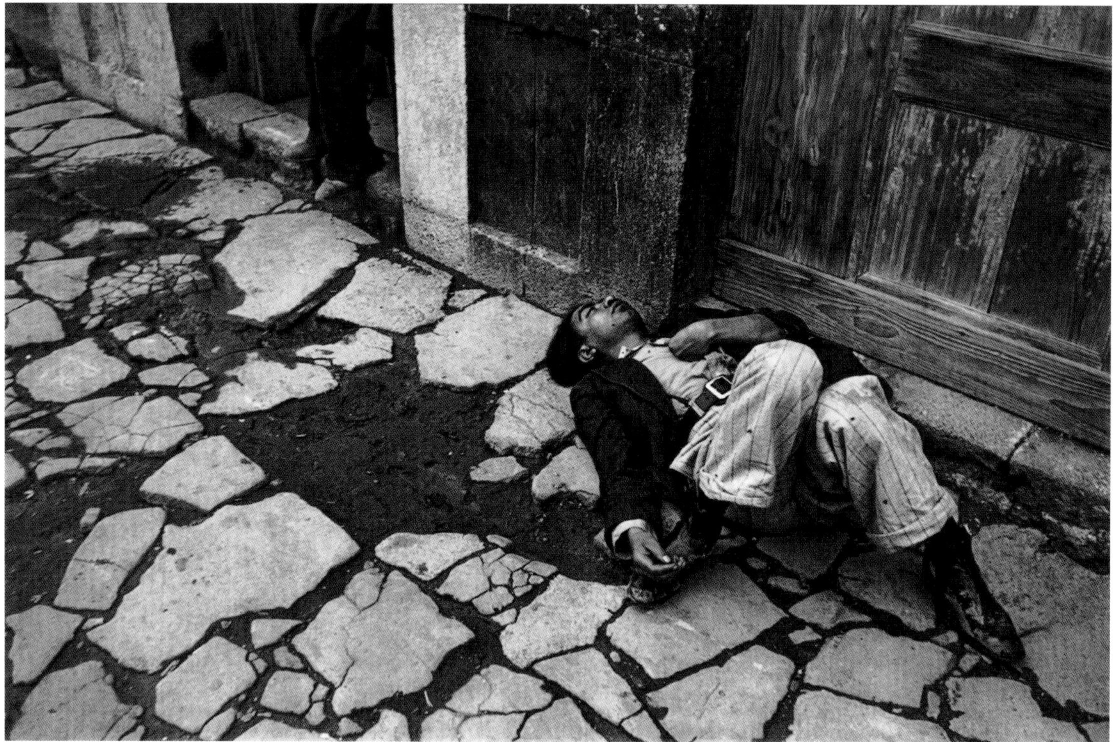

Cartier-Bresson was only 25 when he joined a scientific expedition led by Dr Julio Brandán, an Argentinian anthropologist, former diplomat and radical. Brandán's expedition had the ambitious objective of determining the route for a new Pan-American highway to link Mexico City with Buenos Aires, crossing Guatemala, El Salvador, Honduras, Nicaragua, Costa Rica, Panama, Colombia, Ecuador, Peru and Bolivia before reaching Argentina.[32]
A documentary film, set to regional music, was to be made in each country to highlight its natural beauty, local traditions and architectural and artistic riches, with the aim of presenting as complete a picture of daily life as possible. Furthermore, each country's economic situation and trade relations were to be assessed with the visionary idea of proposing an economic union of the three Americas (North, Central and South).[33] When those involved arrived in Mexico City on 14 July 1934, however, they soon discovered that no funds existed for the expedition, which was quickly abandoned (cats 76, 77).[34]

Despite this setback, Cartier-Bresson, who was quoted as saying how excited he was by what he called the most important opportunity of his life, decided to stay in Mexico. He wrote to his parents

76

Henri Cartier-Bresson
(1908–2004)
Mexico, 1934.
Vintage gelatin silver print,
16.7 x 24.7 cm. Collection Fondation
Henri Cartier-Bresson, Paris

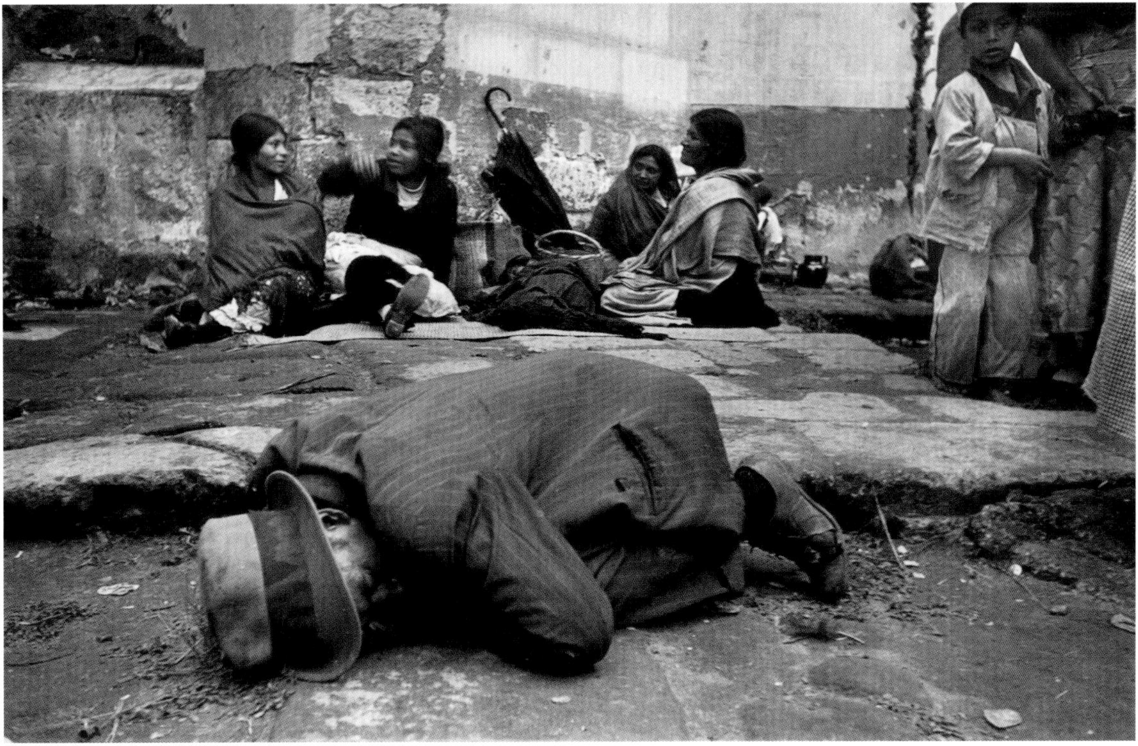

requesting permission for his younger sister Jacqueline to join him there, which she did in August. Cartier-Bresson took an apartment with Hughes, the young Zapotec writer Andrés Henestrosa and the Mexican artist Ignacio 'Nacho' Aguirre, who later posed for one of Cartier-Bresson's most famous photographs during this, his first visit (cat. 78). Cartier-Bresson was drawn to the seamy side of Mexican street life, with its slums, ruined buildings and the world of outcasts who lived near the La Lagunilla market, an area full of bars and brothels (cats 79, 80).[35] He also took photographs in Tehuantepec, where he travelled with Manuel Álvarez Bravo, who was making a film of the isthmus at the time. Thus Cartier-Bresson's work on his first visit to Mexico juxtaposed suffering and decline in the urban centre of Mexico City with the vitality of life in the southern idyll of Tehuantepec (cat. 81).[36] The Honduran writer Rafael Heliodoro Valle observed: 'Cartier-Bresson has a precise position in this modernising movement of the art of the camera, joining those who have placed themselves at the vanguard together: Weston, Modotti, Álvarez Bravo, Agustín Jiménez and all those who have made photography one of the plastic arts that conveys the message of our times.'[37]

77

Henri Cartier-Bresson (1908–2004)
Mexico, 1934.
Gelatin silver print, 27 x 34.2 cm. Collection Fondation Henri Cartier-Bresson, Paris

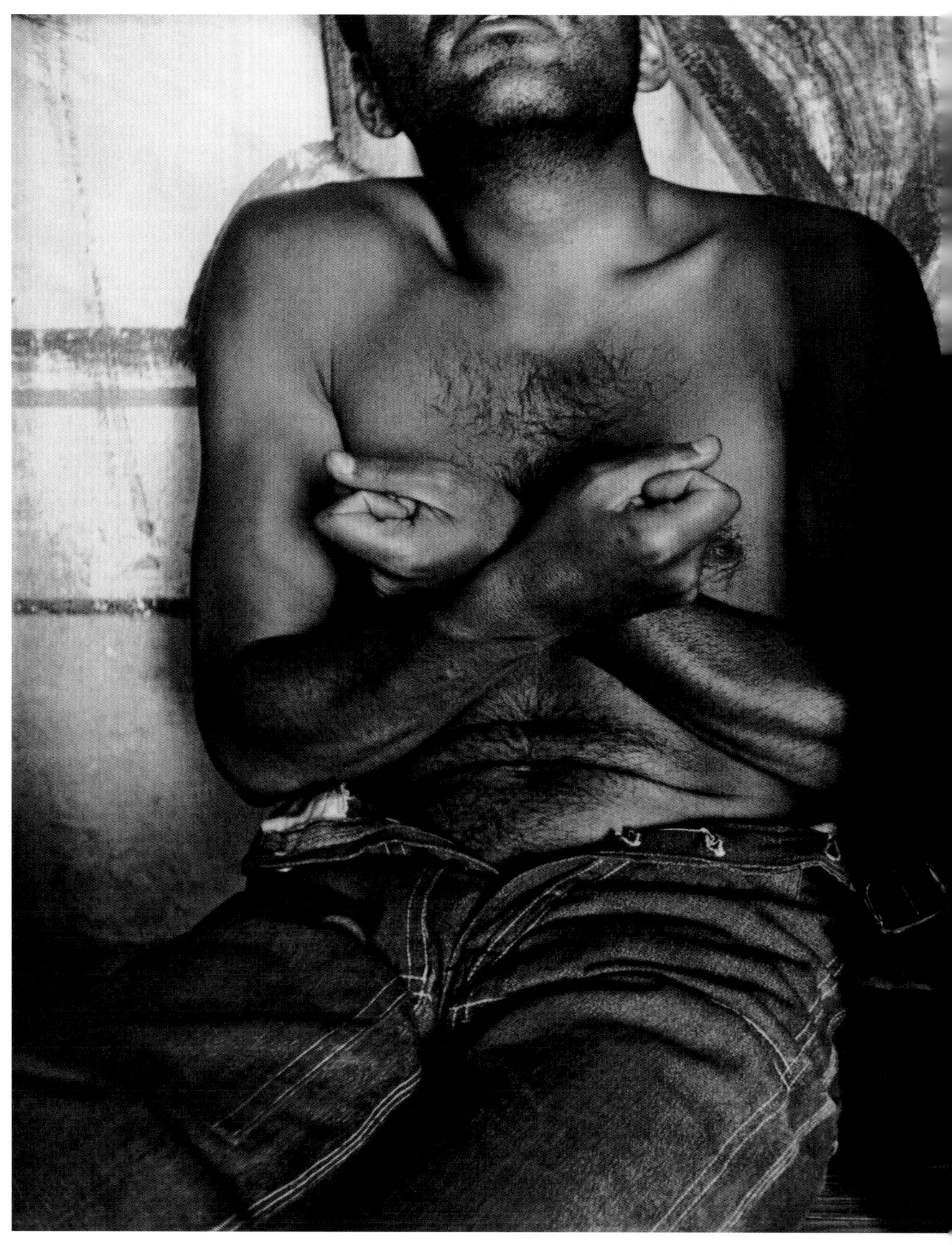

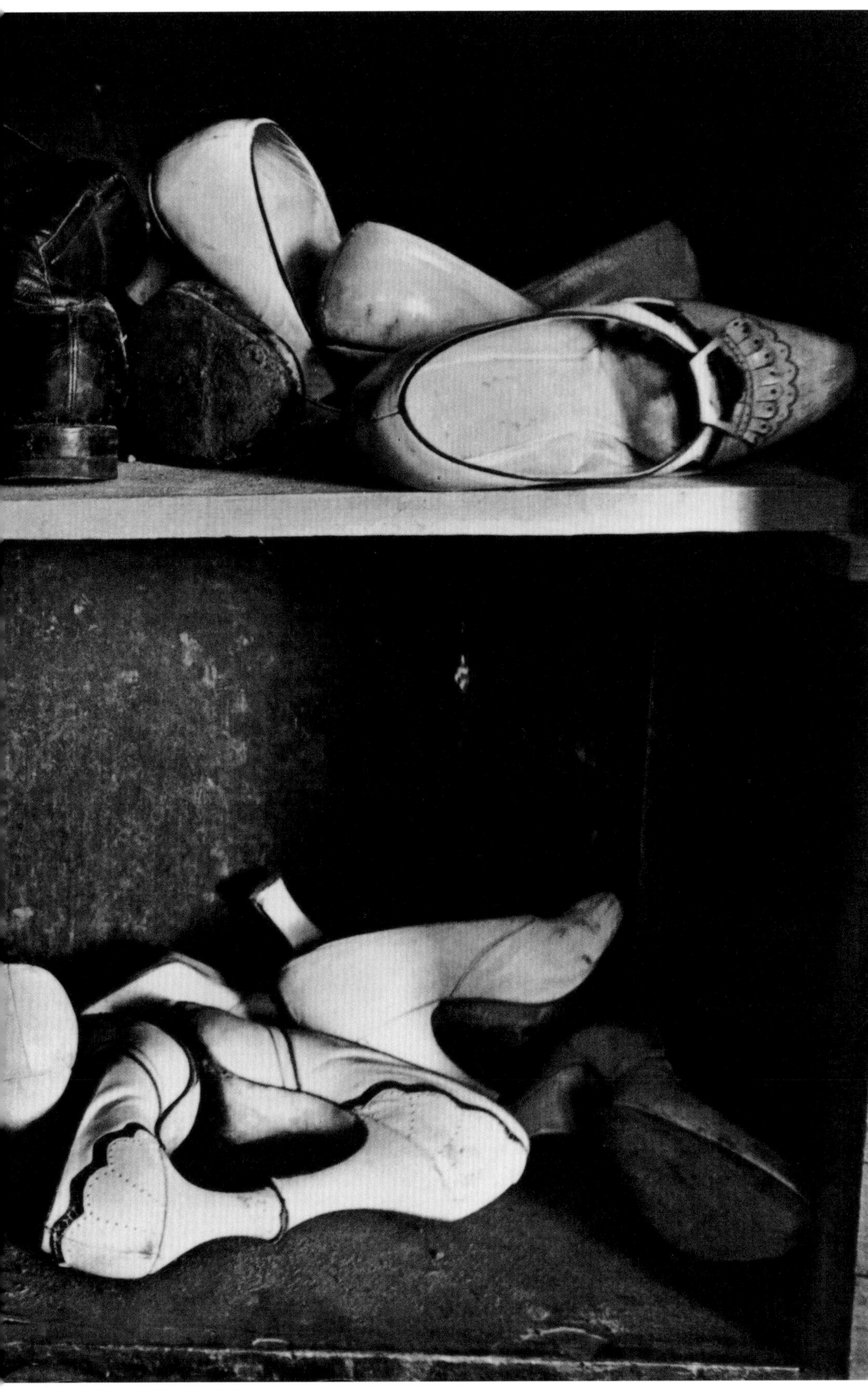

78

Henri Cartier-Bresson
(1908–2004)
Nacho Aguirre,
Santa Clara, Mexico, 1934.
Gelatin silver print,
8 x 12.4 cm. Collection Fondation
Henri Cartier-Bresson, Paris

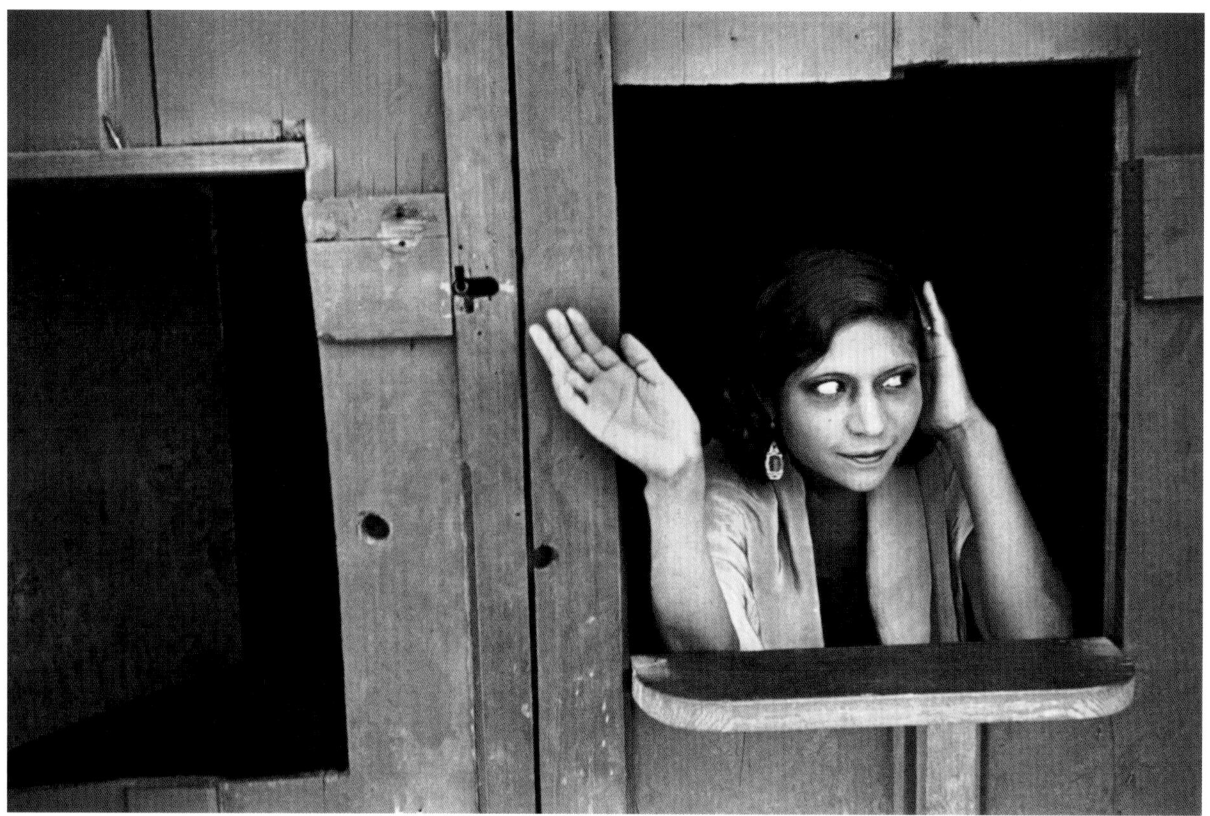

79

Henri Cartier-Bresson
(1908–2004)
Prostitute, Calle Cuauhtemoctzin, Mexico, 1934.
Gelatin silver print,
16.6 x 24.8 cm. Collection Fondation Henri Cartier-Bresson, Paris

80

Henri Cartier-Bresson
(1908–2004)
Prostitute, Calle Cuauhtemoctzin, Mexico, 1934.
Gelatin silver print,
12 x 8.1 cm. Collection Fondation Henri Cartier-Bresson, Paris

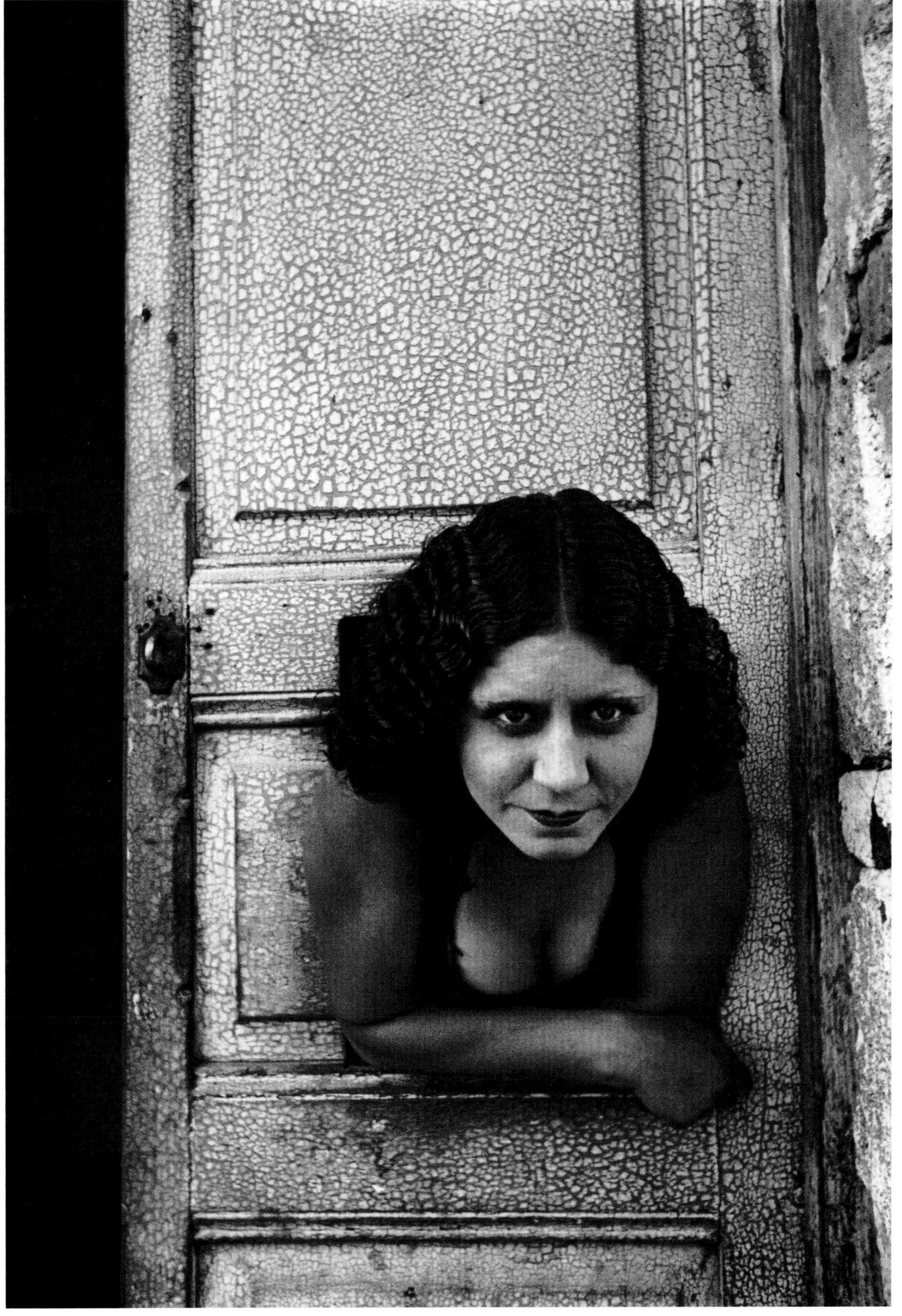

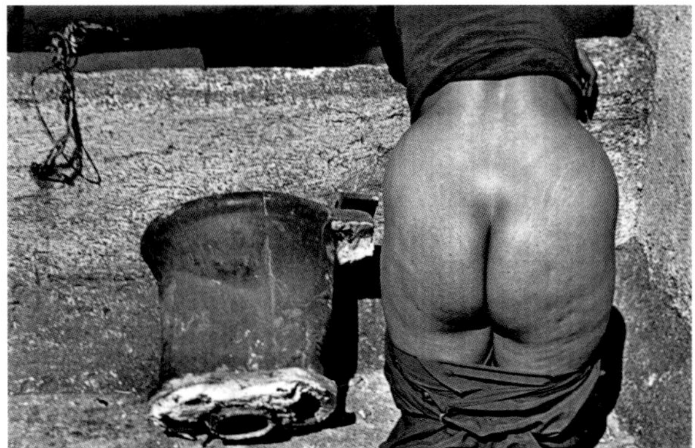

Fig. 51 Henri Cartier-Bresson, **Lupe Marín**, 1934. Gelatin silver print, 16.6 x 24.9 cm. Collection Fondation Henri Cartier-Bresson, Paris, HCB1934001W0064B//1

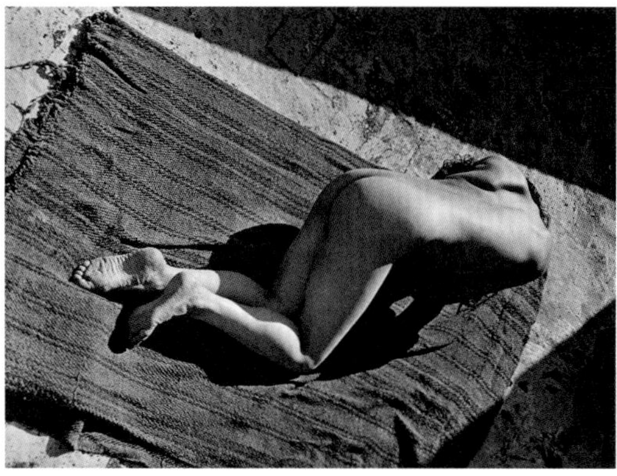

Fig. 52 Edward Weston, **Tina Modotti on the Azotea**, 1924. Gelatin silver print, 18.8 x 27.3 cm. Center for Creative Photography, University of Arizona, Tucson, 81.268.108

In 1935 Cartier-Bresson and Manuel Álvarez Bravo exhibited together in 'Exposición Fotografías: Cartier-Bresson/Álvarez Bravo' at the Palacio de Bellas Artes in Mexico City. Cartier-Bresson left for New York on 1 April, and the exhibition opened there as 'Anti-graphic Photographs' on 23 April at the Julien Levy Gallery, with the addition of work by the American photographer Walker Evans. Although Cartier-Bresson was interested in the life of the streets and the ordinary people, especially women and children, there are some posed photographs, such as that of Aguirre (cats 76–78), one or two landscapes and an extraordinarily daring and playful photograph of Lupe Marín, Rivera's second wife. Marín leans over a wall on the rooftop of an unknown building, exposing her naked buttocks (fig. 51). Next to her rests an uprooted and redundant lavatory bowl. The parallel between the two forms is striking, yet the viewer's gaze is held by the animate and inanimate, as if Cartier-Bresson were mischievously poking fun at Weston's series of Mexican photographs that aestheticised a lavatory bowl (cat. 37) and a sink, as well as his notion of the rooftop terrace, the *azotea*, where he took photographs of the nude Tina Modotti (fig. 52).[38] Cartier-Bresson was not to return to Mexico until 1964, but his fascination with the ordinary, like that of Manuel Álvarez Bravo, helped to create a sense of Mexico as an extraordinary country. These were not consciously Surrealist images, but rather scenes of daily life, commonplace in streets and markets, that encapsulated the essence and endless attraction of Mexico, and which, above all, appealed to the imagination of these young photographers. Captivated by Mexico, Cartier-Bresson wrote: 'Think of the sun of this land, of the curves of the mountains that are so strong, of horizons that stretch further than infinity and the lives of men that count for so little; it is not a curiosity to be visited but a life to be lived.'[39]

Not everyone, however, was so enchanted with Mexico. Settling in Hamburg in July 1933, having left Mexico three months earlier, the

81

Henri Cartier-Bresson (1908–2004)
Mexico, 1934.
Vintage gelatin silver print, 16.7 x 24.9 cm.
Collection Fondation Henri Cartier-Bresson, Paris

American Modernist painter Marsden Hartley wrote to his dealer Edith Halpert in New York: 'As for any glow I may have given Mexico when I last wrote you it has all to be taken back, for a year there was most disastrous to my well-being mentally and physically – and I am only just recovering from its effects here.'[40] Several years later he described Mexico in his autobiography as 'a place that devitalised my energies – the one place I shall always think of as wrong for me'.[41]

These negative reflections on his twelve-month stay in Mexico overshadow the positive feelings he expressed while resident there. Nor do they sit comfortably with the wide-ranging and ambitious body of work that he produced in Mexico, in which he adopted a much bolder and brighter palate to capture the intensity of the light and the landscape that bewitched him in his powerful, symbolic paintings (cat. 82). In part, this contrast can be attributed to ill health – he suffered because of the altitude of Mexico City, moving to Cuernavaca, where he became seriously ill with dysentery, before eventually returning to the capital – and depression brought about by the weather he experienced in Cuernavaca: 'The incessant rain the past months has done nearly everyone in because without sun Mexico is one colossal gloom – for everything gets water soaked – the walls of one's room the floor the bedding even all damp and clammy cold.'[42] Hartley was also broke. He had hoped, like his compatriot the painter Doris Rosenthal, also on a 1931 Guggenheim Fellowship in Mexico, to extend his grant for a further twelve months, which he planned to spend in Germany. Hartley complained in a letter to Halpert: 'If I don't get 2nd year I shall be penniless absolutely', adding '[for] the first time in my life a show has failed but of course no one can be blamed'.[43] Although the 'Exposición Marsden Hartley' at the Galería de la Escuela Central de Artes Plásticas

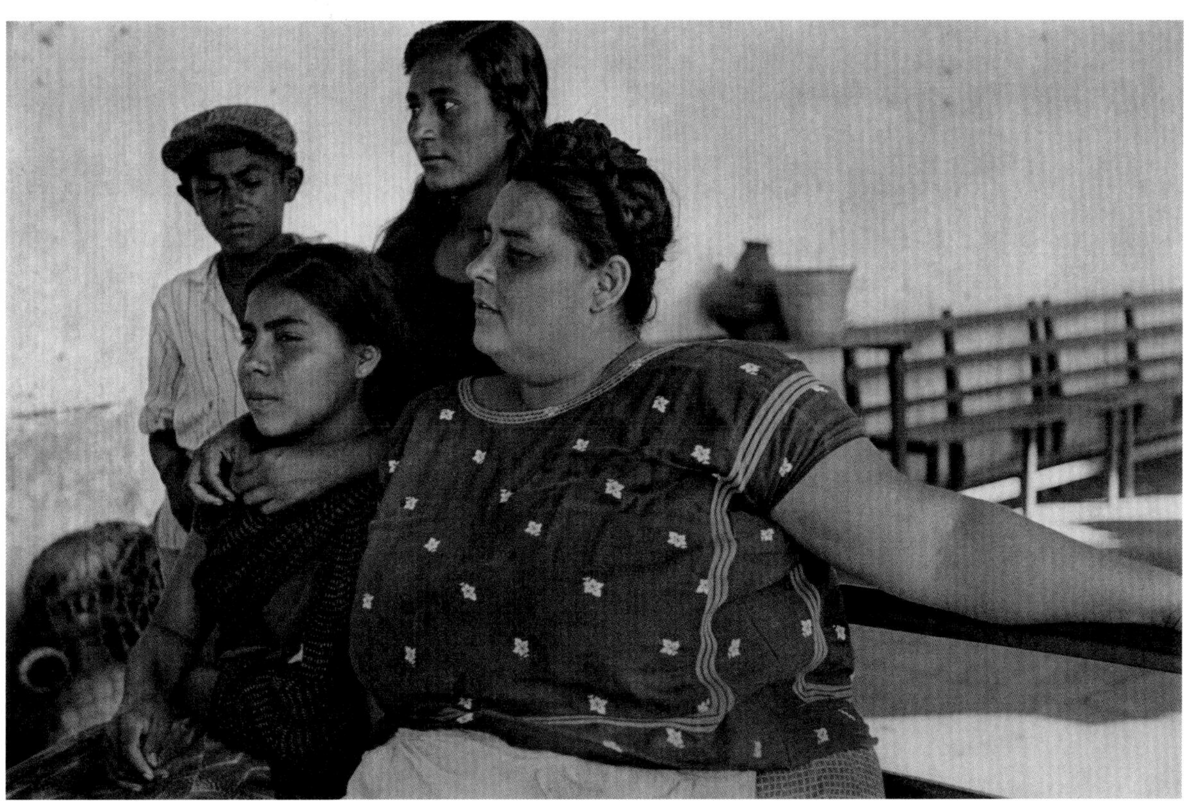

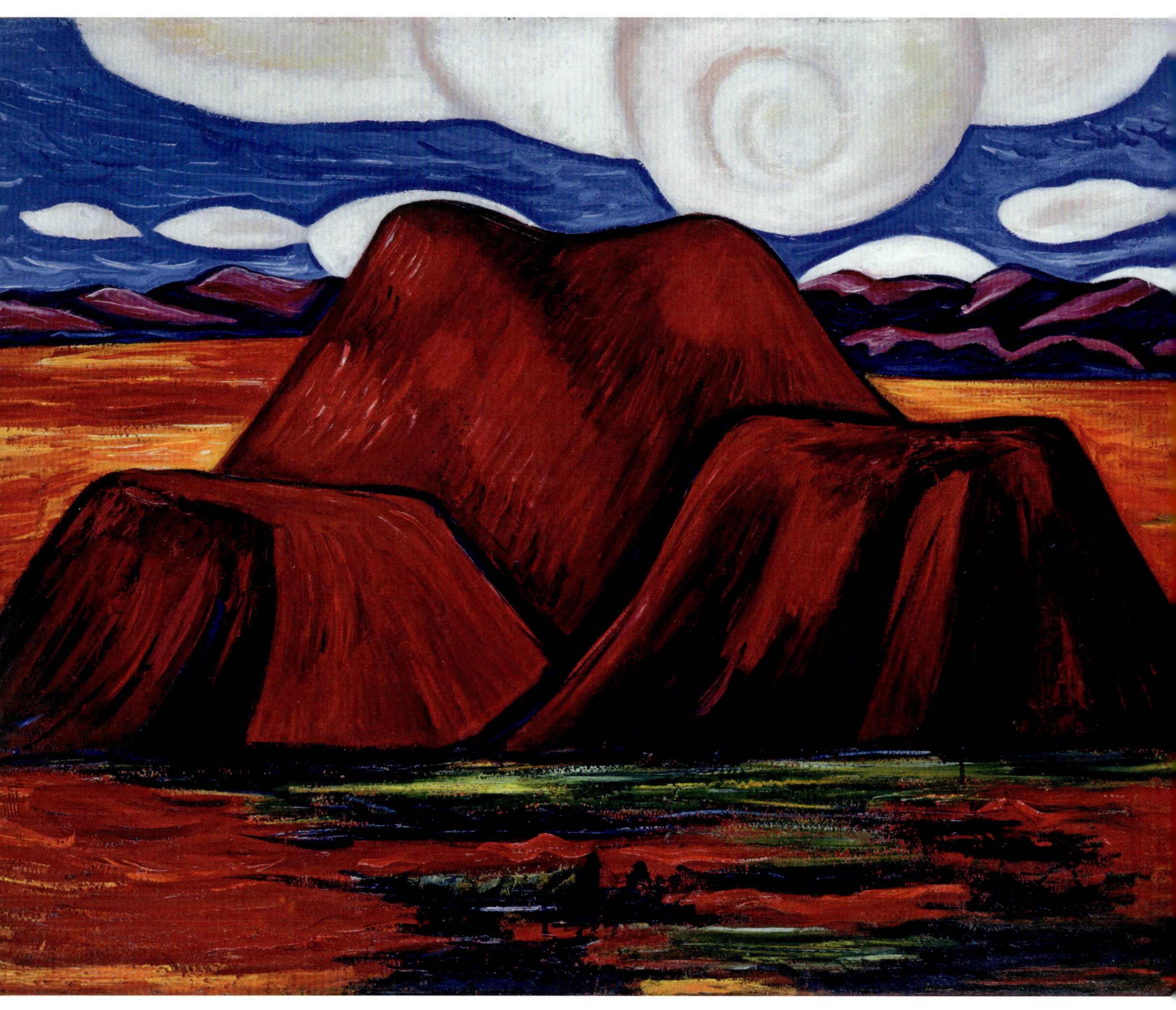

82

Marsden Hartley (1877–1943),
Earth Warming, 1932.
Oil on paperboard,
64.14 x 83.82 cm.
Montgomery Museum of Fine Arts,
Alabama, The Blount Collection

in Mexico City was a critical success, Hartley failed to sell any of its twenty paintings.[44] To cap it all, neither did he much care for Mexican food: 'If I hadn't found this German rancho-pension I couldn't have stayed at all for the food here is simply paralysing to one not born to it.'[45]

Undoubtedly, however, the biggest factor influencing his views on Mexico was the suicide of his 'devoted friend', the American poet Hart Crane, in April 1932. Hartley, who had renewed his friendship with Crane on arrival in Mexico City, having met him years before in France, was devastated by his death. The heavy-drinking Crane had been awarded a Guggenheim Fellowship in 1931 and was encouraged to travel to Mexico in part by his friend and fellow writer Malcolm Cowley, who spoke passionately about the country's landscapes and fused cultures as well as its apparently relaxed attitudes to homosexuality; he led Crane to believe that the 'sexual customs of the Aztecs were much like those of the Arabs'.[46] Crane initially stayed in Mexico City with Katherine Anne Porter, with whom he had an incendiary relationship, and who was likewise in Mexico on a Guggenheim Fellowship. Like many, he was also attracted by the generous financial support offered by the fellowship. Six months after Crane's suicide, Hartley began work on a heavily symbolic painting entitled *Eight Bells Folly, Memorial for Hart Crane* (fig. 53). 'Some of us here', he wrote, 'think we are right when we say that Mexico was too terrific and stimulating for him. It is a breath-taking country and literally takes the breath and demands new apparatus and new energy here.'[47]

During his first two months in Mexico, Hartley spent a great deal of time in the Museo Nacional in Mexico City and also visited the pre-Columbian ruins of Xochicalco and Teotihuacan, where like Lawrence before him he was profoundly moved by the Temple of Quetzalcoatl.[48] Inspired by the heady combination of the Mexican landscape – 'the most amazing light eye has ever encountered' – and the rich and abundant pre-Columbian cultures, Hartley immersed himself in the European mystical texts of Paracelsus, Jakob Böhme and Richard Rolle from the library of local residents Mary and Eric Ostlund, reading them in the garden of his *pension*, the Casa Alemán.[49] These writings provided Hartley with a mechanism with which to approach his painting in Mexico. He was determined to capture the landscape's spiritual energy and timelessness, so that a painting was not simply a likeness of a view but imbued with the power and mysticism that he associated with it. He wanted his paintings to transcend the confines of the canvas and provoke

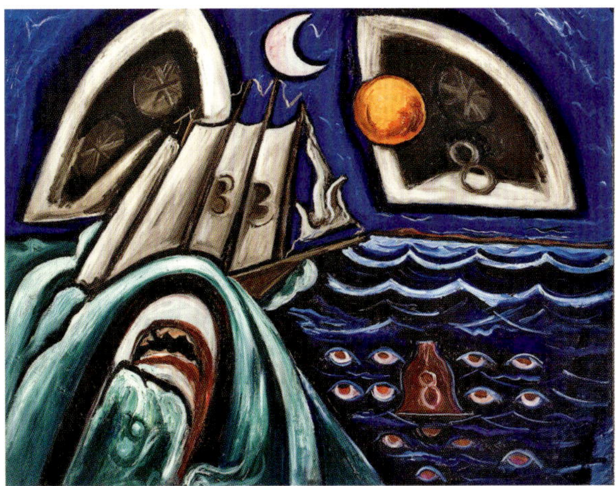

Fig. 53 Marsden Hartley, **Eight Bells Folly, Memorial for Hart Crane**, 1933. Oil on canvas, 77.8 x 100 cm. Frederick R. Weisman Art Museum, University of Minnesota, Minneapolis, 1961.4

a deep, visceral response in the viewer. Of the twenty paintings he exhibited in Mexico City, the 'Eight Panels for an Arcane Library' rank among his finest works, reflecting the profound spiritual connection that Hartley felt with Mexico.[50] Included in this group were two views of 'the majestic rise of Popocatepetl – always in snow – and certainly one of the handsomest volcanoes of the world – such an almost flawless triangle' that Hartley painted from his studio window in Cuernavaca (cat. 83, fig. 54).[51]

The intensity with which Hartley approached his work and the energy that it took to capture both the psychological power and the likeness of each landscape left him drained physically and mentally. As he acknowledged, Mexico provided him with the opportunity to engage with his subject-matter in a very different way, in tandem with his study of the teachings of the European mystics. Despite the scale of the challenge, he achieved what he had set out to do a year earlier: 'Mexico has done a lot of things to me that make me different and ... it has been good for me to have come – that is to say mentally and spiritually it has been excellent for me to have come for I have accomplished certain things which I have wished to do for years.'[52]

Another artist associated primarily with landscape is Gerardo Murillo, who became known as 'Dr Atl' (cat. 84). For Dr Atl, a vulcanologist by training, the landscape of the Valley of Mexico, peppered with the distinctive forms of extinct volcanoes and the dominant presence of the living, snow-capped Popocatepetl and Iztaccihuatl, dominated his work. Dr Atl built on the tradition of the nineteenth-century landscape painter José María Velasco (fig. 55), whose panoramic views of the Valley of Mexico were powerful statements

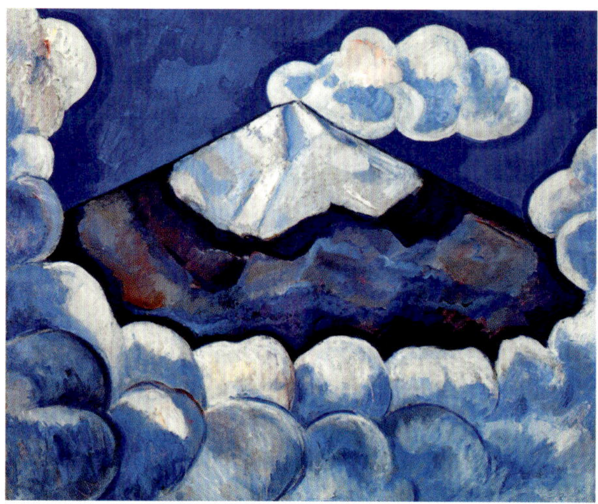

Fig. 54 Marsden Hartley, **Popocatepetl, Spirited Morning – Mexico**, 1932. Oil on board, 63.5 x 73.7 cm. Smithsonian American Art Museum, Washington, DC, 2004.30.3

of national identity celebrating independence, complete with subtle references to the glorious Mexica past and such innovations of the present as the introduction of the railways. Dr Atl's paintings are born out of the landscape; Popocatepetl and Iztaccihuatl appear both as guardians over the Valley of Mexico, witnesses of change from pre-Columbian through colonial to independent rule, and as permanent symbols of Mexico.

Like many others, the American photographer and film-maker Paul Strand, who had been turned down for a Guggenheim Fellowship, was encouraged to travel to Mexico by the Mexican composer Carlos Chávez, whom he met first in New York and then again in Taos, New Mexico, in 1931. Strand, already a well-known and respected photographer, was evidently encouraged by his friend Chávez to see Mexico as a welcome escape from the US, a society he was finding increasingly restrictive in cultural

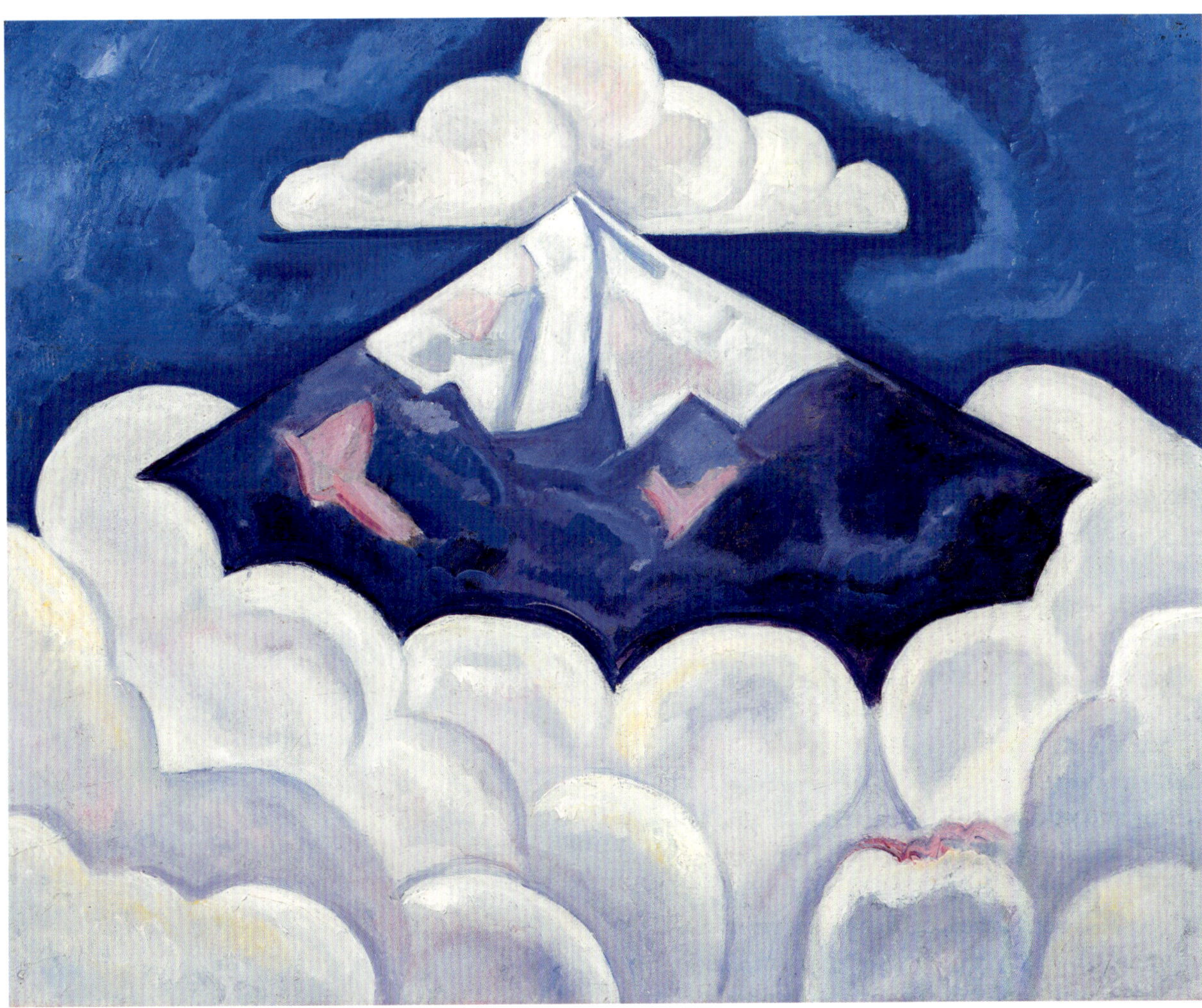

and political terms.[53] Strand drove down to Mexico in a Model A Ford in November 1932, reaching Mexico City in January 1933. He was to stay for two years (cats 86, 87).

Under Chávez's patronage, Strand mounted an exhibition at the Sala de Arte in Mexico City in early February 1933 with 54 prints that he had brought from the US, before setting off to fulfil his commission to take photographs for the Ministry of Public Education as part of an educational campaign. Accompanied by a guide and translator, Strand used an attachment on his camera that enabled him to take photographs of people unawares.[54] Although, like Manuel Álvarez Bravo and Cartier-Bresson, he was drawn to the ordinary people of Mexico, his work was much more about the individual than street

83

Marsden Hartley (1877–1943)
Popocatepetl, One Morning, 1932.
Oil on masonite, 60.3 x 72.8 cm.
Sheldon Museum of Art,
University of Nebraska, Lincoln,
UNL–Howard S. Wilson Memorial

scenes or the unusual. He was deeply depressed about the failure of his marriage to Rebecca Salsbury, who had accompanied him to Mexico but subsequently returned to the US, and his eye was, perhaps subconsciously, drawn to individuals looking tired or melancholy (cats 88–91). He composed beautiful photographs of buildings, often in an ethereal light, as well as a series of images of polychrome baroque processional sculptures (cats 85–87). In these, the stoic suffering of Christ appears to mirror his own turbulent state of mind, as he draws upon the significance of these representations for ordinary people as a means to alleviate their sorrow. In 1940 Strand selected twenty images from his time in Mexico and published them as a portfolio; his loneliness and unhappiness are evident.[55]

Strand avoided taking photographs of urban life, technology, industry or the extremes of wealth or poverty. By the summer of 1933, he had moved into film-making. Chávez had secured him official employment as a primary schoolteacher, which paid him a modest salary and, importantly, allowed him to stay and work in Mexico (cats 88, 89). Inspired by a visit to Alvarado, a fishing village in Vera Cruz, in late October 1933, Strand wrote a story about the exploitation of the local fishermen with a view to a film. Originally intended to be part of a series of educational documentaries financed by the Ministry

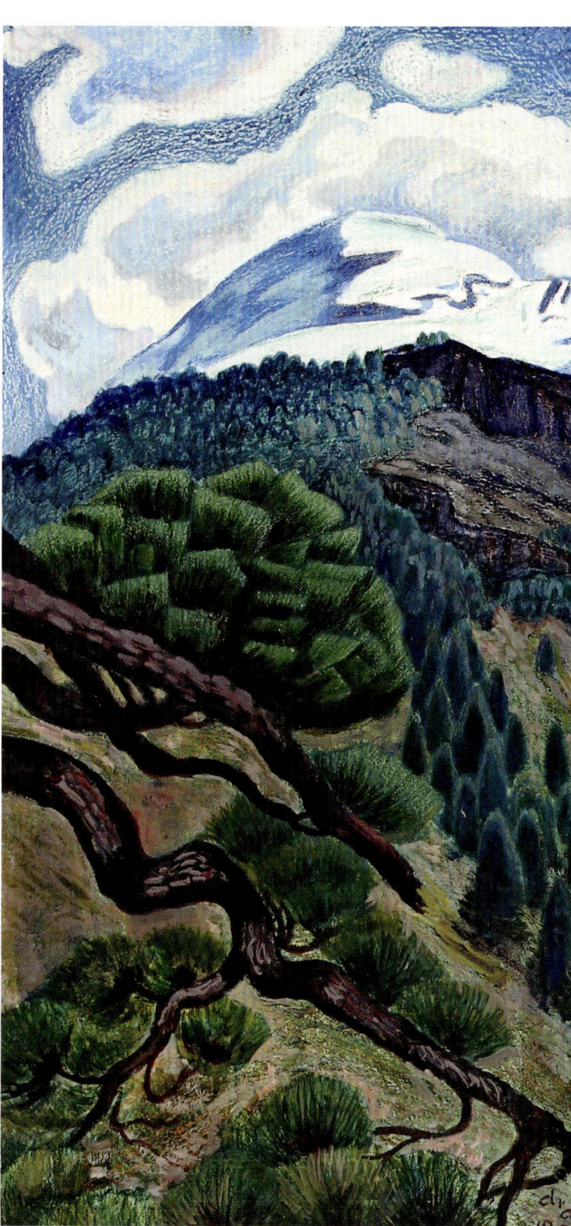

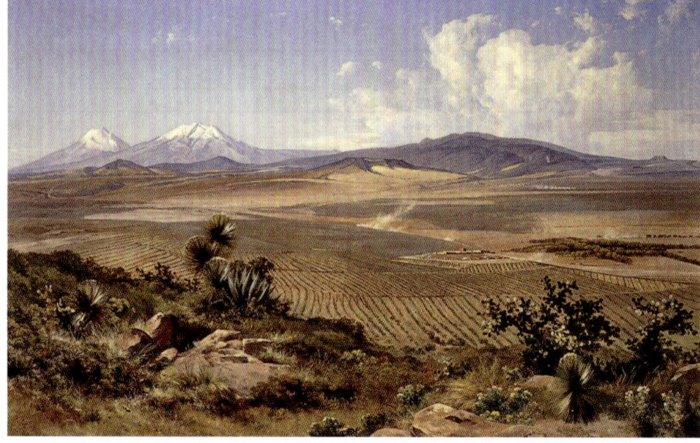

Fig. 55 José María Velasco, **Hacienda of Chimalpa**, 1893. Oil on canvas, 105 x 160 cm. Museo Nacional de Arte (MUNAL) – INBA, Mexico City

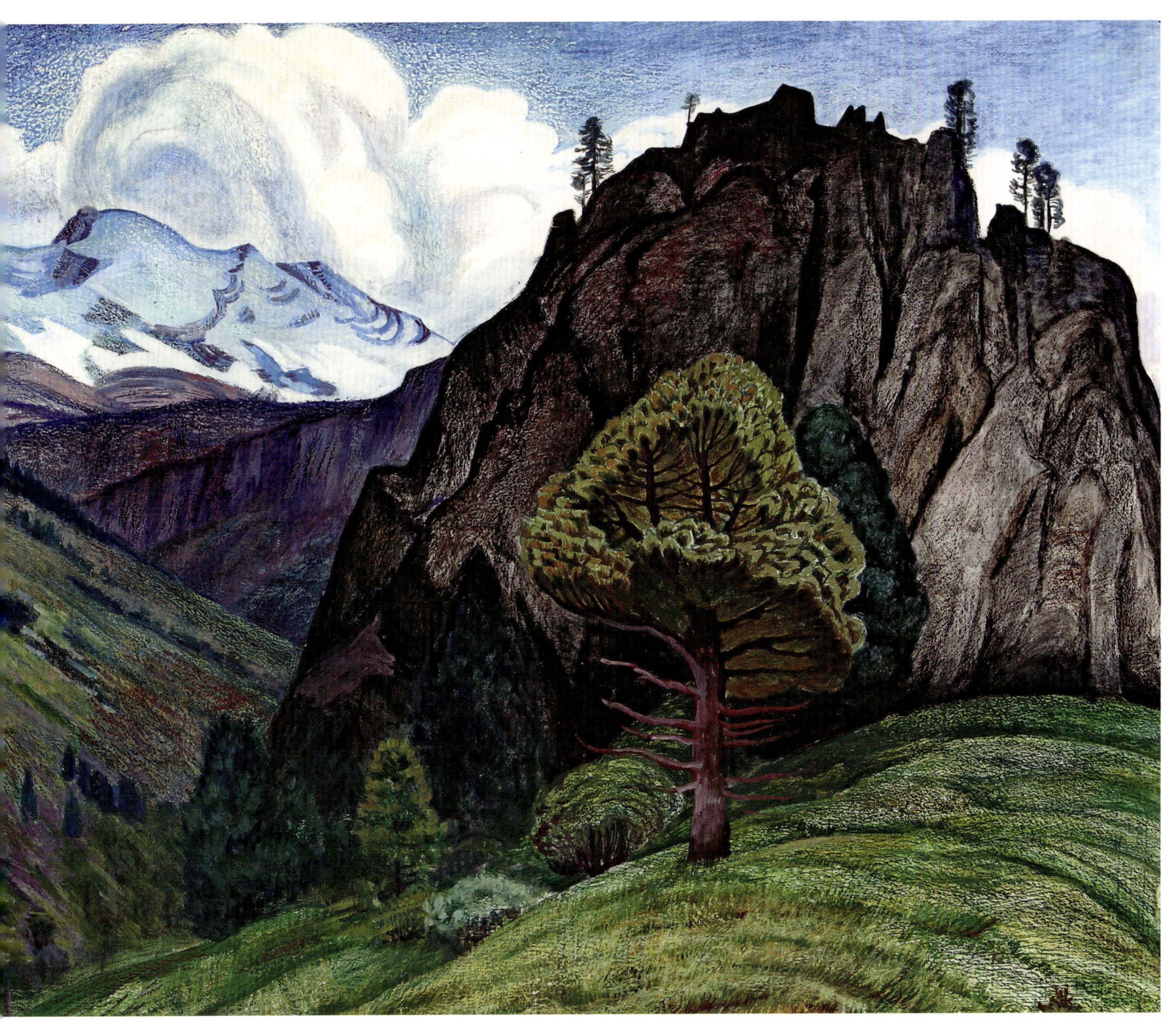

84

Dr Atl (Gerardo Murillo)
(1875–1964)
Landscape with Iztaccihuatl
(Paisaje con Iztaccihuatl), 1932.
Mixed media on wood,
88 x 154 cm.
Colección Andrés Blaisten

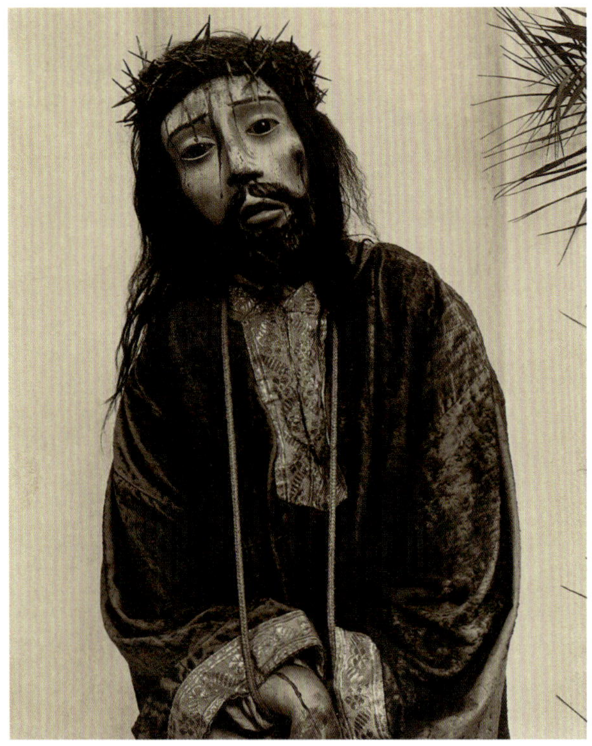

of Public Education, the project presented Strand with an opportunity to express his left-wing political beliefs. Although it occupied him for twelve months, the film was not without its problems, not least the fact that the Mexican government's decision to commission an American to make a documentary about their country was controversial. The budget ran out in October 1934 and Strand's patron Chávez resigned from the Ministry of Public Education; his successor was the writer and intellectual Antonio Castro Leal. The ministry assumed control of the post-production of the film and the musical score was taken away from Chávez and given to the young *avant-garde* composer Silvestre Revueltas.[56] Initially called 'Pescados', the film was eventually released in 1936 as *Redes*.[57] Strand's productive time in Mexico had come to an end, and he left Mexico in dispute over the film; he was not to return until thirty years later, in 1966 (cats 85, 88, 90).

Redes is a powerful, overtly political film. A group of impoverished and hard-working fishermen from a small village are forced to sell their catch to a wealthy capitalist. There is no other work in the region and the capitalist runs a monopoly, gradually paying less and less for each catch. As he increases his profit margins, the fishermen, already wearing torn clothing, are driven further into poverty. Behind the scenes the local authorities collaborate with the capitalist to preserve the *status quo*. Desperate, the fishermen strike as a collective for a better price for their catch, although some from another community refuse to go on strike and continue to sell their fish. At an opportune moment the fishermen's leader is assassinated to break the strike. The message of the film is brutally stark: despite the Revolution, the working class continue to be exploited, while those who abuse them remain above the law. The film, which challenged the government instead of celebrating its achievements, was very controversial. Strand's influence can be seen in the bold composition of many of the scenes and the unambiguous simplicity of the plot, in which the disenfranchised and exploited poor confront the privileged and protected rich. *Redes* remains as powerful and tragic as it must have seemed when it was first released. Ultimately Strand 'sought during his sojourn in Mexico to create a visual record of the

85

Paul Strand (1890–1976)
Cristo with Thorns, Huexotla, Mexico, 1933.
Platinum print,
24.8 x 19.2 cm. The J. Paul Getty Museum, Los Angeles

86

Paul Strand (1890–1976)
Church, Mexico, 1932–33.
Platinum print,
11.7 x 14.8 cm. The J. Paul Getty Museum, Los Angeles

87

Paul Strand (1890–1976)
Village, Tlaxcala, Mexico, 1933.
Platinum print,
11.4 x 14.6 cm. The J. Paul Getty Museum, Los Angeles

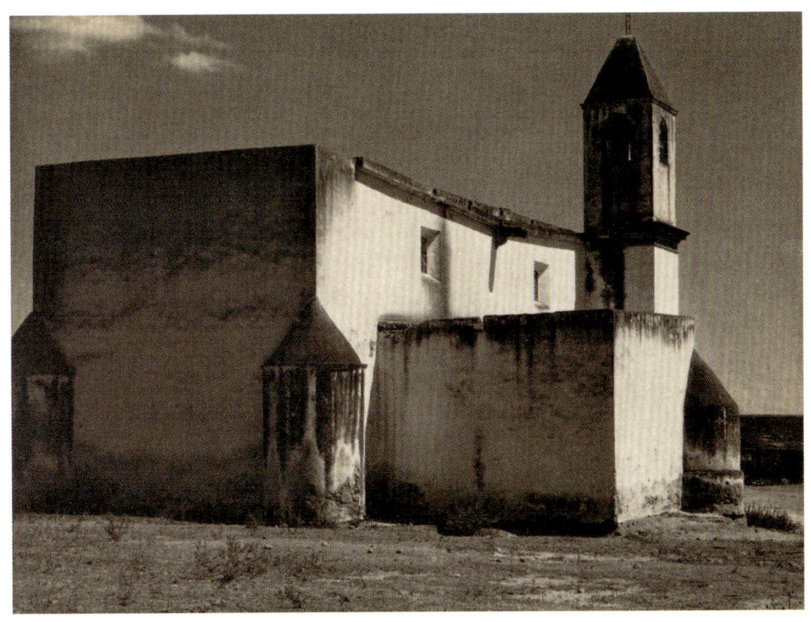

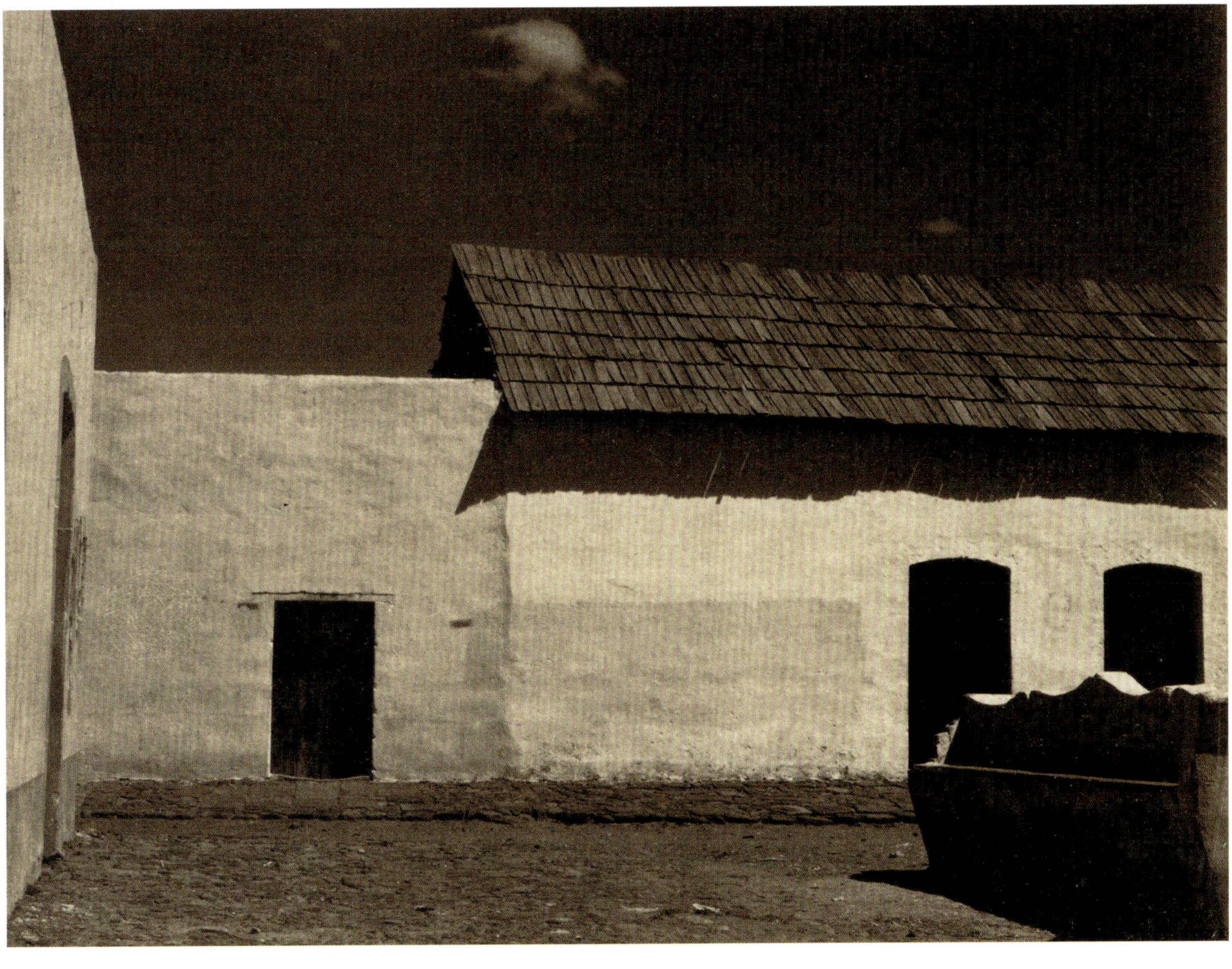

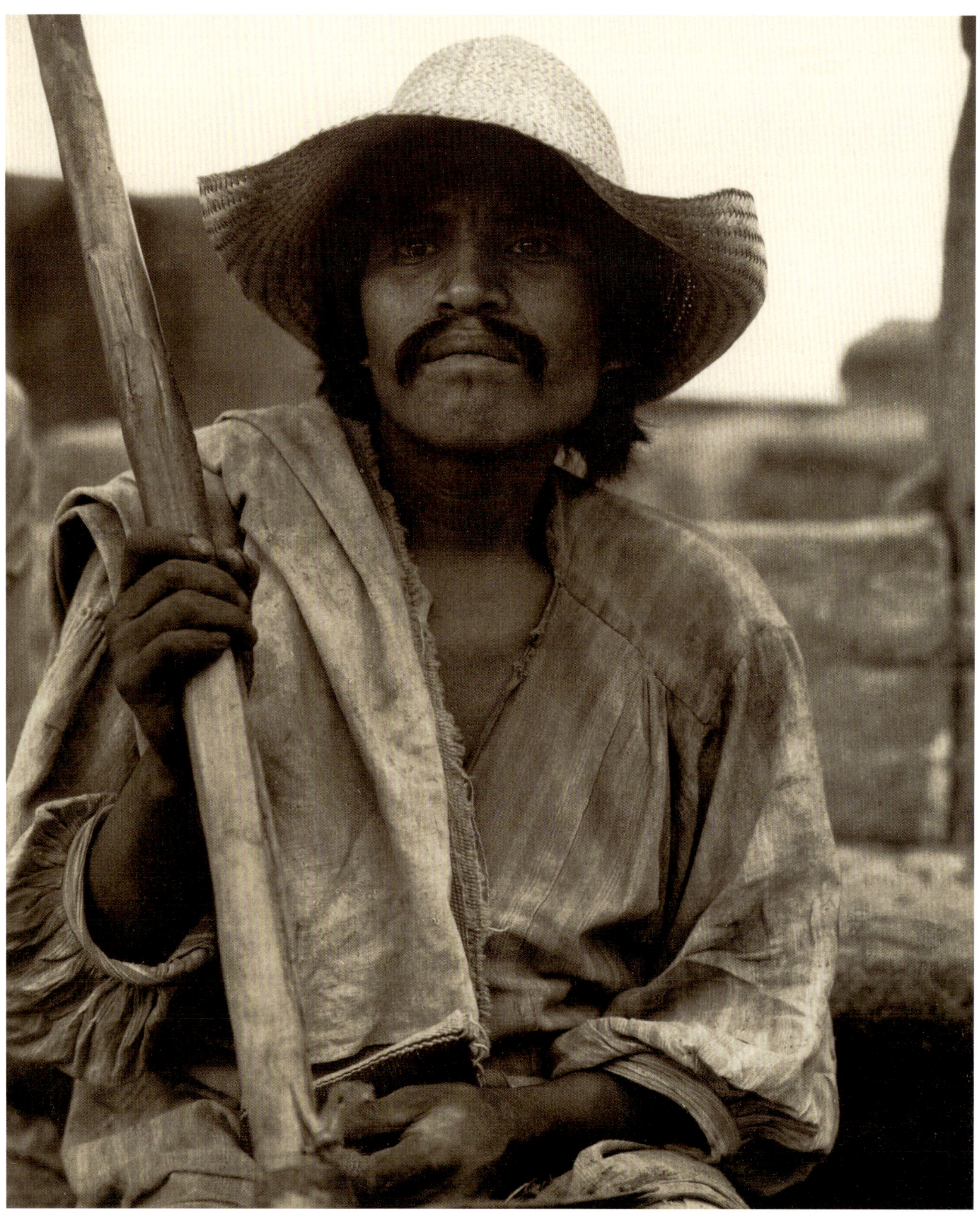

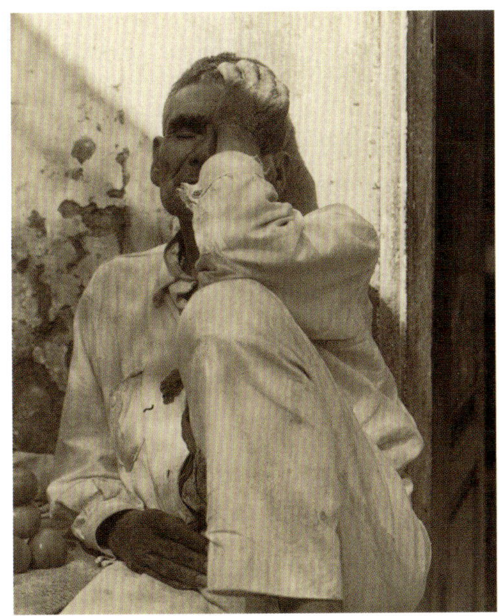

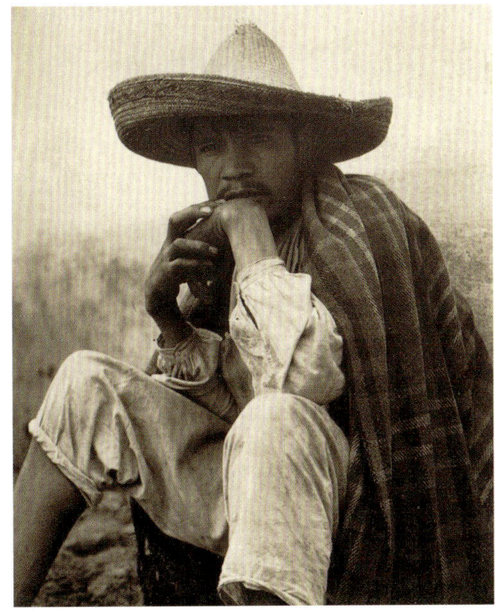

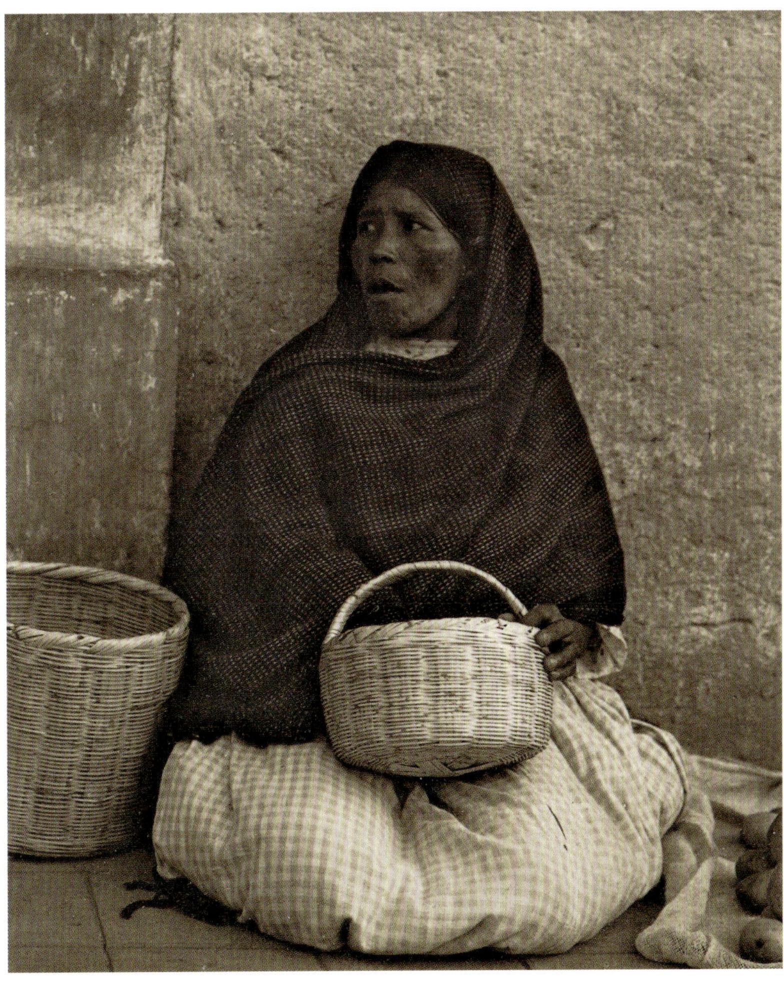

88

Paul Strand (1890–1976)
Man with a Hoe,
Los Remedios, Mexico, 1933.
Platinum print, 14.8 x 11.7 cm.
The J. Paul Getty Museum,
Los Angeles

89

Paul Strand (1890–1976)
Seated Man, Uruapan
del Progreso, Michoacan,
Mexico, 1933.
Platinum print, 14.9 x 11.7 cm.
The J. Paul Getty Museum,
Los Angeles

90

Paul Strand (1890–1976)
Milpa Alta, Mexico, August, 1933.
Platinum print, 14.9 x 11.9 cm.
The J. Paul Getty Museum,
Los Angeles

91

Paul Strand (1890–1976)
Woman, Patzcuaro,
Mexico, 1933.
Platinum print, 14.8 x 11.7 cm.
The J. Paul Getty Museum,
Los Angeles

place, chronicling what he thought of as the country's essential character, while fostering its revolutionary transformation through the tools of photography and film-making'.[58]

Strand and Cartier-Bresson both found Mexico a pivotal influence in their political development.[59] With its forward-thinking arts programme and left-wing politics, Mexico attracted numerous other artists from abroad, including a group of three young and politically like-minded friends: Philip Guston (then known as Phillip Goldstein), Reuben Kadish and Jules Langsner.

Having seen photographs of the mural that Guston and Kadish, assisted by Sanford Pollock (brother of Jackson), had produced for the Workers' Alliance Center in Los Angeles in early 1934, David Alfaro Siqueiros promised to help any of its artists to find work in Mexico. Guston and Kadish, with the poet and art critic Langsner, all in their early twenties and ready for adventure, took up the invitation and travelled down to Mexico City by car.[60] Siqueiros, Rivera and Pablo O'Higgins secured them a commission to decorate the interior patio of a colonial building in Morelia, capital of the state of Michoacan. The building, run by the Universidad Michoacana de San Nicolás de Hidalgo and used primarily as a state museum, already boasted murals by the American painters Grace Greenwood and Ryah Ludins, as well as the Mexican Alfredo Zalce. Marion Greenwood had also painted a mural in a nearby building.

Guston, Kadish and Langsner began work on their mural in August 1934, and were provided with six months' board and lodging plus assistants and materials (figs 56, 57).[61] It is significant that they worked as a collective. *The Struggle against Terrorism* was completed by 21 January 1935. Guston

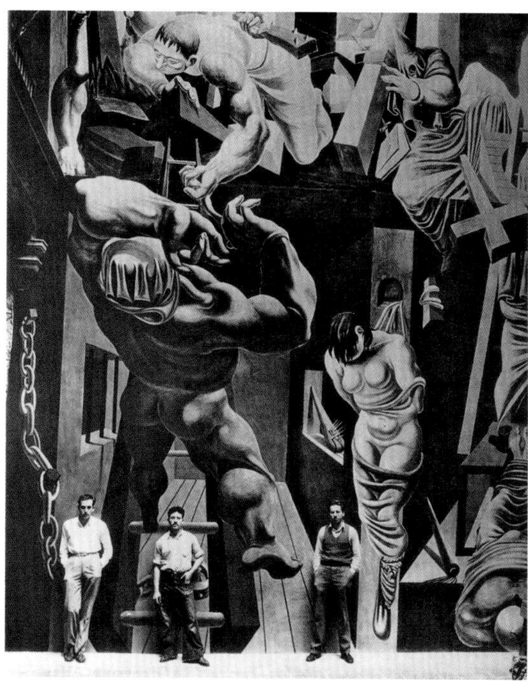

Fig. 56 Casa López(?), **Philip Guston, Reuben Kadish and Jules Langsner in front of their mural, 'The Struggle against Terrorism'**, 1935. Photograph. Museo Regional Michoacan, Morelia, Michoacan

was a great fan of Siqueiros's technique, especially his ability to work within compromised spaces, using distortion to great effect. Having seen photographs of Siqueiros's mural *Plastic Exercise* in Quinta Los Granados, Buenos Aires, in 1933 (fig. 58), he wrote: 'The shape of the room is half-cylinder shape. Huge and he painted the floor also, not a bit of space unpainted. Not being a flat plane on the wall, he had problem of distortion. So he painted his nudes very distorted so that they would appear not distorted. Understand? And tremendous movement – he composed it so that as the spectator moves, the figures move and rotate with him'.[62] Guston was less enthusiastic about the work of Orozco and highly

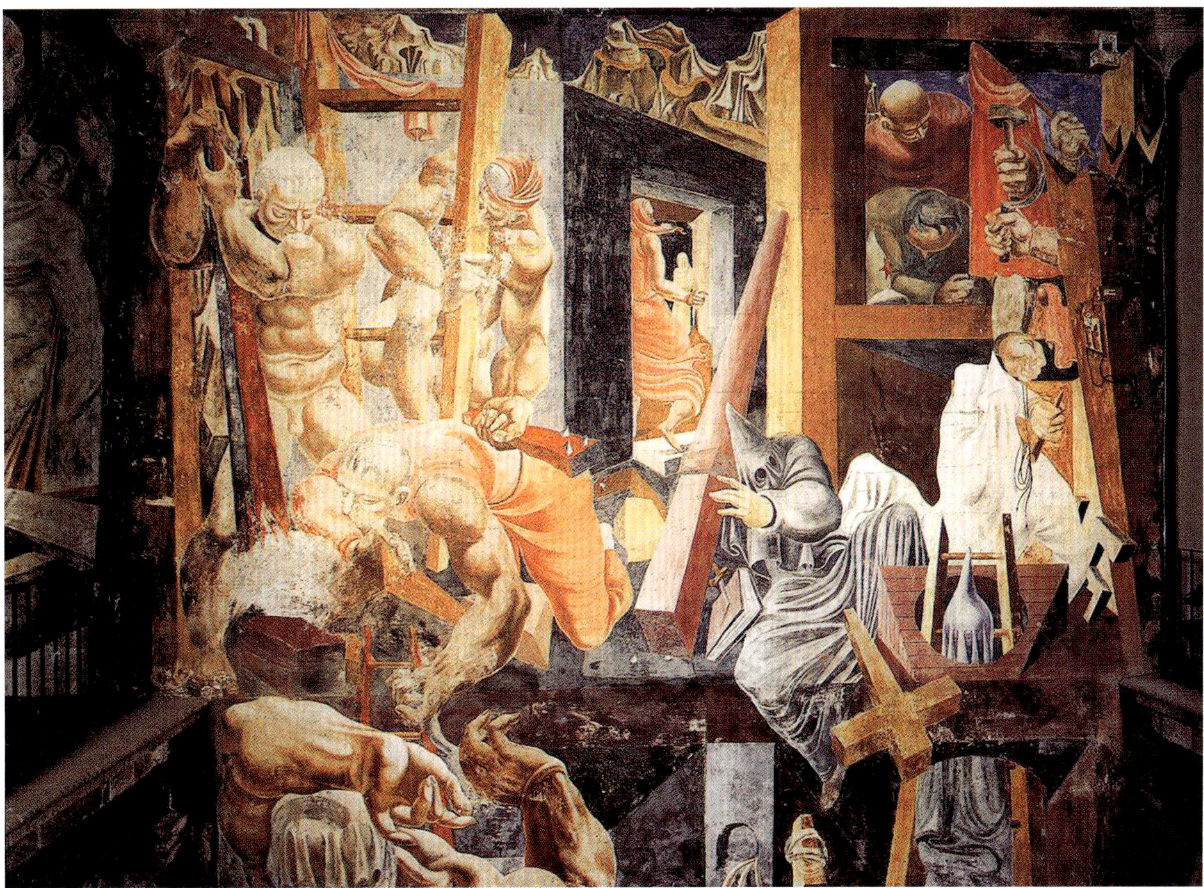

Fig. 57 Philip Guston, Reuben Kadish and Jules Langsner, **The Struggle against Terrorism**, 1934–35. Mural, 95.13 sq. m. Museo Regional de Michoacan, Morelia, Michoacan

critical of Rivera, whom he dismissed as opportunistic.[63] The influence of Siqueiros can be further seen in Guston's circular painting *Bombardment* (fig. 59), in which the explosion at the centre of the composition blasts outwards in all directions, creating a sense that the victims in the foreground of the painting are being literally blown out of the work.

Guston, Kadish and Langsner were given free train passes to attend Lázaro Cárdenas's inauguration as president in Mexico City in December 1934, and portraits that they painted at the time – such as Guston's depiction of the Supreme Court justice Manuel Moreno Sánchez (location unknown), who was patron of a poetry magazine – show that they were friendly with local politicians as well as keen to earn money.[64] The completion of *The Struggle against Terrorism*, with its compressed, vertiginous representation of racial hatred and intolerance, was covered in *Time* magazine and the *Los Angeles Times,* although the work was later forgotten and only rediscovered in 1973, hidden behind a false wall.[65]

As Guston, Kadish and Langsner were completing their work in Mexico and returning to the US, Lola and Manuel Álvarez Bravo separated after ten years of marriage. As well as developing her husband's prints, Lola had begun to take photographs herself, and her early work shares similarities with that of Manuel.[66] She had also encountered the work and ideas of both Strand and Cartier-Bresson. Once separated from Manuel Álvarez Bravo, she decided to become a photographer in her own right, and in order to support this ambition she taught drawing at a primary school in Mexico City. Like many photographers, she had been influenced by the 1924 exhibition of Weston's work at the Palacio de Minería in Mexico City, which was sponsored by the Ministry of Public Education. Lola acknowledged the debt of Mexican photographers to Weston: 'Before the arrival of Edward Weston in Mexico, photography was pictorialist. One had to photograph either people in a lifeless studio, or trees and lakes surrounded by little clouds. The Mexican light, the people and the moods of the country allowed Weston to discover new forms'.[67]

Work was hard to come by, especially for women, but Lola Álvarez Bravo's big break came when Héctor Pérez Martínez named her chief photographer of *El Maestro Rural*, a monthly magazine published by the Ministry of Public Education for primary schoolteachers in rural areas. The work involved a considerable amount of travelling, and as she was the only woman photojournalist in a male-dominated profession and often had to accompany ministers on official tours, Lola Álvarez Bravo had to be tough, both physically and mentally.[68] She also photographed subjects drawn from her circle of friends, among them painters, musicians, poets, intellectuals, politicians and visitors, and she was regarded by many as the pre-eminent portrait photographer in Mexico.[69] 'If my photographs have any value,' she later stated, 'it's because they show a Mexico that no longer exists.'[70] She was one of only a handful of artists who pioneered the development of modern photography in her native country (cats 92, 93).[71]

Lola Álvarez Bravo created two distinct bodies of work, namely street photography and portraiture. She was also very active in other branches of the arts. With Maria Izquierdo, she was a member of the Liga de Escritores y Artistas Revolucionarios (LEAR) from its creation in 1934, and established the first film

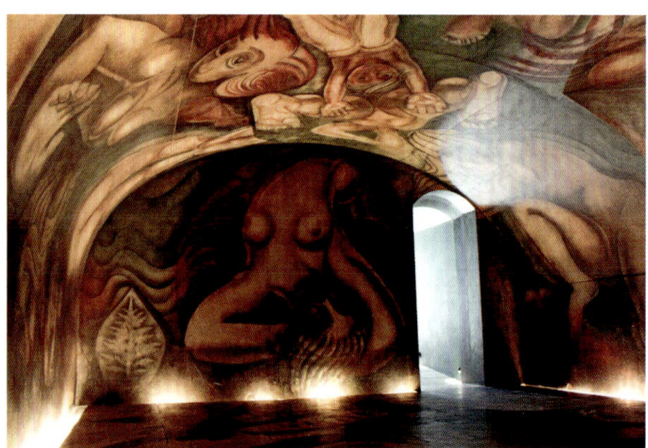

Fig. 58 David Alfaro Siqueiros, **Plastic Exercise (Ejercicio plastico)**, 1933. Mural, spray gun and nitrocellulose pigments on cement. Former basement room at Quinta Los Granados, Buenos Aires (dismantled 1990, reconstructed and restored 2008), 60.84 sq. m. Museo del Bicentenario, Buenos Aires

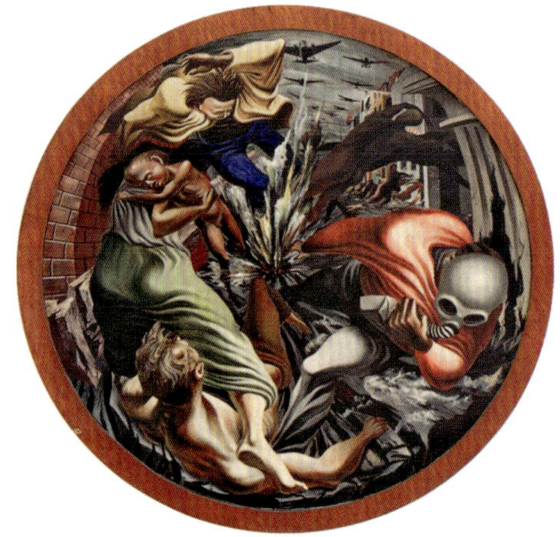

Fig. 59 Philip Guston, **Bombardment**, 1937–38. Oil on masonite, 106.7 cm diameter. Philadelphia Museum of Art, 2011-2-1

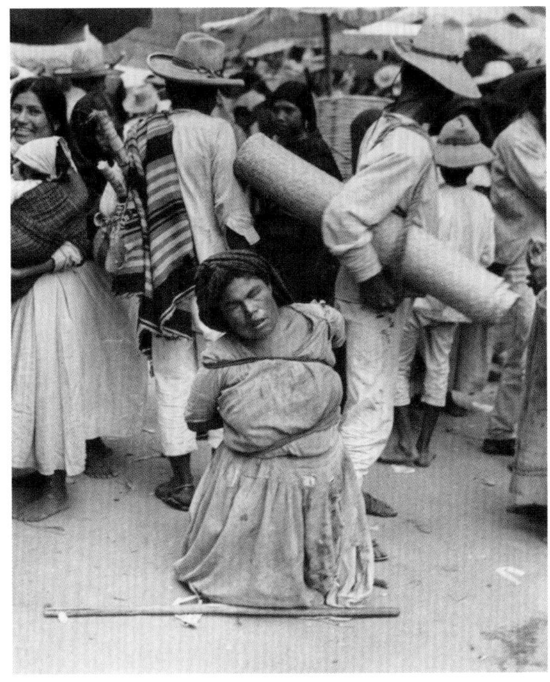

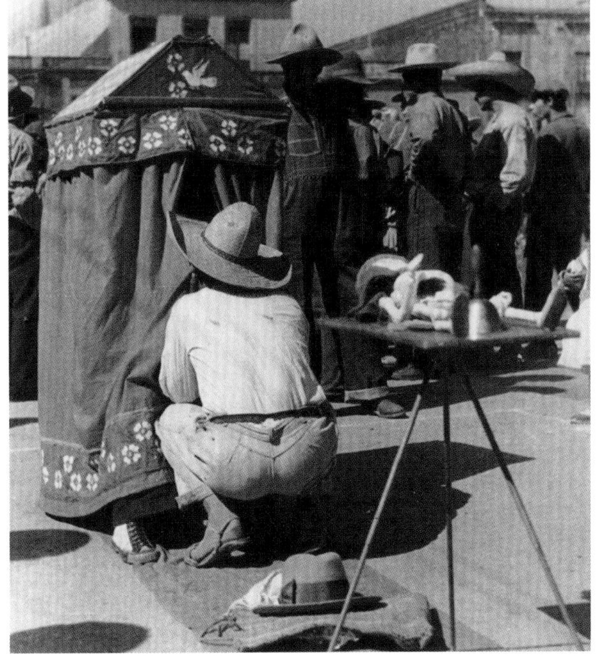

society in Mexico with Manuel Álvarez Bravo, the pioneering photographer Emilio Amero and the painter Julio Castellanos. It was at Lola Álvarez Bravo's Galería de Arte Contemporáneo, which opened in Mexico City in 1951, that Frida Kahlo two years later had her first solo exhibition in Mexico (cats 94, 95).

Another female photographer active in Mexico at this time was Laura Gilpin, who was American. In 1930 and 1931 Gilpin developed a great interest in the Native American cultures of the US, and enjoyed considerable success with her 'Pictorial Lantern Slides of the Southwest'. She applied twice without success for a Guggenheim Fellowship to travel first to Scandinavia and then, the following year, to the Yucatan, where she planned to make another set of lantern slides. In the event Edward Weston was to become the first photographer to receive a Guggenheim Fellowship, some years later in 1937. Despite these setbacks, in 1932 Gilpin accompanied a group of teachers and six boys from the Fountain Valley School, Colorado Springs, on a voyage that took them by ship, train and Model A Ford to Chichen Itza, where Field Director Sylvanus G. Morley granted her access to the darkroom of the Carnegie Institute Maya Expedition (cats 96, 97).

92

Lola Álvarez Bravo (1907–1993)
Indifference
(Indiferencia), *c.* 1940.
Gelatin silver print, 24 x 18.5 cm.
Center for Creative Photography, University of Arizona, Tucson, Lola Álvarez Bravo Archive

93

Lola Álvarez Bravo (1907–1993)
Popular Psychiatrists 2
(Psiquiatras populares 2), 1930s.
Gelatin silver print, 25.5 x 17 cm.
Center for Creative Photography, University of Arizona, Tucson, Lola Álvarez Bravo Archive

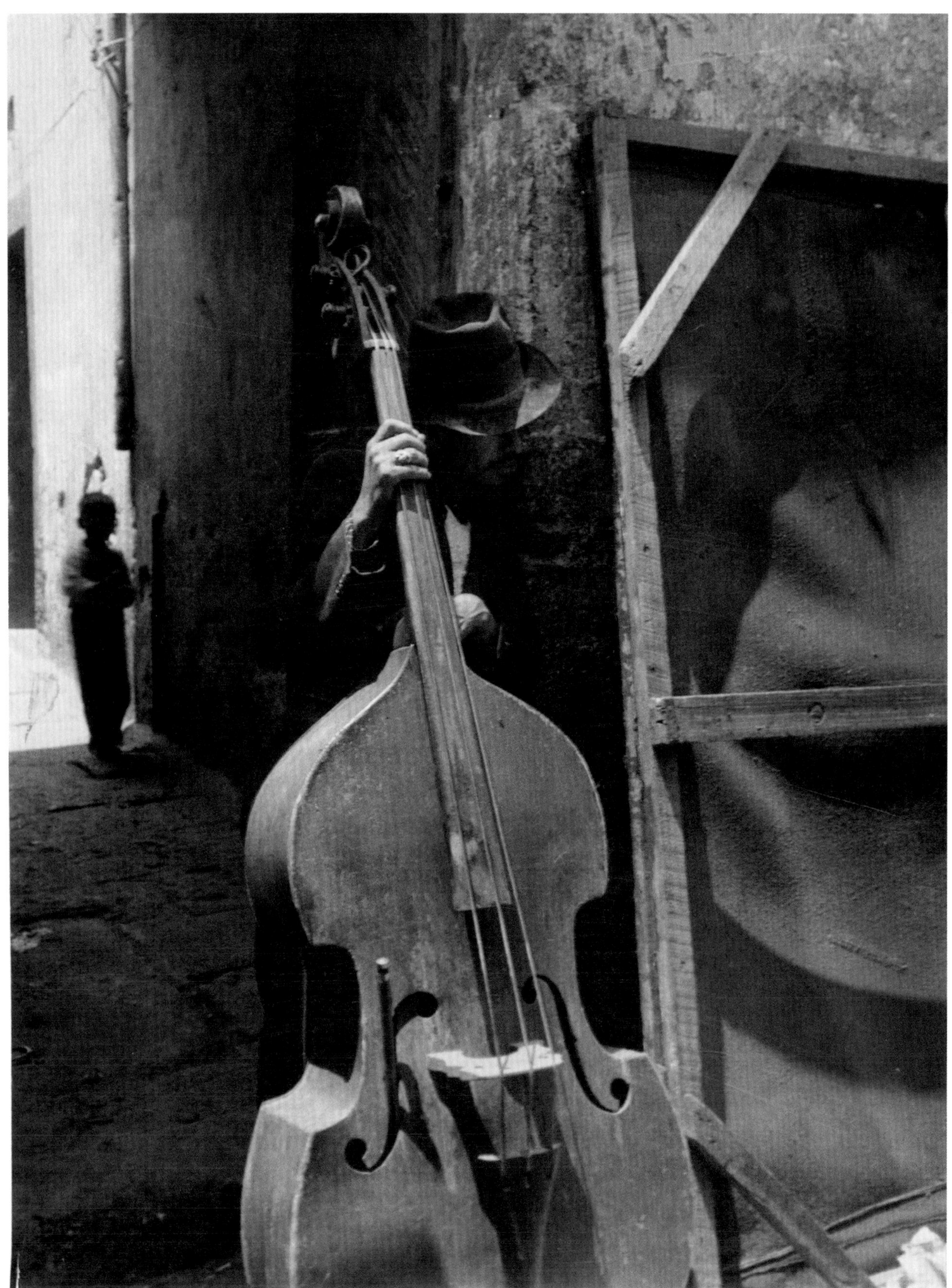

Having worked with the Navajo and Pueblo peoples in the American Southwest, Gilpin was fascinated by the connections between the 'ancient' world view and the modern. She was eager to explore the relevance of an American past to which she and her contemporaries were linked through a common landscape, cultural artefacts and the accumulated knowledge of historical memory. Gilpin approached this subject by contrasting the historical, through surviving architecture and sculpture, with the present, through the modern inhabitants of the same places. In *Temples in Yucatán: A Camera Chronicle of Chichén Itzá* (New York, 1948) she combined images of the Mayan site of Chichen Itza and the nearby villages of Piste and Dzitas. In her photography Gilpin strove for an effect that was at once decorative and historically evocative.[72] She seems to have had an almost intuitive approach to her subject-matter. Her photograph of the sun setting on one of the main pyramids at Chichen Itza captured an event that happens only twice a year, during the spring and autumn equinoxes. The pyramid is dedicated to the Feather Serpent deity Kukulcan. It is constructed in such a way that when the sun sets, a shadow is thrown down the building's entire height; when combined with the jagged form of the pyramid's steps, this shadow creates the appearance of the body of a serpent. At the foot of the pyramid's steps a stone serpent's head joins the body perfectly, completing the vision of the snake deity. Gilpin later confessed that she was unaware of the significance of her photograph until years afterwards (cats 98, 99).[73] In an interview in 1942 she commented:

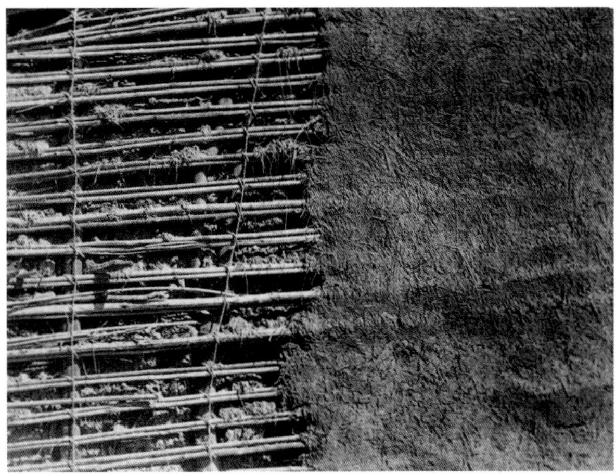

> *One difficulty in photographing these great temples is to retain their remarkable proportions and decorations and the beautiful surface qualities of the material, and at the same time retain the austere and the barbaric qualities which are also present. From the practices of their religion we know that the Mayans were a barbaric people, but they had a marvellous sense of true design ... Many enter the field of photography with the impulse to record a scene. They often fail to realise that what they wish to do is to record the emotion felt upon viewing that scene ... a mere record photograph in no way reflects that emotion.*[74]

94

Lola Álvarez Bravo (1907–1993)
Let's See Who Can Hear Me (Will Anyone Hear Me?) (A ver quién me oye (¿Me oirán?)), 1939.
Gelatin silver print, 23.5 x 17 cm.
Center for Creative Photography, University of Arizona, Tucson, Lola Álvarez Bravo Archive

95

Lola Álvarez Bravo (1907–1993)
Wattle and Daub (Bajareque), *c.* 1938.
Gelatin silver print, 17.2 x 22.1 cm. Center for Creative Photography, University of Arizona, Tucson, Lola Álvarez Bravo Archive

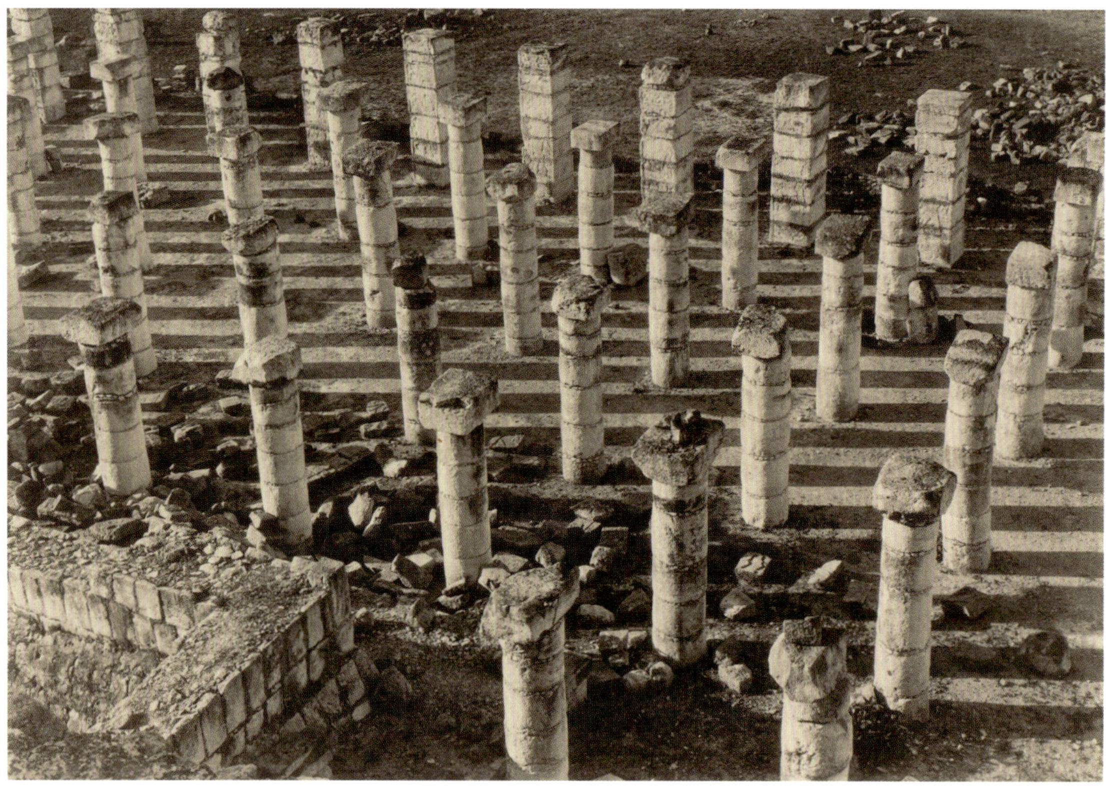

On her return to the US in April 1932, Gilpin printed her images of Chichen Itza on to Gevaluxe paper and toured them to several venues. The Library of Congress bought 42 prints for $500.[75]

In a draft manifesto written in New York in 1934, Siqueiros wrote: 'Our movement is based on critical analysis of the two great contemporary art experiences: the Paris movement and the modern Mexican movement usually known as the Mexican Renaissance. Both these movements are disintegrating today.'[76] That Siqueiros likened to Paris the burst of post-revolutionary creativity that was taking place in Mexico gives a sense of its scale and ambition. After all, Paris was the hedonistic capital of Europe, an artistic crossroads of unparalleled vitality, the destination of all artists searching for freedom and inspiration during the interwar period.[77] However, by 1934 economic depression was beginning to hit artists hard in Paris, and the shadow cast over Europe by the bloody

96

Laura Gilpin (1891–1979)
North Colonnade, Chichen Itza, Yucatan, 1932.
Gelatin silver print,
26.04 x 35.6 cm.
Amon Carter Museum of American Art, Fort Worth.
Gift of the artist

97

Laura Gilpin (1891–1979)
Untitled (Castillo and Temple of Warriors, Chichen Itza, Yucatan), 1932.
Gelatin silver print,
35.1 x 26.04 cm.
Amon Carter Museum of American Art, Fort Worth.
Bequest of the artist

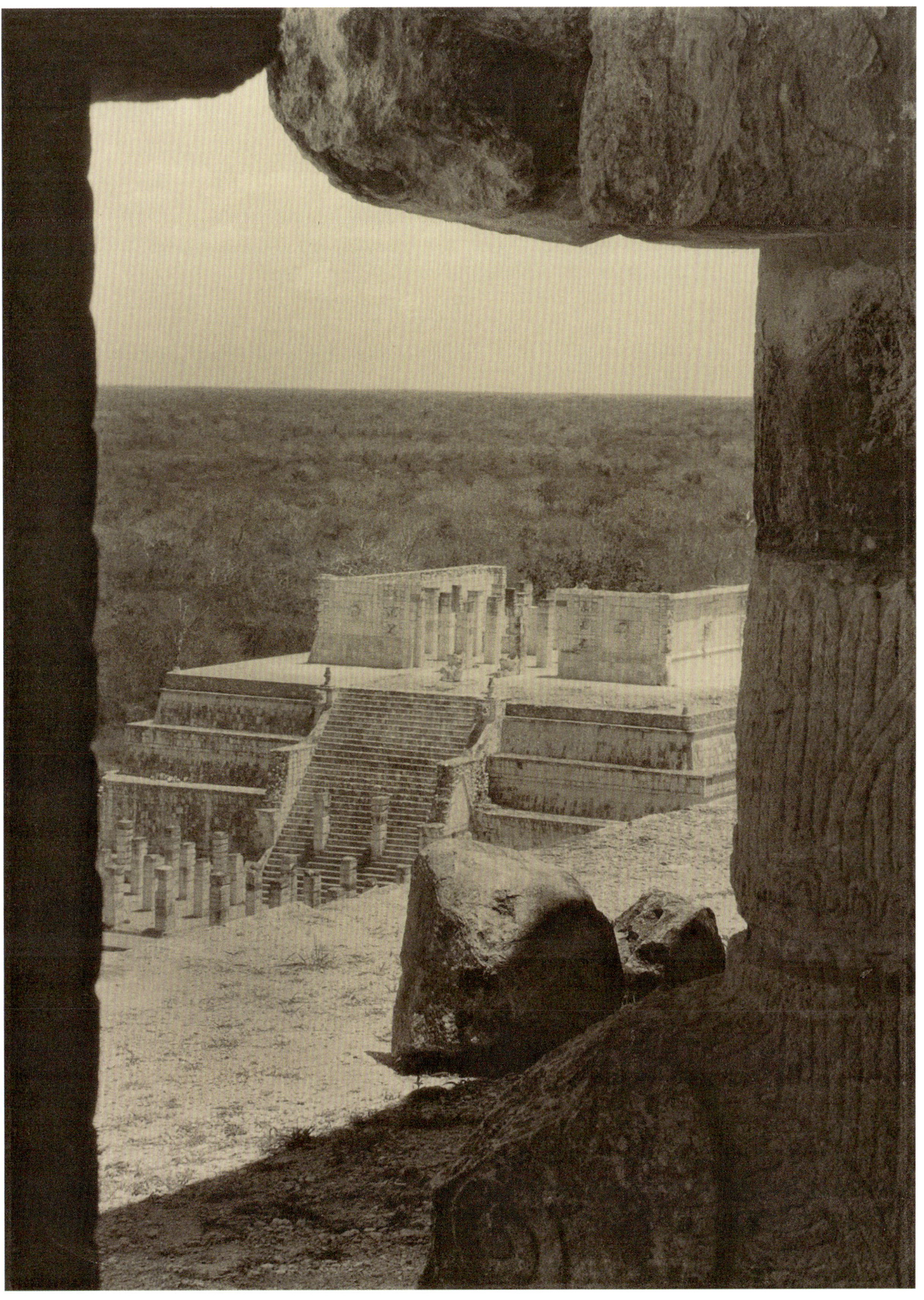

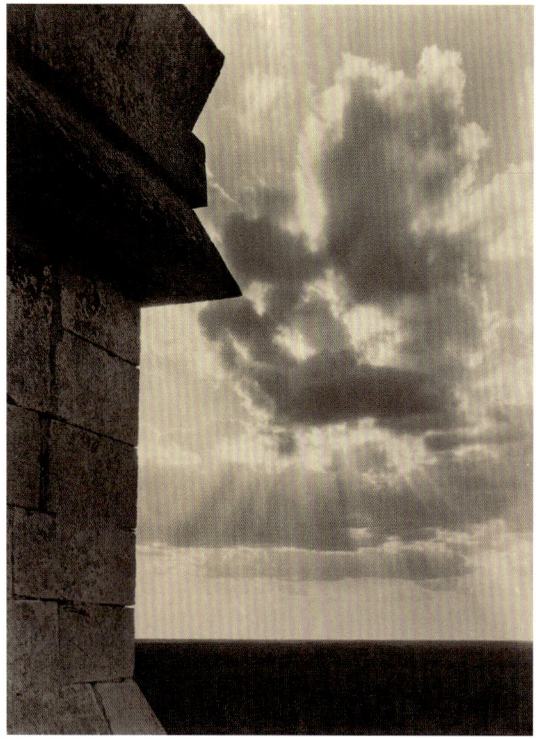

events of the Spanish Civil War was lengthening, with rising tension between Soviet Russia and Germany. Siqueiros was concerned not with external events or the economy but with the quality of the art being produced in Mexico. Artists must avoid 'the tourist-oriented bureaucracy of Mexican art' and rid themselves 'of Mexican demagogic opportunism. We must put an end to superficial folk art, of the type called "Mexican Curious" which predominates in Mexico today.' He continued: 'We must put an end to ... the false collectivism of official Mexican art, with its "socialism".'[78] Siqueiros felt that creativity and individualism were being sacrificed in pursuit of an artistic language prescribed by the self-serving political interests of the government. He wanted to see a new art that would embrace the latest technological advances and allow for greater artistic expression.

Siqueiros was not advocating that public art – murals – be abandoned. In fact he believed quite the opposite, arguing that the exteriors of buildings should be used for murals in strategic locations where they would be seen: 'We must put an end to tourist-inspired Mexican muralism with its archaic technique, and bureaucracy; murals painted in out of the way places and which only emerge from hiding in select monographs published for foreign amateurs.'[79]

The political situation in Mexico, meanwhile, had been destabilised by the assassination of Alvaro Obregón, the president-elect, in 1928 at the hands of a radical Catholic. Behind the scenes, Plutarco Elías Calles, the outgoing president, ensured that the candidates he favoured assumed the presidency. Emilio Portes Gil took office until fresh elections could take place. The victor, Pascual Ortiz Rubio, lasted only two years before a disagreement on policy with Calles led to his replacement by General Abelardo L. Rodríguez. All the time the government was moving further to the right, gradually abandoning the ambitious programmes of social reform that had hitherto been its principal objective. The Communist Party was virtually outlawed, the Mexican army was professionalised and corruption began to infiltrate the newly reorganised party of government, the Partido Nacional Revolucionario, led by Calles.

98

Laura Gilpin (1891–1979)
Sunburst, Kukulcan, Chichen Itza, Yucatan, 1932.
Gelatin silver print,
35.56 x 25.4 cm.
Amon Carter Museum of American Art, Fort Worth.
Gift of the artist

99

Laura Gilpin (1891–1979)
[Castillo and Temple of Warriors] [Chichen Itza, Yucatan], 1932.
Gelatin silver print,
35.1 x 26.04 cm.
Amon Carter Museum of American Art, Fort Worth.
Bequest of the artist

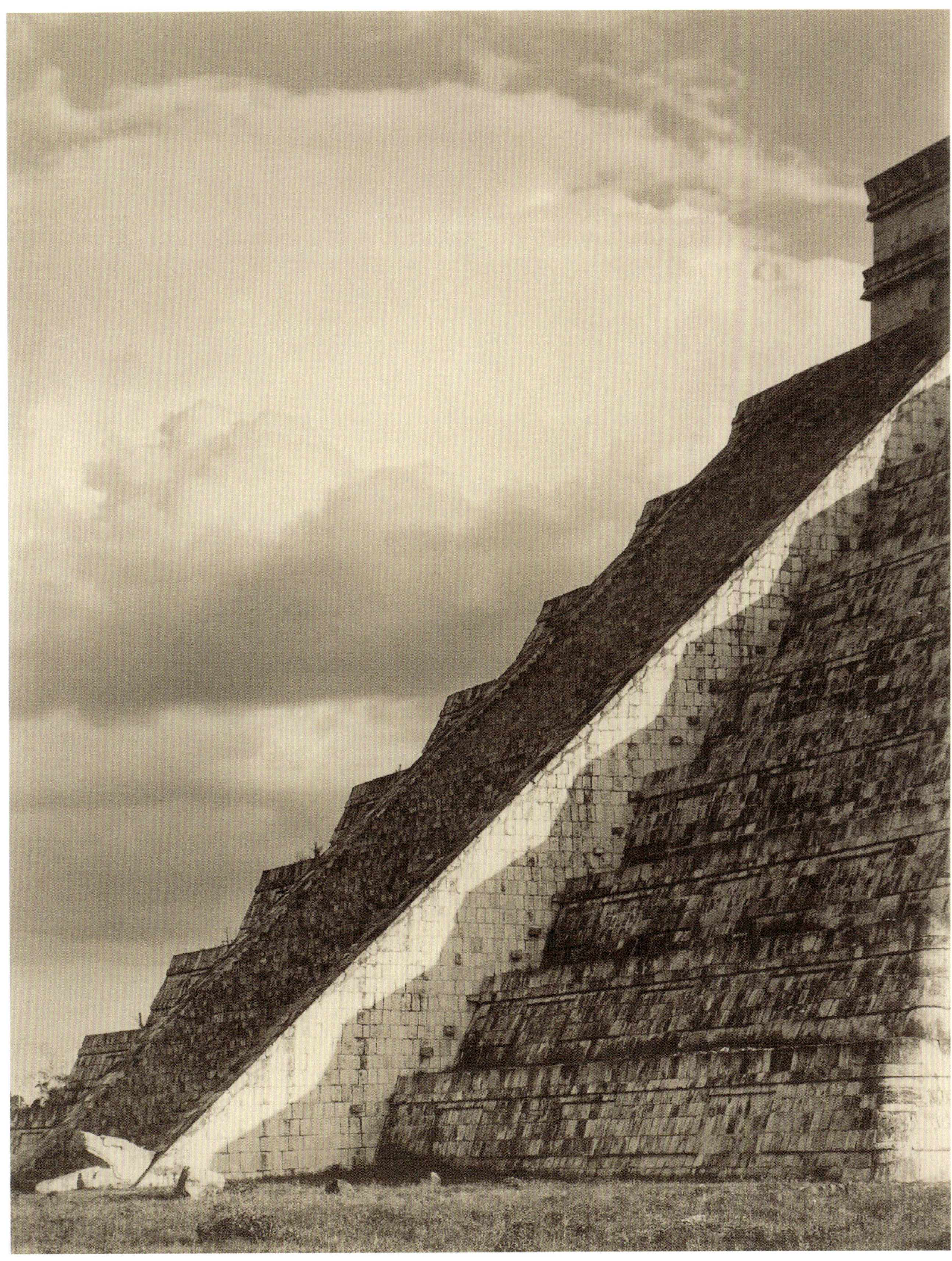

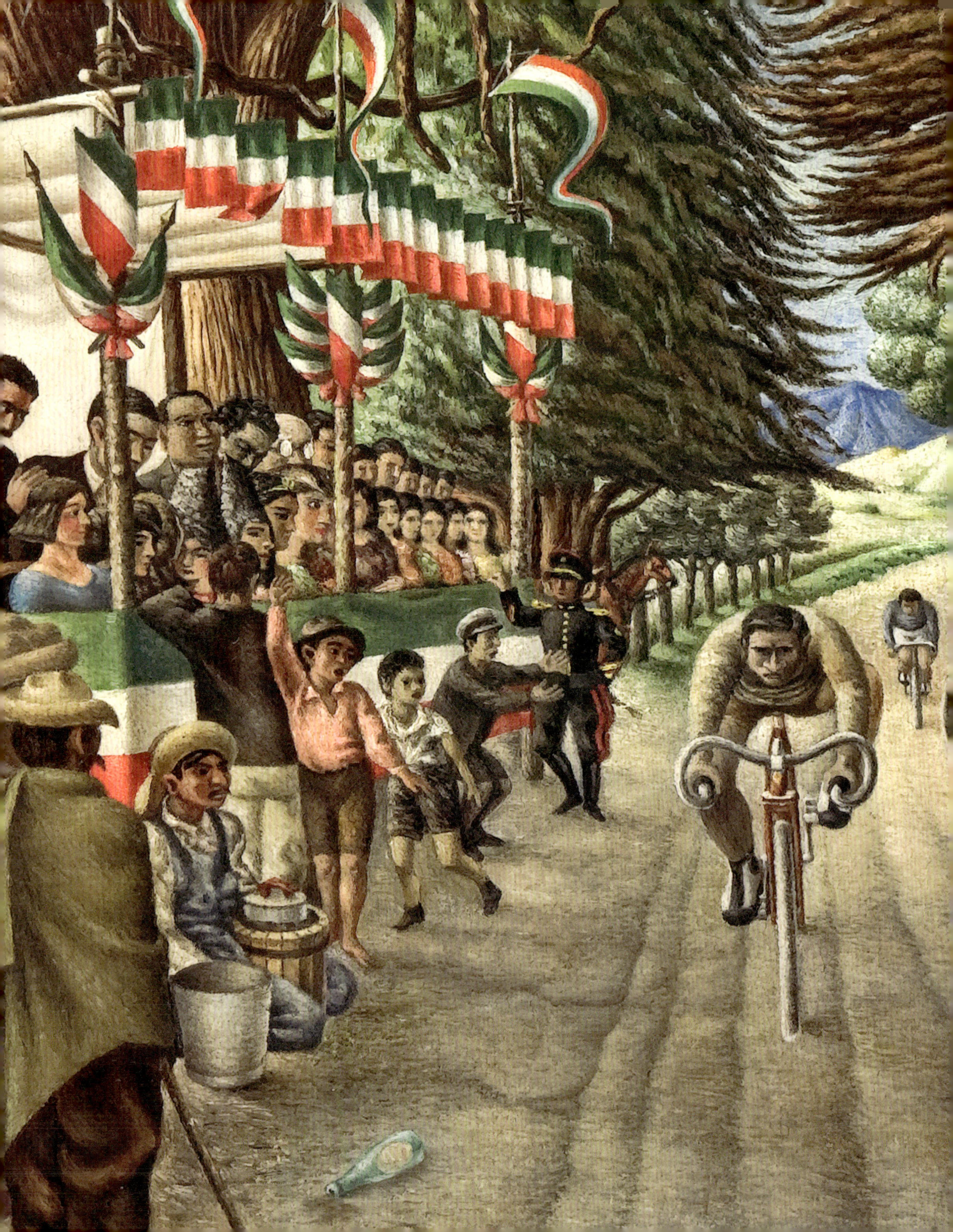

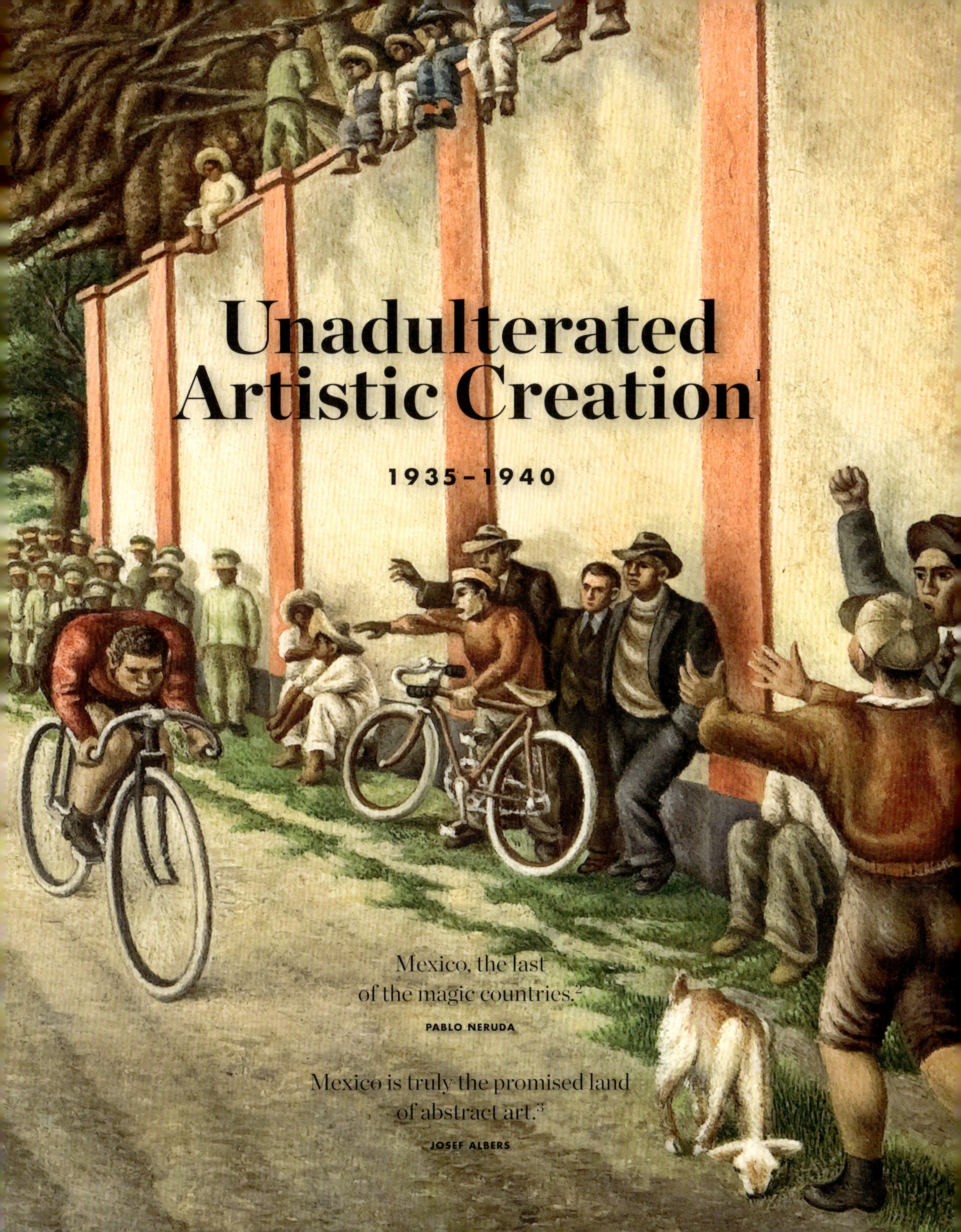

Unadulterated Artistic Creation[1]

1935–1940

Mexico, the last
of the magic countries.[2]

PABLO NERUDA

Mexico is truly the promised land
of abstract art.[3]

JOSEF ALBERS

IN 1933 THE GERMAN-BORN ARTISTS Josef and Anni Albers left Europe for the US following the closure by the Nazis of the Bauhaus, where they had both worked. Josef had been invited to lead the art department at the newly established and progressive Black Mountain College, in North Carolina. The following year, at the invitation of the Cuban-born designer and architect Clara Porset, who had studied at Black Mountain, the Alberses, who were inveterate travellers, visited Cuba with their friends the Dreiers. A left-wing activist, Clara Porset left Cuba for Mexico in 1936, where she married the artist Xavier Guerrero, who was later to facilitate the Alberses' introduction to other artists in Mexico. The Alberses had visited Mexico themselves for a month over Christmas and New Year 1935–36, the first of their thirteen trips to Mexico. Indeed, Anni Albers wrote after their last visit in 1967: 'Mexico which we love and admire is also puzzling to us in some ways. We still have to discover more of it ...'[4]

The Alberses usually drove down by car. They explored Mexico tirelessly and often returned to favourite places, among them the colonial town of Oaxaca and the pre-Columbian sites of Monte Albán, Mitla and Tenayuca. Both artists were greatly inspired by what they saw on their trips. After their second visit in 1936, Anni produced two large weavings: *Ancient Writing* (fig. 60) and *Monte Albán* (fig. 61). Both textiles appear to respond to the plans and elevations of the sites they visited. *Ancient Writing* is an almost intuitive reaction to the cosmological significance of the layout of ceremonial precincts within pre-Columbian cities, whereas the relief profiles of the buildings in *Monte Albán* suggest the carefully considered manner in which they merge with the landscape.[5]

Josef Albers approached these Mexican trips in the same way that he had worked at the Bauhaus, using a 35-mm camera to record his impressions. He took hundreds of photographs of the people and places he encountered on every journey. At home in North Carolina, he would select certain images from contact sheets. Some he enlarged and attached, with the postcards he had acquired on his trips, to filing cards that he then carefully annotated. During this process of selection and rejection, Albers was effectively curating the visual record of his visits,

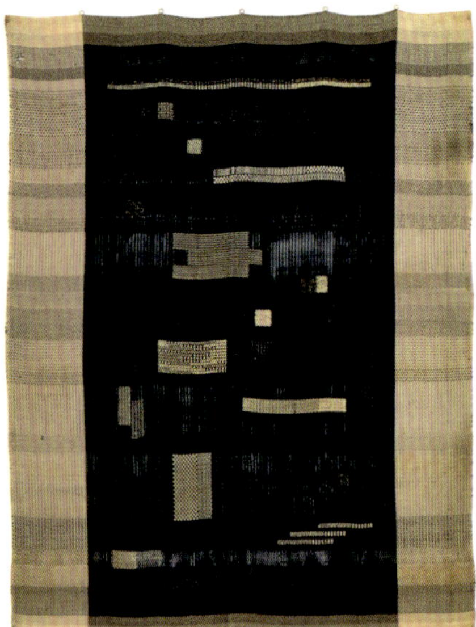

Fig. 60 Anni Albers, **Ancient Writing**, 1936. Rayon, cotton, linen and jute, 149.8 x 111 cm. Smithsonian American Art Museum, Washington, DC, 1984.150

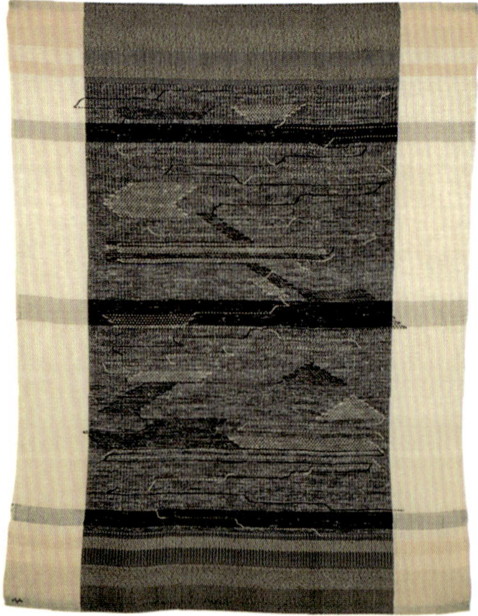

Fig. 61 Anni Albers, **Monte Albán**, 1936. Silk, linen and wool, 146 x 112 cm. Harvard Art Museums, Busch-Reisinger Museum, Cambridge, BR81.5

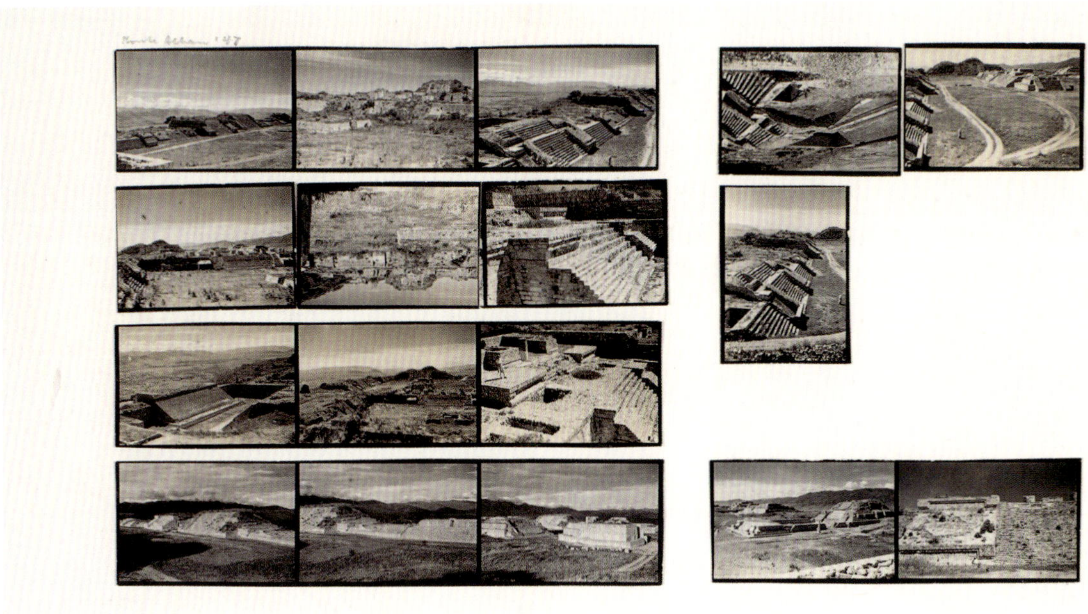

distilling his images to reflect the views and sequences that most appealed to him. These ranged from distant panoramas to close-ups of architectural details. His files also included people (Anni and their friends the Dreiers, for example), markets and colonial buildings (cats 100–102). In this way Albers built up a meticulous visual record of Mexico (albeit in black and white) that was later to inform his work. Although he may have derived the geometric designs that inspired much of his art from his images of pre-Columbian ruins – he named several works after such sites as Monte Albán, Mitla and Tenayuca – his overall recollection of each visit was shaped by his memories of those who had accompanied them and other elements that had helped to mark the occasion, whether a colonial church, a vernacular building, a local inhabitant or a bustling market. These memories seem inseparable from his carefully selected images of architecture, suggesting that Albers's photographs somehow incorporated these more personal elements. These remarkable files, which have been referred to as his sketchbooks, only came to light after his death in 1976.[6]

Albers spent a long time working on his paintings, doubtless often referring to his filing system. He produced around eighty studies for the painting *Adobe* between 1947 and 1956.[7] Similarly *Tenayuca* (fig. 62) passed through a large number of studies over a five-year period, revealing his fascination with process and his tireless reworking

100

Josef Albers (1888–1976)
Monte Albán, 1947.
Photographs (17)
on cardboard, 18.5 x 25.5 cm.
The Josef and Anni Albers Foundation, Bethany, CT

101

overleaf:
Josef Albers (1888–1976)
Mitla, 1935, 1939, 1949.
Contact prints (46)
on cardboard, 25.5 x 41.8 cm.
The Josef and Anni Albers Foundation, Bethany, CT

102

pages 162–3:
Josef Albers (1888–1976)
Monte Albán, c. 1939.
Postcards (3) and contact prints (23) on cardboard, 20.5 x 30.5 cm.
The Josef and Anni Albers Foundation, Bethany, CT

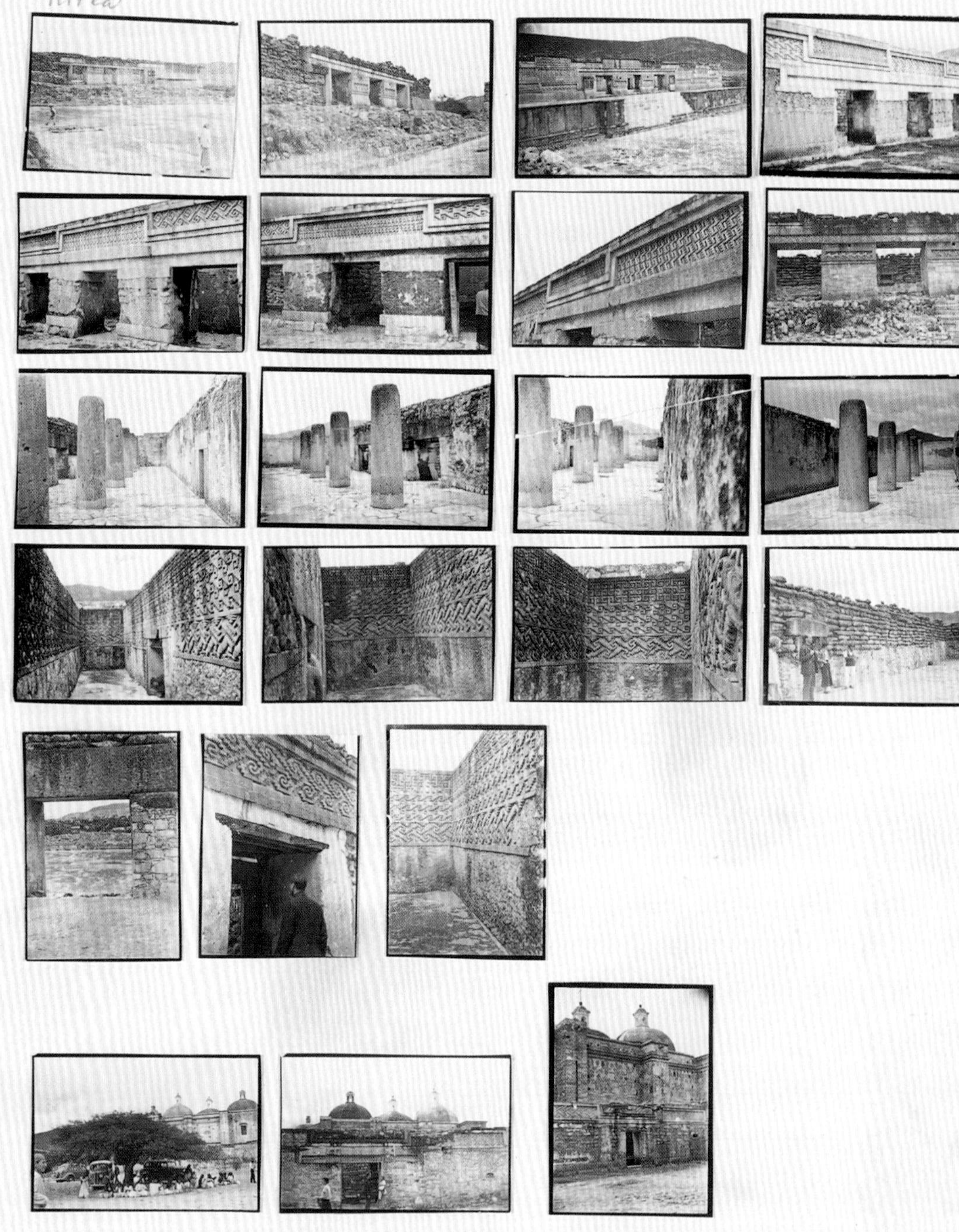
Mitla

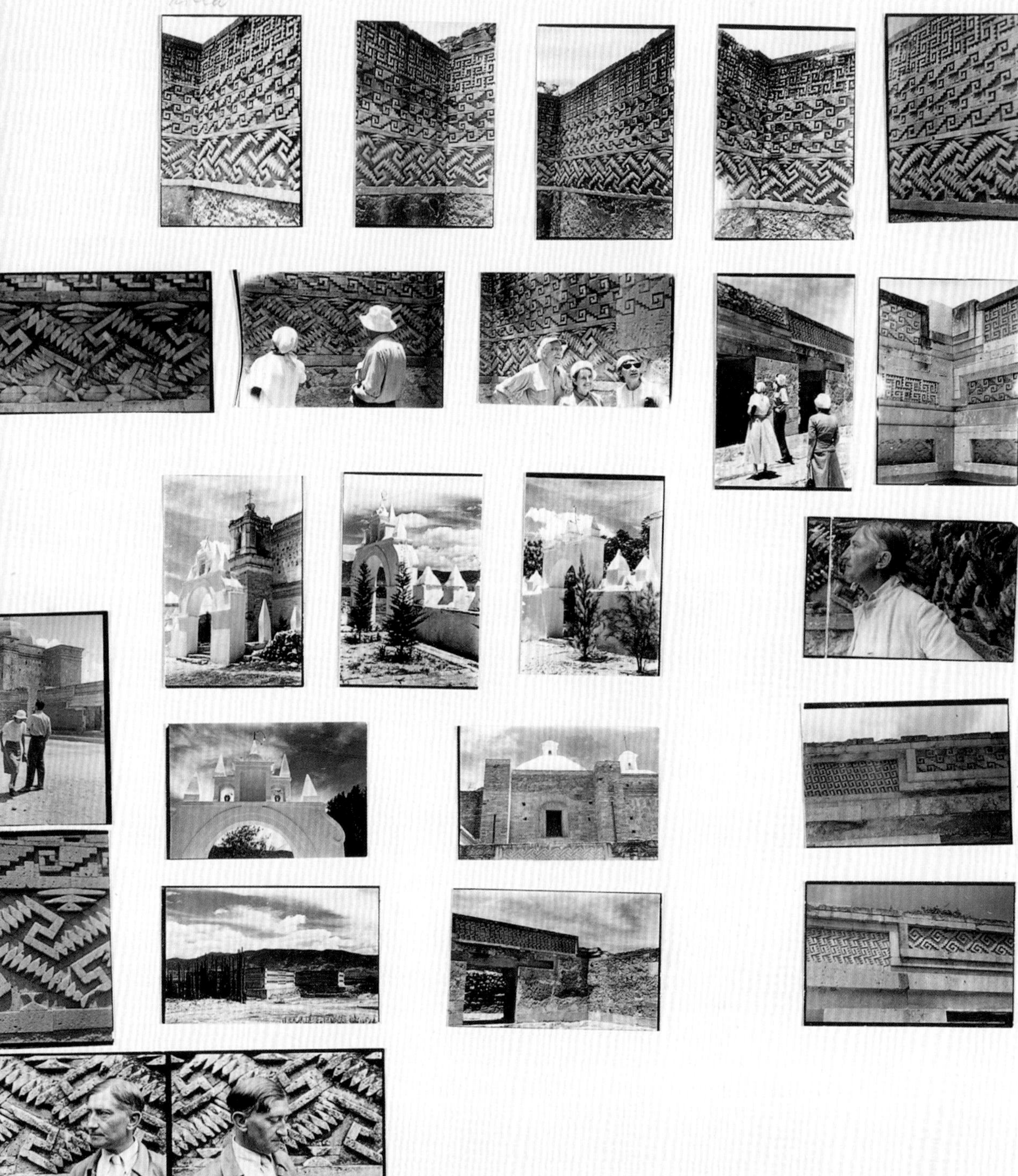
Mitla

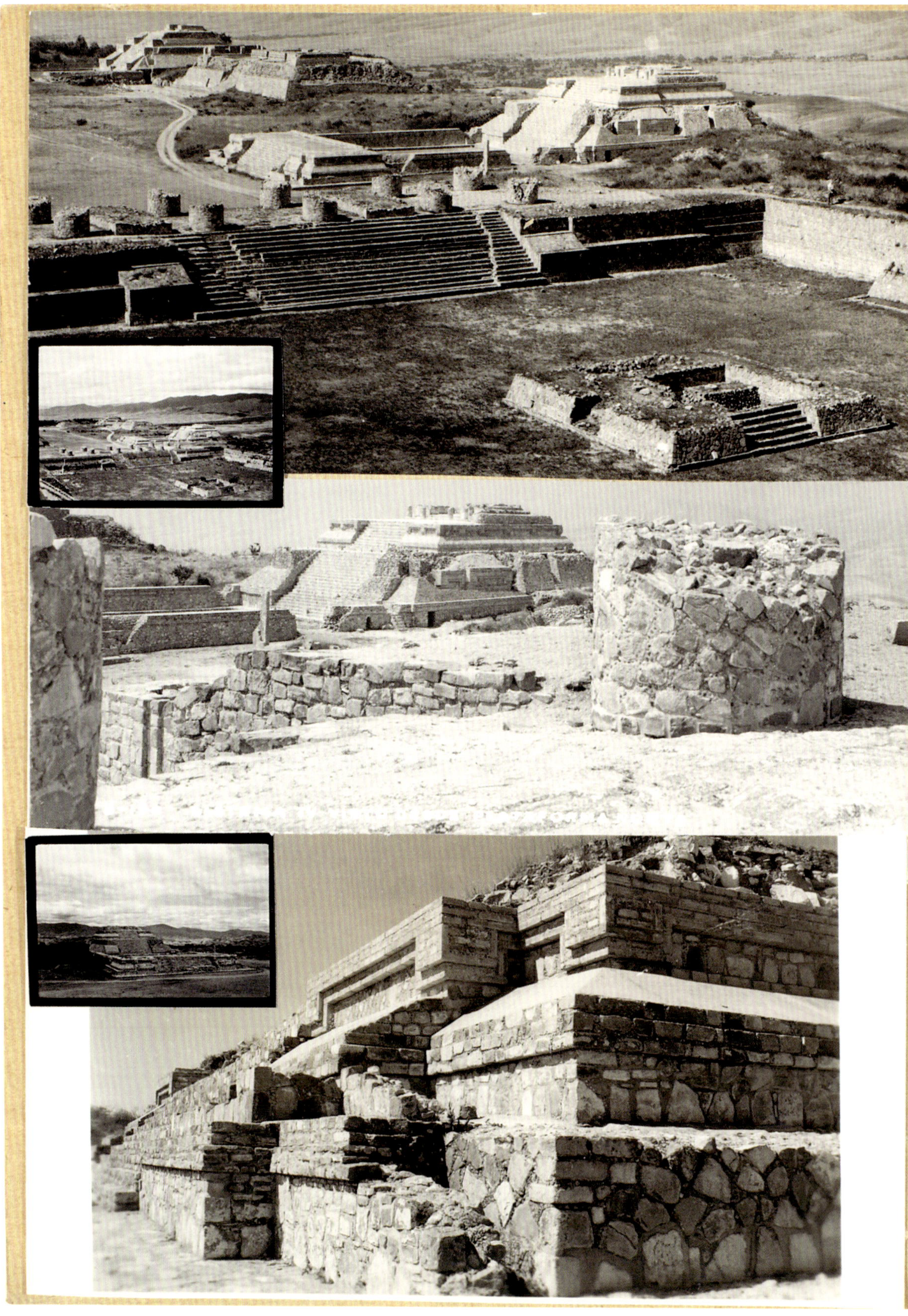

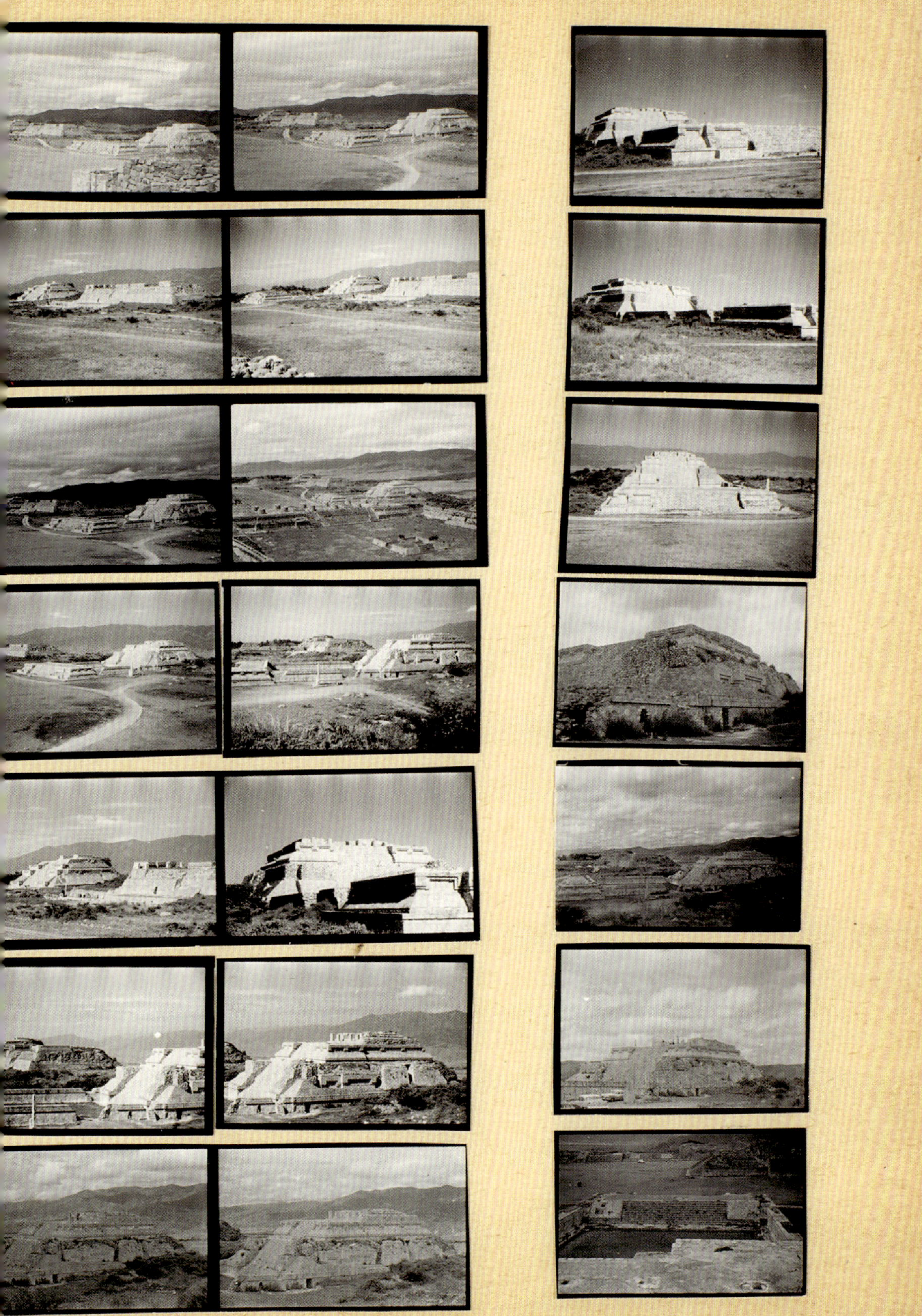

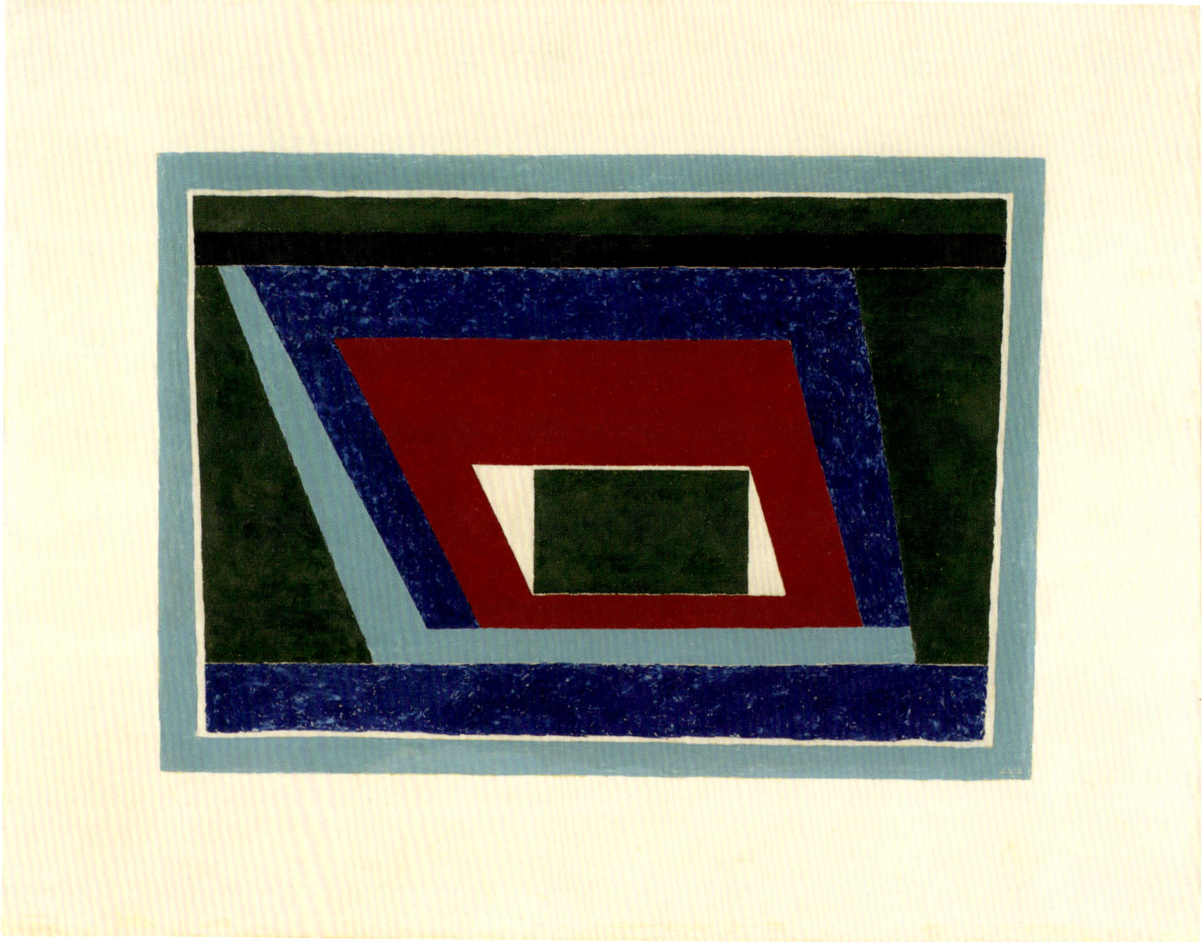

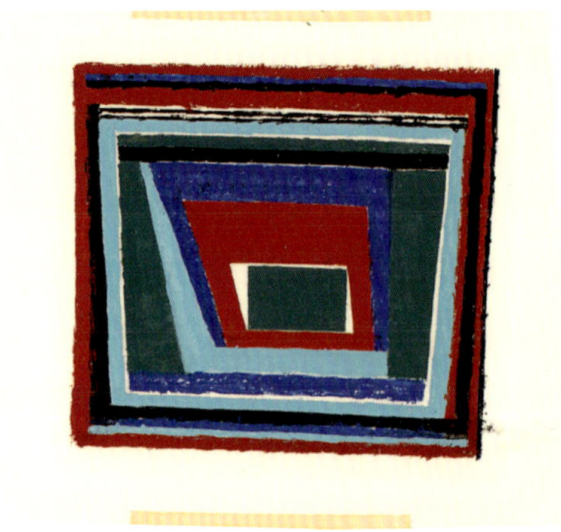

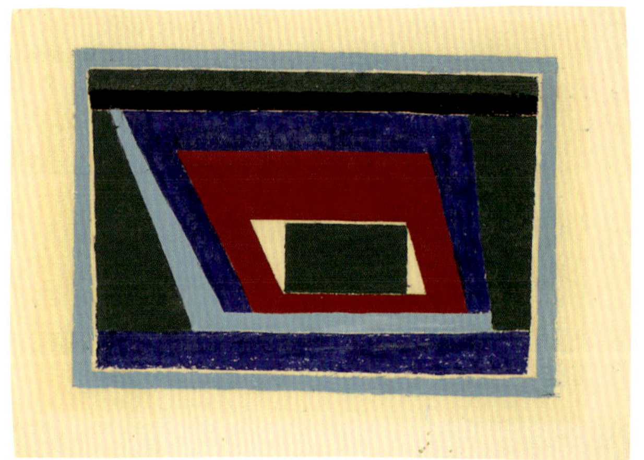

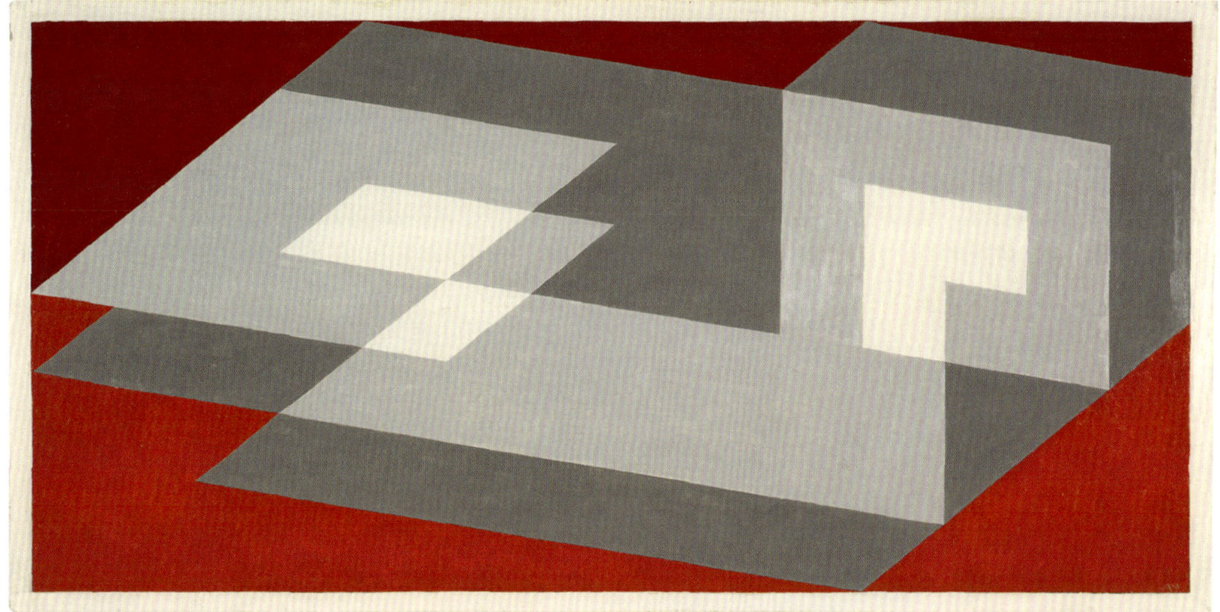

Fig. 62 Josef Albers, **Tenayuca**, 1943. Oil on masonite, 57.2 x 110.5 cm. San Francisco Museum of Modern Art, 84.1

of Mexican themes. Albers's smaller group of studies for *Mantic* (cats 103–105) likewise demonstrates his fascination with geometry and colour. The viewer looks back through what might be a window along a vista of different shapes towards a final block of colour, perhaps a representation of a building or an open space. We cannot be sure whether the forms are shaped by architectural constructions, nor is it clear whether Albers is depicting an internal or an external space. Certainly he appears to be responding to tricks of the sunlight and the different hues of the shadows it casts. Albers was very taken with the vibrant culture and colours of Mexico, perhaps a response to the oppressive situation in Germany and the economic depression consuming the US. These strong colours began to infiltrate his work in 1936, following that first visit to Mexico, and gradually came to dominate it.[8] Colour took on an increasingly significant role in Albers's painting, underpinned by the structural organisation that he derived from the pre-Columbian and vernacular architecture of Mexico.[9] Ultimately Albers's exposure to Mexico led him to create his *Homage to the Square* paintings from 1949, of which he painted over a thousand versions.[10]

If the Alberses were drawn to the visual and chromatic power of Mexico, the French poet and playwright Antonin Artaud was initially attracted to the politics of the country. Disillusioned with life

103

top:
Josef Albers (1888–1976)
Mantic, 1940.
Oil on composition board, 71 x 89 cm. The Josef and Anni Albers Foundation, Bethany, CT

104

below left:
Josef Albers (1888–1976)
Study for 'Mantic', *c.* 1940.
Oil on blotting paper, 32 x 34.9 cm. The Josef and Anni Albers Foundation, Bethany, CT

105

below right:
Josef Albers (1888–1976)
Untitled Abstraction (Mantic), *c.* 1940.
Oil on paper, 30.7 x 40.9 cm. Josef Albers Museum Quadrat, Bottrop

in Europe, he arrived at Vera Cruz on 7 February 1936. Although he considered himself a Surrealist, he felt that, by joining the Communist Party, their leader André Breton had constricted the Surrealists' independence and compromised their artistic freedom. He believed that, by definition, Surrealists should resist ideologies.[11] In his Theatre of Cruelty, Artaud had attempted to forge his own new vision of drama, with varying degrees of success. His obsession with converting his presentation of ideas into reality had, however, brought on bouts of mental illness. Artaud developed a profound interest in Mexico, especially its pre-Columbian writing systems, and included a version of his *The Conquest of Mexico* in a performance of the Theatre of Cruelty in 1931. The idea of travelling to Mexico greatly appealed to him, as he wanted both to witness the impact of the Revolution and to study the belief systems and cultures of the indigenous populations.

Once in Mexico City, Artaud wrote a number of articles for the newspaper *El Nacional Revolucionario* and delivered several lectures at the University of Mexico, the Alliance Française and for LEAR, where he spoke against a Marxist revolution in favour of an indigenous revolution.[12] Although he was fêted in Mexico City, where his rhetoric of revolution and artistic experimentation found an enthusiastic and receptive audience, he found Mexico a huge disappointment, having discovered that the country was dominated by European cultural influences and that the indigenous people had not been successfully incorporated into society. He was horrified that the government still persecuted them and marginalised their cultures. Attracted by the idea of a civilisation uncorrupted by Europeans and unencumbered by material possessions, he decided to spend time with the Tarahumara in the Sierra Madre. Permission was required from the Mexican government, which entailed an irritatingly slow bureaucratic process, but numerous intellectuals in Mexico City supported him and successfully petitioned President Lázaro Cárdenas on his behalf; they even secured him a government grant to cover the cost of his trip. Artaud left Mexico City in late August 1936 and, in order to immerse himself properly in the experience, abandoned his heroin habit *en route*. He stayed with the Tarahumara for five weeks, experimenting with the psychedelic powers of peyote, a cactus native to Mexico that is venerated by the Tarahumara for the potency of the visions it can evoke during ritual use. He observed:

> *Perhaps it is a baroque idea for a European to go to Mexico in search of the living foundations of a culture the notion of which seems to be crumbling away here; but I admit that the idea obsesses me; in Mexico there is to be found, linked to the earth, lost in the outflows of volcanic lava, vibrant in the Indian blood, the magic reality of a culture, and little would be required, no doubt, for its fires to be materially revived.*[13]

On 31 October 1936 Artaud returned to France. His time with the Tarahumara stayed with him for the rest of his life and profoundly changed his view of the world. He wrote about his experiences and incorporated elements of them into his writing and stage performances. He published an account in *D'un voyage aux pays de Tarahumaras*, part of Henri Parisot's series *L'Age d'Or* (Paris, 1945; fig. 63). Artaud's Mexican experiences certainly resonated

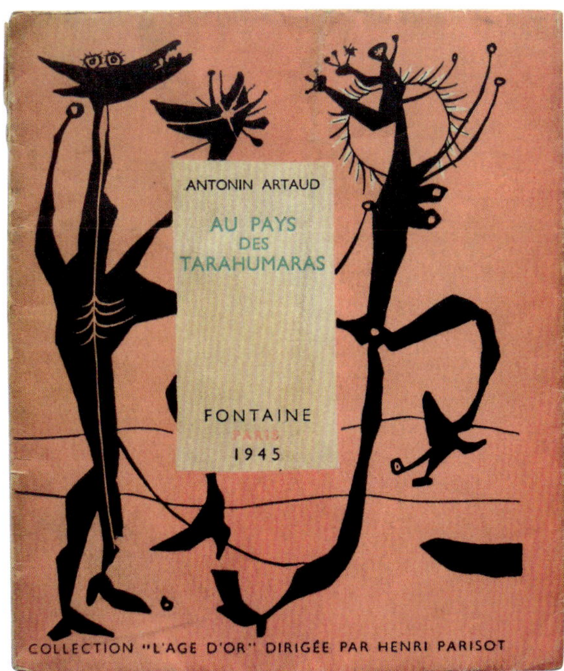

Fig. 63 Cover of Antonin Artaud's **D'un voyage aux pays de Tarahumaras**, designed by Mario Prassinos, published by Fontaine (Paris, 1945). Printed book, 14 x 11.5 cm

with Aldous Huxley, whose own experiments with mescaline were to inform his *Doors of Perception* (London, 1954), and with later generations who experimented with psychotropic drugs, including Carlos Castaneda, who described his time with a Yaqui from Sonora in his famous account *The Teachings of Don Juan: A Yaqui Way of Knowledge* (Berkeley, 1968), the first of many books he published on the subject.

The same month, October 1936, saw the British novelist Malcolm Lowry and his wife Jan Gabrial depart from San Diego bound for Acapulco for what was to be a twenty-month stay; it was almost inevitable that Lowry's arrival in Mexico should coincide with the Day of the Dead celebrations. The previous year they had met Waldo Frank, the left-wing New York intellectual who was the first president of the League of American Writers and editor of *The Collected Poems of Hart Crane* (New York, 1933). Lowry was deeply affected by Hart Crane, 'the drunken sea-obsessed poet', and his fascination with Mexico.[14] Frank knew Mexico well and undoubtedly encouraged Lowry and Gabrial to go there.[15] Living in Los Angeles and writing film scripts, Lowry was disillusioned and needed little encouragement to move to Mexico, not least because his monthly allowance would stretch further than it did in Hollywood.[16] After a brief sojourn in Mexico City they settled in a house at 62 Calle Humboldt, Cuernavaca, sharing it initially with their 'fellow wanderer' the Spanish-speaker Alan Mondragon, whom they had met in Taxco.[17] Lowry and Gabrial spent a week of each month in Mexico City, at the Hotel Canada on Cinco de Mayo, to collect Lowry's allowance from his father.

One day the three friends took the bus to the nearby village of Cuatla. During the journey the bus made an unscheduled stop: an Indian had been stabbed and was lying by the side of the road. As he lay there dying, one of the passengers robbed him, later boasting of the fact. This incident made such an impression on Lowry that he rapidly completed a short story called 'Under the Volcano'. Within three months, this had become the first draft of the novel of the same name, which he showed to his former tutor and mentor Conrad Aiken during a visit Aiken made in 1937 accompanied by Edward Burra, described below.[18] The novel is set over a turbulent twenty-four-hour period and is, in large part, autobiographical, a description of Lowry's own fragile state of mind. Racked by self-doubt and guilt, he descends into alcoholism and despair. An inescapable darkness dominates the book:

> *It was thus far a favourite walk, though not taken since before the rains. The leaves of cacti attracted with their freshness; green trees shot by evening sunlight might have been weeping willows tossing in the gusty wind which had sprung up; a lake of yellow sunlight appeared in the distance below pretty hills like loaves. But there was something baleful now about the evening. Black clouds plunged up to the south. The sun poured molten glass on the fields. The volcanoes seemed terrifying in the wild sunset.*[19]

Lowry's drinking began to get out of control soon after he arrived in Mexico and discovered tequila, and he often disappeared on binges for days on end. His marriage to Gabrial collapsed under the strain in 1938 and he went to Oaxaca seeking escape from his demons. There he befriended Juan Fernando Márquez, who worked for the Banco Nacional de Crédito y Ejidal, at the *pulqueria* 'La Covadonga', and accompanied him on a trip to villages in the mountains to arrange bank loans for small-scale farmers. Tensions were running high in Mexico at this time because of the expropriation of the oil industry by the government under Lázaro Cárdenas; as a consequence, as Graham Greene also discovered, foreigners were viewed with great wariness. Lowry's residency permit expired on 18 March 1938, the very day the expropriation became law.[20] Often blind-drunk, Lowry attracted much suspicion from the police, who monitored his activities closely: 'Everywhere I go I am pursued and even now, as I write, no less than five policemen are watching me.'[21] He was jailed on several occasions for drunkenness before being expelled from Mexico on 23 July 1938.

He returned to Mexico in 1945 with his second wife Margerie Bonner, and went to Oaxaca looking for his old drinking companion only to discover that he was dead. Lowry based the character Juan Fernando Martínez on Márquez in his bleak novel *Dark as the Grave wherein my Friend is Laid* (London, 1969), an account of Lowry's traumatic return to Mexico. During this trip he received a letter rejecting the manuscript of *Under the Volcano* for publication and fought his alcohol addiction.

One of the few people to visit Lowry in Cuernavaca was the unconventional British artist Edward Burra. He did so as the result of an unexpected and unplanned trip to Mexico. In 1937, two years after his first visit to the US, Burra decided to visit his old friend, the American writer Conrad Aiken, who lived in Charlestown, Massachusetts. Aiken was jubilant, having discovered that quick divorces could be obtained in Mexico. He was anxious to divorce his second wife, Clarissa M. Lorenz, so that he could marry his new companion, Mary Augusta Hoover. Although Burra had not planned for such a trip, he needed little persuasion to accompany his friend. Despite poor health, Burra was an enthusiastic traveller and loved adventure: 'Owing to pressure of circumstance we leave tomorrow for Mexico City

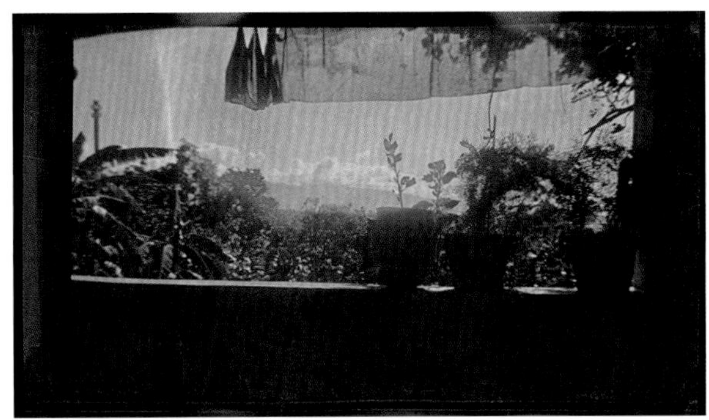

Fig. 64 Edward Burra, 'Popacatepetl from the veranda of 62 Calle Humboldt, Cuernavaca', 1937. Black and white photograph, 5 x 7 cm. Tate Archive, London, M01199

nobody is more surprised than me for I never thought these old eyes would live to see Mexico.'[22]

The two set off with Mary Hoover, travelling overland by train.[23] On arrival in Mexico City, they were advised that they would do better to seek the divorce in the nearby town of Cuernavaca, where, five years earlier, Marsden Hartley had spent several months. Burra's experiences on arrival in Mexico were not dissimilar to Hartley's: he too suffered problems with the altitude in Mexico City, disliked the food, despaired of the incessant rain in Cuernavaca and was debilitated by dysentery. Burra exclaimed to his sister: 'However I got here [Mexico City] I cannot imagine I never expected to reach such a queer place. 7,000 ft high so soon as you do anything you feel like a dead dog.'[24] In a letter to his mother, in reference to his own illness, he added: 'In mexico all the best brown little maladies of the tropics are very prevalent here such as dihorrea etc etc.'[25]

Aiken was very happy to travel on to Cuernavaca, especially as his former pupil Malcolm Lowry, with whom he had maintained a very close friendship, had been living there with his wife Jan Gabrial since late the previous year, and Aiken was eager to introduce him to Hoover. Burra had known Lowry since they had met in Spain in 1933. Cuernavaca at this time was a small town of some 13,000 people, popular as a weekend resort because of its agreeable climate and lush vegetation. Although Burra photographed the town from the first-floor balcony of the Palacio de Cortés, where Rivera's murals are located (see fig. 38), he failed to mention them, commenting instead: 'The Emperor Maximilian had his palace here rather a pretty building fallen somewhat in decay with a covered terrace with a marvellous view of landscape & distant mountains.'[26]

Unlike his wife, Lowry was delighted to see Aiken, with whom he shared a complex and tempestuous friendship fuelled by their mutual love of alcohol. Desperate for Aiken to approve his manuscript, Lowry began to drink heavily. He and Burra did not get on ('Ed is at heart an arid and contemptible fellow').[27] The atmosphere at Lowry's house was tense, especially as Gabrial resented Aiken's encouragement of Lowry's drinking; they also had to deal with a maid who was contemptuous of her employers. Burra slept in a cot on the first-floor veranda. 'There is', he wrote, 'an extraordinary view when not wreathed in rainy season from the veranda of Popacatepetle looking exactly like Fujiama capped with eternal snows realy fantastic at times' (fig. 64).[28] So poor was Burra's health that his friends insisted he return to the US to recover. In total he was in Mexico for a month. He wrote to his sister Anne on his return to Charlestown:

I returned here above very much the worse for wear for I had a terrible attack of dysentery in Mexico where everything is of the dirtiest having gone for two weeks & no better & feeling like the wrath of god & looking a yellowish skeleton I finally said I must leave so went off in a taxi from Cuernavaca to Mexico City that was quite comfortable tho it had its bad moments in Mexico City of course as no one knew anything about anything but 1st class fare Mexicans being on a pinnacle of dishonesty far outdoing any mere European manifestation however I got a ticket to Laredo the frontier & managed the journey pretty well I went to Laredo Pullman & day coach and they are realy very comfortable air conditioned & you can go in the diner up through Texas was a furnace & St Louis I waited 4 hrs was mercifully air conditioned in the waiting rooms by that time I was beginning to develop rheumatism in the feet so you may imagine I am now fairly crippled with it (for heavens sake don't say so to Ma) but I think Ime getting on & the dysentery is pretty well done with of course I never should have got over it in Mexico the filth in the kitchen was in the realms of phantasy it was so terrific a pity because it's a wonderful place but so unfortunate Cortez didn't do a better job very different from the Spanish I may say who are souls of honesty … Conrad Aiken & la IIIième Mdme A are still struggling with dysentery & their Mexican divorce groaning and moaning & feeling like death however I wouldn't have missed it for the world.[29]

According to Gabrial (although this is not corroborated anywhere else), Burra and Hoover visited Patzcuaro, a small colonial market town in Michoacan.[30] Lake Patzcuaro and the island of Janitzio, famous for its Day of the Dead celebrations, were popular destinations for tourists and the artistic community alike. In order to reach Patzcuaro from Cuernavaca by car or bus they would

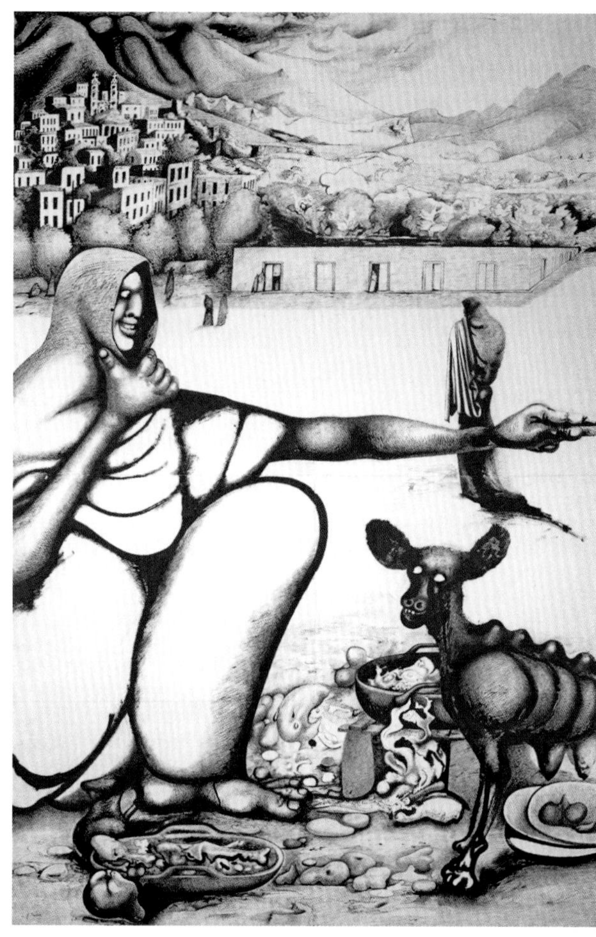

Fig. 65 Edward Burra, **Landscape with Comestibles Seen en route to Mexico City**, c. 1937. Pen and ink wash drawing on paper, 197.5 x 122 cm. Private collection

have travelled via Morelia and Toluca. It was in Morelia that the young American painters Philip Guston and Reuben Kadish and the poet and art critic Jules Langsner had recently completed *The Struggle against Terrorism* (see fig. 57). If Burra did indeed make this trip, it is extremely likely that he visited the recently inaugurated mural. Certainly the elongated form of the woman selling food by the railway in *Landscape with Comestibles Seen en route to Mexico City* (fig. 65) has echoes of the deliberately distorted figures and changing perspectives of *The Struggle against Terrorism*. This large landscape, which is very little known, must rate among the most powerful images that Burra ever produced.

After recovering his health in America, Burra returned to England towards the end of 1937. At home in Rye, he completed three works with Mexican subjects which are reproduced together for the first time here (cats 106, 107, fig. 65). Burra was famous for painting from memory and rarely produced sketches, although he did refer to large scrapbooks of photographs, postcards and newspaper and magazine cuttings when working. Ironically, since Burra had had to leave before Aiken's divorce was granted, the first of these paintings was probably *Landscape with Comestibles Seen en route to Mexico City*, which commemorated the train journey they had made together to Mexico.[31] Of the work Aiken wrote to Lowry:

> *Both Mary and I have so often pined to see it all again* [Cuernavaca], *but without the physiological and psychological miseries that beset us so persistently. Ed* [Burra] *too: I wish you could see what he has kept of it: on our diningroom wall, over the refractory table, scene of those prodigious alcoholic pingpong matches, hangs the world's largest pen-and-ink drawing: eight feet by five of purest beautifullest dreadfullest Mexico: a hooded leering figure in the desert foreground, seated by a fire of sticks, on which a cauldron of dry bones, is about to throw a stick for an emaciated cadaverous bitch, with enormous swollen dugs; the bitch regards the stick-thrower sidelong with an ironic nerts-to-you expression which is quite appalling: at their feet lie other fragments and shards of bones, and a few (they look like the crumbled skeleton of an infant) have been gathered into a wooden bowl. But, back turned to this sinister pair, who are about to perform their sceptical and evil communication, a classically serene figure, hooded too, glides away towards the eternal magical hill-town that rises from the eternal barranca and jungle, and the twin-towered cathedral, and the bitter black mountains above it, and the afrit-black bitter clouds that brew above them. The whole landscape is magically sinister and beautiful, and altogether it's probably the finest thing Ed has done – we're buying it on the nickel-a-year-for-life principle, as you might imagine.*[32]

In his *A Heart for the Gods of Mexico* (London, 1939), a barely disguised fictional account of the trip that Aiken, Hoover and Burra made to Mexico, Aiken described leaving Saltillo by train in a passage that could almost be a description of Burra's work:

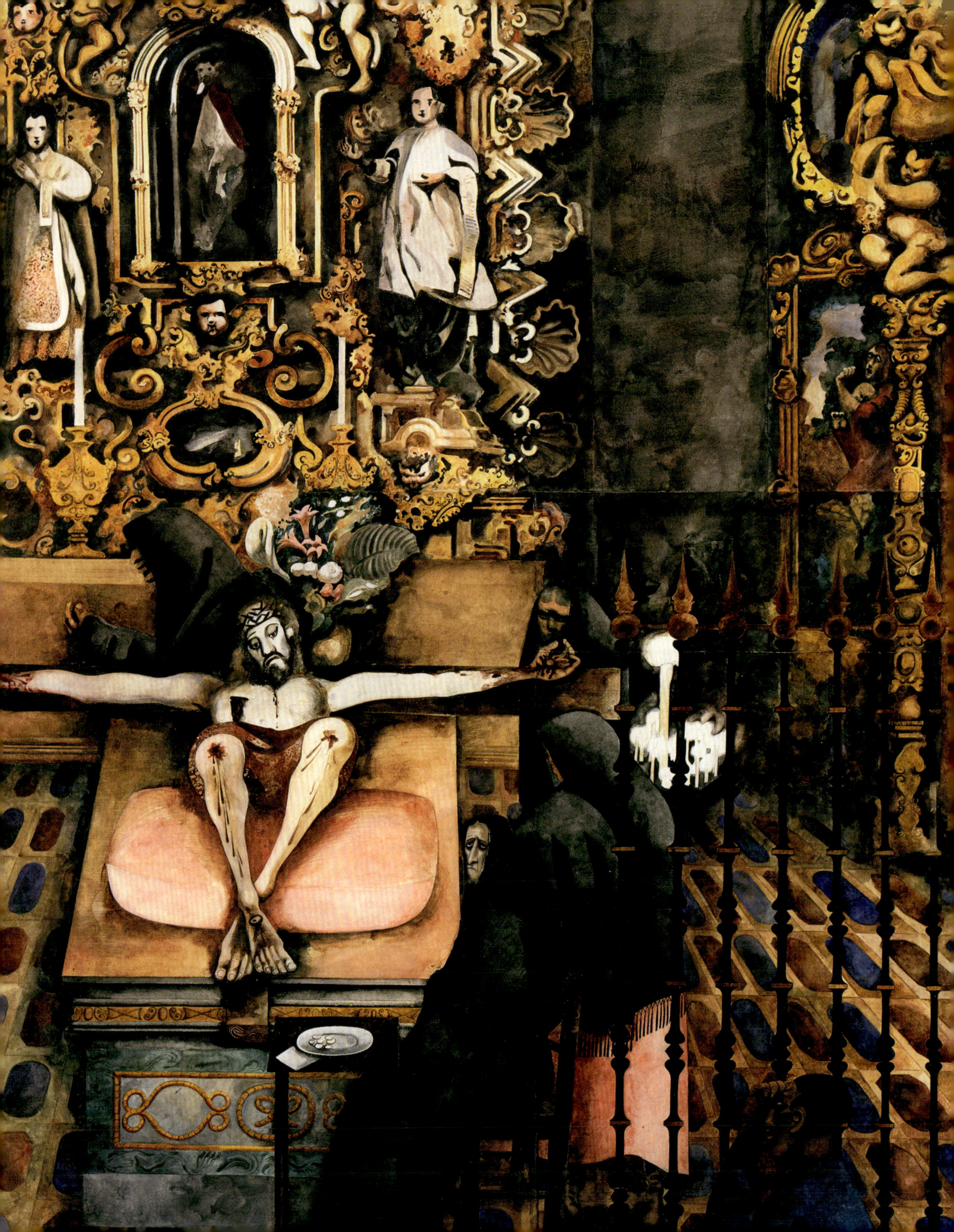

In the profound stillness of early morning, the train then began to move, it glided away from the forlorn and deserted station, where not a soul was to be seen. A little mud-walled town was now visible, on the dark scrubby slope of the mountain, as forlorn and deserted as the station; and then, standing alone in the desert, his back to the sharply outlined mountains in the east, a solitary shrouded figure came into view, an Indian, wrapped closely in his sarape, standing immovable and secret as a rock to watch the passage of the train. It was incredible; it was a dream.[33]

Many years later, in 1976, after Burra's death, Mary Aiken described his drawing:

It is the landscape of that dawn we awakened to the sunrise glimmering through and over the mountains onto a village on the barren Mexican plateau below. The sky, mountains and village are at the top, and have an ominous feel about them. Then in the foreground is a large peasant woman, wrapped in a serape and ragged shawl, like a squatted Fate figure, stirring a large flat-lipped pot containing fleshy bones, set over a small fire. Her face is expressionless, as only an Indian's, or someone's without hope, could be. Not glowering – merely being. Looking on, with a prayer in its piteous eyes that some morsel will, by an unhoped for good luck, come its way, is a mongrel bitch with great swollen dragging teats. Mexico: it is all there.[34]

The other two works are *Mexican Church* (cat. 106) and *El Paseo* (cat. 107; see Appendix, pp. 202–4).

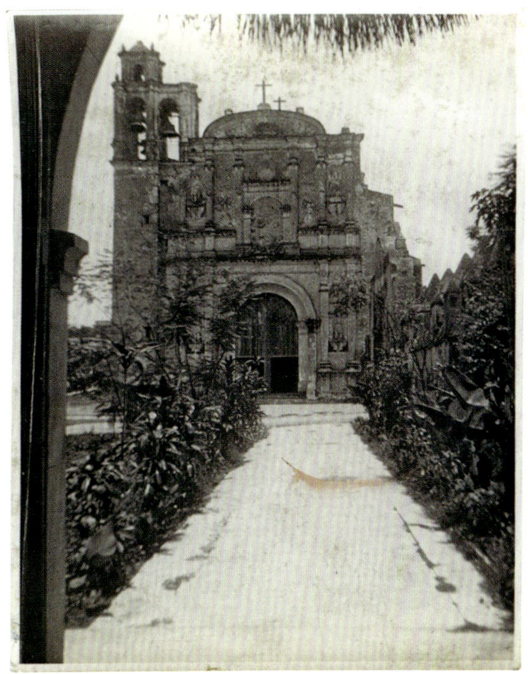

Fig. 66 Edward Burra, 'The exterior of the Tercera Orden de San Francisco, Cuernavaca', 1937. Black and white photograph, 10 x 8 cm. Tate Archive, London, M01198

Mexican Church reveals the building's gloomy colonial baroque interior. It has been suggested that the work is a composite view taken from two postcards that Burra purchased in Mexico.[35] Among his large collection of postcards there are a surprising number of religious images, including polychrome statues and church façades, although these are mostly Spanish. Burra's interest in baroque Catholic buildings and sculptures is demonstrated by a photograph he took of the exterior of the Tercera Orden de San Francisco, a picturesque colonial church in Cuernavaca (fig. 66). As it is the only one

106

Edward Burra (1905–1976)
Mexican Church, c. 1938.
Gouache and ink wash
on paper, 132.1 x 103.5 cm.
Tate, London. Purchased 1940

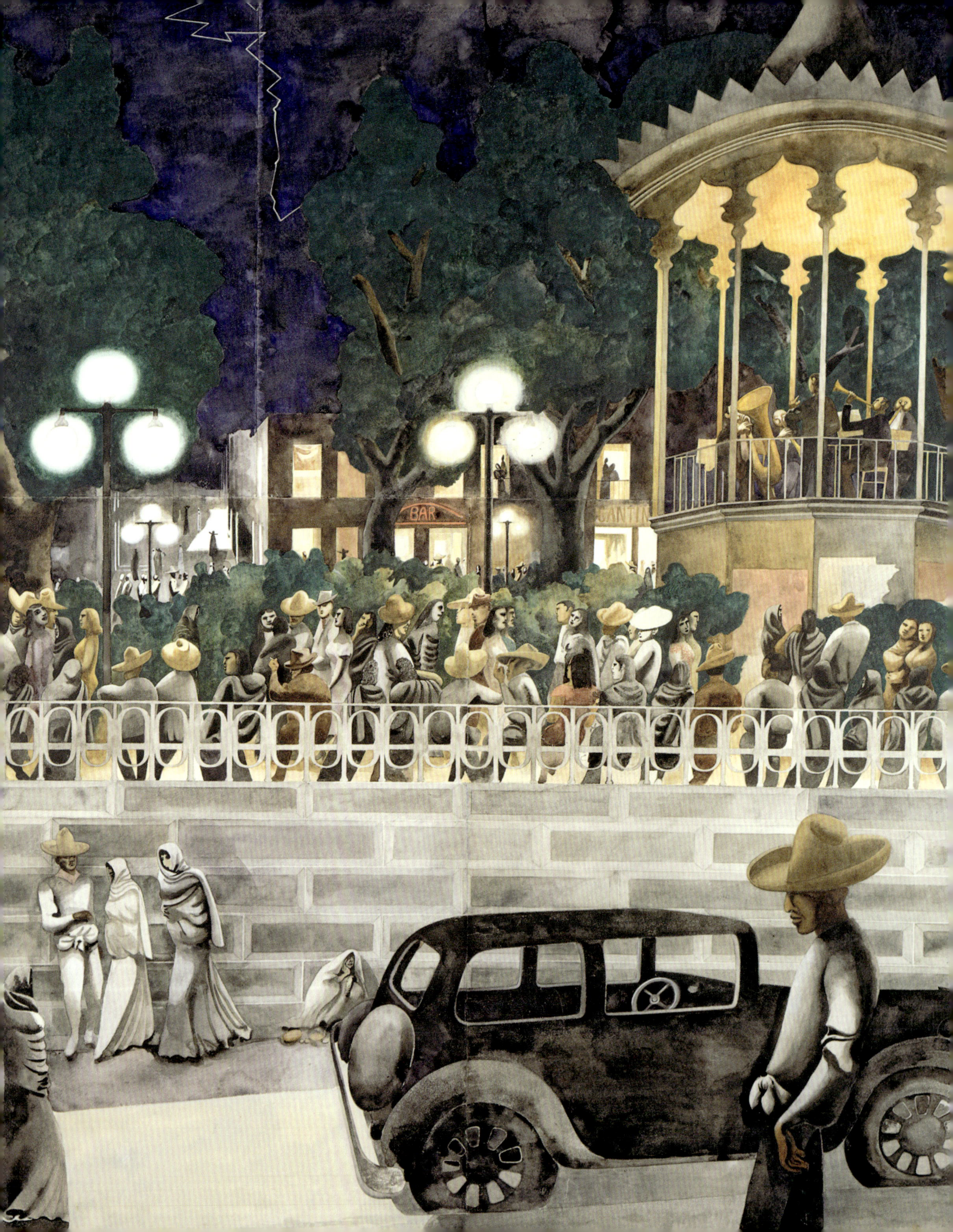
BAR

of the three works in a public collection, *Mexican Church* has received a great deal more interest and commentary than the other two. Mary Aiken wrote, 'As soon as he returned to Rye, he [Burra] made a large painting of one of the chapels done from an amazing perspective view, and including, with the figure on the tomb, all the surrounding bric-à-brac and a total ambience so extraordinary, that it was as if one could see and be the whole interior of the Cathedral at the same time. What a genius! to do it all from memory.'[36]

El Paseo captures an evening scene in the Jardin Juárez, a public square in Cuernavaca. Beneath a closed canopy of mature trees, street lamps cast a bright glow over couples and chaperones walking in the square, accompanied by the music emanating from the bandstand. Promenading in public was typical of courtship in Mexico, and Burra has captured the scene with great brilliance and in his characteristically effortless style. He injects a degree of humour into the painting by recording the strain on the inflated cheeks of the band members as they play with gusto, and something of the macabre with the deathly, almost skull-like faces of the perambulating couples. In the foreground, phantom-like women appear, wrapped in their *rebozos* against the cold or out of modesty.

Despite his visit being overshadowed by ill health and the tense atmosphere at Lowry's house, Burra retained a great admiration for the art of Mexico. He visited the big post-war exhibition of Mexican art at the Musée d'art moderne in Paris in 1952, and on two more occasions when it came to the Tate Gallery in London early the following year as the 'Exhibition of Mexican Art from Pre-Columbian Times to the Present Day'.[37] In many ways it is difficult to gauge the impact that Burra's trip to Mexico had on him. Paintings such as *The Three Fates* (fig. 67) allude to the baroque architecture of Mexico but could also be seen to reflect the religious architecture of Spain, a country Burra knew much better and in which admittedly he had a greater interest. Although undoubtedly shocked by the conditions he experienced in Mexico, his work of this period was predominantly driven by events in Europe, firstly the Spanish Civil War and then the Second World War. Nonetheless, these three works from Mexico are significant and reveal his

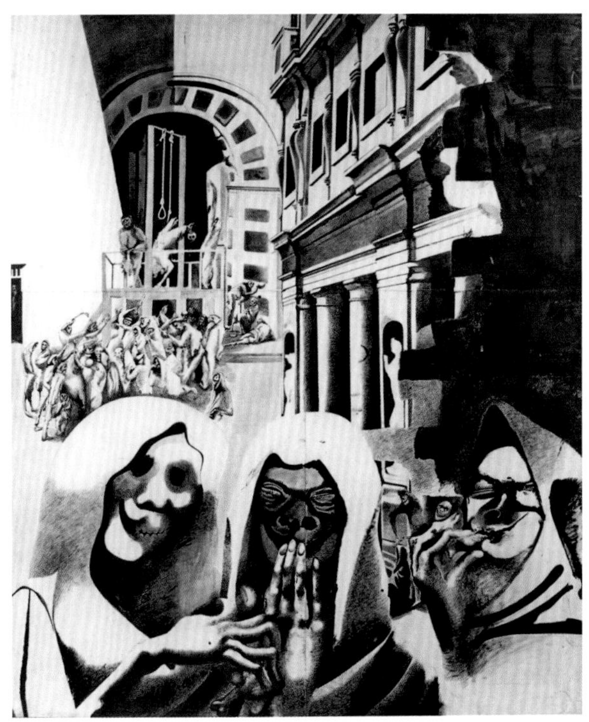

Fig. 67 Edward Burra, **The Three Fates**, *c.* 1937. Watercolour on paper, 132.1 x 111.8 cm. Private collection

107

Edward Burra
(1905–1976)
El Paseo, *c.* 1938.
Watercolour on paper,
113.3 x 110.5 cm.
Private collection, London

fascination with certain characteristics of the country. The fervour of the Catholic faith and the dark interiors of the churches, with their striking processional images that had so impressed Strand (see cat. 85), clearly attracted his interest. Likewise, he was drawn to the evening promenades and the old-fashioned courtship that took place in public places with lively music, which he loved. The poverty and filth that he wrote about in his letters were part of the lasting first impression that Mexico made upon Burra as he awoke on the overnight train from Laredo as it made its way towards the capital.

Another British novelist who travelled to Mexico was Graham Greene. A member of the socialist Independent Labour Party since 1933, he must have been interested to see the impact of the Mexican Revolution at first hand. Before he went to Mexico, Greene had told his literary agent, 'I'm feeling rather bored with everything. I don't know how I shall get the vitality to think of another novel unless I can get out of bloody Europe.'[38] He had been discussing two projects that never came to fruition. The first was to have been a race around the world involving Evelyn Waugh and based on Jules Verne's *Around the World in Eighty Days*. Referring to the participants as professional tourists, Waugh thought the idea interesting but suggested there should be more competitors, including the Byzantine scholar and writer Robert Byron: 'I think it should be a race not in time but economy. Each competitor to start with no luggage and a limited sum – say £100 – and the one who arrives with most cash in hand to get a prize.'[39] The second of Greene's unrealised projects was to have been a collaboration with the journalist and writer Malcolm Muggeridge, in which the two writers were to approach the Palestinian civil war from different sides – Greene from Syria, presenting an Arab perspective, and Muggeridge from Tel Aviv, presenting a Jewish perspective – before meeting at the Holy Sepulchre in Jerusalem.[40]

Ever since reading Lawrence's *The Plumed Serpent* as a twenty-one-year-old, Greene had yearned to visit Mexico, and he was further inspired to do so by Evelyn Waugh's biography of the martyred Jesuit priest Edmund Campion. Campion ran an underground Catholic ministry in Protestant England until his capture in 1581; his subsequent execution mirrored the persecution of priests in contemporary Mexico.[41] After protracted negotiations, Greene secured backing from the publisher Longman to travel to Mexico to report on the suppression of Catholics by the government.[42] He spent five weeks there, and the result was *The Lawless Roads: A Mexican Journey* (London, 1939).[43] The trip was arduous and at times dangerous. As Lowry had found in Oaxaca, the government's seizure of the oil industry had caused Mexicans to view foreigners with suspicion, and police informants were everywhere. Despite the formal end of the Cristero Rebellion in 1929, Catholic priests were still outlawed in many states; although driven underground, they continued to hold masses, baptisms and other religious rites in secret. Greene's journey to Palenque from Salto by mule brought him extreme discomfort and sickness (including dysentery) but provided him with the foundations for *The Power and the Glory* (London, 1940), arguably one of the greatest novels of the twentieth century, and his finest. Greene recounts the last months of a priest who lives in hiding because of state suppression of Catholicism in Tabasco. Governor Tomás Garrido Canabal, a fervently anti-Catholic and anticlerical ally of former President Plutarco Elías Calles, imposed draconian legislation in Tabasco that forced priests to go into hiding or exile. Apart from beer, alcohol was banned there. Garrido Canabal's 'Red Shirts', a group of paramilitary enforcers, terrorised the state, pursuing priests and destroying churches at will.

Greene's nameless priest moves from village to village, seeking sanctuary and performing rites for the villagers (for which he charges fees). A self-confessed 'whisky priest', he is always one step ahead of the pursuing enforcers. The novel is a moral tale about an obsessed lieutenant who is so desperate to capture a cowardly priest and prove his own worth that he resorts to a campaign of terror. In the end, on the point of crossing the state line and reaching safety, the priest turns back to confront his fate, determined to face death and seek redemption after the realisation that his life had been hollow and self-serving. Through this act of sacrifice the priest forces the lieutenant to question his own values and the cost, in human life, of his actions. As the priest calmly accepts his day of judgement, his principles outweigh those of the triumphant but by now deflated lieutenant, who has caught the priest only because he knowingly walked into a trap. The novel draws heavily on Greene's own experiences in Mexico, which provide the book with an authentic sense of the hardships of impoverished rural communities and European immigrants struggling to survive.

As a Catholic and a socialist, Greene witnessed clandestine masses in Mexico and was very conscious of the suspicion that his foreignness aroused. The physical trials of his visit, captured so effectively in *The Lawless Roads*, exhausted him, as did the unpredictable nature of the country and its people. While in Mexico City he wrote to Ben Hubsch of Viking Press, 'I hate this country and this people', and was relieved to be leaving the city, for which he had little affection, for Orizaba.[44] Greene's time in Mexico soured him:

> *Puebla was the only Mexican town in which it seemed to me possible to live with some happiness. It had more than the usual wounded beauty: it had grace. Something French seemed to linger there from Maximilian's time ... even the arts and crafts of Puebla were civilised in a Victorian, European way.*[45]

The aspects of Mexico that had attracted so many were not, after all, what Greene wanted. Following the hardships he had endured on his travels, he harked back to Europe and the conventional concept of civilisation that it offered. And yet Greene did find impressions etched into his memory: 'Only the bullet hole in the porch showed the flaw in Paradise – that this was Mexico.'[46]

If Greene travelled rough and alone during his time in Mexico, the same cannot be said of his compatriot and fellow Catholic Evelyn Waugh. Travelling via New York with his second wife Laura Herbert, Waugh was cosseted throughout and confined himself to the relatively prosperous Valley of Mexico and excursions from the capital.[47] Waugh had been approached in early 1938 by Cecil Pearson, second son of Viscount Cowdray, acting as a representative of his family's extensive business interests in Mexico. Pearson and his family were looking to Waugh to write a popular book that would advertise the injustice of the expropriation by Cárdenas of their hugely profitable oil business.[48] Initially entitled 'Pickpocket Government', the book was published as *Robbery under Law: The Mexican Object-lesson* (London, 1939).[49]

The Pearsons were munificent patrons.[50] Waugh received a cheque for £989, generous expenses and comprehensive travel insurance. Arriving in Mexico in August 1938, they stayed for two months. Waugh's robustly worded contract stipulated that he was not to disclose any information about the agreement, nor was he allowed to state that he was receiving financial assistance from Pearson without written permission.[51]

Waugh was contemptuous of Mexico and the artists who travelled there:

> *In contrast to this type of transitory visitor [insurance agents] there are a large number of Americans who find, or profess to find in Mexico a spiritual home. These are the painters and writers who make such a large and charming section of the English speaking colony. Here in the hills they find an antidote for all the ills of their native civilisation. Although, almost all of them, dependent on invested capital for their livelihood, they express generous sympathy with General Cardenas' socialist regime ... they see a land where ambition, and particularly financial ambition, is not the dominant passion ... They see it, as Dr. Munthe saw San Michele, and it is largely due to their sentimental vision, that the legend has spread and earned credence, of the parasitic white tyrant and the patient savage. The new mood in the Mexican governing clique is destructive of all they value but few of them seem to recognise this; quite soon they may have a rude shock but at the moment they are happy with their tropical plants, collections of bric-a-brac, and albums of Diego Rivera ... the writer who has given most people their ideas about Mexico is D. H. Lawrence; and he hated it ... He came there hoping for an antidote to the poison of industrialism and he left in disgust; he never forgot it.*[52]

Unsurprisingly, Waugh later dismissed the book. The commission was highly partisan and the result was an unbridled attack on Mexico and the politics of its government. He concluded acidly, 'They [the Mexicans] see what, through annexation, has become of California and obstinately prefer their own comparative disorder and desolation.'[53]

Although neither Greene nor Waugh paid much attention to the process of economic development that was taking place across Mexico, many others did. The Mexican painter Antonio Ruiz, known as El Corcito ('Little Corzo') for his likeness to the Spanish bullfighter Manuel Corzo, had worked in Hollywood as a set designer for Universal Studios. He returned to Mexico in 1929 and pursued a career in art education. His output was small – his friend Rivera reported that his entire *oeuvre* would have fitted into a cabinet[54] – and he sold only three paintings in his lifetime. Of these, the Museum of Modern Art, New York, acquired *The New Rich* (1941) in 1943 and the

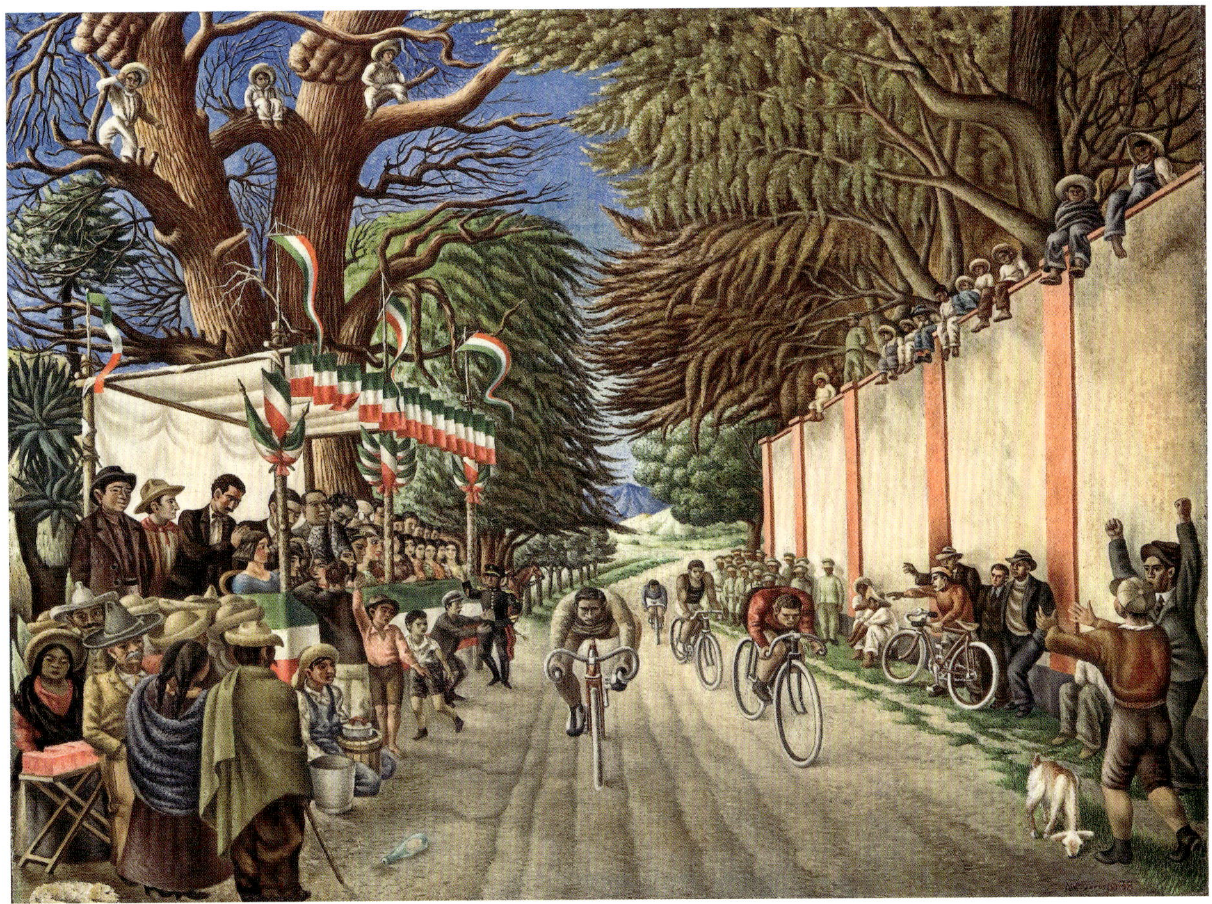

Philadelphia Museum of Art bought *Bicycle Race* (cat. 108) in 1949. Ruiz was represented by two paintings in the 'International Exhibition of Surrealism' at the Galería de Arte Mexicano in Mexico City.[55]

After 1937 Ruiz began to make paintings that were critical of the political regime. Although their content engages immediately with the viewer and appears at first glance to be humorous and light-hearted, their message is hard to avoid. Ruiz exposes the gulf of inequality between traditional Mexico, as represented by the peasant, and the new, modern country, symbolised by technological innovation such as the racing bicycle or the goods on sale in a shop. The absurdity of peasants looking at the latest beachwear designed for the seaside resorts

108

Antonio Ruiz (1892–1964)
Bicycle Race (Carrera de cintas en Texcoco), 1938.
Oil on canvas, 33.3 x 43.2 cm.
Philadelphia Museum of Art. Purchased with the Nebinger Fund, 1949

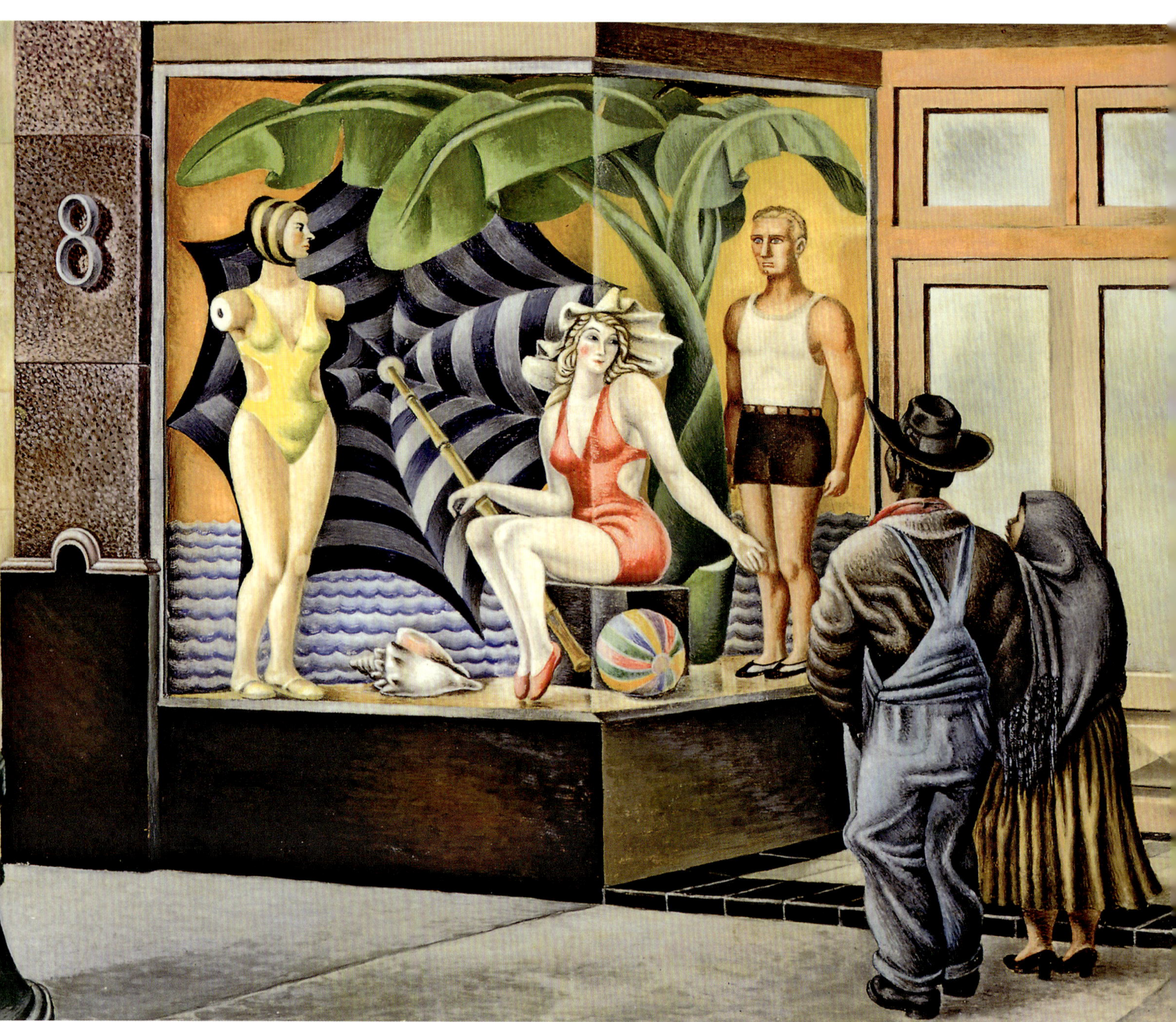

109

Antonio Ruiz (1892–1964)
Summer (El verano), 1937.
Oil on wood, 28.5 x 34.7 cm.
Acervo Patrimonialde la
Secretaría de Hacienda y
Crédito Público, Mexico City

of the Pacific or Gulf coasts in a window display (cat. 109) is both witty and unsettling. In its pursuit of modernity the Mexican state had neglected to address economic equality; although it had pretensions to compete with the US economically, it had failed to integrate the peasant class into society, leaving them marginalised, disenfranchised and increasingly isolated. In *Bicycle Race*, the fast pace of the racing cycles leaves the sedentary peasants behind, literally in a cloud of dust; perhaps this is Ruiz's interpretation of Aesop's fable about the hare and the tortoise. The long wall running along the right of the painting demarcates an unseen but presumably grand property, a physical barrier between private and public space: a division that the Revolution had conspicuously failed to remove.

Although he did not count Ruiz among the first tier of Surrealist artists, André Breton certainly liked his work. The cash-strapped poet had jumped at the offer of a lucrative commission from the French Ministry of Foreign Affairs to lecture at the National University in Mexico City on the state of poetry and painting in Europe.[56] He and his wife Jacqueline arrived at Vera Cruz on 18 April 1938. In the end he was only to give one of his five advertised talks, 'L'Art et le surréalisme', having been prevented from delivering the rest when he was stripped of his official mission.[57] While they were in Mexico the Bretons stayed with Rivera and Kahlo at their new house, designed by Juan O'Gorman, in San Angel (see cats 72, 73). Kahlo found her guest vain and arrogant, nicknaming him the 'old cockroach' and commenting acerbically, 'I never knew I was a Surrealist until André Breton came to Mexico and told me I was one.'[58]

Breton was an ardent admirer of Leon Trotsky and had aligned the Surrealists with the

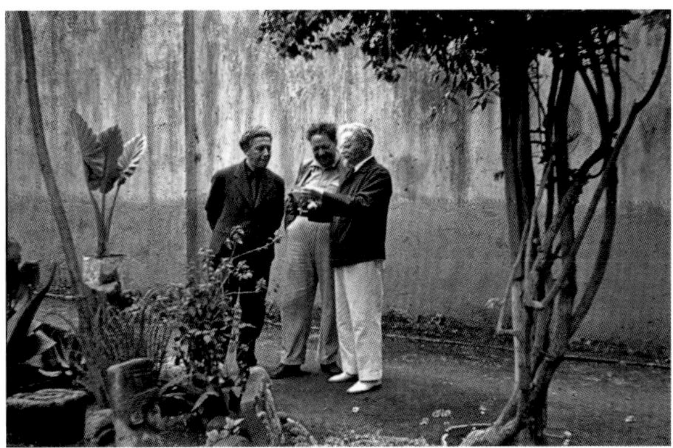

Fig. 68 Manuel Álvarez Bravo, **André Breton, Diego Rivera and Leon Trotsky**, 1939. Gelatin silver print, 20.3 x 25.4 cm. Asociación Manuel Álvarez Bravo, Mexico City

Russian, partly as a gesture of support since his expulsion from France in 1936 and partly out of respect for his intellect. Trotsky – unceremoniously usurped by Joseph Stalin after the death of Vladimir Lenin in 1924 in the contest for the leadership of the Communist Party in Soviet Russia – believed in a Marxist revolution led by the proletariat as opposed to the urban bourgeoisie. In other words, he considered that revolution could take place in an economically backward country, led by the working classes; Mexico, with its largely rural population and economy, was a good example.

When he met Trotsky for the first time in Coyoacan, Breton was awestruck. Their respect for Trotsky brought Rivera and Breton very close; indeed, over the nearly four months of his stay in Mexico, Breton spent virtually all his time with either Trotsky or Rivera, and they often travelled together. Photographs by Manuel Álvarez Bravo, whose work Breton saw for the first time in an exhibition in Guadalajara, show the three of them enjoying time together in Coyoacan (fig. 68).[59]

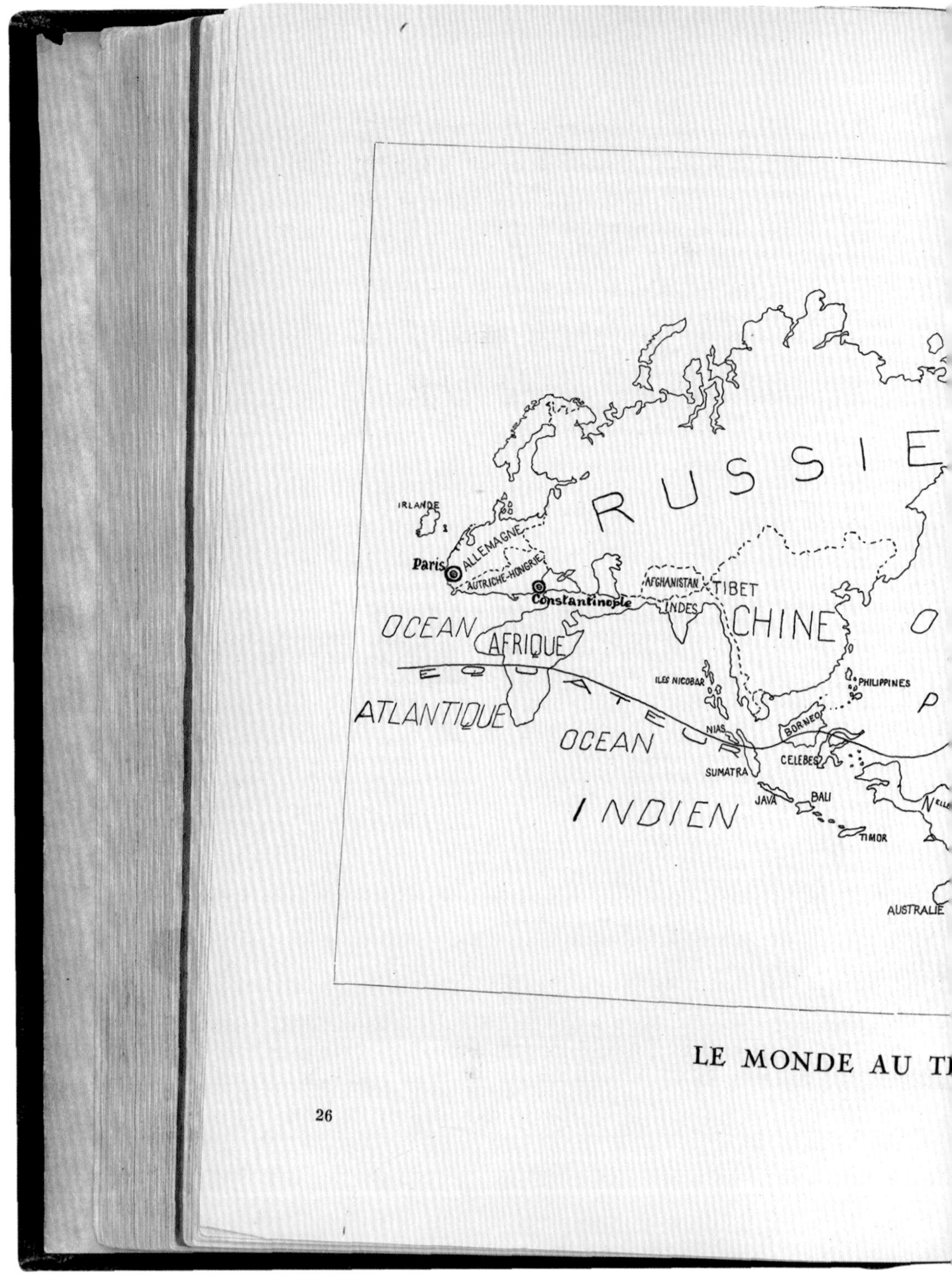

Fig. 69 Unknown artist, 'Le monde au temps des Surréalistes', from *Le Surréalisme en 1929*, pp. 26–7, supplement of *Variétés*, Brussels, June 1929. Printed book, 25.2 x 17.8 cm. The Museum of Modern Art, New York, PN605.S8 S87 1929g

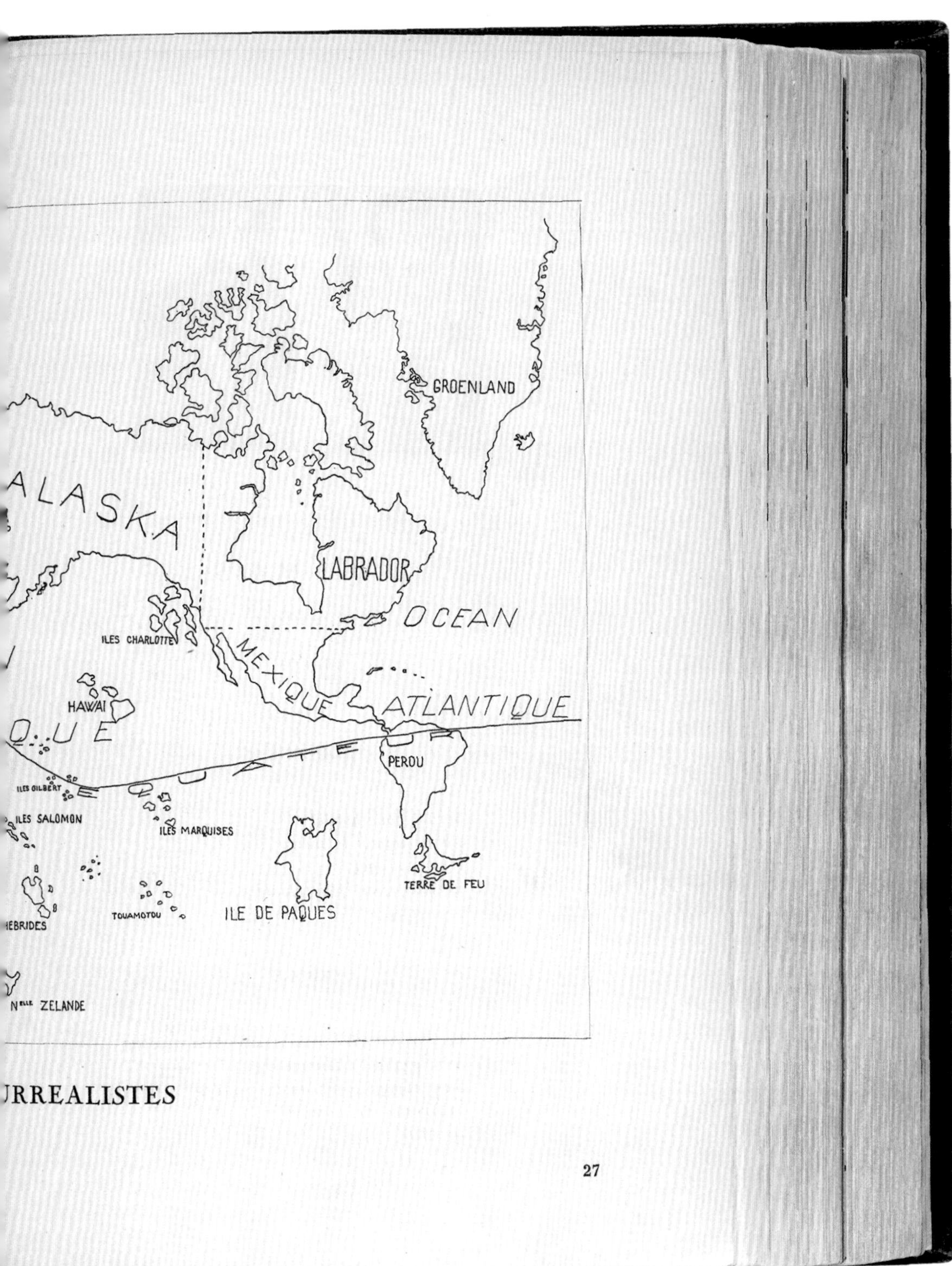
GROENLAND
ALASKA
LABRADOR
OCEAN
ILES CHARLOTTE
MEXIQUE
ATLANTIQUE
HAWAI
PEROU
ILES GILBERT
ILES SALOMON
ILES MARQUISES
TERRE DE FEU
TOUAMOTOU
ILE DE PAQUES
N ELLE ZELANDE
27

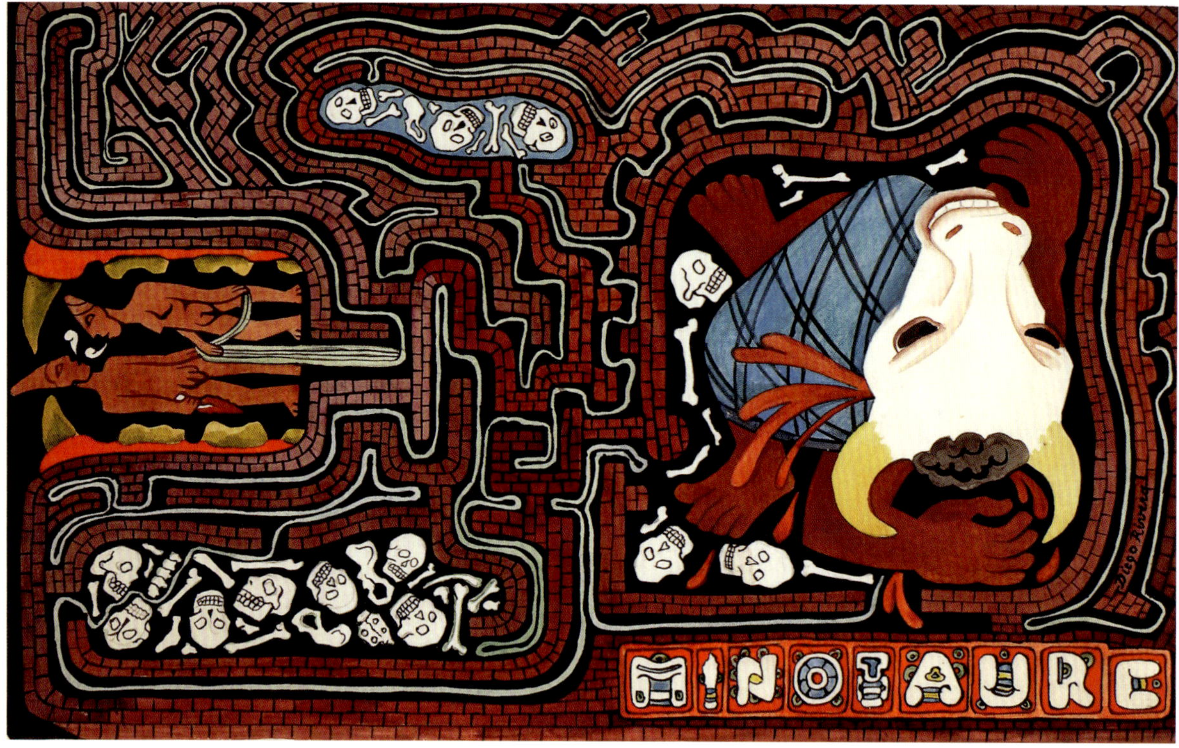

Fig. 70 Diego Rivera, design concept for the interior cover of 'Souvenir du Mexique', contained in the magazine *Minotaure*, No. 12–13, Paris, 1939. Gouache on paper. Private collection

Breton, Trotsky and Rivera travelled to Michoacan to record a series of discussions called 'Conversations in Patzcuaro', but this project was not realised. Trotsky and Breton particularly enjoyed walking together, along with fishing and catching butterflies.

Trotsky urged Breton to write a manifesto on revolutionary art but Breton, hugely intimidated by Trotsky's intellect, prevaricated. Eventually Trotsky helped and *Pour un art révolutionnaire independent* (*Manifesto for an Independent Revolutionary Art*) was completed and dated 25 July 1938. Signed off with the rousing phrases 'The independence of art – for the Revolution. The Revolution – for the complete independence of art!', the manifesto attacks the art censorship exercised by the regimes of Hitler and, in particular, Stalin. Quoting Marx, the authors state that while a writer (read artist) needs to make money to live and write, he does not live and write in order to make money. In a key passage, the manifesto states:

> *The free choice of these themes and the absence of all restrictions on the range of his exploitations – these are possessions which the artist has a right to claim as inalienable. In the realm of artistic creation, the imagination must escape from all constraint and must under no pretext allow itself to be placed under bonds. To those who urge us,*

whether for today or for tomorrow, to consent that art should submit to a discipline which we hold to be radically incompatible with its nature, we give a flat refusal and we repeat our deliberate intention of standing by the formula complete freedom for art.[60]

Trotsky insisted that Rivera be named alongside Breton as co-author of the manifesto, at the same time removing his own name from the document.[61] Breton returned to France on 1 August 1938, his suitcases full of popular art including *ex-votos* stolen from churches as well as thirteen prints he had purchased from Manuel Álvarez Bravo. Many of these items were included in the 1939 exhibition 'Mexique' and published in 'Souvenir du Mexique', a special essay he wrote in 1939 for the journal *Minotaure* (fig. 70). Breton was inspired by Mexico and enchanted by its traditions, not least the Day of the Dead, in which life and death were, to his way of thinking, reconciled. The mingling of different cultures, from the pre-Columbian through the colonial to the modern; the wide range and expressive nature of the popular arts; and the generally relaxed, liberal nature of society likewise appealed to him. These manifested themselves most evidently in the street markets, religious processions and in general aspects of daily life, making everything appear free of the constraints of Europe and America; they inspired Breton's famous observation that Mexico was the Surrealist place par excellence (fig. 69).[62] He encouraged the German-born painter Wolfgang Paalen and the Peruvian poet César Moro to organise an exhibition of Surrealist art in Mexico City. The landmark 'Exposición internacional del surrealismo' (International Exhibition of Surrealism), held in 1940 at the Galería de Arte Mexicano in Mexico City, was the fourth such exhibition (fig. 71).[63] Many international and

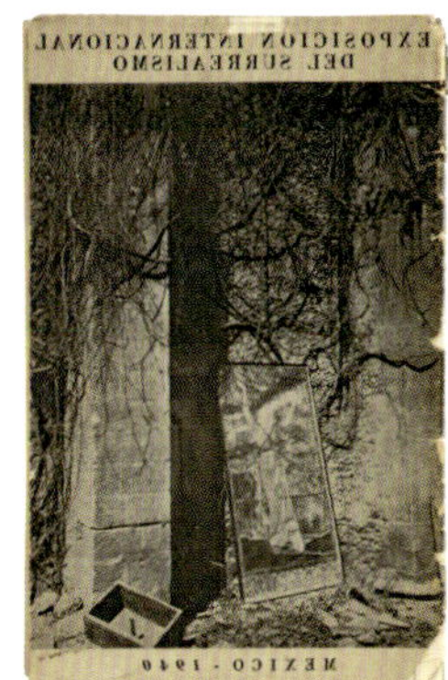

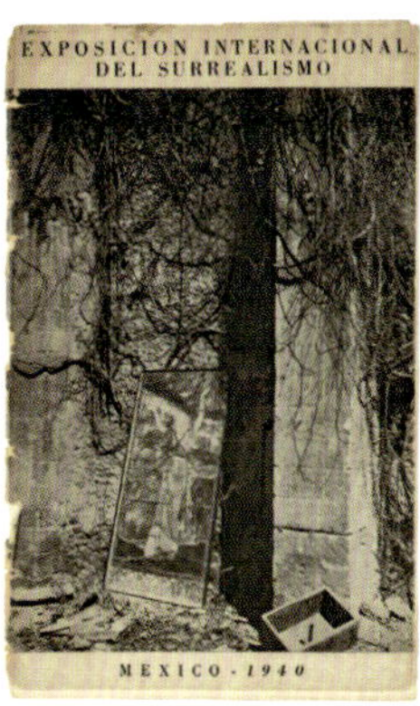

Fig. 71 Catalogue of 'Exposición internacional del surrealismo', featuring Manuel Álvarez Bravo's *On Winter* (*Sobre el invierno*), 1939–40. Galería de Arte Mexicano, Mexico City, 1940. Private collection

Mexican artists were included, alongside ceramics of western Mexico from Rivera's collection and objects from Paalen's Oceanic art collection.[64] Moro wrote in the exhibition catalogue:

For the first time in centuries we witness a heavenly combustion in Mexico. A thousand tokens mingle and are seen in the conjugation of constellations which renew the brilliant pre-Columbian night. The most pure night of the new continent where great dream potentialities made the powerful jaws of civilisations in Mexico and Peru clash together. Countries which keep, in spite of the invasion of the Spanish barbarians and their followers of today, a thousand luminous points which must join very soon with the line of fire of international surrealism.[65]

However, despite all Breton's efforts to harness Mexican art and artists for the Surrealist project, many remained sceptical and did not embrace the movement. Indeed, for many Mexicans, even with its anticolonial position, Surrealism remained too

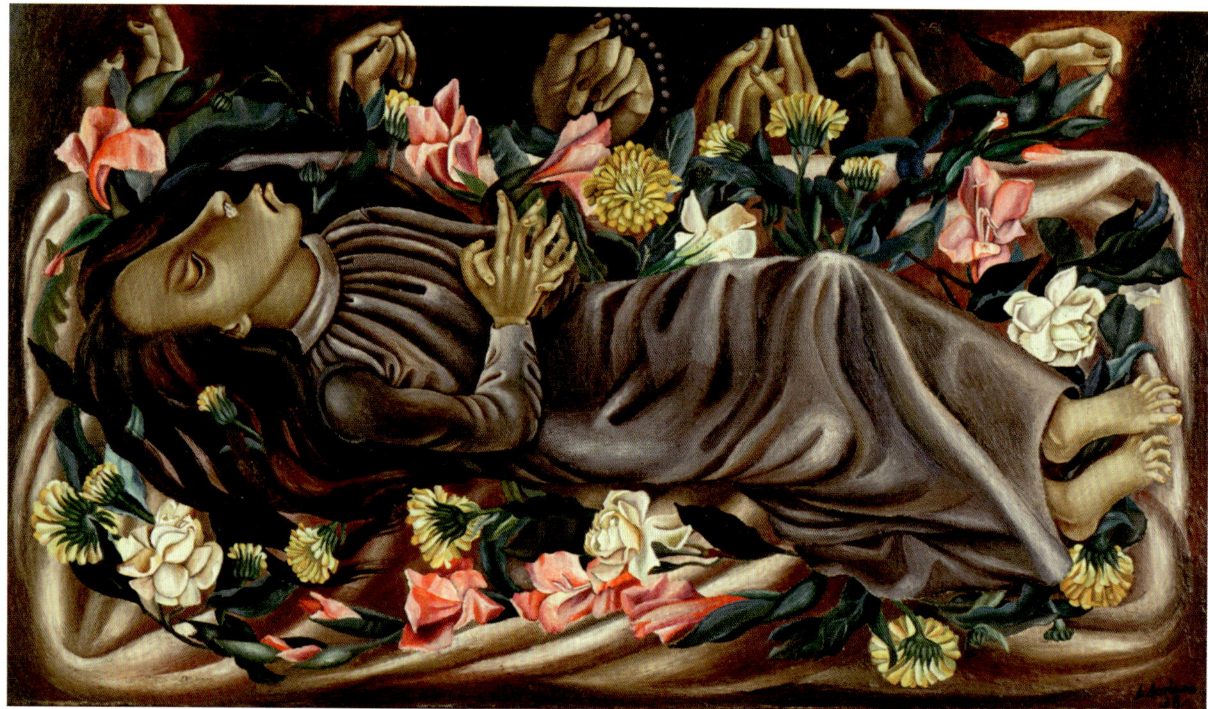

European in outlook.[66] No doubt Breton's reading of Mexican culture was also deemed patronising and somewhat superficial by some.

The Dead Girl by Juan Soriano (cat. 110) is typical of the type of painting that appealed to Breton. During a visit to Vera Cruz, Soriano walked past a house and saw, in the front window, the body of a dead girl, beautifully dressed and lying in state. The body had been placed in the window by her family to alert the neighbourhood to her premature death, so that people could come and pay their respects to the girl and her family. Such public displays of dead bodies were traditional in Mexico; the bodies of young children were dressed in their best clothes and those who could afford it would have a portrait, usually photographic, taken as a keepsake. This would be hung on the wall of the house for all to see, to preserve their memory of the loss. Soriano was sufficiently moved by this scene to paint it, and his work is made all the more poignant by his depiction of the row of clasped hands in the background. In 1937 Frida Kahlo had painted *The Deceased Dimas* (fig. 72) to commemorate the death of the three-year-old son of an Indian family in Ixtapalapa, the Rosas, whose members Rivera had used as models. In fact, Rivera was godfather to Dimas. The tradition of preserving images of dead children dates back at least to the nineteenth century, when studio portraits were regularly taken. During the colonial period, portraits of deceased nuns were likewise commonplace. Although Soriano's painting might have been seen as Surrealist by Breton (in much the

110

Juan Soriano (1920–2006)
The Dead Girl
(La niña muerta), 1938.
Oil on panel, 47 x 80 cm.
Philadelphia Museum of Art.
Gift of Mr and Mrs Henry
Clifford, 1947

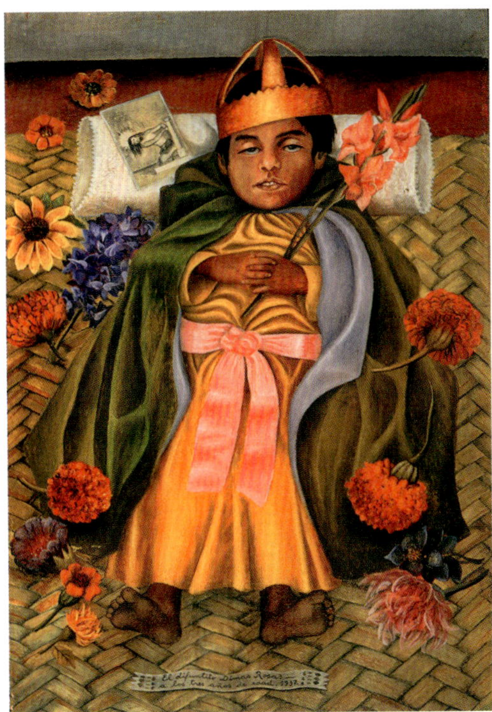

Fig. 72 Frida Kahlo, **The Deceased Dimas (El difunto Dimas)**, 1937. Oil on masonite, 48 x 31 cm. Museo Dolores Olmedo Patiño, Mexico City

same way as he had classified Manuel Álvarez Bravo's photographs), in its local context it was nothing more than a distinctive and commonplace form of venerating the dead. Thus the reality of Mexico was embraced as something 'other', simply because it was different from the European norm.

Breton did not return to Mexico after the assassination of Trotsky. Despite his initial enthusiasm for its art and artists, he was unable to absolve the country from some degree of responsibility for his hero's death, and it could also be argued that he never quite forgave Mexican artists for not wholeheartedly embracing Surrealism. He did, nonetheless, retain a fascination for Mexico and its pre-Columbian cultures for the rest of his life.[67] The Surrealists' tendency to regard Mexico as a representative of the non-European 'other' can be seen as part of a fantasy that embraced the popular, primitive and naive and placed this at odds with the sophisticated critique of modernism and *avant-garde* aesthetics currently being promoted by many of its artists.[68] Such a contrived view of Mexico later led Manuel Álvarez Bravo and Frida Kahlo, among others, to reject the Surrealist label, although as Paz noted it would be absurd to deny the influence of Surrealism on the work of Kahlo.[69] Indeed, Kahlo was initially drawn by the exposure the movement provided, before she determined otherwise.[70]

The exhibition marked the end of what has been described as the 'first Mexican School',[71] in part because it coincided with the influx of artists, among them Leonora Carrington, Remedios Varo, Gordon Onslow Ford, Luis Buñuel and Kati Horna, who were fleeing the Civil War in Spain and its aftermath, which introduced an attractive and viable alternative to Mexican Modernism. Their activities, supported by the active role played by the Galería de Arte Mexicano in the capital, changed the Surrealist landscape in Mexico. A number of Mexican artists, such as Agustín Lazo, Manuel Rodríguez Lozano, Guillermo Meza and Juan Soriano – encouraged by this alternative form of creativity which, with its universality, liberated artists from a specifically Mexican visual language – embraced the movement and consciously adhered to a Surrealist style, ensuring that the legacy of the 1940 exhibition endured. Although the production of murals along the lines of Mexican Modernism continued, these served more to present an appearance of ideological continuity than as an integral part of any social or educational programme, marking the end of an era.[72]

The assassination of Trotsky in 1940 sent shockwaves across the world. Trotsky had been granted political asylum in Mexico as a result of lobbying by Rivera, a recently joined member of the Mexican section of the (Trotskyite) International Communist League, and his fellow member Octavio Fernández. Having arrived in 1937 from Oslo, Trotsky and his wife Natalia lived in the Blue House, Coyoacan, the family home of Frida Kahlo, for the next two years. In 1937, over a period of some four months, Kahlo and Trotsky, who had a keen interest in women, had a brief love affair, in part fuelled by Kahlo's desire for revenge following a liaison between her husband Rivera and her sister Cristina. In November, months after the end of their dalliance, Kahlo presented Trotsky with a self-portrait (fig. 73) dedicated to him and dated 7 November 1937, his fifty-eighth birthday and the twentieth anniversary of the Russian Revolution. Breton much admired this painting when he saw it hanging in Trotsky's office, and he made the following comment about Kahlo: 'We are privileged to be present as in the most glorious days of German romanticism, at the entry of a young woman endowed with all the gifts of seduction, one accustomed to the society of men of genius', concluding that her art was like a 'ribbon around a bomb'.[73] Another self-portrait by Kahlo, also a love token, dates from this period (cat. 111).[74] However, in April 1939, when Trotsky, under pressure from his wife Natalia, moved to a nearby house in Coyoacan, he left the portrait behind, leaving little doubt about the distance that had subsequently come between him and Kahlo. On its first exhibition in New York at the Julien Levy Gallery, the painting (whose ownership had reverted to Kahlo) was entitled *Between the Curtains – Self-portrait Dedicated to Trotsky*. On 20 August 1940 Ramón Mercader, a Spanish-born Russian agent who had insinuated himself into Trotsky's inner circle and Kahlo's confidence (they had met in Paris in January 1939 when she attended the opening of 'Mexique', in which she was the principal artist), assassinated Trotsky with an ice pick as he sat at his desk.[75]

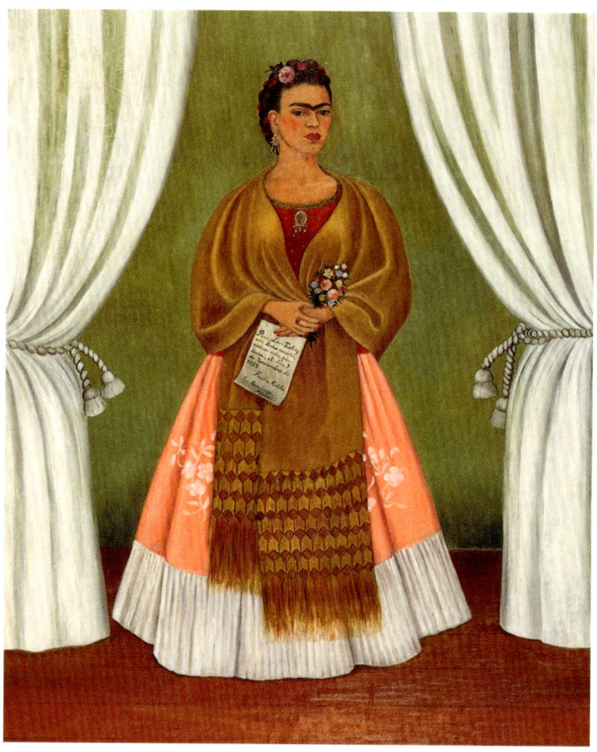

Fig. 73 Frida Kahlo, **Self-portrait Dedicated to Leon Trotsky**, 7 November 1937. Oil on masonite, 76.2 x 61 cm. National Museum of Women in the Arts, Washington, DC

The Hungarian-born photojournalist Robert Capa happened to be in Mexico when Trotsky was murdered. He had exhausted his US visa and the immigration authorities had refused to renew it, with the result that Capa was forced to leave America for six months while his immigration status was resolved. *Life* sent him to Mexico in June 1940 on assignment; the country was in the throes of a presidential election and was being unsettled by Nazi *agents provocateurs* whose aim was to distract American attention from events in Europe through their actions in Mexico.[76] Capa followed the two main presidential candidates, General Manuel Avila Camacho of the government's Partido Revolucionario Mexicano (PRM) and Juan Andreu Almazán of the conservative Partido de Acción Nacional (PAN), on their election campaigns and to their respective ranches (cats 112, 113). The day of the election, 7 July 1940, began with a demonstration in front of the central Post Office in Mexico City by Almazanistas; the Camachistas opened fire and killed a young man (cat. 114). Capa photographed his body lying in the street surrounded by fellow Almazanistas; the photograph, which has eerie echoes of Horne's *Victim of the Executing Squad* (1913; see cat. 13) and Álvarez

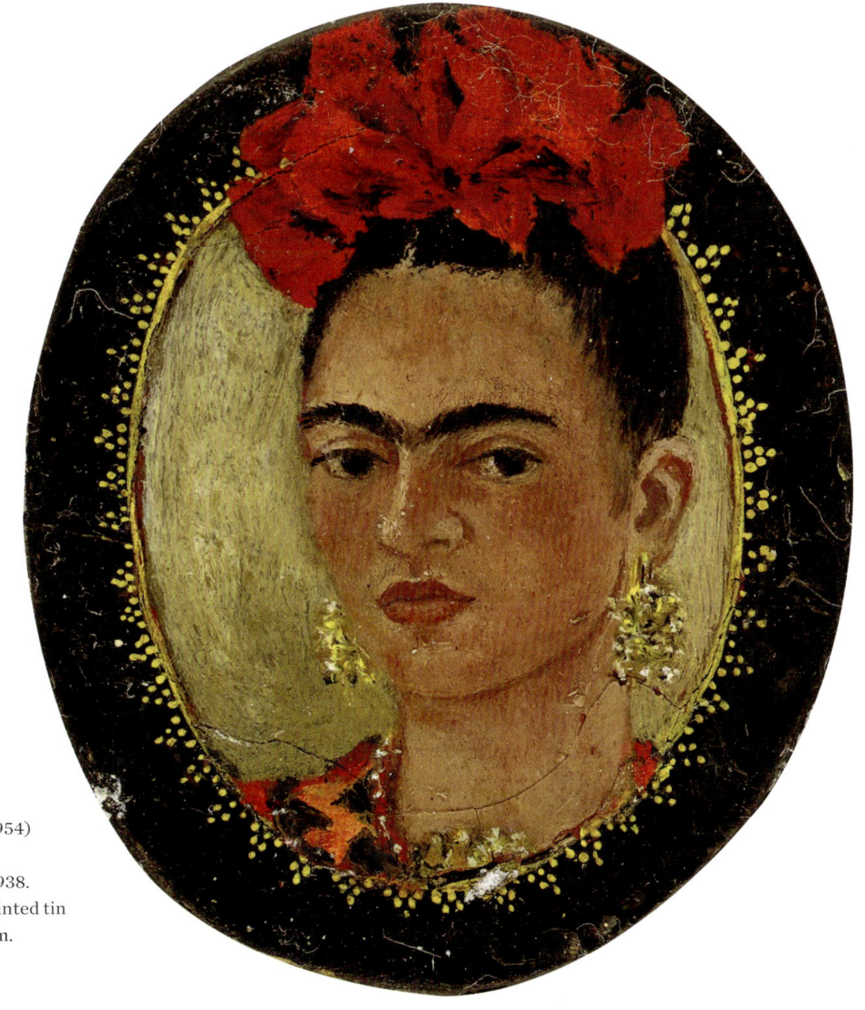

111

Frida Kahlo (1907–1954)
Self-portrait (Autorretrato), *c.* 1938.
Oil on board with painted tin border, 5.08 x 4.32 cm.
Courtesy Sotheby's

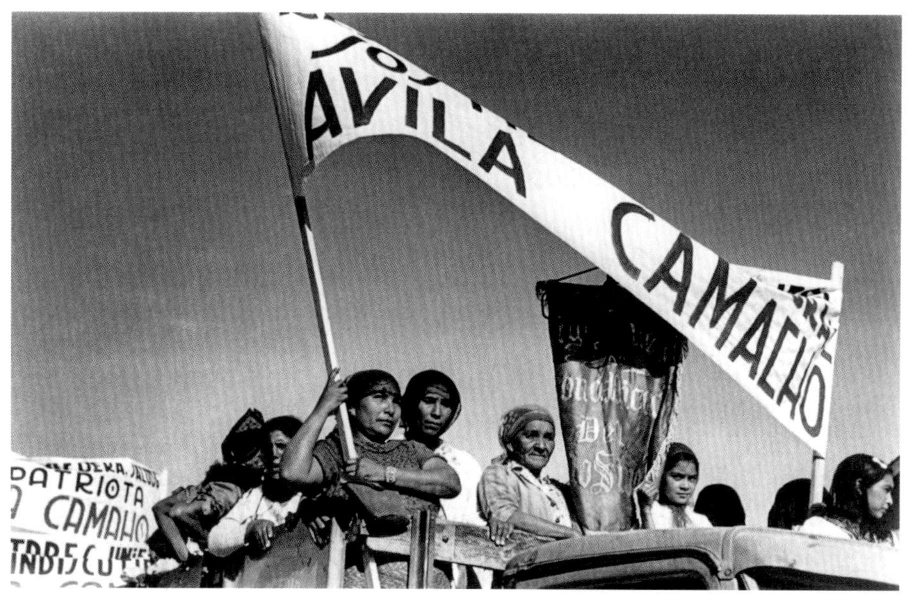

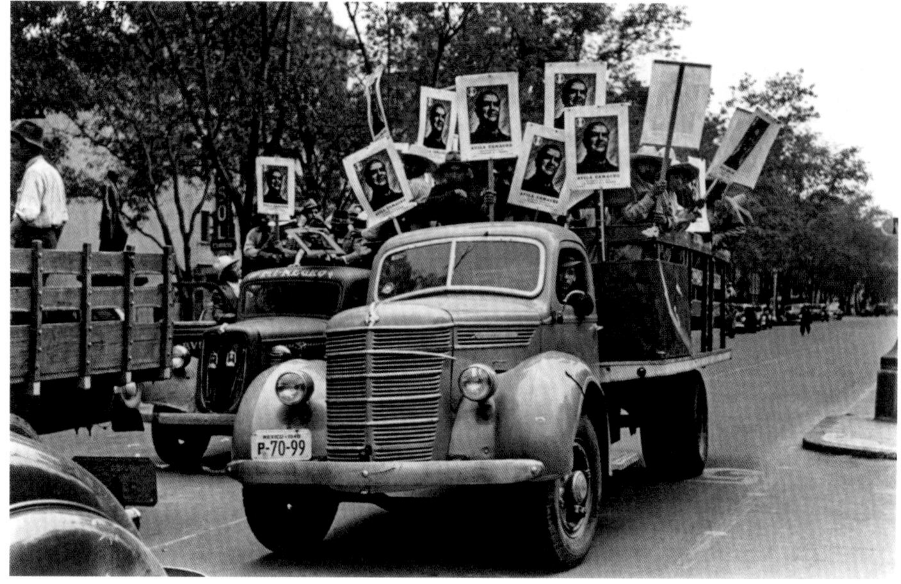

112

Robert Capa (1913–1954)
Women in Truck with Banners Supporting Presidential Candidacy of General Manuel Avila Camacho, Mexico City, June – July 1940.
Gelatin silver print,
40.64 x 50.8 cm.
International Center of Photography, New York, Robert Capa and Cornell Capa Archive. Gift of Cornell Capa and Edith Capa, 1992 (2852.1992)

113

Robert Capa (1913–1954)
Men in Truck with Signs Supporting Presidential Candidacy of General Manuel Avila Camacho, Mexico City, June – July 1940.
Gelatin silver print,
40.64 x 50.8 cm.
International Center of Photography, New York, Robert Capa and Cornell Capa Archive. Gift of Cornell Capa and Edith Capa, 1992 (2851.1992)

114

Robert Capa (1913–1954)
First Fatality on the Day of the Presidential Elections, Mexico City, 7 July 1940.
Gelatin silver print,
40.64 x 50.8 cm.
International Center of Photography, New York, Robert Capa and Cornell Capa Archive. Gift of Cornell Capa and Edith Capa, 1992 (2860.1992)

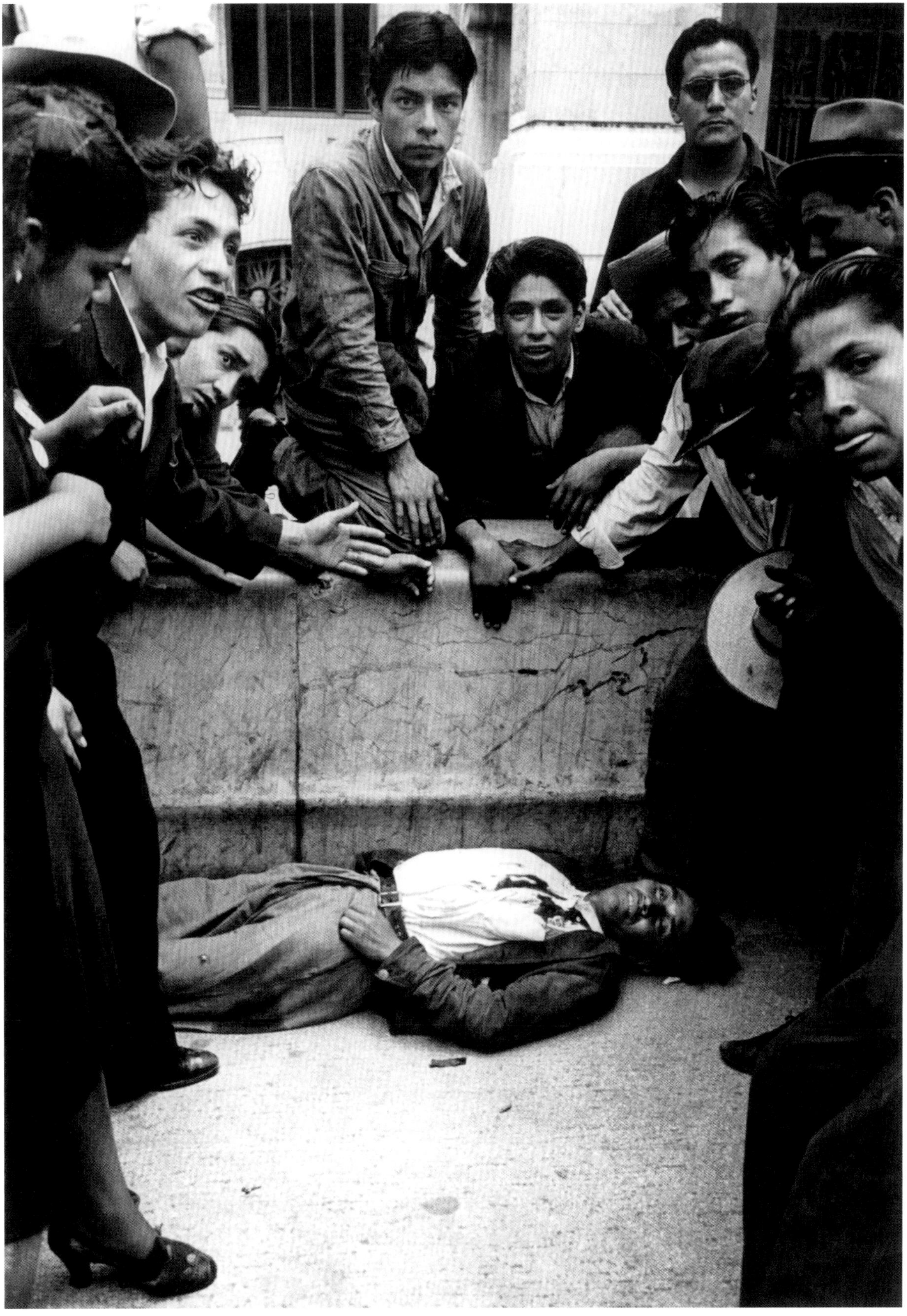

Bravo's *Striking Worker Murdered* (cat. 115), captures the undercurrent of violence that continued to permeate Mexican society during this period. By the end of the day a further thirty people had been killed and several hundred injured in electoral disturbances. Believing (correctly as it turned out) that Avila Camacho had won the election, Capa went to interview him at his estate at Teziutlan for a story that *Life* eventually ran on 1 December 1940.[77]

As soon as he heard of Trotsky's assassination Capa rushed to Coyoacan, but he was too late to take any photographs because the police had already cordoned off the area around the house. He did, however, cover Trotsky's cremation for *Time* in an unillustrated article that described the traumatic events of the ceremony:

> *As the body of Trotsky entered the furnace, the door jammed, would not shut. Fire licked at Trotsky's black suit, at his hair and wispy beard. They began to blaze. In the terrible heat and light and stench that filled the room, with the fire roaring and smoke pouring out of the open door, his last attendants saw Trotsky burning, his face turning black and shrivelling away, his body shrinking so fast that he seemed to be writhing in pain.*[78]

Unsurprisingly, given this appalling turn of events, Trotsky's widow Natalia fainted and was carried out of the building. Capa's immigration papers arrived on 10 October 1940 and he travelled to the US via Laredo. Like so many other visitors to Mexico, he never returned.[79]

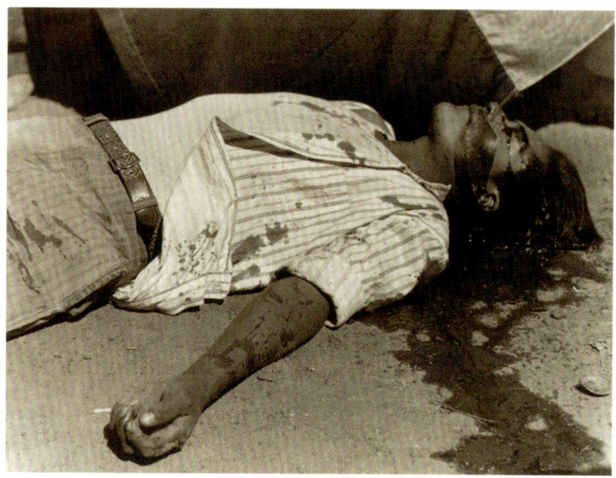

The same year, 1940, saw Pablo Neruda, the distinguished Chilean poet and Communist, assume the position of Chilean Consul General in Mexico. In his memoirs, Neruda wrote: 'Mexico with its prickly pear and serpent; Mexico blossoming and thorny, and dry and lashed by hurricane winds, violent in outline and colour, violent in eruption and creation, surrounded me with its magic and its extraordinary light.'[80]

Neruda was no Trotskyist, however, as his friendship with Siqueiros attested. In fact, Siqueiros was imprisoned for his part in an earlier bungled assassination attempt, when a group of Stalinists drove past Trotsky's house on 24 May 1940 and machine-gunned the bedroom. The Trotskys, who were in the property at the time, were traumatised but otherwise unharmed. The warden of Siqueiros's

115

Manuel Álvarez Bravo (1902–2002)
Striking Worker Murdered (Obrero en huelga, asesinado), 1934. Palladium print, 19.7 x 21.6 cm. The J. Paul Getty Museum, Los Angeles

prison, Pérez Rulfo, accompanied him to quiet bars where he and Neruda could drink together unnoticed.[81] Eventually, after some planning during these evening sorties and daytime visits to the prison, Neruda gave Siqueiros and his wife Angélica Arenales visas for travel to Chile, an act for which he was suspended from his consular duties for two months.[82] During his exile in Chile between 1940 and 1942, Siqueiros was confined to the southern town of Chillán, and he executed a mural in the Escuela República de México there as a gift from the people of Mexico to Chillán as an act of solidarity, following the destruction of the previous school building during the earthquake of January 1939. At the same time Xavier Guerrero painted a mural in the entrance hall, *From Mexico to Chile*, while Siqueiros's mural in the Pedro Aguirre Cerda Library, part of the school, is entitled *Death to the Invader* (fig. 74). Neruda left for Chile in 1943 and wrote, in an echo of Anni Albers's comment on her last departure from Mexico (quoted above): 'When I decided to return to my country, I understood less about Mexican life than when I came to Mexico.'[83]

The painting *Carnival in Huejotzingo* (cat. 116) by José Chávez Morado refers to an annual event that takes place in the town of Huejotzingo, in the state of Puebla, immediately before Lent in the build-up to Easter. Carnivals were very popular with the artistic community in Mexico as well as the more intrepid tourists. They were viewed as popular manifestations that reflected the authenticity and creativity of the Mexican people and, because they drew on pre-Columbian, colonial and republican traditions, mirrored the country's rich mix of cultural influences. The modern carnival of Huejotzingo, which dates back to the last third of the nineteenth century, commemorates three distinct events: the kidnapping of the daughter of an official by a bandit; the Battle of Puebla, which took place on 5 May 1862 between Mexico and the French troops of the Emperor Maximilian; and the first Catholic marriage of indigenous Mexicans. The British folklorist Rodney Gallop captured his first impressions of the carnival in *Mexican Mosaic* (London, 1939), an illustrated account of his travels across Mexico in search of traditional music and dance:

> *When we arrived at about eleven in the morning on Shrove Tuesday, this square was alive with brightly dressed figures in pink and white masks, bearded and moustachioed, all busily engaged with dancing, if the word can properly be applied to their grotesque hopping step, and in filling and firing off ancient muzzle-loading muskets as fast as they could.*[84]

The painter and printmaker Chávez Morado, who travelled in the US (as far north as Alaska) while seeking work as a teenager, then studied briefly at the Chouinard School of Art in Los Angeles at the same time that Siqueiros was painting his mural *The Street Meeting*. Chávez Morado returned to Mexico around 1932 and enrolled in the Escuela Nacional de Artes Plásticas in Mexico City. He was soon immersed in the art scene, and was very active. A member of LEAR,

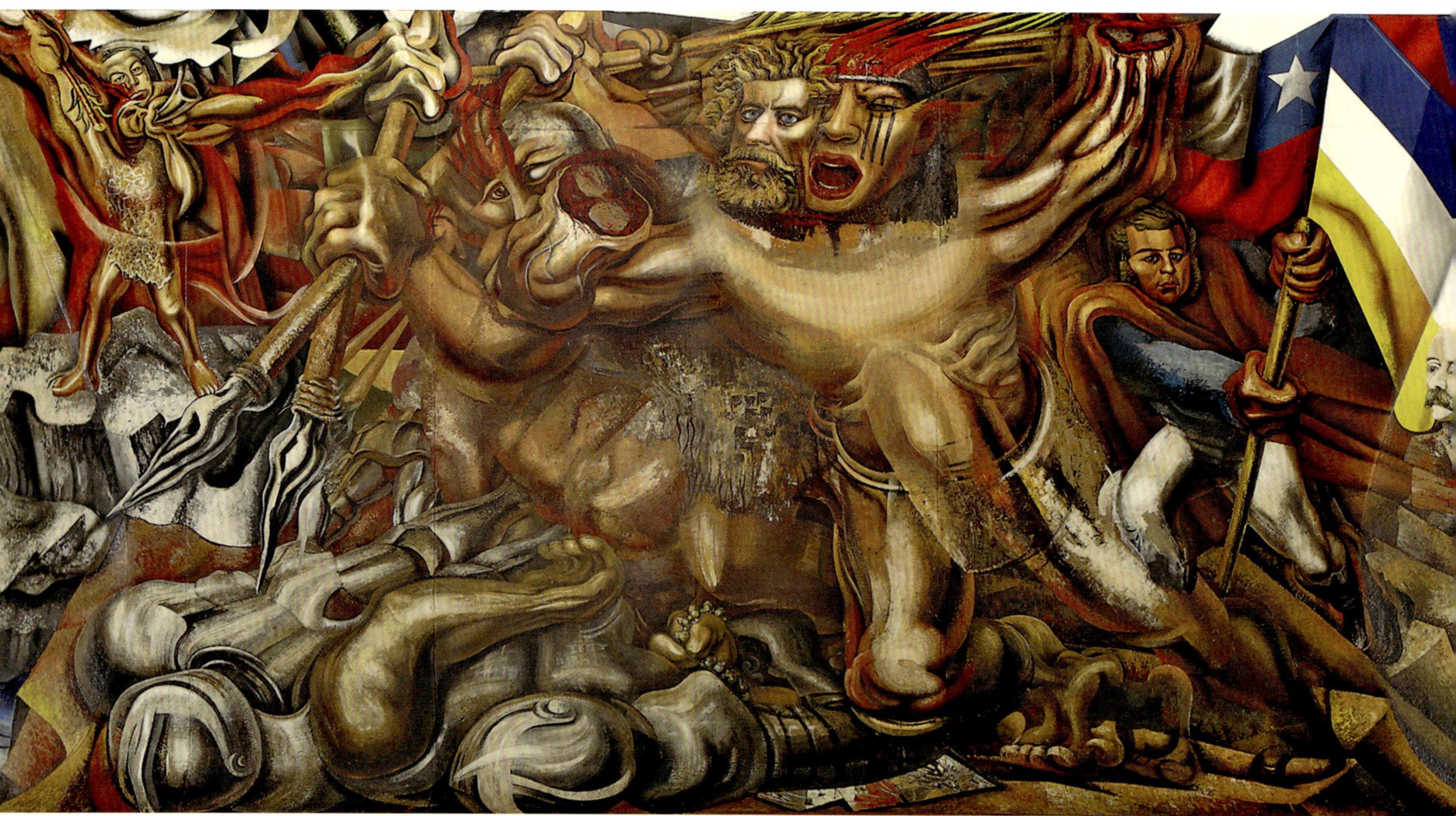

he also joined the Taller de Gráfica Popular in 1937, after which he focused on political graphic art. He married the German-born artist Olga Costa, who had moved to Mexico in 1925 at the age of twelve. Costa's painting *Dead Child* (fig. 75) is in the same vein as the paintings of deceased children by Soriano and Kahlo (cat. 110, fig. 72), demonstrating the significance these portraits still retained in Mexico in the 1940s.

The similarity between Chávez Morado's *Carnival in Huejotzingo* and Philip Guston's

Fig. 74 David Alfaro Siqueiros, **Death to the Invader**, 1941–42. Mixed media (oil, pyroxylin and industrial materials) on masonite and wooden frame, overall 225.2 sq. m. Pedro Aguirre Cerda Library, Escuela República de México, Chillán

Gladiators (cat. 117) is striking. Guston depicts the children with their faces hidden, in an animated mock-battle in the street, where a dog joyously joins in the fun. Armed with bits of discarded timber and trashcan lids, the children wear hats made from newspaper, cooking pans and cloth. The object of the game appears to be to unmask one's opponent. Chávez Morado's participants, whose faces are also hidden by handkerchiefs or masks, appear to be resting. In fact they are fully dressed as characters ready to take part in a more organised, annual ritual. As in Guston's painting, one character, astride a pretend horse, carries a wooden sword. Another holds an indistinguishable weapon. Although it is extremely unlikely that Guston would ever have seen Chávez Morado's earlier work, the similarity between these two paintings is intriguing. Indeed, it is not clear that Guston ever returned to Mexico after his visit in 1934, and by 1940 he was painting in Woodstock, New York. Perhaps Chávez Morado, passing through or visiting Morelia, saw *The Struggle against Terrorism* (see fig. 56) and was struck by the powerful depiction of individual figures against the starkly empty backgrounds that dominate the mural. Perhaps both painters had seen and responded to Giorgio de Chirico's gladiator paintings, such as *End of Combat* (fig. 76).[85]

On 15 May 1940 the Museum of Modern Art, New York, issued a press release, announcing the opening of 'the largest and most comprehensive exhibition of Mexican art ever assembled in this or any other country'.[86] 'Twenty Centuries of Mexican Art', a collaboration between MoMA and the Mexican government, contained several thousand objects (fig. 77). Nothing on this scale had been attempted before. Starting with the pre-Columbian era, the exhibition charted the entire history of Mexico through its art, including the colonial, folk or popular traditions, and concluding with contemporary works. In his introduction

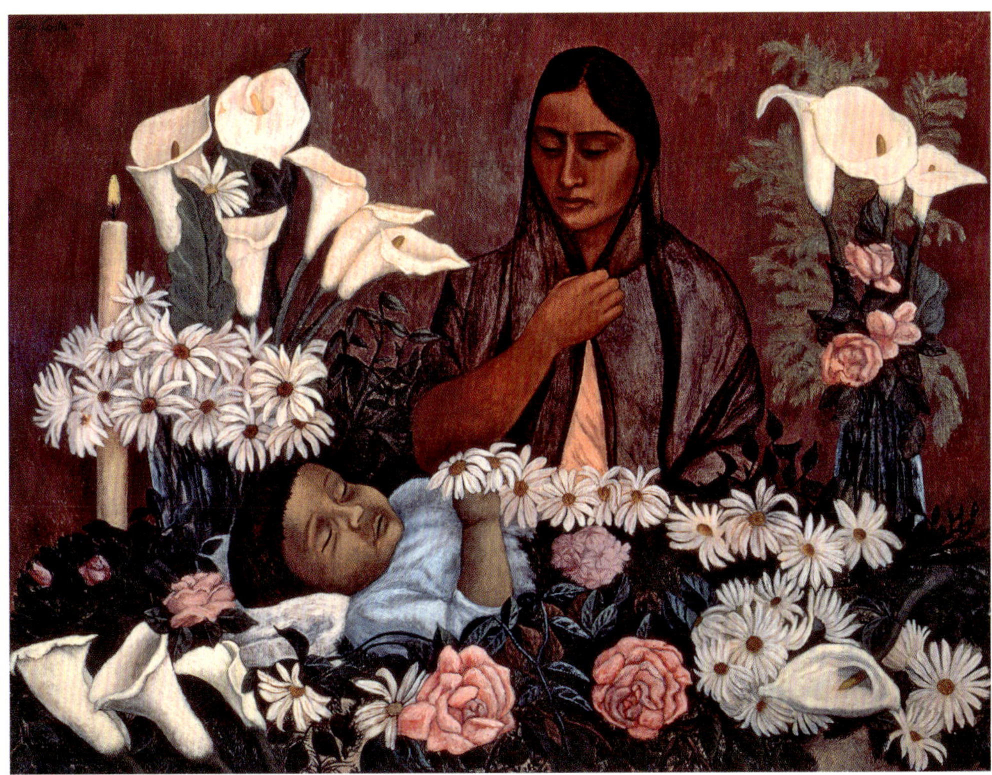

Fig. 75 Olga Costa, **Dead Child (Niño muerta)**, 1944. Oil on canvas, 83.5 x 105.5 cm. Museo de Olga Costa y José Chávez Morado, Guanajuato

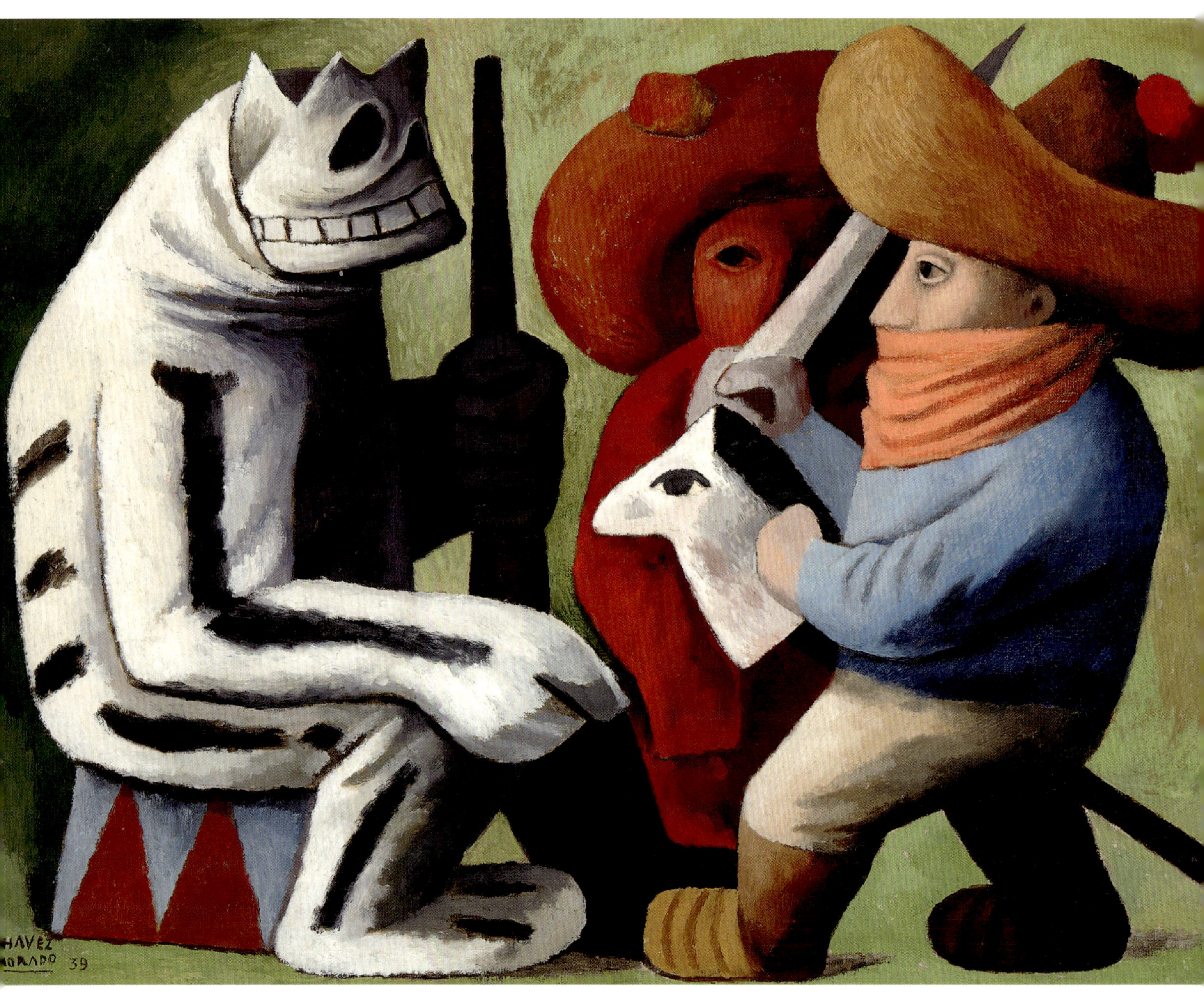

116

José Chávez Morado (1909–2002)
Carnival in Huejotzingo
(Carnaval en Huejotzingo), 1939.
Oil on canvas, 71.1 x 96.5 cm.
Collection of Phoenix
Art Museum. Gift of
Dr and Mrs Loyal Davis

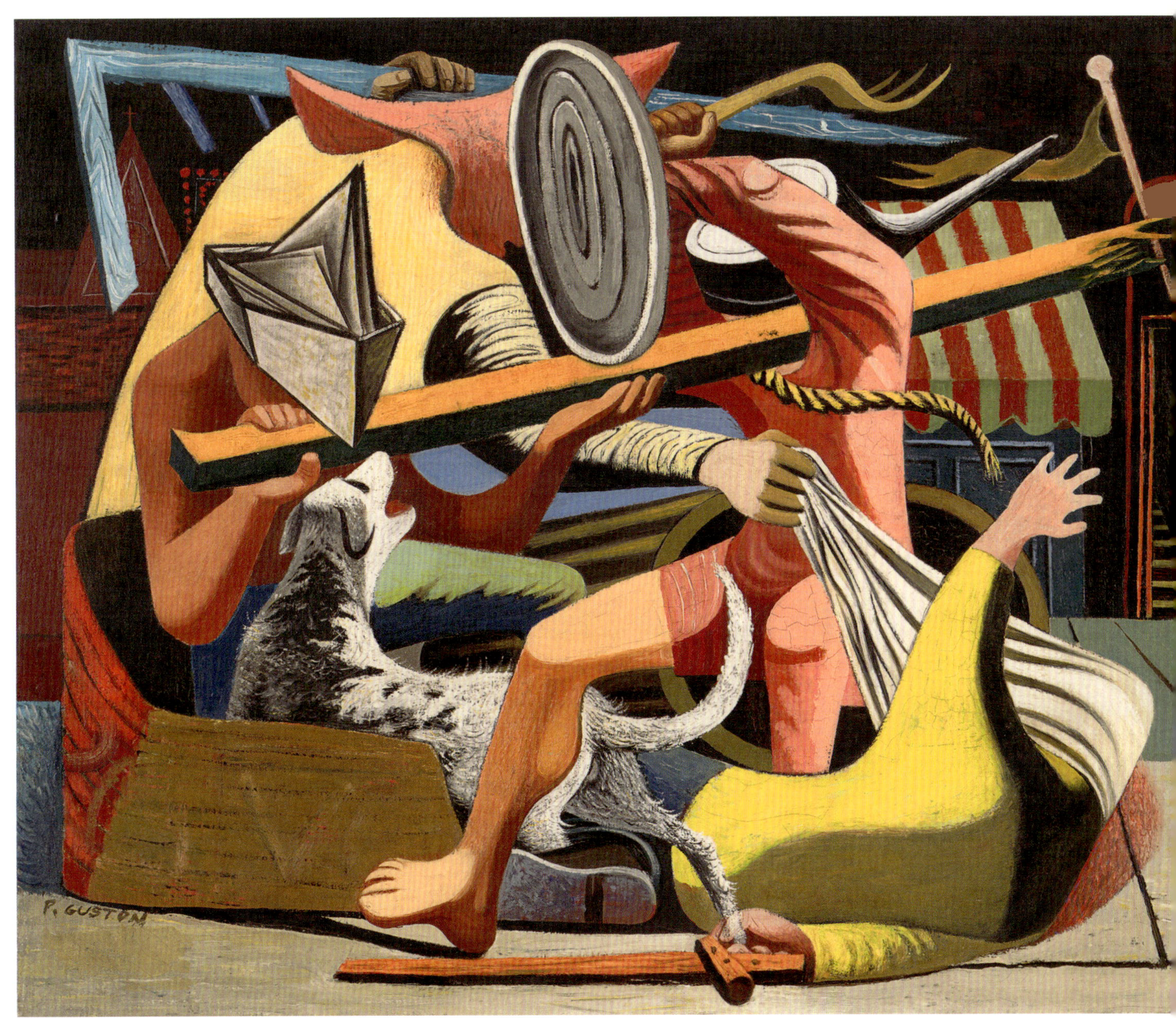

117

Philip Guston
(1913–1980)
Gladiators, 1940.
Oil and pencil on canvas,
62.2 x 71.4 cm. Museum
of Modern Art, New York.
Gift of Edward R. Broida, 2005

to the illustrated catalogue Alfred H. Barr Jr, the director of MoMA, somewhat disingenuously wrote: 'The Mexicans, of course, have one great advantage over us. They have an incomparably richer artistic past – two pasts, in fact – a European and a native, both of which survive in modified form today.'[87] In his foreword he said: 'The more thoughtful of us will not see the exhibition without provocative reflections about the nature and value of our two civilisations, for Mexican culture, as expressed in art, seems in general to be more varied, more creative, and far more deeply rooted among the people, than ours',[88] concluding:

> *An exhibition such as this can do little more than introduce one to the nation's history and culture. Seen in New York, much of the varied art of Mexico will seem bizarre, amusing, picturesque. But to those who know and love Mexico its plastic forms are more than this: they are the symbols of a way of life which still preserves that gayety, serenity, and sense of human dignity which the world needs.*[89]

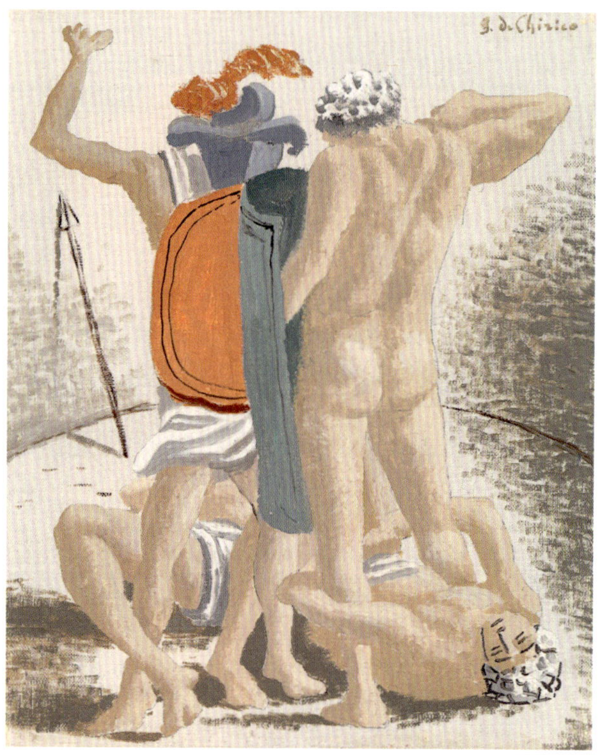

Fig. 76 Giorgio de Chirico, **End of Combat**, c. 1925. Oil on canvas, 41 x 33.3 cm. Barnes Foundation, Philadelphia, BF835

Despite the political backdrop, the exhibition at MoMA, the largest ever held outside Mexico, heralded a truly significant moment in the appreciation of the art of Mexico. It was made possible by the enthusiastic support of Lázaro Cárdenas during the last year of his presidency.

MoMA had no doubt been encouraged by its record-breaking Rivera retrospective some eight years earlier, whose subject was only the second living artist after Henri Matisse to have been accorded such an honour there.[90] 'Twenty Centuries of Mexican Art' celebrated the long and diverse cultural history of Mexico. Its appearance at such a prestigious and conspicuous venue in the US is significant, as Mexico was thereby acknowledged to be a leading centre of contemporary artistic production. This could be interpreted as recognition of the importance of the Revolution and the impact that it had had on Mexican art and artists, as well as the vital role that 2,000 years of continuous cultural development had played in that process. In a sense

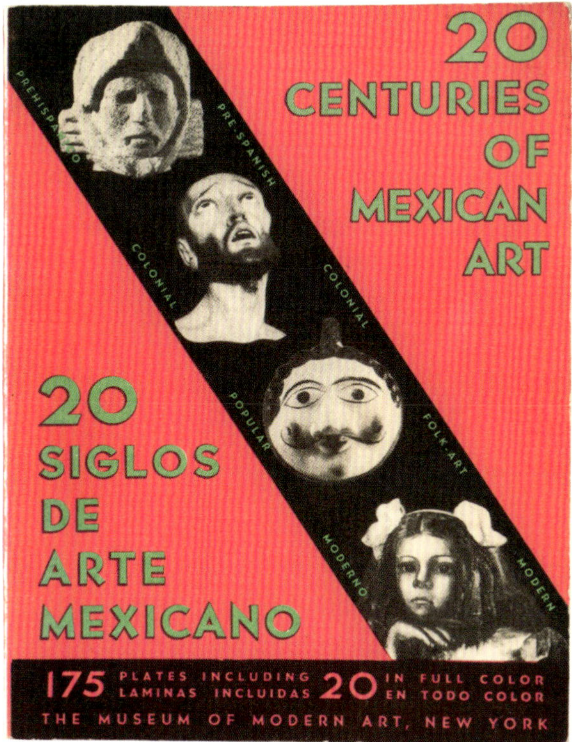

Fig. 77 Catalogue of **Twenty Centuries of Mexican Art**. The Museum of Modern Art, New York, 1940. Printed book, 25.2 x 18.9 cm. Collection of the author

the MoMA exhibition was an analysis of the evolution of art in Mexico. There can be little doubt that it was also a demonstration of Pan-American unity. It was a wonderful opportunity for Mexico to use culture to promote itself as a country of great potential and one worthy of investment, especially given the outbreak of war in Europe. Mexico, it seemed to say, is much less radical than it is usually thought to be, and the strength of its artistic community is a reflection of a stable and creative environment in a wealthy society that can afford to sustain many different artists.

During his travels across Mexico in the 1920s the American journalist Carleton Beals captured the sense of a country inherently corrupt, dominated by political cronyism and favouritism following the Revolution. He described visiting the Tarascan town of Paracho where Don Melchor, a loyal member of the National Revolutionary Party, town constable, landowner, shopkeeper and chief of the Social Defence Corps, presided:

> *Don Melchor, with his wicked eye, his swagger, his heavy Mauser, his rifles, his long poniard, his right to dispense liquor, his participation in the spoils of the revolution, his status as land-holder and an employer and a granter of favors, with one foot planted on good economic self-interest, the other on the good-will of federal higher-ups, bearing aloft and unsullied the ideal banner of the revolution, in addition to his deadly weapons, is typical of the new ruler in rural Mexico. Don Melchor can almost say – 'I am the Revolution'.*[91]

Some twenty years later Miguel Covarrubias painted *El Hueso* (cat. 118), which shows an immaculately dressed teacher wearing the colours of the political party Partido Revolucionario Mexicano (PRM) in a badge on his lapel. Next to the chair on which he is seated, a large clean bone lies on the tiled veranda floor. In Mexico *el hueso* (literally, the bone) is slang for a sinecure: 'to give a bone' is thus to provide jobs for party supporters or as a favour to friends and family. Covarrubias's painting is a powerful comment

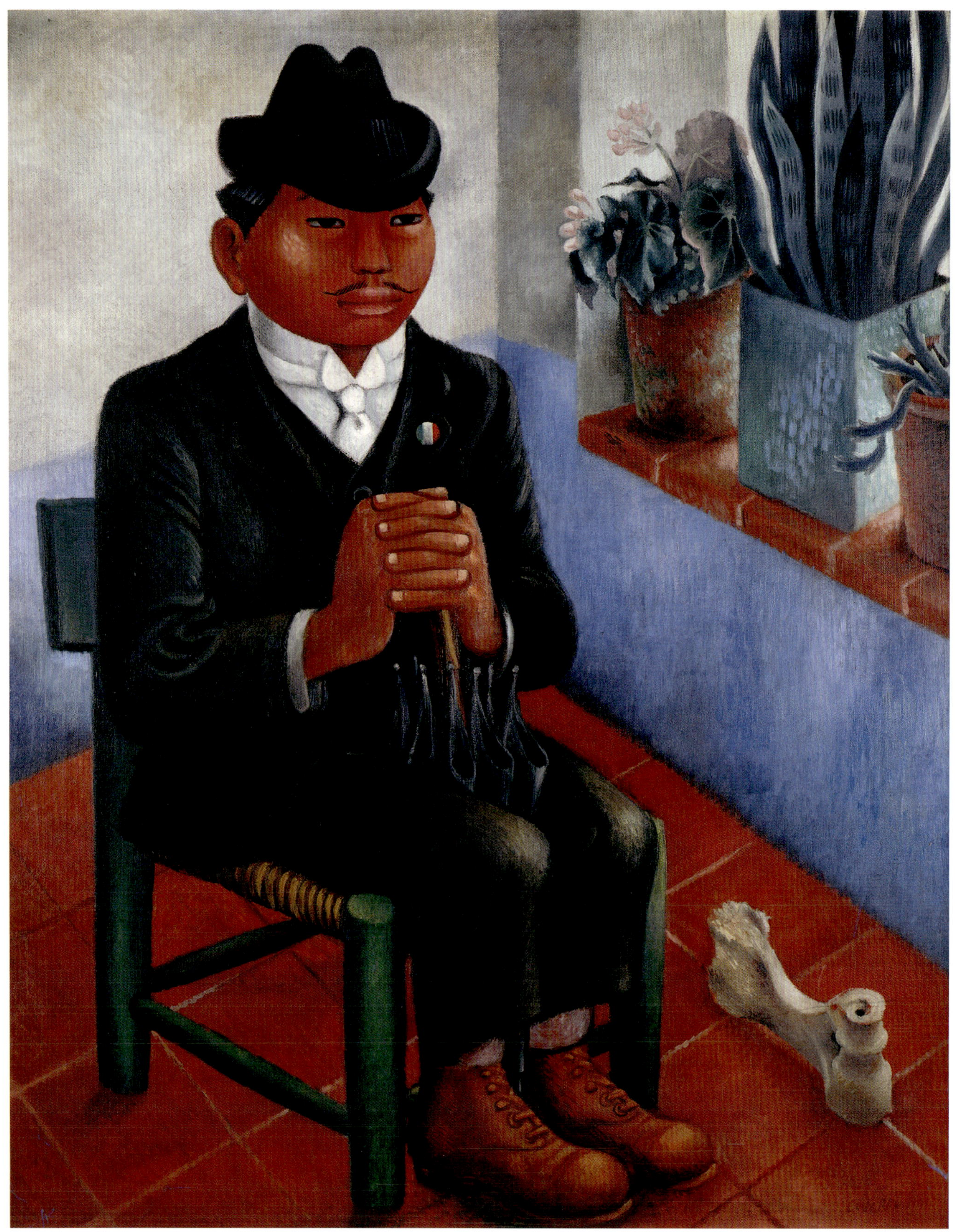

on the continuation of political corruption; despite the events of the Revolution and the many changes Mexico had undergone since, democracy was still compromised and politics continued to be dominated by affiliations.

Capa's images of the 1940 presidential campaign reveal the tension inherent in Mexican politics, which very often led to violent confrontations, further illustrating the clear and highly emotive divisions between political parties. Under the Mexican constitution, presidential terms are fixed for a period of six years and restricted to a single term. Elections are held in July of the final year of a presidency, and the incumbent takes office the following December. Thus elections take place while the outgoing president, who is theoretically barred from campaigning for any of the candidates, is still in office. In 1940, as was customary, the president 'chose' his party's candidate, or in the case of the PRM, his successor.[92] Cárdenas chose his Secretary of War, Avila Camacho, who, because of his low profile, was nicknamed 'The Unknown Soldier'. The 1940 elections were a genuine turning point in the implementation of the ambitions of the Mexican Revolution. Avila Camacho presided over a fundamental change in the political system, moving from revolution to a process of evolution. The socialist state was abandoned in favour of private initiative.[93] Politics became much less radical and a new era of conservatism dawned across Mexico. In his inaugural presidential address, Avila Camacho declared: 'Each new epoch demands a rebirth of ideas. The clamour of the entire republic now demands the material and spiritual consolidation of our social conquests in a prosperous and powerful economy. It demands an era of construction of abundant life, of economic expansion.'[94] Change may have been gradual at first, but the inexorable process that was to transform Mexico through the ideals of the Revolution that had begun thirty years before, with so much promise and expectation, had commenced.

118

Miguel Covarrubias (1904–1957)
The Bone (Rural Schoolteacher) (El Hueso (El maestro rural)),
c. 1940.
Oil on canvas, 76.8 x 61.5 cm.
Museo Nacional de Arte/
Instituto Nacional de
Bellas Artes y Literatura

APPENDIX

EDWARD BURRA: *EL PASO* (1935) OR *EL PASEO* (c. 1938)?

'Burra busies himself with the movements of gay people – crowds of them, with music and dazzling lights. His massive water colours, in which he introduces his figures one-sixth life-size, are extremely impressive things, and one wishes that he had tarried longer in that paintable land and brought back more of his vital work.'[1]

INTRODUCTION

Between 1942 and 1973 Edward Burra's painting *El Paseo* (*c.* 1938; cat. 107), the property of a private collection, was included in five exhibitions:

> 'British Impressions of Mexico in Art and Literature, 1555–1942: An Exhibition of Books, Pictures, Engravings and Other Printed Matter Organised by the British Council with the Co-operation of the British-Mexican Society', Royal Water-Colour Society's Gallery, 26 Conduit Street, London, 15–22 October 1942, and Manchester City Art Gallery, 24 November – 31 December 1942: *El Paseo*, no date (cat. 6, illustrated)
>
> 'The Recent Work of Edward Burra', Ernest Brown & Phillips Ltd, The Leicester Galleries, London, June 1949: *El Paseo*, 1935 (cat. 16, not illustrated)
>
> 'Edward Burra, Derrick Greaves, Hubert Dalwood: Three Contemporary British Artists', Whitworth Art Gallery, Manchester, 17 November – 8 December 1959: *El Paseo*, 1935 (cat. 2, not illustrated)
>
> 'Edward Burra: The Early Years (1923–1950)', Lefevre Gallery, London, 7–30 October 1971: *El Paso*, 1935 (cat. 15, not illustrated)
>
> 'Edward Burra', Tate Gallery, London, 23 May – 8 July 1973: *El Paso*, 1935 (cat. 46, illustrated). Lender: D. W. E. Eckart, Harrogate, Yorkshire

During this 31-year exhibition history, the painting's title changed from *El Paseo* to *El Paso*. I contend that the title of the painting was changed inadvertently, most probably through a typographical error, and that the dating of the work to 1935, which first appears in 1949, was wrong. Although these might appear to be minor changes, their implications, in Spanish and in the dating, are more significant than first appears.

The single most important implication of the date is to distance this work geographically and chronologically from Mexico and to place it instead in Texas on Burra's first visit to the US in 1933–34, whereas the subject-matter and location are without doubt Cuernavaca in Morelos, the town in which Burra, accompanying Conrad Aiken and Mary Augusta Hoover, stayed with Malcolm Lowry and Jan Gabrial in May and June 1937.

The painting was the only work by Burra to be included in an exhibition organised by the British Council in 1942 as a gesture of thanks for the support of the Mexican government during the Second World War, for which an illustrated catalogue was produced.[2] The work is entitled *El Paseo* in that catalogue, as it was for the following two exhibitions in 1949 and 1959.

The next time the work was shown, at the Lefevre Gallery in 1971, its title had changed to *El Paso*. It was catalogued as such by John Rothenstein in the retrospective exhibition at the Tate Gallery in 1973. Andrew Causey, in his *Edward Burra: Complete Catalogue* (Oxford, 1985), also catalogued it as *El Paso*.

The title and date currently ascribed to the work – *El Paso*, 1935 – are, it seems to me, incorrect.

TITLE

In Spanish, the verb *pasear* means 'to take a walk', 'to take for a walk' (as in to take a dog for a walk) or 'to show off'. The noun *paseo* refers to a relaxed stroll (as in stepping out) or a promenade, typically taken with one's spouse or sweetheart at the weekend or in the evening. Burra's painting depicts numerous couples strolling through a park where a band is playing in a public bandstand, thereby suggesting that the artist had in mind the definition of *el paseo*.

Conversely, the Spanish noun *paso* translates literally as 'step', but it is also used to refer to a crossing or a passing (ceding) point. Geographically, El Paso, the Texas border town opposite Ciudad Juárez in the Mexican state of Chihuahua, is an abbreviation of El Paso del Rio del Norte, referring to the crossing point of the Rio Grande (which in Mexico is known as the Río Bravo del Norte).[3] *El paso* has no link with the subject-matter of Burra's painting. Furthermore, Burra never visited El Paso. His crossing from the US into Mexico in 1937 took place further east, through the Texan border town of Laredo, which also lies on the Rio Grande, across from Nuevo Laredo, Tamaulipas. Nor does El Paso possess a public open space or a square boasting a bandstand.

In fact, the very spot in Cuernavaca from where Burra took the view can be identified. The viewpoint is looking north to northeast across the Jardin Juárez (a public square also known as the Zócalo), which still retains its distinctive bandstand, from the arcaded façade of the Government Palace of the State of Morelos on Ignacio Reyes Street, just before the corner where it meets Hermenegildo Galeana Street in the centre of the town. The elevated wall that Burra included in his painting runs along the south side of the park. Given that we know Burra stayed in Cuernavaca in 1937, on his only visit to Mexico, there can be little doubt that the painting was inspired by this visit: it is a view Burra saw for himself. Indeed, the Tate Archive preserves a small number of photographs that Burra took in Cuernavaca, including one that appears to show the Jardin Juárez (fig. 78).[4]

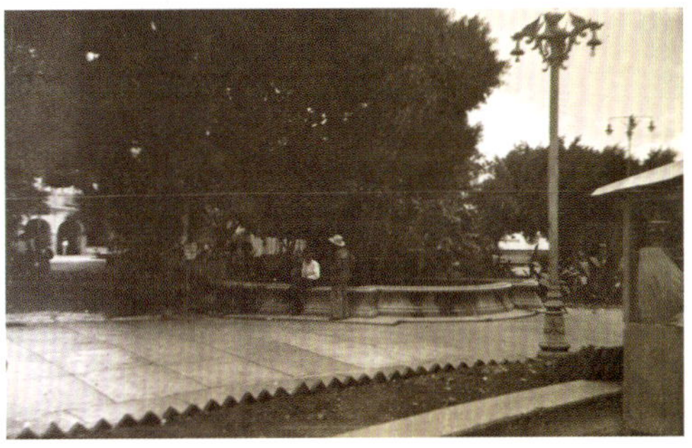

Fig. 78 Edward Burra, 'Jardin Juárez, Cuernavaca', 1937. Black and white photograph, 5 x 7 cm. Tate Archives, London, M01197

Burra told Rothenstein that he never gave titles to his works until they were selected and installed in an exhibition, at which point, he explained, 'somebody comes along and stamps them with my signature with a rubber stamp, and presses me to invent titles for them'.[5] Thus he probably gave this work its name in 1942, when it was first shown in London. It seems highly likely that, when it came to be shown at the Lefevre Gallery nearly thirty years later, the title was transcribed incorrectly from a previous catalogue or an error was made in the editing process. Whatever happened, the title was inadvertently changed and the new name has been copied ever since.

DATE

Burra visited Mexico only once, during May and June 1937. If the painting is set in Cuernavaca, as I contend, then the original date given to the work, 1935, must be incorrect. Indeed, the date was only attributed to the work when it was shown in London in June 1949, more than ten years after it was painted and some seven years after it was first exhibited. Burra is known to have been vague about the dates of his works, as he described in the only documentary film made during his lifetime:

CAROLE SMITH *Do you look back on any of the pictures you did? Do you like some more than others?*
EDWARD BURRA *I suppose so, yes.*
CS *Which?*
EB *I don't know. I like some, yes. I suppose one likes others; one more than another. You know, I don't remember them.*
CS *You don't remember them?*
EB *I don't remember things. It becomes a blank.*
CS *I think you have a very good memory.*
EB *In a way,* [pause] *some things. I don't remember the paintings. I don't remember when I did them. People are always asking me the date. I never can remember, not the right date you know.*
CS *No?*
EB *And I've never written the date on them or hardly ever.*

Later Burra adds:

EB *I enjoy painting.* The *painting. I enjoy* the *painting [laughs]. And then I don't mind, you know. I get tired of it after that. I don't particularly want to keep the painting. I never hang any paintings up or hardly ever. They're all kept in piles and carted off. Before that happy time they were left on the floor or poked in a cupboard.*[6]

Once a work was completed, Burra moved on to the next painting, both physically and mentally, retaining little sentimental attachment to the finished canvas. It is not difficult to see how he might forget the date of a work's completion. In some cases paintings must have been left a considerable time before being exhibited, further distancing the artist from the time and place of their execution, even though Burra was renowned for his ability to paint from memory: 'From the middle 1920s, when he made fairly frequent visits to the Continent, his use of postcards diminished, and he came to rely increasingly on his memory – a memory so precisely retentive that he had no need even to make sketches and he returns from tours or expeditions to possible subjects with his mind charged with a wide range of images exactly envisaged.'[7]

CONCLUSION

My contention is that when the painting was first dated in 1949, which I am suggesting was some eleven years after he painted it, Burra was confused about its date and ascribed it to his first trip to the US, from October 1933 to March 1934, and his celebrated Harlem series. Indeed, both Rothenstein and Bryan Robertson incorrectly assert that Burra visited Mexico at this time, whereas in fact he was in New York and Boston.[8] Yet in May 1937 Burra wrote to his sister: 'Owing to pressure of circumstance we [Burra, Aiken and Hoover] leave tomorrow for Mexico City nobody is more surprised than me for I never thought these old eyes would live to see Mexico.'[9] Clearly he had never been before.

The original title of the work was *El Paseo*, and I contend that this title should be reinstated and that the painting's date should be changed from 1935 to *c.* 1937 or *c.* 1938, to conform with the dates conventionally given to the other two works that Burra is known to have painted in Rye, East Sussex, after his trip to Mexico: *Landscape with Comestibles Seen en route to Mexico City* (*c.* 1937; fig. 65), in a private collection, and *Mexican Church* (*c.* 1938; cat. 106), in the Tate collection.

As Robertson concluded: 'The reason for this close scrutiny of dates and places is that Burra rarely dated a picture, and although he was a prolific correspondent, he almost never dated a letter or postcard. Only a topical reference or the letter being preserved in its postmarked envelope can determine dates in Burra's life. He was not so much secretive over his movements as totally unconcerned about anyone else's interest in him.'[10]

ENDNOTES

PROLOGUE

1 Paz 1985, p. 144.
2 London 1942, p. 4.
3 Meyer and Sherman 1979, p. 511.
4 Philadelphia 2006 and London 2009 are two important recent exhibitions and expositions on the subject.
5 Mayakovsky 2005, p. 11.

CHAPTER 1

1 Saturday 26 December 1925. Glusker 2010, vol. 1, p. 29.
2 Azuela 1992, p. 58.
3 Knight 1986, pp. 55–6.
4 Charlot 1939, pp. 62–3. The article from which this quote is taken, '"Pulqueria" Painting', was originally published in *Forma: Revista de Artes Plásticas,* vol. 1, no. 1, October 1926.
5 Knight 1986, p. 2.
6 Knight 1986, pp. 1–36, gives a brilliant summary of the Porfiriato.
7 Roth 1997, p. 218.
8 Knight 1986, p. 123.
9 Roth 1997, p. 218.
10 Villa was paid $25,000 plus 50% of motion-picture royalties as part of the agreement. Roth 1997, p. 218.
11 Reed's book was later made into a film, *Mexico in Flames* (1982), directed by Sergei Bondarchuk.
12 Reed 1983, p. 22.
13 The first English-language edition, *The Underdogs* (New York, 1929), was translated by Enrique Munguía Jr, with a foreword by Carleton Beals and illustrated by José Clemente Orozco. Azuela wrote two more novels on the Revolution: *Los caciques* (Mexico City, 1917) and *Las moscas* (Mexico City, 1918). Other famous novels about the Revolution, such as Martín Luis Guzmán's *El águila y la serpiente* (Madrid, 1928) and *La sombra del caudillo* (Bilbao, 1929) and José Rubén Romero's *Apuntes de un lugareño* (Barcelona, 1932) and *Desbandada* (Mexico City, 1934), were published much later, unlike Azuela's work, which came out during the conflict and as a consequence conveys a greater sense of the immediacy of the Revolution.
14 Azuela 1992, pp. 106–7.
15 Mraz 2009, p. 64.
16 See Sarber 1986 and Bennett 2010 for a more detailed account of Horne.
17 Sarber 1986, p. 9.
18 Sarber 1986, pp. 11–12.
19 Mraz 2009, pp. 34–5.
20 Brehme published *México pintoresco* (Mexico City, 1923).
21 Mraz 2009, pp. 67–9.
22 See, for example, Philadelphia 2006 (figs 264–5 and 286–7), Mexico City 2008B (pp. 110–11) and Mraz 2009 (figs 12–13).
23 Kiehl 1990, p. 540.
24 Jean Charlot, 'Un precursor del movimiento de Arte Mexicano: El grabador Posadas', in *Revista de Revistas*, vol. 16, no. 799, 30 August 1925, p. 25. The article was translated and reprinted as 'Mexican Popular Print-Makers II: Posada' in Charlot 1939, pp. 85–93 (and the original publication erroneously credited to *Universal Illustrado*, August 1925). The first monograph on Posada was published in 1930 (Mexico City) by Frances Toor, Pablo O'Higgins and Blas Vanegas Arroyo for *Mexican Folkways*.
25 Favela 1990, pp. 575–6, refers to *The Plantain Vendor* (1914) and Lozano 1999, p. 13, to *The Glass Mill* (1909) as reflecting Herrán's interest in themes from everyday life, perhaps with an undertone of social criticism.
26 Quirarte 1990, pp. 581–4.
27 Herrera 1990, p. 565.
28 Brenner 1929, p. 294.
29 Brenner 1929, p. 297.
30 Mraz 2009, p. 59.

CHAPTER 2

1 Friday 11 June 1926. Glusker 2010, vol. 1, p. 180.
2 Mayakovsky 2005, p. 15.
3 Taken from interviews carried out by John Charlot on 18 October 1970 and 14 May 1971. See 'Jean Charlot: Interviews with John Charlot, September 14, 1970 – August 7, 1971; September 26–29, 1975; March 24 – April 24, 1978', edited by John Charlot and Janine Richardson, 2010. Published online at www.jeancharlot.org. © The Jean Charlot Estate LLC. With permission.
4 Jean Charlot interview, 14 May 1971 (see note 3 above).
5 Franco 1967, p. 52.
6 See Boas 1915.
7 Cordero Reiman 1993, p. 13.
8 Franco 1969, p. 195.
9 London 1982, p. 11.
10 Debroise 1983, p. 49.
11 The denunciation of easel painting was at its strongest in the Soviet Union in the writings of Nikolai Tarabukhin and Boris Arvatov as well as the manifestos of the Constructivists. Wollen 1989, p. 16.
12 Debroise 1983, p. 62. After Vasconcelos left office, only two muralists were retained by the Ministry of Public Education, Rivera and Montenegro.
13 Blunt's article, 'The Art of Diego Rivera', praised Rivera's murals which he had seen illustrated in *Portrait of America* (New York, 1934/London, 1935) by Rivera and Bertram D. Wolfe. Blunt 1935.
14 A notable exception was the artist Xavier Guerrero, who studied political theory in Moscow between 1928 and 1932.
15 19 November 1924. Newhall 1961, p. 104. © 1981 Center for Creative Photography, Arizona Board of Regents.
16 Jean Charlot interview, 12 June 1971 (see note 3 above).
17 From 'Towards a Transformation of Plastic Arts', plans for a manifesto and study programme written in New York. Siqueiros 1975, p. 47.
18 Lawrence 1981, p. 58.
19 17 December 1925, quoted in San Francisco 1983, p. 23.
20 Paz 1993, p. 259.
21 London 1989A, p. 126.
22 Jean Charlot, *The Mexican Mural Renaissance, 1920–1925*, New Haven, 1963; Debroise 1983, p. 42; Wollen 1989, p. 16.

23 Wollen 1989, pp. 17–18.
24 San Francisco 1983, p. 44.
25 Mexico City 1940, p. 17. © 1940 The Museum of Modern Art, New York.
26 Siqueiros 1975, pp. 45–6.
27 His first visit was March to July 1923; the second visit was September to November 1923; the third and final visit was October 1924 to March 1925.
28 Lawrence's first piece on Mexico, 'Au revoir USA', was published in *Laughing Horse*, a literary journal, one of whose editors was Johnson, in 1923 (vol. 8, pp. 1–3).
29 Nehls 1958, p. 219.
30 Lawrence and Somerset Maugham lunched on 6 November 1924. 'We met Somerset Maugham in Mexico City. He hates it here: has gone to Yucatán. He'll hate it there. I didn't like him. A bit rancid.' Letter to Curtis Brown, dated 14 November 1924, Hotel Francia, Oaxaca, in Boulton 1989, p. 166.
31 Sunday Evening [2 November 1924]. Newhall 1961, p. 101. © 1981 Center for Creative Photography, Arizona Board of Regents.
32 Tuesday Evening [4 November 1924]. Newhall 1961, pp. 101–2. © 1981 Center for Creative Photography, Arizona Board of Regents.
33 Letter dated 19 December 1924, Av. Pino Suarez #43, Oaxaca, in Boulton 1989, p. 185.
34 The four essays on Mexico are 'Corasmin and the Parrots', 'Walk to Huayapa', 'The Mozo' and 'Market Day'.
35 Roberts 1987, p. 455; Boulton 1989, p. 207.
36 Beals 1931, p. 300.
37 Friday 11 June 1926. Glusker 2010, vol. 1, p. 180.
38 July/August 1926. Newhall 1961, p. 181. © 1981 Center for Creative Photography, Arizona Board of Regents.
39 Lawrence 1981, p. 33.
40 Worthen 2005, pp. 321–2.
41 San Francisco 1983, p. 4.
42 Philadelphia 1995, p. 20.
43 Weston and Modotti had first met at one of Robo's frequent parties at his Hollywood studio.
44 Philadelphia 1995, p. 21.
45 San Francisco 1983, p. 15.
46 San Francisco 1983, p. 36.
47 San Francisco 1983, pp. 15–16.
48 Charlot was later to publish *The Mexican Mural Renaissance, 1920–1925*, the result of a two-year Guggenheim Fellowship spent in Mexico between 1945 and 1947.
49 Morris, Charlot and Axtell Morris 1931; Axtell Morris 1931, with illustrations by Jean Charlot.
50 Brenner 1929, p. 296.
51 Philadelphia 1995, p. 46.
52 The British artist Catherwood and the American writer Stevens travelled through Guatemala, Chiapas, Tabasco and the Yucatan in 1839. The lavishly illustrated accounts of their travels and the abandoned Mayan sites they encountered and recorded were hugely popular on publication: Stevens 1841 and 1843; Catherwood 1844.
53 The Carnegie Institute began excavations, known as Project Chichén, in 1924 following agreement with the Ministry of Public Education. The joint project was led by José Erosa Piniche of Monumentos Prehispánicos and the Carnegie Institute Maya Expedition, led by Sylvanus G. Morley.
54 Henry Moore Institute Archive, 2000.0046.
55 Henry Moore Institute Archive, 2000.0046.
56 Henry Moore Institute Archive, 2000.0046.
57 Henry Moore Institute Archive, 2000.0046.
58 Both Edward Weston and Jean Charlot had significant collections of Modotti's photographs of the murals, which are preserved in their respective archives at the Center of Creative Photography, University of Arizona, Tucson, and the Jean Charlot Collection, University of Hawai'i at Manoa Library.
59 Henry Moore Institute Archive, 2000.0046.
60 Underwood taught at the Royal College of Art, London from 1920 to 1923. Among the life-class students who asked him to continue to tutor them in special evening classes after his resignation was Henry Moore (Neve 1974, p. 76). Edward Burra was a student and contemporary of Moore at the RCA in 1923 (Robertson 1982, p. 13).
61 Moore may have seen the British Museum's small stone Mexica Chacmool (Am1825,1210.4), collected by William Bullock in 1823.
62 Neve 1974, p. 89.
63 Letter to Edward Weston, dated 11 September 1927, partially transcribed in Aikin 1986, p. 26.
64 Letter to Edward Weston, dated 24 October 1927, partially transcribed in Aikin 1986, p. 27. Charlot likewise drew Shore: *Portrait of Henrietta Shore*, 1927, graphite on paper (whereabouts unknown).
65 Letter to Edward Weston, dated 24 November 1927, partially transcribed in Aikin 1986, p. 27.
66 Letter to Edward Weston, dated 11 September 1927, partially transcribed in Aikin 1986, p. 26.
67 Morrow Lindbergh 1973, p. 5.
68 Letter to Sue Beck *en route* from Panama to Managua, 5 October 1929, transcribed in Morrow Lindbergh 1973, p. 103.
69 Nuttall gave her name to a Mixtec codex that she traced from the Monastery of San Marco in Florence to the collection of Sir Robert Curzon, 14th Baron Zouche. The Codex Zouche-Nuttall entered the collections of the British Museum in 1917 (Am1902,0308.1/BM Add. MSS 39671). Nuttall published *Codex Nuttall; Facsimile of an Ancient Mexican Codex* (Cambridge, MA, 1902). See Alfred M. Tozzer's obituary in *American Anthropologist*, July–September 1933, new series 35, vol. 3, pp. 475–82.
70 Letter to Charles Lindbergh, dated 25 March 1929, transcribed in Morrow Lindbergh 1973, p. 30.
71 Mayakovsky 2005, p. 11.
72 Mayakovsky 2005, p. 28.
73 Siqueiros 1975, pp. 24–5.
74 Tina Modotti, 'On Photography', *Mexican Folkways*, vol. 5, no. 4, October–December 1929, transcribed in London 1982, p. 28.
75 Gallo 2005, p. 1.

CHAPTER 3

1 Hartley 1997, p. 146.
2 Sire 2012, p. 17.
3 Debroise 1983, p. 89.
4 Paz 1993, pp. 246–9.
5 Quirarte 1988, pp. 22–31.
6 The John Simon Guggenheim Memorial Foundation was established in 1925 and stipulated that all recipients spend their fellowships outside the US.
7 Paz 1993, pp. 261–2.
8 Paz 1993, p. 256.
9 Paz 1993, p. 259.
10 From an interview with the artist recorded in Cuernavaca, quoted in Genauer 1974, pp. 17–18. © 1975 by Emily Genauer. Used by permission of Harry N. Abrams, Inc., New York. All rights reserved.
11 Neruda 1978, p. 155.
12 New York 1997, pp. 16–17.
13 New York 1997, pp. 23–4.
14 New York 1997, pp. 21–2.
15 Gallo 2005, p. 187.

16 Oles 1998, p. 274.
17 10–25 March 1939.
18 London 1989A, p. 216.
19 Albiñana 1998A, p. 266.
20 Albiñana 1998A, p. 266.
21 Albiñana 1998A, p. 266.
22 Letter to Victoria Ocampo, dated June 1934, quoted in Karetnikova 1991, p. 28.
23 Salazkina 2009, p. 1.
24 Karetnikova 1991, p. 13.
25 Salazkina 2009, p. 86.
26 Karetnikova 1991, p. 5.
27 Karetnikova 1991, pp. 16–30.
28 It has been suggested that the different sections of the film were dedicated to distinct artists: 'Prologue' to David Alfaro Siqueiros; 'Sandunga' to Jean Charlot; 'Fiesta' to Francisco de Goya; 'Maguey' to Diego Rivera; 'Soldadera' to José Clemente Orozco; and 'Epilogue' to José Guadalupe Posada. See Jay Leyda and Zina Voynov, *Eisenstein at Work* (New York 1982), quoted in García-Romeu 1998, p. 261.
29 Karetnikova 1991, p. 29.
30 Gundlach 2006, p. 233.
31 Langston Hughes (original English text in manuscript dated 6 March 1935, subsequently translated and published as 'Fotografías más que fotografías' in *Todo*, 12 May 1935).
32 The other members were the Argentine architect Federico Álvarez de Toledo, French film-maker Bernard de Colmont, the El Salvadorian artist Antonio 'Toño' Salazar, the Mexican ethnographer Ignacio 'Tata Nacho' Fernández Esperón, French journalist Gérard Tacvor writing for *Le Petit Parisien* and *Le Miroir du Monde*, the Cuban novelist (who would later win the Nobel prize for literature) Alejo Carpentier, and two French camera assistants, Nourhan Tacvor (brother of Gérard) and Lionel de Charmoy. The expedition was encouraged by Paul Rivet and Georges Rivière of the Musée de Trocadero, and Guillaume Grandidier and Nemours Larronde of the Geographic Society of France.
33 'Llegó una comisión científica que estu diaria el trazando ideal de la ruta panamericana', in *El Pais Excelsior*, Habana, 5 July 1934.
34 It has been suggested that Cartier-Bresson was also commissioned to collect objects of ethnographic interest for the Musée de l'Homme, Paris. Certainly a number of unpublished prints by Cartier-Bresson are held in the library of the museum. Valencia 1998, p. 278.
35 Albiñana 1998B, p. 278.
36 Albiñana 1998B, p. 279.
37 Rafael Heliodoro Valle, 'Luces instantáneas' in *Reforma Social*, 25 August 1934.
38 Weston's *Escusado* (1925) was reproduced in *Forma: Revista de Artes Plásticas*, vol. 1, no. 6, 1928, a journal published by the Ministry of Public Education between 1926 and 1928 and edited by the artist Gabriel Fernández Ledesma. The photograph proved so contentious that the magazine was withdrawn from sale and discontinued, revealing a previously unseen censoriousness in the once-progressive ministry. Fernández 1998, p. 242.
39 Henri Cartier-Bresson, dated 25 February 1935, quoted in Sire 2012, p. 17. I am grateful to Patrick José Bergot for the translation from French.
40 Letter to Edith Halpert quoted in McCoy 1997, p. 12. Halpert owned the Downtown Gallery in New York, which represented Hartley.
41 Hartley 1997, p. 145.
42 Letter to Edith Halpert, dated 20 September 1932, transcribed in McCoy 1997, p. 13.
43 Letter to Edith Halpert, dated 20 September 1932, transcribed in McCoy 1997, p. 15.
44 Hokin 1990, p. 36.
45 Letter to Edith Halpert, dated 20 September 1932, transcribed in McCoy 1997, p. 13.
46 Fisher 2002, p. 442.
47 Taken from Marsden Hartley, 'In Memoriam – Hart Crane', an unpublished essay of 1932 (Hartley/Berger Archive, Beinecke Rare Books and Manuscripts Library, Yale University, Collection of American Literature), quoted in Hokin 1990, p. 34.
48 Hartley described visiting the Temple of Quetzalcoatl at Teotihuacan as the 'grandest experience of my life'. Letter to Adelaide Kuntz, dated 4 April 1932, quoted in Hokin 1990, p. 34. In a letter to Edith Halpert, dated 3 May 1932, he wrote that 'the Aztec remains are astounding in beauty and nobility'; transcribed in McCoy 1997, p. 12. See also Hartley 1997, p. 149.
49 See Jonathan Weinberg, 'Marsden Hartley: Writing on Painting', in Hartford 2003, pp. 133–4, and Ludington 1992, pp. 308–9. The Swiss-born sixteenth-century alchemist Philippus Aureolus Theophrastus Bombastus von Hohenheim, known as Paracelsus, coined the term 'Yliaster' referring to primal matter. Böhme was a seventeenth-century German Christian mystic and Rolle a fourteenth-century English Christian mystic. Hartley dedicated the titles of *Yliaster (Paracelsus)*, 1932 (Smithsonian American Art Museum, Washington, DC), *Morgenrot*, 1932 (Private collection) and *The Transference of Richard Rolle*, 1932 (Private collection) to these three. The other five works of the 'Eight Panels for an Arcane Library' are *Popocatepetl, One Morning*, 1932 (Sheldon Museum of Art, University of Nebraska, Lincoln), *Popocatepetl, Spirited Morning – Mexico*, 1932 (Smithsonian American Art Museum, Washington, DC), *Carnelian Country*, 1932 (The Regis Collection, Minneapolis), *Cascade of Devotion*, 1932 (University Art Museum, University of California, Berkeley) and *Tollan, Aztec Legend – Mexico*, 1933 (The Regis Collection, Minneapolis).
50 Kornhauser 2003, p. 23.
51 Letter to Adelaide Kuntz, dated 24 August 1932, quoted in Hokin 1990, p. 35.
52 Letter to Edith Halpert, dated 12 January 1933, transcribed in McCoy 1997, p. 15.
53 Miami 2010, p. 9.
54 Miami 2010, p. 35.
55 *Photographs of Mexico* (1940) contained twenty photogravures. It was printed by The New York Photogravure and Color Company and published by Virginia Stevens, New York, in an edition of 250 copies.
56 Miami 2010, pp. 84–6.
57 The title of the film, *Redes*, is ambiguous. It may refer to the nets upon which the fishermen depend for their livelihood, or imply that the fishermen are enmeshed in the local political network that exploits them. The film's premiere took place at the Teatro Juárez in Alvarado on 4 June 1936. Released in the US as *The Wave*, it premiered at the Filmarte Theatre, West 58th Street, New York on 20 April 1937. The film was released in France as *Révoltés d'Alvarado*.
58 Miami 2010, p. 9.
59 Chéroux 2012, p. 32.
60 Guston and Kadish had originally wanted to go to Italy to see frescoes at first hand. When they realised how expensive the passage to Europe was, they decided to go to Mexico instead, buying a car to make the journey. They were desperate to get out of Los Angeles. Mayer 1991, p. 19.

61 Oles 1993, p. 199.
62 Letter to Harold Lehman, Mexico City, dated 14 July 1934. Boime 2008, p. 455.
63 Landau 2007, p. 86.
64 Landau 2007, p. 86.
65 Landau 2007, p. 75.
66 New York 1994, p. 17.
67 New York 1994, p. 19.
68 New York 1994, p. 27.
69 New York 1994, p. 21.
70 New York 1994, p. 27.
71 Ferrer 1994, p. 211.
72 Fort Worth 1986, p. 61.
73 Fort Worth 1986, p. 61.
74 'Historic Architecture Photography; The Southwest', in *Complete Photographer*, vol. 6, 20 July 1942, quoted in Fort Worth 1986, p. 61.
75 Fort Worth 1986, p. 62.
76 Siqueiros 1975, p. 45.
77 Fraquelli 2002, p. 106.
78 Siqueiros 1975, pp. 45–6.
79 Siqueiros 1975, p. 47.

CHAPTER 4

1 Adapted from André Breton, 'Souvenir du Mexique', in *Minotaure*, vol. 12/13 (May 1939), 'In Mexico ... artistic creation is not adulterated as it is here', quoted in London 1989A, p. 216.
2 Neruda 1978, p. 151.
3 Josef Albers in a letter to Wassily and Nina Kandinsky from Calle de Paris 23, Mexico City, dated 22 August 1936, partially transcribed in Csoma 2007, p. 211.
4 Letter to Inés Amor, dated 30 June 1967, partially transcribed in Danilowitz 2007B, p. 205.
5 Brugnoli and Hoces de la Guardia 2007, p. 66.
6 Gilderhus 2007, pp. 125–6.
7 Danilowitz 2007A, p. 28.
8 Oles 1993, p. 167; Danilowitz 2007A, p. 27.
9 Danilowitz 2007A, p. 27.
10 Gilderhus 2007, p. 128, quoting Irving Finklestein, 'The Life and Art of Josef Albers', PhD thesis, Institute of Fine Arts, New York, 1968. See also Oles 1993, p. 167.
11 Knapp 1980, pp. 133–4.
12 The three lectures at the University of Mexico on 26, 27 and 29 February 1936 were 'Surrealism and Revolution', 'Man against Destiny' and 'The Theatre and the Gods'. On 18 March he lectured on the recent history of French theatre at the Alliance Française, and later that month for LEAR (see letter addressed to Jean Paulhan, dated 26 March 1936, transcribed in Antonin Artaud, *Oeuvres Complètes, Vol. VIII: de quelques problèmes d'actualité; aux messages révolutionnaires; lettres du Mexique, Paris*, 1971, pp. 359–60). See also Schneider 1978.
13 Quotation from *Los Tarahumaras* (1955), quoted in Sellin 1968, p. 19.
14 Bowker 1993, p. 195.
15 Bowker 1993, pp. 194–5.
16 Lowry received a US$150 monthly stipend from his father, Arthur O. Lowry, a successful businessman in England. Day 1974, p. 213.
17 Gabrial 2000, p. 103.
18 Day 1974, pp. 216–19.
19 Lowry 1963, p. 15. From *Under the Volcano* by Malcolm Lowry, published by Jonathan Cape, reprinted by permission of the Random House Group Ltd. Reprinted by permission of SLL/Sterling Lord Literistic, Inc. Copyright by Estate of Malcolm Lowry, 1975.
20 Bowker 1993, p. 237.
21 Letter to John Davenport (Hotel Francia, Oaxaca de Oaxaca, Mexico, no date), transcribed in Breit and Bonner Lowry 1967, pp. 11–13.
22 Letter to his sister Anne Burra, Lady Ritchie of Dundee, dated 11 May 1937 (from 17 Elwood Street, Charlestown, Mass.). Tate Archive, TGA 939/2/1.
23 It would have been a long journey, starting with Boston to New York and then connecting to St Louis, Missouri. The National Railways of Mexico offered a Pullman sleeping-car service between St Louis and Mexico City via Laredo with a journey time of 61 hours. The 1935 edition of *The South American Handbook* advises that the train journey from New York to Mexico takes 3½ days.
24 Letter to his sister Anne Burra, no date (c/o Wells Fargo Express, Av. Madero, Mexico D.F.). Tate Archive, TGA 939/2/1.
25 Letter to his mother Ermentrude Anne Robertson-Luxford, no date (c/o Lowry, Calle Humboldt 62, Cuernavaca, Morelos). Tate Archive, TGA 939/2/1.
26 Letter to his mother Ermentrude Anne Robertson-Luxford, no date (c/o Lowry, Calle Humboldt 62, Cuernavaca, Morelos). Tate Archive, TGA 939/2/1.
27 Gabrial 2000, p. 140.
28 Letter to his mother Ermentrude Anne Robertson-Luxford, no date (c/o Lowry, Calle Humboldt 62, Cuernavaca, Morelos). Tate Archive, TGA 939/2/1.
29 Letter to his sister Anne Burra, dated 29 June 1937 (from 17 Elwood Street, Charlestown, Mass.). Tate Archive, TGA 939/2/1.
30 Gabrial 2000, pp. 141–4, recollected leaving Cuernavaca for Patzcuaro via Morelia after Mary Hoover and Burra went in June 1937; by the time she returned, Burra had left. Mary Hoover, however, makes no mention of this trip in Aiken 1982.
31 The exhibition 'Edward Burra' contained a painting called *Mexican Landscape* (*Edward Burra: Catalogue of an Exhibition Held at Redfern Gallery*, London, 19 November – 24 December 1942, cat. 18), which could be this work, given that the Tate Gallery had acquired *Mexican Church* in 1940 and *El Paseo* was shown in the 1942 British Council exhibition in London and Manchester with that title. It is also possible that this is an unidentified work.
32 Letter to Malcolm Lowry, dated 4 September 1946 (Jeake's House, Rye, Sussex), transcribed in Sugars 1992, pp. 196–7.
33 Aiken 1964, pp. 460–1.
34 Aiken 1982, p. 92.
35 London 1985, p. 119.
36 Aiken 1982, p. 92.
37 Causey 1985, p. 62.
38 Sherry 1989, p. 659.
39 Sherry 1989, p. 606.
40 Sherry 1989, p. 662.
41 Evelyn Waugh, *Edmund Campion: Jesuit and Martyr in the Reign of Queen Elizabeth*, London, 1935.
42 Mockler 1994, p. 140.
43 The book was published in the US as *Another Mexico* (New York, 1939).
44 Sherry 1989, p. 724.
45 Greene 2002, p. 201. Published by Vintage, Random House.
46 Greene 2002, p. 143.
47 Stannard 1986, p. 480.
48 Stannard 1986, pp. 478–9.
49 The book was published in the US as *Mexico: An Object Lesson* (New York, 1939).
50 Sykes 1975, p. 182.
51 Hastings 1994, p. 375.
52 Waugh 1939, pp. 9–10. Extracts from *Robbery Under Law* by Evelyn Waugh. Copyright © 1939, Evelyn Waugh, used by permission of The Wylie Agency (UK) Limited.
53 Waugh 1939, p. 269.
54 Rewald 1990, pp. 651–61.
55 *The Dream of Malinche*, 1939 (Collection Mariana Pérez Amor, Mexico City) and *The Orator*, 1939 (Collection Mr and Mrs Stanley Marcus, Dallas).

56 Barber 1993, p. 80.
57 On 13 May 1938; the remaining talks were blocked by the League of Revolutionary Artists (LEAR). Fernández 1998, p. 257. There were many articles hostile to Surrealism in the press and, as a Trotskyist, Breton's presence was opposed by the Stalinist camp. Before his lecture he did open an art exhibition and also spoke at the Mexican premiere of *Un chien andalou* (1929, directed by Luis Buñuel and Salvador Dalí). His last public appearance was at a poetry reading on 26 June 1938. Polizzotti 1995, p. 459.
58 Polizzotti 1995, p. 455.
59 Breton acquired thirteen prints by Manuel Álvarez Bravo, which he took back to Paris with him.
60 Translated by Greg Adargo; see Nate Schmolze and David Walters (for marxists.org, 2001), 'Marxists Internet Archive' (http://marxists.org/subject/art/lit_crit/works/rivera/manifesto.htm).
61 Polizzotti 1995, pp. 460–64.
62 Recorded during a conversation with Rafael Heliodoro Valle for *L'Universidad*, 22 June 1938. Tythacott 2003, p. 182.
63 The three previous international Surrealist exhibitions were 'Exposición Surrealista' (El Ateneo, Santa Cruz de Tenerife, 11–24 May 1935); 'International Surrealist Exhibition' (New Burlington Galleries, London, 11 June – 4 July 1936); and 'Exposition Internationale du Surréalisme' (Galérie Beaux-arts, Paris, 17 January – 24 February 1938).
64 The eleven Mexican artists in the exhibition were Manuel Álvarez Bravo, Frida Kahlo, Agustín Lazo, Manuel Rodríguez Lozano, Carlos Mérida, Guillermo Meza, Roberto Montenegro, Diego Rivera, Antonio Ruiz, Moreno Villa and Xavier Villaurrutia.
65 Mexico City 1940, n. p. © 1940 The Museum of Modern Art, New York.
66 Greeley 2003, p. 223.
67 Tythacott 2003, p. 182.
68 Greeley 2003, pp. 223–4, n. 72.
69 Paz 1993, p. 261.
70 Debroise 1983, p. 181.
71 Debroise 1983, p. 12.
72 Cordero Reiman 1993, pp. 45–7.
73 Herrera 2003, p. 214.
74 Kahlo's miniature self-portrait was created for an intimate friend. It resembles a personal keepsake given to a lover, such as a photograph contained in a locket. She eventually gave it to the Spanish painter José Bartoli, a refugee from the Spanish Civil War, with whom she had a passionate affair. Herrera 2011, pp. 40–41.
75 Herrera 2003, pp. 192–214.
76 Whelan 1985, p. 168.
77 Whelan 1985, p. 170.
78 Transcribed in Whelan 1985, p. 311.
79 He filed four pieces from Mexico: 'Nazis and Communists in Mexico' in *Life* (10 June 1940); 'Mexican Presidential Election' in *Life* (1 July 1940); 'Election Day Violence, Mexico' in *Life* (22 July 1940); and 'Trotsky's Cremation' (text only) in *Time* (9 September 1940).
80 Neruda 1978, p. 150.
81 Neruda 1978, p. 154.
82 Neruda 1978, pp. 154–5.
83 Neruda 1978, p. 163.
84 Gallop 1990, p. 106.
85 Guston had first seen the work of de Chirico in the Louise and Walter Arensberg collection in New York, most probably in 1930. He remained deeply affected by *The Poet and his Muse* (c. 1925, Philadelphia Museum of Art). Mayer 1991, p. 15; Ashton 1990, p. 21.
86 Museum of Modern Art Archives, 40511–34 (15 May 1940).
87 New York 1940, p. 11. © 1940 The Museum of Modern Art, New York.
88 New York 1940, p. 11. © 1940 The Museum of Modern Art, New York.
89 New York 1940, p. 12. © 1940 The Museum of Modern Art, New York.
90 'Diego Rivera' ran for five weeks, from 22 December 1931 to 30 January 1932, setting new attendance records. It was the fourteenth exhibition at the Museum of Modern Art, which opened in 1929.
91 Beals 1931, pp. 211–12. Beals was awarded a Guggenheim Fellowship in 1931 to write a biography of Porfirio Díaz.
92 The Partido Nacional Revolucionario (PNR) and its subsequent manifestations, the Partido Revolucionario Mexicano (PRM) and the Partido Revolucionario Institucional (PRI), held the presidency for 71 years until 2000, when Vicente Fox Quesada of the Partido de Acción Nacional (PAN) wrested the presidency from their control.
93 Meyer and Sherman 1979, pp. 627–8.
94 Meyer and Sherman 1979, p. 628.

APPENDIX

1 Signed P. D./A. A. L., 'British Impressions of Mexico', in *Bulletin of Spanish Studies*, vol. 20, no. 77, pp. 71–6 (p. 72).
2 This scarce catalogue is held in only three academic libraries in the UK: the edition produced for London can be found in the Walter Strachan Collection at the John Rylands Library, University of Manchester and at the Tate Library in London, and the edition produced for Manchester is held by the National Art Library at the Victoria and Albert Museum in London.
3 The town was named by the Governor of New Spain, Juan de Oñate y Salazar, when he took formal possession in the name of the Spanish King Felipe II in 1598.
4 Tate Archive, TGA 939/3/2.
5 London 1973, p. 29.
6 *Edward Burra*, Arts Council of Great Britain, 1973 (Balfour Films, produced by Carole Smith, directed by Peter Smith). Transcribed by the author.
7 London 1973, p. 17.
8 London 1973, p. 19; London 1980, p. 2; Robertson 1982, p. 19.
9 Letter to his sister Anne Burra, dated 11 May 1937 (from 17 Elwood Street, Charlestown, Mass.). Tate Archive, TGA 939/2/1.
10 Robertson 1982, p. 13.

BIBLIOGRAPHY

Aiken 1964
Conrad Aiken, *The Collected Novels of Conrad Aiken [Blue Voyage, Great Circle, King Coffin, A Heart for the Gods of Mexico, Conversation]*, New York, 1964

Aiken 1982
Mary Augusta Aiken, 'The Best Painter of the American Scene' in William Chappell (ed.), *Edward Burra: A Painter Remembered by his Friends*, pp. 84–99, London, 1982

Aikin 1986
Roger Aikin, 'Henrietta Shore. A Retrospective Exhibition: 1900–1963' in Monterey 1986, pp. 8–38

Aikin 1992
Roger Aikin, 'Henrietta Shore and Edward Weston' in *American Art*, Vol. 6, No. 1, 1992, pp. 42–61

Albiñana 1998A
Salvador Albiñana, 'Agustín Jiménez' in Valencia 1998, pp. 266–70

Albiñana 1998B
Salvador Albiñana, 'Henri Cartier-Bresson' in Valencia 1998, pp. 278–80

Ashton 1990
Dore Ashton, *A Critical Study of Philip Guston*, Berkeley, 1990

Axtell Morris 1931
Ann Axtell Morris, *Digging in Yucatán*, New York, 1931

Azuela 1992
Mariano Azuela, *The Underdogs*, Pittsburgh, 1992

Barber 1993
Stephen Barber, *Antonin Artaud: Blows and Bombs*, London, 1993

Beals 1931
Carleton Beals, *Mexican Maze*, New York, 1931

Bennett 2010
Charles Bennett, 'Picturing the Revolution: The Real-Photo Postcards of Walter H. Horne' in *El Palacio*, Vol. 115, No. 1, 2010, pp. 59–65

Blunt 1935
Anthony Blunt, 'The Art of Diego Rivera' in *The Listener*, Vol. XIII, No. 327 (April 17) 1935, pp. 652–3

Boas 1915
Franz Boas, 'Summary of the Work of the International School of American Archeology and Ethnology in Mexico, 1910–1914' in *American Anthropologist*, New Series, Vol. 17, No. 2 (April – June 1915), pp. 59–65, 384–95

Boime 2008
Al Boime, 'Breaking Open the Wall: The Morelia Mural of Guston, Kadish and Langsner' in *The Burlington*, Vol. 150, No. 1264, 2008, pp. 452–9

Boulton 1989
James T. Boulton (ed.), *The Letters of D. H. Lawrence*, Cambridge, 1989

Bowker 1993
Gordon Bowker, *Pursued by Furies: A Life of Malcolm Lowry*, London, 1993

Bradbury, Mottram and Franco 1971
Malcolm Bradbury, Eric Mottram and Jean Franco (eds), *The Penguin Companion to Literature, Volume 3: United States and Latin American Literature*, Harmondsworth, 1971

Braun 1993
Barbara Braun, *Pre-Columbian Art and the Post-Colonial World: Ancient American Sources of Modern Art*, New York, 1993

Breit and Bonner Lowry 1967
Harvey Breit and Margerie Bonner Lowry (eds), *Selected Letters of Malcolm Lowry*, London, 1967

Brenner 1929
Anita Brenner, *Idols behind Altars*, New York, 1929

Brenner 1971
Anita Brenner, *The Wind that Swept Mexico: The History of the Mexican Revolution, 1910–1942*, Austin, 1971

Bronx 1988
The Latin American Spirit: Art and Artists in the United States, 1920–1970, exh. cat., Bronx Museum of the Arts, 1988; El Paso Museum of Art; San Diego Museum of Art; Instituto de Cultura Puertoriqueña, San Juan; Center for the Arts, Vero Beach, FL

Brugnoli and Hoces de la Guardia 2007
Paulina Brugnoli and Soledad Hoces de la Guardia, 'Albers and her Great Teachers, the Andean Weavers' in Madrid 2007, pp. 61–71

Bynner 1951
Witter Bynner, *Journey with Genius: Recollections and Reflections Concerning the D. H. Lawrences*, New York, 1951

Caplow 2002
Deborah Caplow, 'José Chávez Morado' in Riggs 2002, pp. 129–31

Caplow 2007
Deborah Caplow, *Leopoldo Méndez: Revolutionary Art and the Mexican Print*, Austin, 2007

Cardiff 1979
A. D. Fraser Jenkins, *Leon Underwood: Mexico and After: Sculpture, Paintings, Drawings and Prints 1928–36*, exh. cat., National Museum of Wales, Cardiff, 1979

Casado 1984
Arturo Casado Navarro, *Gerardo Murillo: El Dr Atl*, Mexico City, 1984

Catherwood 1844
Frederick Catherwood, *Views of Ancient Monuments in Central America, Chiapas, and Yucatán*, London, 1844

Causey 1985
Andrew Causey, *Edward Burra: Complete Catalogue*, Oxford, 1985

Chappell 1982
William Chappell (ed.), *Edward Burra: A Painter Remembered by his Friends*, London, 1982

Charlot 1939
Jean Charlot, *Art from the Mayans to Disney*, London, 1939

Charlot 1963
Jean Charlot, *The Mexican Mural Renaissance, 1920–1925*, New Haven, 1963

Chéroux 2012
Clément Chéroux, 'Le mexique en partage, un tropisme politique' in Paris 2012, pp. 23–41

Coffrey 2012
Mary K. Coffrey, *How a Revolutionary Art became Official Culture: Murals, Museums, and the Mexican State*, Durham, 2012

Cordero Reiman 1993
Karen Cordero Reiman, 'Constructing a Modern Mexican Art, 1910–1940' in New Haven 1993, pp. 10–47

Córdova 2005
Carlos A. Córdova, *Agustín Jiménez y la vanguardia fotográfica Mexicana*, Mexico City, 2005

Csoma 2007
Jessica Csoma, 'A Chronology' in Madrid 2007, pp. 207–22

Danilowitz 2007A
Brenda Danilowitz, '"We are not alone." Anni and Josef Albers in Latin America' in Madrid 2007, pp. 17–31

Danilowitz 2007B
Brenda Danilowitz, 'Towards an Ending: Anni and Josef Albers's Final Journey to Mexico' in Madrid 2007, pp. 201–5

Day 1974
Douglas Day, *Malcolm Lowry: A Biography*, London, 1974

Debroise 1983
Olivier Debroise, *Figuras en el tropico, plástica mexicana 1920–1940*, Barcelona, 1983

Delpar 1992
Helen Delpar, *The Enormous Vogue of Things Mexican: Cultural Relations between the United States and Mexico, 1920–1935*, Tuscaloosa, 1992

Detroit 1998
Linda Downs and Ellen Sharp, *Diego Rivera: A Retrospective*, exh. cat., Detroit Institute of Arts, 1998; Philadelphia Museum of Art; Museo del Palacio de Bellas Artes, Mexico City; Salas Pablo Ruiz Picasso, Madrid; Staatliche Kunsthalle, Berlin; Hayward Gallery, London

Dr Atl 1922
Dr Atl (Gerardo Murillo), *Las Artes Populares en México* (2 vols), Mexico City, 1922

Ellis 1998
David Ellis, *D. H. Lawrence: Dying Game 1922–1930*, Cambridge, 1998

Favela 1990
Ramón Favela, 'Saturnino Herrán, *The Plantain Vendor*, 1912' in New York 1990, pp. 575–6

Fernández 1998
Horacio Fernández, 'Edward Weston' in Valencia 1998, pp. 242–4

Ferrer 1994
Elizabeth Ferrer, 'Lola Álvarez Bravo: A Modernist in Mexican Photography' in *History of Photography*, Vol. 18, No. 3, 1994, pp. 211–17

Ferrer 2006
Elizabeth Ferrer, *Lola Álvarez Bravo*, New York, 2006

Fisher 2002
Clive Fisher, *Hart Crane: A Life*, New Haven, 2002

Fort Worth 1986
Martha A. Sandweiss, *Laura Gilpin: An Enduring Grace*, exh. cat., Amon Carter Museum of American Art, Fort Worth, 1986; IBM Gallery, New York; Colorado Historical Society, Denver; Saint Louis Art Museum; Museum of Fine Arts, Santa Fe; Center of Creative Photography, University of Arizona, Tucson

Franco 1967
Jean Franco, *The Modern Culture of Latin America: Society and the Artist*, London, 1967

Franco 1969
Jean Franco, *An Introduction to Spanish American Literature*, Cambridge, 1969

Frankfurt 1987
Erika Billeter (ed.), *Imagen de México: Der Beitrag Mexikos zur Kunst des 20. Jahrhunderts*, exh. cat., Kunsthalle, Frankfurt, 1987

Fraquelli 2002
Simonetta Fraquelli, 'Montparnasse and the Right Bank: Myth and Reality' in London 2002, pp. 106–17

Gabrial 2000
Jan Gabrial, *Inside the Volcano: My Life with Malcolm Lowry*, New York, 2000

Gallo 2005
Rubén Gallo, *Mexican Modernity: The Avant-Garde and the Technological Revolution*, Cambridge, 2005

Gallop 1990
Rodney Gallop, *Mexican Mosaic: Folklore and Tradition*, London, 1990

García-Romeu 1998
Emilia García-Romeu, 'Sergei Eisenstein: ¡Que Viva México!' in Valencia 1998, pp. 261–3

Genauer 1974
Emily Genauer, *Rufino Tamayo*, New York, 1974

Gilderhus 2007
Kiki Gilderhus, 'Homage to the Pyramid: The Mesoamerican Photocollages of Josef Albers' in Madrid 2007, pp. 123–9

Glusker 2010
Susannah Joel Glusker (ed.), *Avant-Garde Art and Artists in Mexico: Anita Brenner's Journals of the Roaring Twenties* (2 vols), Austin, 2010

Greeley 2003
Robin Adèle Greeley, 'For an Independent Revolutionary Art: Breton, Trotsky and Cárdenas's Mexico' in Spiteri and LaCoss 2003, pp. 204–25

Greene 1949
Graham Greene, *The Power and the Glory*, London, 1949

Greene 2002
Graham Greene, *The Lawless Roads*, London, 2002

Gundlach 2006
F. C. Gundlach (ed.), *Martin Munkacsi*, London, 2006

Gunn 1974
Drewey Wayne Gunn, *American and British Writers in Mexico, 1556–1973*, Austin, 1974

Harlem 1996
Lizzetta Le-Falle-Collins and Shifra M. Goldman, *In the Spirit of Resistance: African-American Modernists and the Mexican Muralist School*, exh. cat., Studio Museum in Harlem, 1996; African American Museum, Dallas; Edsel and Eleanor Ford House, Grosse Pointe Shores, MI; Diggs Gallery, Winston-Salem State University, NC; Dayton Art Institute; The Mexican Museum, San Francisco

Hartford 2003
Marsden Hartley, exh. cat., Wadsworth Atheneum Museum of Art, Hartford, 2003; Phillips Collection, Washington, DC; Nelson-Atkins Museum of Art, Kansas City

Hartley 1997
Marsden Hartley, *Somehow a Past: The Autobiography of Marsden Hartley*, Cambridge, 1997

Hastings 1994
Selina Hastings, *Evelyn Waugh: A Biography*, London, 1994

Herrera 1990
Hayden Herrera, catalogue entries 285–91: Francisco Goitia, '*Landscape of Zacatecas I*, c. 1914'; '*Landscape of Zacatecas II*, c. 1914'; '*The Witch*, 1916'; '*Pyramid of the Sun, Teotihuacán*, 1925'; '*Tata Jesucristo (Father Jesus)*, 1926–27'; '*Man Seated on a Trash Heap*, 1926–27'; '*Santa Mónica, Zacatecas, by Moonlight*, c. 1946' in New York 1990, pp. 562–75

Herrera 2003
Hayden Herrera, *Frida: The Biography of Frida Kahlo*, London, 2003

Herrera 2011
Hayden Herrera, 'Lot 12: Frida Kahlo *Autorretrato en miniatura*' in *A Discerning Eye: Latin American Masterpieces from a Private Collection*, Sotheby's New York (25 May 2011), pp. 38–41

Hokin 1990
Jeanne Hokin, 'Marsden Hartley: Volcanoes and Pyramids' in *Latin American Art*, Vol. 2, No. 1, 1990, pp. 32–6

Hokin 1993
Jeanne Hokin, *Pinnacles and Pyramids: The Art of Marsden Hartley*, Albuquerque, 1993

Honnef 2006
Klaus Honnef, 'Photographic Heights: The Berlin Years 1928–1934' in Gundlach 2006, pp. 295–339

Hooks 1993
Margaret Hooks, *Tina Modotti: Photographer and Revolutionary*, London, 1993

Huxley 1934
Aldous Huxley, *Beyond the Mexique Bay*, London, 1934

Karetnikova 1991
Inga Karetnikova, *Mexico According to Eisenstein*, Albuquerque, 1991

Kiehl 1990
David W. Kiehl, 'Printmaking: Posada and his Contemporaries' in New York 1990, pp. 539–41

Knapp 1980
Bettina L. Knapp, *Antonin Artaud: Man of Vision*, Chicago, 1980

Knight 1986
Alan Knight, *The Mexican Revolution. Volume 1: Porfirians, Liberals and Peasants*, Cambridge, 1986

Kornhauser 2003
Elizabeth Mankin Kornhauser, 'Marsden Hartley: "Gaunt Eagle from the Hills of Maine"' in Hartford 2003, pp. 11–30

Landau 2007
Ellen G. Landau, 'Double Consciousness in Mexico: How Philip Guston and Reuben Kadish painted a Morelian mural' in *American Art*, Vol. 21, No. 1, 2007, pp. 75–97

Lawrence 1956
D. H. Lawrence, *Mornings in Mexico and Etruscan Places*, London, 1956

Lawrence 1981
D. H. Lawrence, *The Plumed Serpent*, Harmondsworth, 1981

London 1942
British Impressions of Mexico in Art and Literature, 1555–1942. An Exhibition of Books, Pictures, Engravings and other printed matter organised by the British Council with the co-operation of the British-Mexican Society, exh. cat., Royal Watercolour Society Gallery, London, 1942; Manchester City Art Gallery

London 1973
John Rothenstein, *Edward Burra*, exh. cat., Tate Gallery, London, 1973

London 1980
Edward Burra: Paintings from America, exh. cat., Lefevre Gallery, London, 1980

London 1982
Laura Mulvey and Peter Wollen, *Frida Kahlo and Tina Modotti*, exh. cat., Whitechapel Art Gallery, London, 1982

London 1985
Edward Burra, exh. cat., Hayward Gallery, London, 1985; Southampton Art Gallery; Leeds City Art Gallery; Norwich Castle Museum

London 1989A
Dawn Ades, *Art in Latin America: The Modern Era, 1820–1980*, exh. cat., Hayward Gallery, London, 1989; Nationalmuseum and Moderna Museet, Stockholm; Palacio de Velázquez, Madrid

London 1989B
Julian Rothenstein (ed.), *J. G. Posada: Messenger of Mortality*, exh. cat., South Bank Centre, London, 1989; Museum of Modern Art, Oxford; Camden Arts Centre, London; Cornerhouse, Manchester; Gardner Centre, Brighton; Chapter Arts Centre, Cardiff; Warwick Arts Centre, Coventry; Victoria Arts Gallery, Bath; City Art Centre, Plymouth

London 2002
Paris: Capital of the Arts 1900–1968, exh. cat., Royal Academy of Arts, 2002; Guggenheim Museum, Bilbao

London 2009
Dawn Ades and Alison McClean, *Revolution on Paper: Mexican Prints 1910–1960*, exh. cat., British Museum, London, 2009

Lowe 1994
Sarah M. Lowe, 'The Immutable Still Lifes of Tina Modotti: Fixing Form' in *History of Photography*, Vol. 18, No. 3, 1994, pp. 205–10

Lowry 1963
Malcolm Lowry, *Under the Volcano*, Harmondsworth, 1963

Lowry 1972
Malcolm Lowry, *Dark as the Grave wherein my Friend is Laid*, Harmondsworth, 1972

Lozano 1999
Luis-Martín Lozano, 'Mexican Modern Art: Rendezvous with the Avant-Garde' in Montreal 1999, pp. 11–27

Ludington 1992
Townsend Ludington, *Marsden Hartley: The Biography of an American Artist*, Boston, 1992

Madrid 2007
Anni and Josef Albers: Latin American Journeys, exh. cat., Museo Nacional Centro de Arte Reina Sofia, Madrid, 2007; Josef and Anni Albers Museum, Bottrop; Antiguo Colegio de San Ildefonso, Mexico City

Mayakovsky 2005
Vladimir Mayakovsky, *My Discovery of America*, London, 2005

Mayer 1991
Musa Mayer, *Night Studio: A Memoir of Philip Guston*, London, 1991

McCoy 1997
Garnett McCoy, 'South of the Border with Marsden Hartley: Letters to Edith Halpert, 1931–1933' in *Archives of American Art Journal*, Vol. 37, No. 1/2, 1997, pp. 11–19

Mérida 1937
Carlos Mérida, *Modern Mexican Artists: Critical Notes*, Mexico City, 1937

Mexico City 1940
Exposición internacional del surrealismo: Aparición de la gran esfinge nocturna. Relojes videntes. Perfume de la 5a dimension. Marcos radioactivos. Invitaciones quemadas, exh. cat., Galeria de Arte Mexicano, Mexico City, 1940

Mexico City 1993
Carole Naggar and Fred Ritchin (eds), *México: Through Foreign Eyes [Visto por ojos extranjeros], 1850–1990*, exh. cat., Museo de Arte Contemporáneo Internacional Rufino Tamayo, Mexico City, 1993; Museo de Arte Contemporáneo, Monterrey; International Center of Photography, New York

Mexico City 2007
Adriana Zavala, *Un arte nuevo: El aporte de María Izquierdo*, exh. cat., Colección Blaisten/Centro Cultural Universitario Tlatelolco, UNAM, Mexico City, 2007; Instituto Cultural Cabañas, Guadalajara; Museo de Arte Contemporáneo, Monterrey

Mexico City 2008A
Agustín Jiménez: Memoirs of the Avant-Garde, exh. cat., Museo de Arte Moderno, Mexico City, 2008

Mexico City 2008B
Pilar García and James Oles (eds), *Gritos desde el archive: Grabado politico del Taller de Gráfica Popular. Colección Academia de Artes*, exh. cat., Colección Blaisten/Centro Cultural Universitario Tlatelolco, UNAM, Mexico City, 2008

Mexico City 2011
Dr Atl: Obras maestras, exh. cat., Colección Blaisten/Centro Cultural Universitario Tlatelolco, UNAM, Mexico City, 2011

Meyer and Sherman 1979
Michael C. Meyer and William L. Sherman, *The Course of Mexican History*, New York, 1979

Miami 2010
James Crippner, *Paul Strand in Mexico*, exh. cat., Patricia and Phillip Frost Art Museum, Florida International University, Miami, 2010; Aperture Gallery, New York; El Paso Museum of Art; Palacio de Bellas Artes, Mexico City

Mockler 1994
Anthony Mockler, *Graham Greene: Three Lives*, The Guynd by Arbroath, Angus, Scotland, 1994

Monterey 1986
Henrietta Shore. A Retrospective Exhibition: 1900–1963, exh. cat., Monterey Peninsula Museum of Art, 1986

Montreal 1999
Mexican Modern Art, 1900–1950, exh. cat., Montreal Museum of Fine Arts, 1999; National Gallery of Canada, Ottawa

Morris, Charlot and Axtell Morris 1931
Earl H. Morris, Jean Charlot and Ann Axtell Morris, *The Temple of the Warriors at Chichén Itzá, Yucatán*, Washington, DC, 1931

Morrow Lindbergh 1973
Anne Morrow Lindbergh, *Hour of Gold, Hour of Lead: Diaries and Letters of Anne Morrow Lindbergh, 1929–1932*, New York, 1973

Mraz 2009
John Mraz, *Looking for Mexico: Modern Visual Culture and National Identity*, Durham, 2009

Nehls 1958
Edward Nehls (ed.), *A Composite Biography of D. H. Lawrence, Vol. 2: 1919–1925*, Madison, 1958

Neruda 1978
Pablo Neruda, *Memoirs*, Harmondsworth, 1978

Neve 1971
Christopher Neve, 'The Importance of being Aztec: Leon Underwood's Mexican Period' in *Country Life*, Vol. CL, No. 3884 (18 November), 1971, pp. 1,358–9

Neve 1974
Christopher Neve, *Leon Underwood*, London, 1974

New Haven 1993
James Oles, *South of the Border: Mexico in the American Imagination, 1914–1947*, exh. cat., Yale University Art Gallery, New Haven, 1993; Phoenix Art Museum; New Orleans Museum of Art; Museo de Monterrey

New York 1940
Twenty Centuries of Mexican Art, exh. cat., Museum of Modern Art, New York, 1940

New York 1982
Bryan Robertson and Andrew Causey, *A Sense of Place: The Paintings of Edward Burra and Paul Nash*, exh. cat., Grey Art Gallery and Study Center, New York University, New York, 1982

New York 1990
Mexico: Splendors of Thirty Centuries, exh. cat., Metropolitan Museum of Art, New York, 1990; San Antonio Museum of Art; Los Angeles County Museum of Art

New York 1994
Olivier Debroise, *Lola Álvarez Bravo: In Her Own Light*, exh. cat., Americas Society, New York, 1994

New York 1997
Susan Kismaric, *Manuel Álvarez Bravo*, exh. cat., Museum of Modern Art, New York, 1997

Newhall 1961
Nancy Newhall (ed.), *The Daybooks of Edward Weston: Volume 1. Mexico*, Rochester, 1961

Oles 1993
James Oles, 'South of the Border: American Artists in Mexico, 1914–1947', in New Haven 1993, pp. 48–213

Oles 1998
James Oles, 'The Modern Photography and Cementos Tolteca: An Utopian Alliance' in Valencia 1998, pp. 273–5

Oles 2001
James Oles, 'Noguchi in Mexico: International Themes for a Working-Class Market' in *American Art*, Vol. 15, No. 2, 2001, pp. 10–33

Oles 2006
James Oles, 'The Mexican Experience of Marion and Grace Greenwood' in Mary Kay Vaughan and Stephen E. Lewis (eds), *The Eagle and the Virgin: Nation and Cultural Revolution in Mexico, 1920–1940*, Durham, 2006, pp. 79–89, 93–4

Oles and Ramírez 2007
James Oles and Fausto Ramírez (eds), *Arte moderno de México: Colección Andrés Blaisten*, Mexico City, 2007

Ortiz Moasterio 2002
Pablo Ortiz Moasterio (ed.), *Mirada y memoria: Archivo fotográfico Casasola. Mexico: 1900–1940*, Madrid, 2002

Paris 2004
'Documentary and Anti-Graphic Photographs'. Manuel Álvarez Bravo, Henri Cartier-Bresson, Walker Evans, exh. cat., Fondation Henri Cartier-Bresson, Paris, 2004; Musée de l'Elysée, Lausanne

Paris 2012
Henri Cartier-Bresson/Paul Strand: Mexique, 1932–1934, exh. cat., Fondation Henri Cartier-Bresson, Paris, 2012; Le Point du Jour Centre d'art, Cherbourg

Paz 1985
Octavio Paz, *The Labyrinth of Solitude*, Harmondsworth, 1985

Paz 1993
Octavio Paz, 'María Izquierdo, Seen in her Surroundings and Set in her Proper Place' in Octavio Paz, *Essays on Mexican Art*, New York, 1993, pp. 246–65

Philadelphia 1995
Sarah M. Lowe, *Tina Modotti: Photographs*, exh. cat., Philadelphia Museum of Art, 1995; Museum of Fine Arts, Houston; San Francisco Museum of Modern Art

Philadelphia 2006
John Ittmann (ed.), *Mexico and Modern Printmaking: A Revolution in the Graphic Arts, 1920 to 1950*, exh. cat., Philadelphia Museum of Art, 2006; Frist Center for the Visual Arts, Nashville; Phoenix Art Museum; McNay Art Museum, San Antonio

Polizzotti 1995
André Polizzotti, *Revolution of the Mind: The Life of André Breton*, London, 1995

Pontevedra 1997
A Colección Andrés Blaisten: Pintura moderna de México, exh. cat., Museo de Pontevedra, 1997

Quirarte 1988
Jacinto Quirarte, 'Mexican and Mexican American Artists in the United States: 1920–1970' in Bronx 1988, pp. 14–71

Quirarte 1990
Jacinto Quirarte, 'Saturnino Herrán, *Our Gods* mural project, 1914–1918' in New York 1990, pp. 581–4

Reed 1983
John Reed, *Insurgent Mexico*, Harmondsworth, 1983

Rewald 1990
Sabine Rewald, catalogue entries 338–44: Antonio M. Ruiz, '*Jesús "Chucho" Bribiesca*, 1923'; '*The Lottery Ticket*, 1932'; '*Schoolchildren on Parade*, 1936'; '*Bicycle Race, Texcoco*, 1938'; '*The Orator*, 1939'; '*The New Rich*, 1941'; '*The Soprano*, 1949' in New York 1990, pp. 651–61

Riggs 2002
Thomas Riggs (ed.), *St James' Guide to Hispanic Artists: Profiles of Latino and Latin American Artists*, Detroit, 2002

Roberts, Boulton and Mansfield 1987
Warren Roberts, James T. Boulton and Elizabeth Mansfield (eds), *The Letters of D. H. Lawrence, Volume IV: June 1921 – March 1924*, Cambridge, 1987

Robertson 1982
Bryan Robertson, 'Edward Burra (1905–1976)' in New York 1982, pp. 9–33

Roth 1997
Mitchel P. Roth, *Historical Dictionary of War Journalism*, Westport, 1997

Russell 1929
Phillips Russell, *Red Tiger: Adventures in Yucatan and Mexico*, New York, 1929

Salazkina 2009
Masha Salazkina, *In Excess: Sergei Eisenstein's Mexico*, Chicago, 2009

San Diego 1990
Revelaciones: The Art of Manuel Álvarez Bravo, exh. cat., Museum of the Photographic Arts, San Diego, 1990; The Friends of Photography, San Francisco; Detroit Institute of Arts; Presentation House Gallery, Vancouver; Nelson-Atkins Museum of Art, Kansas City; Santa Barbara Museum of Art; Comfort Gallery, Haverford College, Haverford, PA; Lowe Art Museum, University of Miami, Coral Gables; Harvard University Art Museums, Arthur M. Sackler Museum, Cambridge, MA; Utah Museum of Fine Arts, Salt Lake City; Phoenix Art Museum; Minneapolis Institute of Arts; El Museo del Barrio, New York

San Francisco 1983
Amy Conger, *Edward Weston in Mexico, 1923–1926*, exh. cat., San Francisco Museum of Modern Art, 1983; Albuquerque Museum; Amon Carter Museum, Fort Worth; Minneapolis Institute of Arts; California Museum of Photography, University of California, Riverside; Museum of Fine Arts, St Petersburg, FL; Center for Creative Photography, University of Arizona, Tucson

Sarber 1986
Mary A. Sarber, 'W. H. Horne and the Mexican War Photo Postcard Company' in *Password* [The El Paso County Historical Society], Vol. 31, No. 1, 1986, pp. 5–15, 46

Schmidt 1978
Henry C. Schmidt, 'The American Intellectual Discovery of Mexico in the 1920s' in *South Atlantic Quarterly*, Vol. 77, No. 3, 1978, pp. 335–51

Schneider 1978
Luis Mario Schneider, *México y el surrealismo (1925–1950)*, Mexico City, 1978

Sellin 1968
Eric Sellin, *The Dramatic Concepts of Antonin Artaud*, Chicago, 1968

Sherry 1989
Norman Sherry, *The Life of Graham Greene, Volume One: 1904–1939*, London, 1989

Sims 1990
Lowery S. Sims, catalogue entries 348–9: Rufino Tamayo, '*Mandolins and Pineapples*, 1930'; '*The Muses of Paintings*, 1932' in New York 1990, pp. 665–8

Siqueiros 1975
David Alfaro Siqueiros, *Art and Revolution*, London, 1975

Sire 2012
Agnès Sire, 'Le voyage Mexicain ou la quête de la maturité' in Paris 2012, pp. 7–21

Spiteri and LaCoss 2003
Raymond Spiteri and Donald LaCoss (eds), *Surrealism, Politics and Culture*, Aldershot, 2003

Stannard 1986
Martin Stannard, *Evelyn Waugh: The Early Years, 1903–1939*, London, 1986

Stevens 1841
John Lloyd Stevens, *Incidents of Travel in Central America, Chiapas, and Yucatán*, London, 1841

Stevens 1843
John Lloyd Stevens, *Incidents of Travel in Yucatán*, London, 1843

Stevenson 2007
Jane Stevenson, *Edward Burra: Twentieth-Century Eye*, London, 2007

Sugars 1992
Cynthia C. Sugars (ed.), *The Letters of Conrad Aiken and Malcolm Lowry, 1929–1954*, Toronto, 1992

Sykes 1975
Christopher Sykes, *Evelyn Waugh: A Biography*, London, 1975

Tythacott 2003
Louise Tythacott, *Surrealism and the Exotic*, London, 2003

Valencia 1998
Mexicana: Fotografía moderna en México, 1923–1940, exh. cat., Institut Valencià d'Art Modern (IVAM Centre Julio González), Valencia, 1998

Vanderwood and Samponaro 1988
Paul J. Vanderwood and Frank N. Samponaro, *Border Fury: A Picture Postcard Record of Mexico's Revolution and U.S. War Preparedness, 1910–1917*, Albuquerque, 1988

Washington 2007
Elizabeth Ferrer, *Lola Álvarez Bravo*, exh. cat., Smithsonian Institution (International Gallery, S. Dillon Ripley Center), Washington, DC, 2007; Portland Museum of Art; Naples Museum of Art, FL; Snite Museum of Art, University of Notre Dame, South Bend, IN

Waugh 1935
Evelyn Waugh, *Edmund Campion: Jesuit and Martyr in the Reign of Queen Elizabeth*, London, 1935

Waugh 1939
Evelyn Waugh, *Robbery under Law: The Mexican Object-Lesson*, London, 1939

West 1997
W. J. West, *The Quest for Graham Greene*, London, 1997

Whelan 1985
Richard Whelan, *Robert Capa: A Biography*, London, 1985

Wollen 1989
Peter Wollen, 'Introduction' in London 1989B, pp. 14–23

Worthen 2005
John Worthen, *D. H. Lawrence: The Life of an Outsider*, London, 2005

LENDERS TO THE EXHIBITION

Aguascalientes
Museo de Aguascalientes – Instituto Nacional de Bellas Artes y Literatura

Bethany
The Josef and Anni Albers Foundation

Bottrop
Josef Albers Museum Quadrat

College Station
Cushing Memorial Library and Archives, Texas A&M University

Dallas
DeGolyer Library, Southern Methodist University

Fort Worth
Amon Carter Museum of American Art

Laguna Beach, CA
The Buck Collection

Lincoln
Sheldon Museum of Art, University of Nebraska

London
The British Museum
National Portrait Gallery
Sotheby's
Tate
Victoria and Albert Museum
Wilson Centre for Photography

Los Angeles
The Getty Research Institute
The J. Paul Getty Museum
Los Angeles County Museum of Art

Mexico City
Acervo Patrimonial de la Secretaría de Hacienda y Crédito Público
Colección Andrés Blaisten
Collection of Clarissa and Edgar Bronfman Jr
Cano Shor Family Collection
Archivo Fotográfico Agustín Jiménez
Colección Morales-Olvera
Museo Nacional de Arte, Instituto Nacional de Bellas Artes y Literatura
Collection José Antonio Rodríguez
Colección Raúl Cedeño Vanegas

Montgomery
Montgomery Museum of Fine Arts

New York
Howard Greenberg Gallery
International Center of Photography
The Museum of Modern Art
Throckmorton Fine Art, Inc.

Paris
Collection Fondation Henri Cartier-Bresson

Philadelphia
Philadelphia Museum of Art

Phoenix
Phoenix Art Museum

Tucson
Arizona Historical Society
Center for Creative Photography, University of Arizona

Washington, DC
George Grantham Bain Collection, Library of Congress, Prints and Photographs Division
Hirshhorn Museum and Sculpture Garden, Smithsonian Institution
The Phillips Collection

PHOTOGRAPHIC ACKNOWLEDGEMENTS

Acervo INBA en custodia del Museo de Aguascalientes (Reproducción autorizada por el Instituto Nacional de Bellas Artes y Literatura, 2013): cat. 26
Aguascalientes (Mexico), © Instituto Nacional de Bellas Artes – CONACULTA, Gobierno de la República, México. Photo: Ricardo Vega Muñoz: fig. 15
Courtesy of The Josef and Anni Albers Foundation (© The Josef and Anni Albers Foundation/VG Bild-Kunst, Bonn and DACS, London 2013): cats 100–104
Manuel Álvarez Bravo © Colette Urbajtel, Archivo Manuel Álvarez Bravo SC: figs 47, 68
Archivo Fotográfico Agustín Jiménez: fig. 49, cats 65–66, 68–71
Arizona Historical Society, PC98_43167: cat. 1
Austin, The University of Texas at Austin: fig. 5 (Photography Collection, Harry Ransom Center); fig. 7 (The Robert Runyon Photograph Collection, 0031, The Dolph Briscoe Center for American History)
Colección Andrés Blaisten: cat. 42 (© ARS, NY and DACS, London 2013); cat. 58; cat. 84 (© DACS 2013)
Bristol Museums, Galleries & Archives: fig. 40
Buenos Aires, Presidencia de la Nación, Museo del Bicentenario/© DACS: fig. 58
California, The Buck Collection (© Andrée Dell): cat. 54
Cambridge, Busch-Reisinger Museum, Harvard, Gift of Mr and Mrs Richard G. Leahy, BR81.5. Photo: Imaging Department © President and Fellows of Harvard College/ © The Josef and Anni Albers Foundation/VG Bild-Kunst, Bonn and DACS, London 2013: fig. 61
Cambridge, Harvard University: fig. 8 (Houghton Library bMS Am.1091 [1385]); fig. 39 (courtesy of Peabody Museum of Archaeology and Ethnology 58-34-20/72823)
Cano Shor Family: cat. 18
Colección Raúl Cedeño Vanegas: cats 20–21, 23–25
Collection Center for Creative Photography, The University of Arizona: fig. 22, cat. 56; figs 3, 23, 25–26, 52, cats 35, 41 (© 1981 Arizona Board of Regents); cats 92–95 (© 1995 The University of Arizona Foundation/Diego Álvarez Bravo Martínez)
Courtesy Center for Creative Photography, University of Arizona Foundation: fig. 41 (© Esther Born Estate)
Chicago, Photography © The Art Institute of Chicago: fig. 1
College Station, TX, The John D. Wheelan Collection, Cushing Memorial Library and Archives, Texas A&M University: cat. 6
Dallas, DeGolyer Library, Southern Methodist University: figs 4, 6, 9, cats 2–5, 7, 14, 17, 28
Florence, Scala: fig. 18 (© 2013. Banco de México Diego Rivera Frida Kahlo Museums Trust, Mexico, D.F./DACS); figs 29, 30, 69 (© 2013 Digital Image, The Museum of Modern Art, New York); fig. 38 (Photo Art Resource/Bob Schalkwijk); fig. 72 (Photo Art Resource/ Bob Schalkwijk/© 2013. Banco de México Diego Rivera Frida Kahlo Museums Trust, Mexico, D.F./DACS); fig. 59 (Photo The Philadelphia Museum of Art/Art Resource); fig. 54 (Smithsonian American Art Museum, Partial and promised gift of Sam Rose and Julie Walters); fig. 60 (Smithsonian American Art Museum, Gift of John Young/© The Josef and Anni Albers Foundation/VG Bild-Kunst, Bonn and DACS,

London 2013); cat. 29 (The Museum of Modern Art, New York); cat. 31 (© 2013 Digital Image, LACMA/Art Resource, New York/© Andrée Dell); cats 34, 55 (© 2013 Digital Image, The Museum of Modern Art, New York/© DACS 2013); cat. 117 (© 2013 Digital Image, The Museum of Modern Art, New York/© Estate of Philip Guston, courtesy of Mckee Gallery, New York)
Fort Worth, Amon Carter Museum of American Art: cat. 43 (P1988.6); cats 96–99 (© 1979 Amon Carter Museum of American Art, Fort Worth, Texas, gift of the artist)
Geneva, © Musée d'art et d'histoire, Ville de Geneve/ © 2013. Banco de México Diego Rivera Frida Kahlo Museums Trust, Mexico, D.F./DACS: fig. 70
Honolulu, Jean Charlot Collection, University of Hawaii at Manoa Library: fig. 27
Leeds, © Leeds Museums & Galleries (Henry Moore Institute Archive): figs 31, 32, 34; fig. 20 (Photo: Royal Academy of Arts)
Leeds, © Reproduced by permission of The Henry Moore Foundation: fig. 36
Lincoln, University of Nebraska, Photo © Sheldon Museum of Art: cat. 83
London, The Bridgeman Art Library: fig. 2 (Museo Nacional de Arte, Mexico); fig. 65 (Photo © Lefevre Fine Art Ltd)
London, Edward Burra © Estate of the Artist, c/o Lefevre Fine Art Ltd: figs 65, 67
London, by courtesy of the Conway Library, The Courtauld Institute of Art: fig. 33
London, © DACS 2013: fig. 77
London, Magnum Photos: fig. 51, cats 75–81 (© Henri Cartier-Bresson); cats 112–114 (Robert Capa © International Center of Photography)
London, National Portrait Gallery (Collection Center for Creative Photography © 1981 Arizona Board of Regents): cat. 36
London, Courtesy Roe and Moore/© ADAGP, Paris and DACS, London 2013: fig. 63
London, Society for Co-operation in Russian & Soviet Studies: fig. 42
London, © Tate 2013: figs 64, 66, 78, cat. 106
London, © The Trustees of the British Museum: cat. 19
London, © Victoria and Albert Museum: cat. 38; cats 62–63 (© Colette Urbajtel, Archivo Manuel Álvarez Bravo SC)
London, Wilson Centre for Photography: cats 37, 40 (Collection Center for Creative Photography © 1981 Arizona Board of Regents); cat. 45
Los Angeles, The J. Paul Getty Museum: cat. 30; cats 39, 57 (Collection Center for Creative Photography © 1981 Arizona Board of Regents); cat. 44; cats 64, 115 (© Colette Urbajtel, Archivo Manuel Álvarez Bravo SC); cats 85–91 (© Aperture Foundation, Inc., Paul Strand Archive)
Los Angeles, Getty Research Institute: cats 8–12 (89.R.46); cat. 13 (2002.R.35)
Los Angeles, © The J. Paul Getty Trust 2013. All rights reserved/© DACS: fig. 43
Mexico, © Rafael Doniz: fig. 10 (© 2013. Banco de México Diego Rivera Frida Kahlo Museums Trust, Mexico, D.F./DACS); fig. 75
Mexico City, Jose Antonio Espinosa Sánchez, 2009, Courtesy Virtual Model Project by Leticia Lopez Orozco, Instituto de Investigaciones Estéticas: fig. 45 (© The Isamu Noguchi Foundation and Garden Museum/ARS, New York and DACS, London 2013); fig. 46 (copyright holder unknown)
Mexico City, Museo Nacional de Arte (MUNAL), photo © D.R. Museo Nacional de Arte/ Instituto Nacional de Bellas Artes y Literatura, 2013: fig. 19 (© 2013 Banco de México Diego Rivera Frida Kahlo Museums Trust, Mexico, D.F./DACS); figs 28, 55, cats 27, 47; cat. 118 (© María Elena Rico Covarrubias)
Minneapolis, Collection of the Frederick R. Weisman Art Museum at the University of Minnesota. Gift of Ione and Hudson D. Walker (1961.4): fig. 53
Montgomery, Alabama, Montgomery Museum of Fine Arts, The Blount Collection: cat. 82
Colección Morales-Olvera: cat. 15
Colección Muyaes-Ogazón: cats. 16, 22
New York, Art Resource/© Gilles Mermet: fig. 17
New York, Collection of Clarissa and Edgar Bronfman Jr, courtesy of Sotheby's (© 2013 Banco de México Diego Rivera Frida Kahlo Museums Trust, Mexico, D.F./DACS): cat. 33
New York, © The Guston Foundation: figs 56, 57, 59
New York, courtesy International Center of Photography (© Estate of Martin Munkácsi, courtesy Howard Greenberg Gallery): fig. 50
New York, courtesy of the Reuben Kadish Art Foundation (© the Reuben Kadish Art Foundation and The Guston Foundation): fig. 56
New York, © Estate of Martin Munkácsi, courtesy Howard Greenberg Gallery: cats 72–74
New York, Private collection, courtesy of Sotheby's (© 2013. Banco de México Diego Rivera Frida Kahlo Museums Trust, Mexico, D.F./DACS): cat. 111
New York, courtesy Throckmorton Fine Art, Inc.: cats 46, 48
Nottingham, Manuscripts and Special Collections, The University of Nottingham: fig. 24
Pachuca (Mexico), © (186381) CONACULTA–INAH–SINAFO–FN–MEXICO: fig. 16
Paris, © Association Atelier André Breton, http://www.andrebreton: fig. 48
Philadelphia, Image © 2013 The Barnes Foundation/© DACS 2013: fig. 76
Philadelphia Museum of Art: cats 60–61 (© Colette Urbajtel, Archivo Manuel Álvarez Bravo SC); cat. 108 (© Archivo Antonio Ruiz); cat. 110 (© DACS 2013)
Phoenix, © Collection of Phoenix Art Museum: fig. 14 (© 2013. Banco de México Diego Rivera Frida Kahlo Museums Trust, Mexico, D.F./DACS); cat. 116 (© DACS 2013)
Private collection (Estate of the artist, c/o Lefevre Fine Art Ltd): cat. 107
Private collection: fig. 35, cats 49–53 (Image © Royal Academy of Arts, London, Roy Fox/ Copyright The Leon Underwood Estate, courtesy of The Redfern Gallery)
Quadrat Bottrop, Josef Albers Museum (© The Josef and Anni Albers Foundation/VG Bild-Kunst, Bonn and DACS, London 2013): cat. 105
Coleccion José Antonio Rodríguez: cat. 67
San Francisco, Images courtesy of City College of San Francisco/© 2013. Banco de México Diego Rivera Frida Kahlo Museums Trust, Mexico, D.F./DACS: figs 21, 44
San Francisco, Collection SFMOMA, Purchase with the aid of funds from Mr and Mrs Richard N. Goldman and Madeleine Haas Russell/ © The Josef and Anni Albers Foundation/VG Bild-Kunst, Bonn and DACS, London 2013: fig. 62
Santiago, Consejo de Monumentos Nacionales de Chile/© DACS: fig. 74
Secretaria de Hacienda y Crédito Público de México: cat. 109 (© Archivo Antonio Ruiz)
Henrietta Shore, © Andrée Dell: fig. 37 (Photography by Sean Weaver)
Stanford, Stanford University Libraries: fig. 12
Washington, DC, Hirshhorn Museum and Sculpture Garden, Smithsonian Institution: cat. 32 (Photography by Lee Stalsworth)
Washington, DC, The Honorable Clare Boothe Luce/© 2013. Banco de México Diego Rivera Frida Kahlo Museums Trust, Mexico, D.F./DACS: fig. 72
Washington, DC, The Phillips Collection, acquired 1930: cat. 59 (© ADAGP, Paris and DACS, London 2013)
Washington, DC, Prints and Photographs Division, Library of Congress: fig. 11

INDEX

All references are to page numbers; those in **bold** type indicate catalogue plates, and those in *italic* type indicate figure illustrations

Abitia, Jesús H. 33
Academia de Bellas Artes, Mexico City 72
Academia de San Carlos, Mexico City 53, 61, 109
Acapulco 167
Aesop 181
Agencia Mexicana de Información Gráfica 33
Agua Prieta 22
Aguirre, Ignacio 'Nacho' 129, **130–1**, 134
Aiken, Conrad 167, 168, 171–3, 202
Albers, Anni 158–9, 193; *Ancient Writing* 158, *158*; *Monte Albán* 158, *158*
Albers, Josef 157, 158–65; *Adobe* 159; *Homage to the Square* 165; *Mantic* **164**, 165, **165**; *Mitla* 159, **160**; *Monte Albán* (1947) 159, **159**; *Monte Albán* (c. 1939) 159, **162–3**; *Tenayuca* 159–65; *Untitled Abstraction (Mantic)* **164**
Albiñana, Salvador 16
Alexandrov, Grigory 121
Alliance Française 166
Almazán, Juan Andreu 189
Almazanistas 189
Alvarado 140
Álvarez Bravo, Lola 104, 110, 113–14, 148–9; *Indifference* **149**; *Let's See Who Can Hear Me (Will Anyone Hear Me?)* **150**; *Popular Psychiatrists 2* **149**; *Wattle and Daub* **151**
Álvarez Bravo, Manuel 66, 101, 110, 112–14, 129, 134, 139, 148, 149, 185, 187; *About Winter* 114; *André Breton, Diego Rivera and Leon Trotsky* 181–4, *181*; *Box of Visions* **112**; *The Crouched Ones* **116**; *Furnace Men* 113, **114**; *Girl Looking at Birds* 114, *117*; *Lords of the Dance* 113, **115**; *The Obstacles* **113**; *Striking Worker Murdered* 189–92, **192**; *Tríptico Cemento 2 (La Tolteca)* 113, *117*
Alvorado, Pedro de 97
Amero, Emilio 101, 149
Angel, Abraham 104
Ángeles, General Felipe 47
Anhuacalli, Coyoacán 66
anthropology 64
'Anti-graphic Photographs', New York (1935) 134
archaeology 64, 84–8
Arenales, Angélica 193
Argentina 128
Art Center, New York 110
Artaud, Antonin 110, 165–7; *The Conquest of Mexico* 166; *D'un voyage aux pays de Tarahumaras* 166, *167*; *The Assassination of Pancho Villa, July 20, 1923* 53, **53**
Ateneo de la Juventud 56
'Atl, Dr' (Gerardo Murillo) 66, 138; *Las Artes Populares en México* 66; *Landscape with Iztaccihuatl* **140–1**
Augustinians 57
Avila Camacho, General Manuel 189, 192, 201
Aztecs *see* Mexica
Azuela, Mariano 19; *Los de Abajo* 30–1

Barcelona 63
Barr, Alfred H. Jr 198
Bauhaus 158
Beals, Carleton 71, 199
Best Maugard, Adolfo 116, 121
Black Mountain College, North Carolina 158
Blanco, General Lucio 28
Blue House, Coyoacan 188
Blunt, Anthony 58
Boas, Franz 56
Böhme, Jakob 137
Bolivia 128
Bonner, Margerie 168
Born, Esther, *Fiesta, Día de las Flores, Mexico City)* *101*
Brandán, Dr Julio 128
Brehme, Hugo 33, *34*, 35, 112; *Untitled (Nacional de México, No. 739)* 35, **38–9**; *Zapata* 35, *37*
Brenner, Anita 51, 71, 77; *Idols behind Altars* 66, 117; *The Wind that Swept Mexico* 33
Brentano, Lowell 84
Breton, Adèle 97; *The Annexe of the Nunnery (Chichen Itza)* *100*
Breton, André 114, 116, 166, 181–7, *181*, 188; *Mexique* *117*; *Manifesto for an Independent Revolutionary Art* 184–5; 'Souvenir du Mexique' 185
Breton, Jacqueline 181
Brett, Dorothy 68
British Council 202
broadsheet engravings 21, 40
Buenos Aires 128, 146
Buñuel, Luis 116, 187
Burra, Edward 167, 168–76, 202–4; 'The exterior of the Tercera Orden de San Francisco, Cuernavaca' 173–5, *173*; 'Jardin Juárez, Cuernavaca' *203*; *Landscape with Comestibles Seen en route to Mexico City* *170*, 171–3, 204; *Mexican Church* 171, **172**, 173–5, 204; *El Paseo (El Paso)* 171, 173, **174**, 175, 202–4; 'Popacatepetl from the veranda of 62 Calle Humboldt, Cuernavaca' 169, *169*; *The Three Fates* 175
Bustillo Oro, Juan 116
Bynner, Witter 68, *68*
Byron, Robert 176

Cachú Ramírez, Antonio 33
Cachú Ramírez, Juan 33
Café Paris, Mexico City 104
calaveras (cartoons) 40–4, **42–5**
Calles, Plutarco Elías 97–100, 154, 177
Camachistas 189
Campion, Edmund 176
Cano, Alfonso 56
Cano Manilla, Ramón, *India Oxaqueña* *78*
Capa, Robert 189–92, 201; *First Fatality on the Day of the Presidential Elections, Mexico City* 189–92, **191**; *Men in Truck with Signs Supporting Presidential Candidacy of General Manuel Avila Camacho, Mexico City* **190**; *Women in Truck with Banners Supporting Presidential Candidacy of General Manuel Avila Camacho, Mexico City* **190**
Cárdenas, Lázaro 14, 147, 166, 168, 178, 198, 201
Carnegie Institute 66
Carnegie Institute Maya Expedition 151
carnivals 193
Carranza, Venustiano 25, 34, 47, 52
Carranza Rodríguez, Emilio 96
Carrington, Leonora 187
Cartier-Bresson, Henri 103, 114, 127–34, 139, 146, 148; *Lupe Marín* 134, *134*; *Mexico* **127–9, 135**; *Nacho Aguirre, Santa Clara, Mexico* **130–1**; *Prostitute, Calle Cuauhtemoctzin, Mexico* **132–3**
las Casas, Friar Bartolomé de *20*, 21
Casasola, Agustín Víctor 33
Casasola, Miguel 33
Casasola agency 33, 35
Castaneda, Carlos 167
Castellanos, Julio 104, 149
Castrejón, Sara 33
Castro Leal, Antonio 67, 142
Catherwood, Frederick 84
Catholic Church 16, 44, 100, 176–7, 193
Causey, Andrew 202
Cedillo, Saturnino 53
Cementos Tolteca 113
Chacmools 93–5

Chaplin, Charlie 121
Charlot, Jean 21, 40, 53, **54**, **55**, 60, 77–9, 84–8, 95; *Coiffure* **78**
Chávez, Carlos 68, 138–9, 140, 142
Chávez Morado, José 104, 193–5; *Carnival in Huejotzingo* 193, 194–5, **196**
Chichen Itza 77, 84–8, 93, *100*, 149–52, **152–5**
Chihuahua 24, 35, 52
Chile 192, 193
Chillán 193
Chirico, Giorgio de 95, 195; *End of Combat* 195, *198*
Chouinard Art Institute, Los Angeles 104
Christianity 57
cinema 23, 116–25, 140–6
City College of San Francisco 107
Ciudad Juárez 22, 33
Ciudad Juárez, Battle of (1911) 23, 28, *28*
Coatlicue 44, *47*
Colombia 128
Columbus, New Mexico 34
communism 60, 79, 83, 104, 154, 166, 181–5, 188
conquistadores 20, 21
Cook, Howard 107–9
Cooper, James Fenimore 97
Cortés, Hernán 14, 20, 97
Corzo, Manuel 178
Costa, Olga 194; *Dead Child* 194, *195*
Costa Rica 128
Courbet, Gustave 47
Covarrubias, Miguel 109; *The Bone (Rural Schoolteacher)* 199–201, **200**
Cowley, Malcolm 137
Coyoacan 77, 97, 181–4, 188, 192
Crane, Hart 137, *137*, 167
Cristero Rebellion (1926–29) 100, 176
Cuatla 167
Cuba 158
Cubism 58
Cuernavaca 35, 95–6, 135, 137, 138, 167, 169, 170, 171, 173, 175, 202, 203

Dartmouth College, New Hampshire 104
Daumier, Honoré 47
Day of the Dead 40, 122, 125, 167, 170, 185
Delacroix, Ferdinand-Victor-Eugène 47
Delphic Studios, New York 116
Detroit 104
D'Harnoncourt, René 66, *66*, 71
Dominicans 57
Dos monjes (film) 116
Dreier 158, 159
drugs 166–7
Dunlop, Helena 95
Dzitas 151

Ecuador 128
Eisenstein, Sergei 114, 116–25
El Paso, Texas *23*, *28*, 33, 203
El Salvador 128
elections 201
Ensayo de un crimen (The Criminal Life of Archibaldo de la Cruz) (film) 116
Epstein, Jacob 88
Escobedo, Jesús, *Off to the Front* 35–40, **39**
Escuela Nacional de Artes Plásticas, Mexico City 193
Escuela Nacional de Bellas Artes, Mexico City 116
Escuela Nacional Prepatória 56, 60, 77
Escuela República de México, Chillán 193
Evans, Walker 134
ex-Convent of San Pedro y San Pablo 56
ex-votos 21, 35, **39**, 185
Execution in Mexico **49**
'Exhibition of Mexican Art from Pre-Columbian Times to the Present Day', London (1953) 175
'Exposición Fotografías: Cartier-Bresson/ Álvarez Bravo', Mexico City (1935) 134
'Exposición internacional del surrealismo' ('International Exhibition of Surrealism'), Mexico City (1940) 114, 179, 185, 187
'Exposición Marsden Hartley', Mexico City (1933) 135–7

Fascism 114
Federal Art Project (US) 107–9
Fernández, Horacio 16
Fernández, Octavio 188
films 23, 116–25, 140–6
'first Mexican School' 187
First World War 34, 53, 63
Fort Bliss **27**, 33
Fotografía Artistica Hugo Brehme 35
Fountain Valley School, Colorado Springs 149
France 63
Franciscans 57
Frank, Waldo 167
frescoes 57, *57*, 77
Futurism 58

Gabrial, Jan 167, 168, 169, 170, 202
Galería de Arte Contemporáneo, Mexico City 149
Galería de Arte Mexicano, Mexico City 185, 187
Galería de la Escuela Central de Artes Plásticas, Mexico City 137
Galerie Renou & Colle, Paris 114
Gallop, Rodney, *Mexican Mosaic: Folklore and Tradition* 63–4, 193
Gamio, Manuel 56, 68
Garduño, Antonio 33, 112
Garrido Canabal, Tomás 177
Gastelum, Bernardo 104
Géricault, Théodore 47
German Expressionism 116
Germany 114, 154, 165
Gilpin, Laura 149–52; *Castillo and Temple of Warriors (Chichen Itza, Yucatan)* 151, **153**; *North Colonnade, Chichen Itza, Yucatan* 151, **152**; 'Pictorial Lantern Slides of the Southwest' 149; *Steps of the Castillo, Chichen Itza* 151, **155**; *Sunburst, Kukulcan, Chichen Itza, Yucatan* 151, **154**; *Temples in Yucatán: A Camera Chronicle of Chichén Itzá* 151
Goitia, Francisco 19, 44–9, 61, 83; *Man Seated on a Trash Heap* 83, **84–5**; *Zacatecan Landscape with Hanged Men II* 47, **48**
Goupil, Eugène 77
Goya y Lucientes, Francisco José 47
El Greco 47
Greene, Graham 15, 53, 168, 176–7, 178; *The Lawless Roads: A Mexican Journey* 176, 177; *The Power and the Glory* 15, 176–7
Greenwood, Grace 107, 146
Greenwood, Marion 107, 146; *The Industrialisation of the Countryside* *107*
Guatemala 128
Guedalla, Philip 12
Guerrero, Xavier 158; *From Mexico to Chile* 193
Guggenheim Fellowships 135, 137, 138, 149
Guston, Philip 107–9, 146–7; *Bombardment* 147, *148*; *Gladiators* **16**, 194–5, **197**; *The Struggle against Terrorism* 146, *146–7*, 147–8, 171, 195

Hale, Dorothy 40, *40*
Halley's Comet 20, *20*
Halpert, Edith 135
Hare, James 'Jimmy' 28, *28*
Hartley, Marsden 103, 135–8, 169; *Earth Warming* **136**; *Eight Bells Folly, Memorial for Hart Crane* 137, *137*; *'Eight Panels for an Arcane Library'* 138; *Popocatepetl, One Morning* 138, **139**; *Popocatepetl, Spirited Morning – Mexico* 138, *138*
Havana 15
Hélène, Madame 104
Henestrosa, Andrés 129
Herbert, Laura 177
Herrán, Saturnino 44, 47, 61; *Coatlicue Transformed* 44, *47*; *Our Gods* 44, *47*; *Woman from Tehuantepec* 44, **46**
Hidalgo, Miguel 20
Hitler, Adolf 184
Hollywood 117
Honduras 128
Hoover, Mary Augusta (Mary Aiken) 168, 169, 170–3, 175, 202
Horna, Kati 187
Horne, Walter 28, 33–4 ; *Dr Armstrong's Collection of Twenty-eight Different Bullets used by Rebels in Battle at Agua Prieta* **22**; *Gruesome Scene* (Juarez, Mexico) **31**; *Triple Execution in Mexico* **32**; *A Victim of the Executing Squad* **33**, 189
Hubsch, Ben 177

Huejotzingo 193
Hughes, Langston 127, 129
Humanidad (film) 116
Huxley, Aldous, *Doors of Perception* 167

El Imparcial 33
Impressionism 47
Independent Labour Party 176
International Communist League 188
International School of American Archaeology and Anthropology, Mexico City 56
Italian Hall, Los Angeles 104
Italy 57, 63, 114
Ivan the Terrible (film) 125
Ixtapalapa 186
Izquierdo, Maria 101, 104, 109–10, 148; *The Racket* **110**
Iztaccihuatl 138

Janitzio 170
Jiménez, Agustín 101, 113, 114–16, 129; *The Basilica* **118–19**; *Dustpans* **122**; *Explosion* **123**; *Peaches and Prickly Pears* **122**; *Tehuanas* (from the film project *Tehuantepec*) **120–1**; *Untitled* (from *¡Qué viva México!* shoot) *121*
Jiménez, Luciana ('Luz') 79
Johnson, Willard 68, *68*
journalism 28–30
Julien Levy Gallery, New York 112, 134, 188

Kadish, Reuben 146–7; *The Struggle against Terrorism* 146, *146–7*, 147–8, 171, 195
Kahlo, Cristina 188
Kahlo, Frida 77, 100–1, *125*; affair with Trotsky 188; background 109; exhibitions 114, 149; house in San Angel 127; and Surrealism 181, 187; *The Deceased Dimas* 186, *187*, 194; *Self-portrait (Autorretrato)* 188, **189**; *Self-portrait Dedicated to Leon Trotsky* 188, *188*; *The Suicide of Dorothy Hale* 40, *40*
Kidder, Alfred V. 96, *100*

La Lagunilla market, Mexico City 129
Langsner, Jules 146–7; *The Struggle against Terrorism* 146, *146–7*, 147–8, 171, 195
Laredo 203
Latapí, Aurora Eugenia 113, 116; *Corncobs* **119**; *Worker* **119**
Lawrence, D. H. 15, 67–72, *68*, **70**, 71, 137, 178; *Mornings in Mexico* 69; *The Plumed Serpent* 15, 61, 69–71, *97*, 176
Lazo, Agustín 104, 187
League of American Writers 167
Leal, Fernando 77
LEAR (Liga de Escritores y Artistas Revolucionarios) 148–9, 166, 194
Lefevre Gallery, London 202, 203
Lenin, Vladimir 181
Leon Underwood casting the Red Tiger, at the Mérida Museum 92
Lerma 88, *93*
Library of Congress 152
Life magazine 189, 192
Lindbergh, Anne Morrow 96–7
Lindbergh, Charles 96
London, Jack, *The Mexican* 117
Longman 176
Lorenz, Clarissa M. 168
Los Angeles 104, 146
Los Angeles Times 148
Lowry, Malcolm 15, 167–8, 169, 175, 176, 202; *Dark as the Grave wherein my Friend is Laid* 168; *Under the Volcano* 15, 167–8
Ludins, Ryah 107, 146
Luhan, Mabel Dodge 68

Madero, Francisco 20, 21–2, 23, 33
Madrid 63
El Maestro Rural 148
Majorca 63
La mancha de sangre (film) 116
Marín, Lupe 104, 134, *134*
Márquez, Juan Fernando 168
Marx, Karl 184
Marxism 181
Matisse, Henri 198
Maugham, W. Somerset 68
Maximilian I, Emperor 52, 169, 193
Maya 64, 77, 83, 84, 93, 96, 151
Mayakovsky, Vladimir 16, 51, 58, 97, *101*
Melchor, Don 199
Mella, Juan Antonio 83, *86*
Mercader, Ramón 188
Mérida 100
Mérida, Carlos 77, 112
Mérida Museum 88, *92*
Metropolitan 28
Mexica (Aztecs) 20, 21, 44, 49, 93
Mexican Communist Party 79, 83, 104, 154
Mexican Folkways 66, 77, 101, 113
Mexican Life 116
Mexican Modernism (Mexican Renaissance) 40, 44, 47, 63–7, 79, 95, 100, 109, 152
Mexican Revolution (1910–20) 14, 22–49, 52, 58, 181, 198, 201
Mexican War of Independence (1810–21) 20
Mexican War Photo Postcard Company 33–4
Mexicana: Fotografía moderna en México, 1923–1940, Valencia (1998) 16
México: Through Foreign Eyes, 1850–1990, Mexico City (1993) 16
Mexico City 61–3, 77, 104, 112, 128, 129, 169
Mexico View Co., *Leaving the Danger Zone* **26–7**
'Mexique' exhibition, Paris (1939) 114, *117*, 185, 188
Meza, Guillermo 187
Michoacan 146, 184
Millet, Jean François 47
Milpa Alta 79
Ministry of Foreign Affairs (France) 181
Ministry of Public Education 64–6, 72, 100, 114, 139, 142, 148
Minotaure 114, *184*, 185
Mitla 158, 159, **160**
Mixcoac 113
Modern Mexican Artists 77
Modernism *see* Mexican Modernism
Modotti, Tina 72–7, 95, 129, 134, *134*; and Álvaro Bravo 112–13; interest in *pulquerías* 66; on photography as an art form 101; political agenda 79–84; Tolteca competition 113–14; *'Anniversary', Mexico* **73**; *Circus Tent, Mexico* **108**; *Hands of a Puppeteer* **81**; *Hands Resting on Tool* **80**; *Illustration for a Mexican Song* 83, *83*; *Jean Charlot* **54**; *Mella's Typewriter* *86*; *René D'Harnoncourt Puppet* *66*; *St Francis Helping the Poor* *77*; *Telegraph Wires* **82**; *Untitled (Workers, Mexico)* **79**; *Workers Reading* El Machete **86–7**
Le monde au temps des Surréalistes *182–3*
Mondragon, Alan 167
Monte Albán 158, 159, **159**, **162–3**
Montenegro, Roberto 63, 64; *Maya Women* **63**; *The Tree of Life* 56
Monumentos Prehispánicos 64–6
Moore, Henry 93; *Reclining Figures* 93, *95*
Morelia 171
Morelos 52
Morelos, José María 20, 35
Moreno Sánchez, Manuel 147
Morley, Sylvanus G. 149–51
Moro, César 185
Morris, Ann Axtell 77, 88
Morris, Earl H. 84–8
Morrow, Dwight 95–6
Moscow 58, 107, 117–21
Muggeridge, Malcolm 176
Munkácsi, Martin 125–7; *Frida Kahlo and Diego Rivera, Mexico* *125*, 127; *Mexico* **126**; *Rivera's Studio* **124**, 127; *Rivera's Studio, Mexico* **125**, 127
mural movement 56–61, 77, 88, 95–6, 100, 104–9, 111, 121, 146, 154, 187–8
Murillo, Gerardo *see* 'Atl, Dr'
Murphy, Dudley 104
Musée d'art moderne, Paris 175
Museo Nacional, Mexico City 137
Museum of Modern Art (MoMA), New York 66–7, 195–9, *199*
Mutual Film Corporation 24

El Nacional Revolucionario 166
Naggar, Carole 16
National Museum of Archaeology, Mexico City 109
National University, Mexico 181

Nazis 158, 189
Neruda, Pablo 112, 157, 192–3
New Deal programme (US) 100, 107
New York 104
New York Society of Women Artists 95
newsreels 23, 24
Nicaragua 100, 128
Noguchi, Isamu 107; *History as Seen from Mexico in 1936* *106–7*
Novo, Salvador 60
Nuttall, Zelia 97

Oaxaca 69, 111–12, 158, 168, 176
Obregón, Alvaro 34, 47, 49, 53, 56, 97, 154
Ocampo, Victoria 117
O'Gorman, Juan 66, 127, 181
O'Higgins, Pablo 77, 107, 146
Oles, James 16
Onslow Ford, Gordon 187
Orizaba 177
Orozco, José Clemente 60, 61, *77*, 93, 95, 100, 104, 121, 146 ; *Barricade* **105**
Orozco Romero, Carlos 112
Ortega, Toribio *30*
Ortiz Rubio, Pascual 154
Ostlund, Mary and Eric 137

Paalen, Wolfgang 185
Paine, Frances Flynn 110
Palacio de Bellas Artes, Mexico City 112, 134
Palacio de Cortés, Cuernavaca 35, 96, *98–9*, 169
Palacio de Minería, Mexico City 148
Palenque 176
Palestine 176
Pan-American highway 128
Panama 128
Paracelsus 137
Paracho 199
Paramount Pictures 117
Paris 58, 63, 152
Parisot, Henri, *L'Age d'Or* 166
Parra, Félix, *Fray Bartolomé de las Casas* *20*
Partido de Acción Nacional (PAN) 189
Partido Nacional Revolucionario 154
Partido Revolucionario Mexicano (PRM) 189, 199–201
El Paso del Norte 30
Patzcuaro 63, 170–1
Paz, Octavio 12, 104, 109, 110, 187
Pearson, Cecil 177–8
Pedro Aguirre Cerda Library, Chillán 193
Pérez Martínez, Héctor 148
Pershing, General John J. 34
Peru 128
peyote 166
Piste 151
Pollock, Sanford 146
Pomona, California 104
Popacatepetl 138, 169, *169*
Popol Vuh 83
Porfiriato 20–1, 35, 44, 49, 52, 56
Porfirio Díaz, José de la Cruz 14, 20–3, 23, 33, 52
Porset, Clara 158
Porter, Katherine Anne 137
Portes Gil, Emilio 154
Posada, José Guadalupe 35, 40–4; *Baptism Party for the Son of Emiliano Zapata* **36**; *The Burial of Zapata* 35, **36**, 40, 44; *The Calavera of Emiliano Zapata* **45**; *The Death of Emiliano Zapata* 35, **36**, 40, 44; *Execution by Firing Squad* 44, **44**; *Farewell of a Maderista and his Sad Sweetheart* **41**, 44; *The Great Calavera of Emiliano Zapata* **43**, 44; *The Great Halley's Comet of 1910* *20*; *The Hanged Man* **41**, 44; *Little Calavera of [Arnulfor] Gómez* **42**, 44; *The Suicide of Maria Luisa* *40*
postcards 34, 173
pre-Columbian civilisation 56, 57, *57*, 63–6, 69, 158–9, 165, 185
presidential elections 201
'Primer salón Mexicano de fotografía' (1928) 112
Proletcult Theatre, Moscow 117
Puebla, Battle of (1862) 193
pulquerías 21, *21*, 66
Pyramid of the Sun, Teotihuacan *68*, **69**

¡Qué viva México! (film) 121–5, *121*
Quetzalcoatl 68, 69
Quinta Los Granados, Buenos Aires 146
Quintana Roo 96

Ramos, Manuel 33; *Another Result* **25**; *Another Wreck of a Newspaper Office, Mexico City* **24**; *Result of a Shell in a Room, Mexico City* **25**
Red Army Club, Moscow 107
'Red Shirts' 177
Redes (film) 142–6
Reed, John 28, *30*; *Insurgent Mexico* 28–30
Reid, Mayne 97
Renaissance 57
Revueltas, Silvestre 142
Reyes, Alfonso 56
Richéy, Roubaix de l'Abrie (Robo) 72, 77
Rio Grande *28*, 33, 203
Ritchin, Fred 16
Rivera, Diego 83, 97, 109, 117, *125*, 146, 147, 178, *181*, 186; and André Breton 181–5; celebrates regional identity 64; house in San Angel 127; interest in *pulquerías* 66; murals 35, 56, 57, 58–61, 95–6, 104; Palacio de Cortés, Cuernavaca 35, 96, 169; studio **124**, **125**; success in America 95–6, 100, 198; Tolteca competition 113; and Trotsky 181–5, 188; cover of *Minotaure* 184; *Creation* 56, 77; *The Creative Genius of the South Growing from Religious Fervour and a Native Talent for Plastic Expression* *65*; *Dance in Tehuantepec* **62**; *History of the State of Morelos. Conquest and Revolution* 36, *98–9*; *May Day, Moscow* *58*; *Pan American Unity. The Marriage of the Artistic Expression of the North and of the South on the Continent* *65*, *106*, 107; *Portrait of Zapata* *36*; *Zapatista Landscape – The Guerilla* *59*
Robelo, Ricardo Gómez 72, *72*
Robertson, Bryan 204
Rodó, José Enrique, *Ariel* 56
Rodríguez, Abelardo L. 107, 154
Rodríguez Lozano, Manuel 104, 187
Rolle, Richard 137
Roosevelt, Franklin D. 107
Rosenthal, Doris 135
Rothenstein, John 202, 203, 204
Rubio, Pascual Ortíz 83
Ruiz, Antonio 178–81; *Bicycle Race* 179, **179**, 181; *The New Rich* 179; *Summer* **180**, 181
Pérez Rulfo 193
Runyon, Robert 28; *Military Band* (Matamoros, Tamaulipas) *30*
Russell, Phillips *64*, 84, 88; *Red Tiger: Adventures in Yucatan and Mexico* *64*, 88
Russian Revolution (1917) 57, 58, 107, 188

Sáenz, Moisés 56
Sala de Arte, Mexico City 114, 139
Salsbury, Rebecca 140
Saltillo 171–3
Salto 176
San Angel, Mexico City 127, 181
San Carlos Academy, Mexico City *see* Academia de San Carlos
San Francisco 104, 107
Sandino, Augusto 100
Second World War 175, 202
Shore, Henrietta **55**, 95, 107–9; *Mexican Bathers* 95, *97*; *Women of Oaxaca* 95, **96**
Sierra Madre 166
Sinclair, Upton 116, 121–2
Siqueiros, David Alfaro, and Trotsky 192–3; manifesto 152–4; murals 60–1, 104, 109, 146, 147; *América Tropical* 104–7, *106*; *Death to the Invader* 193, *194*; 'A Declaration of Social, Political and Aesthetic Principles' 100; *Plastic Exercise (Ejercicio plastic)* 146, *148*; *Portrait of Present Day Mexico* 104; *The Street Meeting* 104, 193; 'Towards a Transformation of Plastic Arts' 67; *Zapata* *7*, **61**
Smith, Carole 204
Socialist Realism 58, 109
Sonora 167
Soriano, Juan 104, 187, 194; *The Dead Girl* 186–7, **186**
South of the Border: Mexico in the American Imagination 1914–1947 (New Haven, 1993) 16
Soviet Union 58, 79, 107, 122, 125, 154, 181

Spain 20, 21, 33, 63, 93, 114
Spanish Civil War 83, 154, 175, 187
Spirit of St Louis 96
Stalin, Joseph 122, 181, 184
Stalinism 60, 192
Steichen, Edward 116
Stephens, John Lloyd 84
Strand, Paul 68, 114, 138–46, 148, 176; *Church, Mexico* **143**; *Cristo with Thorns, Huexotla, Mexico* 140, **142**; *Man with a Hoe, Los Remedios, Mexico* **144**; *Milpa Alta, Mexico, August* **145**; *Seated Man, Uruapan del Progreso, Michoacan, Mexico* **145**; *Village, Tlaxcala, Mexico* **143**; *Woman, Patzcuaro, Mexico* **145**
Surrealism 40, 95, 114, 134, 166, 181, 185–7

Tabasco 177
Taller de Gráfica Popular (TGP) 15, 35, 40, 194
Tamayo, Rufino 61, 100, 109, 110–12; *Mandolins and Pineapples* 111–12, **111**
Taos art colony 68
Tarahumara 166
Tate Gallery, London 175, 202
Taxco *34*, 63
Teatro Nacional, Mexico City 44
Tehuantepec 63, 64, 129
Tenayuca 158, 159
Teotihuacan 68, *68*, **69**, 137
Tercera Orden de San Francisco, Cuernavaca 173–5, *173*
Texas 202, 203
Theatre of Cruelty 166
Time magazine 148, 192
Tissé, Edouard 121
Tolteca competition 113
Toltecs 93
Toluca 171
Toor, Frances 66
los tres grandes 60
Trotsky, Leon 181–5, *181*, 187, 188–9, 192–3
Trotsky, Natalia 188, 192–3
Trotskyism 60, 188
'Twenty Centuries of Mexican Art', New York (1940) 66–7, 195–9, *199*

Ullstein Verlag 125–7
Underwood, Leon 84–95, *92*; *El Castillo nr Merida under Reconstruction 93*; *Chaac-Mool's Destiny* 93–5, **94**; *From the Balcony* **89**; *From the Balcony Hotel Palasio, V. H. 88*; *Moctezuma's Voices* **91**; *Red Tiger: Adventures in Yucatan and Mexico 64*, 88; *Untitled* (1930) **90**; *Untitled* (c. 1930) **90**; *Untitled* (drawing of a potter, Lerma, Campeche) *93*; *Untitled* (sketch from the balcony of Hotel Palasio, Villa Hermosa, Tabasco) *88*
Union of Technical Workers, Painters and Sculptors 56–7, 100, 109
United States of America 14–15; depression 165; Mexican murals in 95–6, 104–7; and the Mexican Revolution 23–4, 28, 33–4; New Deal 100, 107
Universidad Michoacana de San Nicolás de Hidalgo 146
University of Mexico 166

Valle, Rafael Heliodoro 129
Valley of Mexico 138
Varo, Remedios 187
Vasconcelos, José 53–6, 57–60, 64, 72, 100, 104
Velasco, José María 138; *Hacienda of Chimalpa 140*
Velázquez, Diego de 47
Vera Cruz 14, 28, 186
Verne, Jules, *Around the World in Eighty Days* 176
Viking Press 177
Villa, Francisco 'Pancho' 24, 28, 28, **29**, *30*, 33, 34, 35, 47, 52–3, *52*, **53**

war correspondents 28–30
Waugh, Evelyn 176, 177–8; *Robbery under Law: The Mexican Object-lesson* 178
Weekley, Frieda 68, *68*
Weston, Edward 72–7, 79, 95, 101, 112, 129; exhibition 148; Guggenheim Fellowship 149; interest in popular art 66; on D. H. Lawrence 68, 71; and Rivera 60, 61; *'Anniversary', Mexico* **73**; *Charrito (Pulquería) 67*; *Circus Tent, Mexico* **109**; *Cloud, Mexico* **74–5**; *D. H. Lawrence* 68, **70**, *71*; *Excusado* **72**, 134; *Heaped Black Pots* **76**; *Pulquería Interior 21*; *Pyramid of the Sun, Mexico* **69**; *Ricardo Gómez Robelo 72*; *Three Oaxacan Pots* **77**; *Tina Modotti on the Azotea* 134, *134*
Wilson, Woodrow 34
Workers' Alliance Center, Los Angeles 146
Works Progress Administration 107–9

Xochicalco 137
Xochimilco 49, 83, 97

Yaqui people 167
Yucatan 64, 96, 149

Zacatecas 47–9
Zacatecas, Battle of (1914) 28, 47
Zalce, Alfredo 146
Zapata, Emiliano 7, 24–5, 35, **36**, *36*, *37*, 40, **43**, **45**, 52–3, *52*, **61**
Zapatistas 35
Zurbarán, Francisco 47

SUPPORTERS OF THE ROYAL ACADEMY

MAJOR BENEFACTORS

The President and the Trustees of the Royal Academy Trust are grateful to all its donors for their continued loyalty and generosity. They would like to extend their thanks to all those who have made a significant commitment, past and present, to the galleries, the exhibitions, the conservation of the Permanent Collection, the Library collections, the Royal Academy Schools, the Learning programme and other specific appeals.

HM The Queen
Her Majesty's Government
The 29th May 1961 Charitable Trust
The Aldama Foundation
The American Associates of the Royal Academy Trust
The Annenberg Foundation
Barclays Bank
BAT Industries plc
Sir David and Lady Bell
The late Tom Bendhem
The late Brenda M Benwell-Lejeune
John Frye Bourne
British Telecom
The Brown Foundation
John and Susan Burns
Mr Raymond M Burton CBE
Sir Trevor Chinn CVO and Lady Chinn
The Trustees of the Clore Foundation
The John S Cohen Foundation
Sir Harry and Lady Djangoly
The Dulverton Trust
Alfred Dunhill Limited
The John Ellerman Foundation
The Eranda Foundation
Ernst & Young
Esso UK plc
Esmée Fairbairn Charitable Trust
The Fidelity UK Foundation
The Foundation for Sports and the Arts
Friends of the Royal Academy
Jacqueline and Michael Gee
The Getty Grant Programme
Mr Thomas Gibson
Glaxo Holdings plc
Diane and Guilford Glazer
Mr and Mrs Jack Goldhill
Maurice and Laurence Goldman
The Horace W Goldsmith Foundation
HRH Princess Marie-Chantal of Greece
Mr and Mrs Jocelin Harris
The Philip and Pauline Harris Charitable Trust
The Charles Hayward Foundation
Heritage Lottery Fund
IBM United Kingdom Limited
The Idlewild Trust
Lord and Lady Jacobs
The JP Jacobs Charitable Trust
The Japan Foundation
Gabrielle Jungels-Winkler Foundation
Mr and Mrs Donald Kahn
The Lillian Jean Kaplan Foundation
The Kresge Foundation
The Samuel H Kress Foundation
The Kirby Laing Foundation
The Lankelly Foundation
The late Mr John S Latsis
The David Lean Foundation
The Leverhulme Trust
Lex Service plc
The Linbury Trust
Sir Sydney Lipworth QC and Lady Lipworth CBE
John Lyons Charity
Ronald and Rita McAulay
McKinsey and Company Inc
John Madejski OBE DL
The Manifold Trust
Marks and Spencer
The Paul Mellon Estate
The Mercers' Company
The Monument Trust
The Henry Moore Foundation
The Moorgate Trust Fund
The late Mr Minoru Mori HON KBE and Mrs Mori
Museums and Galleries Improvement Fund
National Westminster Bank
Stavros S Niarchos
Simon and Midge Palley
The Peacock Charitable Trust
The Pennycress Trust
PF Charitable Trust
The Pidem Fund
The Pilgrim Trust
The Edith and Ferdinand Porjes Trust
The Porter Foundation
John Porter Charitable Trust
Rio Tinto
John A Roberts FRIBA
Sir Simon and Lady Robertson
The Ronson Foundation
Rothmans International plc
RTZ Corporation plc
Dame Jillian Sackler DBE
Jillian and Arthur M Sackler
Mr Wafic Rida Saïd
Mrs Jean Sainsbury
The Saison Foundation
The Sammermar Trust
The Basil Samuel Charitable Trust
Mrs Coral Samuel CBE
Sea Containers Ltd
Shell UK Limited
Miss Dasha Shenkman
William and Maureen Shenkman
The Archie Sherman Charitable Trust
The late Pauline Sitwell
The Starr Foundation
Sir Hugh Sykes DL
Alfred Taubman
Sir Anthony and Lady Tennant
Ware and Edythe Travelstead
The Trusthouse Charitable Foundation
The Douglas Turner Trust
Unilever plc
The Weldon UK Charitable Trust
The Welton Foundation
The Weston Family
The Malcolm Hewitt Wiener Foundation
The Maurice Wohl Charitable Foundation
The Wolfson Foundation

and others who wish to remain anonymous

PATRONS

The Royal Academy is extremely grateful to all its Patrons, who generously support every aspect of its work.

Chair
Robert Suss

Platinum
Celia and Edward Atkin CBE
Mr and Mrs Christopher Bake
Mr and Mrs Patrick Doherty
Ms Ghizlan El Glaoui
Mr Denis Korotkov-Koganovich
Mr and Mrs Jake Shafran
David and Sophie Shalit

Gold
Christopher and Alex Courage
Mr and Mrs Andrew Higginson
Mrs Elizabeth Hosking
Miss Joanna Kaye
Lady Rayne Lacey
Jacqueline and Marc Leland
The Licensing Company, London
Sir Sydney Lipworth QC and Lady Lipworth CBE
Mr and Mrs Ronald Lubner
Sir Keith and Lady Mills
Jean and Geoffrey Redman-Brown
Mrs Stella Shawzin
Mr Kevin Sneader and Ms Amy Munter
Jane Spack
David Stileman
Mrs Elyane Stilling
Mr and Mrs Pierre Winkler
Mr Robert John Yerbury

Silver
Lady Agnew
Miss H J C Anstruther
Lord Ashburton
Mr and Mrs Simon Bamber
Jane Barker
Ms Catherine Baxendale
The Duke of Beaufort
Mrs J K M Bentley, Summers Art Gallery
Mr Nigel Boardman
Eleanor E Brass
Mrs Gary Brass
Mr and Mrs Richard Briggs OBE
Mrs Marcia Brocklebank
Sir Francis Brooke Bt
Mrs Joyce Brotherton
Lady Brown
Jeremy Brown
Lord Browne of Madingley
Mr Martin Burton
Mr F A A Carnwath CBE
Jean and Eric Cass
Sir Charles and Lady Chadwyck-Healey
Sir Trevor Chinn CVO and Lady Chinn
Mr and Mrs George Coelho
Denise Cohen Charitable Trust
Sir Ronald Cohen
Ms Linda Cooper
Mark and Cathy Corbett
Mr and Mrs Ken Costa
Julian Darley and Helga Sands
The Countess of Dartmouth
Mr Daniel Davies
Peter and Andrea De Haan
The de Laszlo Foundation
Professor and Mrs John Deanfield
Mrs Anita Dinkin
Dr Anne Dornhorst
Lord Douro
Mr and Mrs Jim Downing
Ms Noreen Doyle
Janet and Maurice Dwek
Mrs Sheila Earles
Lord and Lady Egremont
Bryan Ferry
Mr Sam Fogg
Mrs Rosamund Fokschaner
Mrs Jocelyn Fox
Mrs Marion F Foster
Mrs Anthony Foyle
Mr and Mrs Eric Franck
Mr Simon Freakley
Arnold Fulton
The Lord Gavron CBE
Jacqueline and Jonathan Gestetner
Lady Getty
Mr Mark Glatman
Lady Gosling
Mr Stephen Gosztony
Piers Gough CBE RA
Mr Gavin Graham
Mrs Mary Graves
HRH Princess Marie-Chantal of Greece
Mrs Margaret Guitar
Mr James Hambro
Sir Ewan and Lady Harper
Mrs Melanie Harris
Richard and Janeen Haythornthwaite
Sir John Hegarty and Miss Philippa Crane
Michael and Morven Heller
Lady Heseltine
Mr and Mrs Alan Hobart
Mr Philip Hudson
Mr and Mrs Jon Hunt
Mrs Deanna Ibrahim
S Isern-Feliu
Mrs Caroline Jackson
Mr Derek Jacobson
Mr Michael Jacobson
Sir Martin and Lady Jacomb
Mrs Raymonde Jay
Fiona Johnstone
Mr Nicholas Jones
Mrs Ghislaine Kane
Dr Elisabeth Kehoe
Mr Duncan Kenworthy OBE
Princess Jeet Khemka
Mr and Mrs Naguib Kheraj
Mr D H Killick
Mr and Mrs James Kirkman
Mrs Aboudi Kosta
Mr and Mrs Herbert Kretzmer
Norman A Kurland and Deborah A David
Joan H Lavender
Mr George Lengvari and Mrs Inez Lengvari
Lady Lever of Manchester
Mr Peter Lloyd
Miss R Lomax-Simpson
The Marquess of Lothian
The Hon Mrs Virginia Lovell
Mr and Mrs Henry Lumley
Mrs Josephine Lumley
Mrs Sally Lykiardopulo
Gillian McIntosh
Andrew and Judith McKinna
Mr Nicholas Maclean
Sir John Mactaggart
Madeline and Donald Main
Mrs Inge Margulies
Mr Charles Martin
Mr and Mrs Richard Martin
Zvi and Ofra Meitar Family Fund
Professor Anthony Mellows OBE TD and Mrs Anthony Mellows
Mrs Ann Miller
Mrs Joy Moss
Mrs Carole Myers
Dr Ann Naylor
Mr Stuart C Nelson
Ann Norman-Butler
North Street Trust
Mr Michael Palin
John H Pattisson
Nicholas B Paumgarten
Mr and Mrs D J Peacock
Mr and Mrs A Perloff
Mr Philip Perry
David Pike
Mr Maurice Pinto
Mr and Mrs Anthony Pitt-Rivers
Mr and Mrs Stuart Popham
Mr Basil Postan
John and Anne Raisman
Mr David Reid Scott
Lady Renwick
Rothschild Foundation
Miss Elaine Rowley
Mr and Mrs K M Rubie
Roland and Sophie Rudd
The Lady Henrietta St George
Mr Adrian Sassoon
H M Sassoon Charitable Trust
Mr and Mrs Christopher Satterthwaite
Carol Sellars
Mr and Mrs Kevin Senior
Christina Countess of Shaftesbury
Mr Robert N Shapiro
Victoria Sharp
Major General and Mrs Jonathan Shaw
Richard and Veronica Simmons
Alan and Marianna Simpson
The Tavolozza Foundation
Mr Anthony J Todd
Miss M L Ulfane
John and Carol Wates
Mrs Angela Webb
Edna and Willard Weiss
Anthony and Rachel Williams
Christopher G Williams Esq
Mr William Winters

Patron Donors
Stephen Barry Charitable Settlement
Mr and Mrs William Brake
Benita and Gerald Fogel
Mrs Bianca Roden
The Michael H Sacher Charitable Trust

and others who wish to remain anonymous

Benjamin West Group Patrons
Chair
Lady Judge CBE

Platinum
Mr Tony Davis
David Giampaolo
Charles and Kaaren Hale
Ms Dambisa Moyo
Mr and Mrs John R Olsen

Gold
Marco and Francesca Assetto
Lady Judge CBE
Mr Christian Levett
Ms Alessandra Morra
Mr John Peter Williams

Silver
Lady J Lloyd Adamson
Mr Dimitry Afanasiev
Mrs Spindrift Al Swaidi
Ms Ruth Anderson
Ms Sol Anitua
Mr Andy Ash
Mrs Leslie Bacon
Naomi and Ted Berk
Mrs Michal Berkner Jenrick
Micaela and Christopher Boas
Jean and John Botts
Mrs Adrian Bowden
Mr Simon Brocklebank-Fowler
Mrs Olga But-Gusaim
Mrs Sophie Cahu
Brian and Melinda Carroll
Mr and Mrs Paul Collins
Vanessa Colomar de Enserro
Ms Karla Dorsch
Mr and Mrs Jeff Eldredge
Mr David Fawkes
Mrs Stroma Finston
Cyril and Christine Freedman
Mrs Mina Gerowin Herrmann
Ms Moya Greene
Mr David Greenwald
Mr and Mrs Timothy Hart
Mr Michael Hatchard
Mr Andrew Hawkins
Ms Alexandra Hess
Mr Rashid Hoosenally
Katie Jackson
Suzanne and Michael Johnson
Syrie Johnson
Lord and Lady Leitch
Mrs Stephanie Léouzon
Mrs Rose-Marie Lieberman
Mr Guido Lombardo
Charles G Lubar
Ted and Patricia Madara
Cornelius Medvei
Mrs Victoria Mills
Scott and Christine Morrissey
Neil Osborn and Holly Smith
Lady Purves
Mr James B Sherwood
Mr Scott and Mrs Kathleen Simpson
Mrs Sahim Sliwinski-Hong
Mr Stuart Southall
Sir Hugh and Lady Sykes
Mr Ian Taylor
Miss Lori Tedesco
Mr and Mrs Julian Treger
Frederick and Kathryn Uhde
Mr Craig D Weaver
Prof Peter Whiteman QC
Mr and Mrs John Winter
Ms Regina Wyles

and others who wish to remain anonymous

Schools Patrons
Chair
Clare Flanagan

Platinum
Mrs Sarah Chenevix-Trench
Matthew and Sian Westerman

Gold
Sam and Rosie Berwick
Christopher Kneale
Mr William Loschert
Mr Keir McGuinness

Silver
Lord and Lady Aldington
Mrs Elizabeth Alston
Mr Nicholas Andrew
Dr Anne Ashmore-Hudson
Mr Jonathan and Mrs Sarah Bayliss
Mrs Gemma Billington
Mrs Jeanne Callanan
Tatiana Cherkasova
Rosalind Clayton
Mr Richard Clothier
Ms Davina Dickson
Mrs Dominic Dowley
John Entwistle OBE
Mrs Catherine Farquharson
Ian and Catherine Ferguson
Ms Clare Flanagan
Mr Mark Garthwaite
Mrs Michael Green
Ms Louise Hallett
Mr Lindsay Hamilton
Mrs Lesley Haynes
Rosalyn Henderson
The Hon Tom Hewlett
Prof Ken Howard OBE RA and Mrs Howard
Mark and Fiona Hutchinson
Mrs Susan Johns
Ms Karen Jones
Mrs Marcelle Joseph
Mr Paul Kempe
Ms Nicolette Kwok
Mrs Anna Lee
Mr and Mrs Mark Loveday
Philip and Val Marsden
The Mulberry Trust
Lord and Lady Myners
Peter Rice Esq
Anthony and Sally Salz
Brian D Smith
Mr Simon Thorley QC
Mr Ray Treen
Mrs Carol Wates
Mrs Diana Wilkinson
Mr and Mrs Maurice Wolridge

and others who wish to remain anonymous

Contemporary Circle Patrons
Chair
Susie Allen-Huxley

Platinum
Robert and Simone Suss

Gold
Mrs and Mrs Thomas Berger
Mr Jeremy Coller
Helen and Colin David
Mrs Alison Deighton
Matthew and Monika McLennan
Mr and Mrs Scott Mead
Ms Miel de Botton
Mr and Mrs Simon Oliver
Mr and Mrs Paul Phillips
Richard Sharp

Silver
Joan and Robin Alvarez
Mrs Charlotte Artus
Jeremy Asher
Mr David Baty
Ms Sara Berman
Viscountess Bridgeman
Dr Elaine C Buck
Ms Debra Burt
Jenny Christensson
Nadia Crandall
Mrs Georgina David
Mrs Elizabeth Davydova
Mr Patrick De Nonneville
Mollie Dent-Brocklehurst
Mrs Sophie Diedrichs-Cox
Mr and Mrs Gerard Dodd
Chris and Angie Drake
Mrs Jennifer Duke
Mr Timothy Ellis
Lady Polly Feversham
Mr Stephen Garrett
Simon Gillespie
Stefa Hart
Mrs Susan Hayden
Margaret A Jackson
Mr Gerald Kidd
Mrs Fiona King
Anna Lapshina
Mrs Sarah Macken
Mrs Chantal Maljers-van Erven Dorens
Mr Penelope Mather
Mrs Sophie Mirman
Victoria Miro
Mr and Mrs Jeremy Nicholson
Mrs Tessa Nicholson
Mrs Yelena Oosting
Veronique Parke
Mrs Tineke Pugh
Mrs Catherine Rees
Edwina Sassoon
Omar Shah
Richard and Susan Shoylekov
Ms Ana Stanic
Jeffery C Sugarman and Alan D H Newham
Anna Watkins
Cathy Wills
Manuela and Iwan Wirth
Mr and Mrs Maurice Wolridge
Ms Cynthia Wu

Patron Donors
Mrs Karen Santi

and others who wish to remain anonymous

Library and Collections Circle
Patron Donors
Mr Mark W Friend
Mr Loyd Grossman
Miss Jo Hannah Hoehn
Mr and Mrs Robert Hoehn
Lowell Libson
Pam and Scott Schafler
Mr and Mrs Bart Tiernan
Mr Andrew Williams
Jonny Yarker

and others who wish to remain anonymous

Young Patrons
Kalita al Swaidi
Miss Maria Allen
Miss Joy Asfar
Rosanna Bossom
May Calil
Mr and Mrs Tom Davies
Mr Stefano Donati
Mr Rollo Gabb
Miss Fernanda Gilligan
Laura Graham
Soliana Habte
The Hon Alexandra Knatchbull
Julie Lawson
Mr Lin Lei
Mr Haakon Lorentzen
Mr Mandeep Singh
Mr Stephen Sobey
LinLi Teh
Miss Annabelle Wills
Miss Burcu Yuksel

and others who wish to remain anonymous

TRUSTS AND FOUNDATIONS

Artists Collecting Society
The Atlas Fund
The Albert Van den Bergh Charitable Trust
The Bomonty Charitable Trust
The Charlotte Bonham-Carter Charitable Trust
William Brake Charitable Trust
R M Burton 1998 Charitable Trust
C H K Charities Limited
P H G Cadbury Charitable Trust
The Carew Pole Charitable Trust
The Clore Duffield Foundation
John S Cohen Foundation
The Evan Cornish Foundation
The Sidney and Elizabeth Corob Charitable Trust
The Dovehouse Trust
The Gilbert and Eileen Edgar Foundation
The John Ellerman Foundation
The Eranda Foundation
Lucy Mary Ewing Charitable Trust
The Margery Fish Charity
The Flow Foundation
The Garfield Weston Foundation
Gatsby Charitable Foundation
The Golden Bottle Trust
The Gordon Foundation
Sue Hammerson Charitable Trust
The Charles Hayward Foundation
Heritage Lottery Fund
Hiscox
Holbeck Charitable Trust
The Harold Hyam Wingate Foundation
The Ironmongers' Company
The Emmanuel Kaye Foundation
The Kindersley Foundation
The de Laszlo Foundation
The David Lean Foundation
The Leche Trust
The Leverhulme Trust
The Maccabaeans
The McCorquodale Charitable Trust
The Machin Foundation
The Paul Mellon Centre
The Paul Mellon Estate
The Mercers' Company
Margaret and Richard Merrell Foundation
The Millichope Foundation
The Mondriaan Foundation
The Monument Trust
The Henry Moore Foundation
The Mulberry Trust
The J Y Nelson Charitable Trust
The Old Broad Street Charity Trust
The Peacock Charitable Trust
The Pennycress Trust
PF Charitable Trust
The Stanley Picker Charitable Trust
The Pidem Fund
The Edith and Ferdinand Porjes Charitable Trust
Mr and Mrs J A Pye's Charitable Settlement
Rayne Foundation
The Reed Foundation
T Rippon & Sons (Holdings) Ltd
Rootstein Hopkins Foundation
The Rose Foundation
Schroder Charity Trust
The Sellars Charitable Trust
The Archie Sherman Charitable Trust
Paul Smith and Pauline Denyer-Smith
The South Square Trust
Spencer Charitable Trust
Oliver Stanley Charitable Trust
Peter Storrs Trust
Strand Parishes Trust
The Joseph Strong Frazer Trust
The Swan Trust
Thaw Charitable Trust
Sir Jules Thorn Charitable Trust
The Bruce Wake Charity
Celia Walker Art Foundation
Warburg Pincus International LLC
Weinstock Fund
Wilkinson Eyre Architects
The Spencer Wills Trust
The Maurice Wohl Charitable Foundation
The Wolfson Foundation
The Worshipful Company of Painter-Stainers

AMERICAN ASSOCIATES OF THE ROYAL ACADEMY TRUST

Burlington House Trust
Mrs James C Slaughter

Benjamin West Society
Mrs Deborah Loeb Brice
Mrs Nancy B Negley

Benefactors
Mr Michael Moritz and Ms Harriet Heyman
Mrs Edmond J Safra
The Hon John C Whitehead

Sponsors
Mrs Drue Heinz HON DBE
David Hockney OM CH RA
Mr Arthur L Loeb
Mr and Mrs Hamish Maxwell
Mr and Mrs Richard J Miller Jr
Diane A Nixon
Ms Joan Stern
Dr and Mrs Robert D Wickham

Patrons
Mr and Mrs Steven Ausnit
Mr and Mrs E William Aylward
Mr Donald A Best
Mrs Mildred C Brinn
Mrs Benjamin Coates
Lois M Collier
Mr and Mrs Stanley De Forest Scott
Mr and Mrs Lawrence S Friedland
Mr and Mrs Leslie Garfield
Ms Helen Harting Abell
Dr Bruce C Horten
Mr William W Karatz
The Hon Eugene A Ludwig and Dr Carol Ludwig
Miss Lucy F McGrath
Mr and Mrs Wilson Nolen
Mrs Mary Sharp Cronson
Ms Louisa Stude Sarofim
Martin J Sullivan OBE
Mr Robert W Wilson

Donors
Mr James C Armstrong
Ms Naja Armstrong
Laura Blanco
Mr Constantin R Boden
Dr and Mrs Robert Bookchin
Laura Christman and William Rothacker
Ms Alyce Faye Cleese
Mr Richard C Colyear
Mr and Mrs Howard Davis
Ms Zita Davisson
Mr Gerry Dolezar
Ms Maria Garvey Dowd
Mrs Beverley C Duer
Mrs June Dyson
Mr Robert H Enslow
Mrs Katherine D Findlay
Mr and Mrs Gordon P Getty
Mr and Mrs Ellis Goodman

Mrs Oliver R Grace
Sir Jeremy and Lady Greenstock
Mr and Mrs Gustave M Hauser
Mrs Judith Heath
Ms Elaine Kend
Mr and Mrs Nicholas L S Kirkbride
Ms Jeanne K Lawrence
The Hon Samuel K Lessey Jr
Mr Henry S Lynn Jr
Ms Clare E McKeon
Ms Christine Mainwaring-Samwell
Ms Barbara T Missett
The Hon and Mrs William A Nitze
Mrs Charles W Olson III
Ms Jennifer Pellegrino
Cynthia Hazen Polsky and Leon B Polsky
Ms Wendy Reilly
Donna Rich
Mr and Mrs Daniel Rose
Mrs Nanette Ross
Mrs Martin Slifka
Mr Albert H Small
Mr and Mrs Morton I Sosland
Mrs Frederick M Stafford
Mr and Mrs Alfred Taubman
Ms Evelyn Tompkins
Mr Peter Trippi
Mrs Judith Villard
Ms Lucy Waring

Corporate and Foundation Support
American Express Foundation
The Blackstone Charitable Foundation
British Airways PLC
The Brown Foundation
Crankstart Foundation
Fortnum & Mason
Gibson, Dunn & Crutcher
The Horace W Goldsmith Foundation
Hauser Foundation
Kress Foundation
Leon Levy Foundation
Loeb Foundation
Henry Luce Foundation
Lynberg & Watkins
Edmond J Safra Philanthropic Foundation
Siezen Foundation
Sony Corporation of America
Starr Foundation
Thaw Charitable Trust

CORPORATE MEMBERS OF THE ROYAL ACADEMY

Launched in 1988, the Royal Academy's Corporate Membership Scheme has proved highly successful. Corporate membership offers benefits for staff, clients and community partners and access to the Academy's facilities and resources. The outstanding support we receive from companies via the scheme is vital to the continuing success of the Academy and we thank all members for their valuable support and continued enthusiasm.

Premier Level Members
A T Kearney Limited
Barclays plc
Bird & Bird
Catlin Group Limited
CBRE
Christie's
Deutsche Bank AG
FTI Consulting
GlaxoSmithKline plc
Insight Investment
JM Finn & Co
Jones Lang LaSalle
JTI
KPMG
Linklaters
Neptune Investment Management
Schroders Private Banking
Smith & Williamson
Sotheby's

Corporate Members
The Boston Consulting Group UK LLP
British American Tobacco
Brunswick
Bupa
Capital International Limited
Clifford Chance LLP
Essex Court
F & C Asset Management plc
GAM
La Mania
Lazard
Lindsell Train
Lloyds TSB Private Banking
Lubbock Fine Chartered Accountants
Marie Curie
Moelis & Company
Oracle Capital Group
The Royal Society of Chemistry
Slaughter and May
Tanya Baxter Contemporary
Tiffany & Co.
Trowers & Hamlins
UBS
Vision Capital Limited
Weil, Gotshal & Manges

Associate
All Nippon Airways
Bank of America Merrill Lynch
BNP Paribas
Bloomberg LP
Bonhams 1793 Ltd
Credit Agricole CIB
Ernst & Young
Generation Investment Management LLP
Heidrick & Struggles
John Lewis Partnership
Morgan Stanley
Pentland Group plc
Realty Insurances Limited
Rio Tinto
Sykes & Sons Limited
Timothy Sammons Fine Art Agents

Supporters of Past Exhibitions
The President and Council of the Royal Academy would like to thank the following supporters and benefactors for their generous contributions towards major exhibitions in the last ten years:

2013
245th Summer Exhibition
Insight Investment
George Bellows
2009–2013 Season supported by JTI
Edwards Wildman
Premiums 2013, RA Schools Annual Dinner and Auction and RA Schools Show 2013
Newton Investment Management
Manet: Portraying Life
BNY Mellon, Partner of the Royal Academy of Arts

2012
Mariko Mori
JTI
RA Now
JTI
Bronze
Christian Levett and Mougins Museum of Classical Art
Daniel Katz Gallery
Baron Lorne Thyssen-Bornemisza
John and Fausta Eskenazi
The Ruddock Foundation for the Arts
Tomasso Brothers Fine Art
Jon and Barbara Landau
Janine and J. Tomilson Hill
Embassy of the Kingdom of the Netherlands
Eskenazi Limited
Lisson Gallery
Alexis Gregory
Alan and Mary Hobart
Richard de Unger and Adeela Qureshi
Rossi & Rossi Ltd
Embassy of Israel
244th Summer Exhibition
Insight Investment
From Paris: A Taste for Impressionism – Paintings from the Clark
2009–2013 Season supported by JTI
Edwards Wildman
The Annenberg Foundation
Premiums, RA Schools Annual Dinner and Auction and RA Schools Show 2012
Newton Investment Management
Johan Zoffany RA: Society Observed
2009–2013 Season supported by JTI
Cox & Kings
Building the Revolution: Soviet Art and Architecture 1915–1935
2009–2013 Season supported by JTI
The Ove Arup Foundation
The Norman Foster Foundation
Richard and Ruth Rogers
David Hockney RA: A Bigger Picture
BNP Paribas
Welcome to Yorkshire: Tourism Partner
Visit Hull & East Yorkshire: Supporting Tourism Partner
NEC

2011
Degas and the Ballet: Picturing Movement
BNY Mellon
Region Holdings
Blavatnik Family Foundation
Eyewitness: Hungarian Photography in the Twentieth Century. Brassaï, Capa, Kertész, Moholy-Nagy, Munkácsi
2009–2013 Season supported by JTI
Hungarofest
OTP Bank
243rd Summer Exhibition
Insight Investment
Premiums, RA Schools Annual Dinner and Auction and RA Schools Show 2011
Newton Investment Management
Watteau: The Drawings
2009–2013 Season supported by JTI
Region Holdings
Modern British Sculpture
American Express Foundation
The Henry Moore Foundation
Hauser & Wirth
Art Mentor Foundation Lucerne
Sotheby's
Blain Southern
Welcome to Yorkshire: Tourism Partner

2010
GSK Contemporary – Aware: Art Fashion Identity
GlaxoSmithKline
Pioneering Painters: The Glasgow Boys 1880–1900
2009–2013 Season supported by JTI
Glasgow Museums
Treasures from Budapest: European Masterpieces from Leonardo to Schiele
OTP Bank
Villa Budapest
Daniel Katz Gallery, London
Cox & Kings: Travel Partner
Sargent and the Sea
2009–2013 Season supported by JTI
242nd Summer Exhibition
Insight Investment
Paul Sandby RA: Picturing Britain, A Bicentenary Exhibition
2009–2013 Season supported by JTI
The Real Van Gogh: The Artist and His Letters
BNY Mellon
Hiscox
Heath Lambert
Cox & Kings: Travel Partner
RA Outreach Programme
Deutsche Bank AG

2009
GSK Contemporary
GlaxoSmithKline
Wild Thing: Epstein, Gaudier-Brzeska, Gill
2009–2013 Season supported by JTI
BNP Paribas
The Henry Moore Foundation
Anish Kapoor
JTI
Richard Chang
Richard and Victoria Sharp
Louis Vuitton
The Henry Moore Foundation
J W Waterhouse: The Modern Pre-Raphaelite
2009–2013 Season supported by JTI
Champagne Perrier-Jouët
GasTerra
Gasunie
241st Summer Exhibition
Insight Investment
Kuniyoshi. From the Arthur R. Miller Collection
2009–2013 Season supported by JTI
Canon
Cox & Kings: Travel Partner
Premiums and *RA Schools Show*
Mizuho International plc
RA Outreach Programme
Deutsche Bank AG

2008
GSK Contemporary
GlaxoSmithKline
Byzantium 330–1453
J F Costopoulos Foundation
A G Leventis Foundation
Stavros Niarchos Foundation
Cox & Kings: Travel Partner
Miró, Calder, Giacometti, Braque: Aimé Maeght and His Artists
BNP Paribas
Vilhelm Hammershøi: The Poetry of Silence
OAK Foundation Denmark
Novo Nordisk
240th Summer Exhibition
Insight Investment
Premiums and *RA Schools Show*
Mizuho International plc
RA Outreach Programme
Deutsche Bank AG
From Russia: French and Russian Master Paintings 1870–1925 from Moscow and St Petersburg
E.ON
2008 Season supported by Sotheby's

2007
Paul Mellon's Legacy: A Passion for British Art
The Bank of New York Mellon
Georg Baselitz
Eurohypo AG
239th Summer Exhibition
Insight Investment
Impressionists by the Sea
Farrow & Ball
Premiums and *RA Schools Show*
Mizuho International plc
RA Outreach Programme
Deutsche Bank AG
The Unknown Monet
Bank of America

2006
238th Summer Exhibition
Insight Investment
Chola: Sacred Bronzes of Southern India
Cox & Kings: Travel Partner
Premiums and *RA Schools Show*
Mizuho International plc
RA Outreach Programme
Deutsche Bank AG
Rodin
Ernst & Young

2005
China: The Three Emperors, 1662–1795
Goldman Sachs International
Impressionism Abroad: Boston and French Painting
Fidelity Foundation
Matisse, His Art and His Textiles: The Fabric of Dreams
Farrow & Ball
Premiums and *RA Schools Show*
The Guardian
Mizuho International plc
Turks: A Journey of a Thousand Years, 600–1600
Akkök Group of Companies
Aygaz
Corus
Garanti Bank
Lassa Tyres

2004
236th Summer Exhibition
A T Kearney
Ancient Art to Post-Impressionism: Masterpieces from the Ny Carlsberg Glyptotek, Copenhagen
Carlsberg UK Ltd
Danske Bank
Novo Nordisk
The Art of Philip Guston (1913–1980)
American Associates of the Royal Academy Trust
The Art of William Nicholson
RA Exhibition Patrons Group
Vuillard: From Post-Impressionist to Modern Master
RA Exhibition Patrons Group

Other Supporters
Sponsors of events, publications and other items in the past five years:

Carlisle Group plc
Castello di Reschio
Cecilia Chan
Country Life
Guy Dawson
Derwent Valley Holdings plc
Dresdner Kleinwort Wasserstein
Lucy Flemming McGrath
Foster and Partners
Goldman Sachs International
Gome International
Gucci Group
Hines
IBJ International plc
John Doyle Construction
Harvey and Allison McGrath
Martin Krajewski
Marks & Spencer
Michael Hopkins & Partners
Morgan Stanley Dean Witter
The National Trust
Prada
Radisson Edwardian Hotels
Richard and Ruth Rogers
Rob van Helden
The Wine Studio